Class and Class Conflict
in Industrial Society

Class
and Class Conflict
in Industrial Society

RALF DAHRENDORF

STANFORD UNIVERSITY PRESS
STANFORD, CALIFORNIA
1959

This work originally appeared in Germany in 1957 under the title *Soziale Klassen und Klassenkonflikt in der industriellen Gesellschaft* and has been translated, revised, and expanded by the author

Stanford University Press
Stanford, California

© 1959 by the Board of Trustees of the
Leland Stanford Junior University

Library of Congress Catalog Card Number: 59-7425
Printed in the United States of America

Preface to the First (German) Edition

In the middle of the twentieth century, the sociologist finds himself in an awkward position. While he is just beginning to lay and secure the foundations of his discipline, an impatient public demands with increasing urgency both immediately applicable and comprehensive solutions from him. Following almost every sociological conference, confident journalists charge sociologists with being either ignorant of practical problems or incapable of solving them. Like an angry creditor, the public pursues the sociologist's every move in order to lay its hands on every penny he may produce. Is it surprising that under these conditions many a sociologist has begun to forge currency? The public deserves no better; but unfortunately the false currency, the overly rapid as well as the all-embracing solutions harm the progress of sociology as well. They remove sociological discussion from the sphere of scholarly criticism which inspires ever new efforts to that of a sterile quarrel of opinions. It is therefore necessary to make a decision.

The sociologist certainly is a debtor of the society in which he lives in a way unparalleled in most other disciplines of scholarship. But this debt merely forces him to choose the subjects of his research in such a way that its results—if any—might contribute to informing society about itself. This is all. In developing his theories, methods, and techniques, the sociologist is bound exclusively by the rules of all scholarship, which demand from him accuracy and adherence to that pedestrian path of science which nobody else can take for him and which no magic force can abridge. Inevitably, this path involves byways and detours; it is a long way, and its destination may disappoint his and others' expectations; perhaps somebody else soon shows that the path chosen was altogether wrong. But if an ill-advised public does not understand the process of scientific inquiry and demands more, the sociologist may and must be sufficiently proud and confident to defend his scholarly responsibility in face of a misconceived obligation to society which is all too often informed by little more than a desire to please. *Hic Rhodus, hic salta!*

These remarks are in place at the beginning of a study, the subject of which is as extensive as its results are tentative, modest, and in need of supplementation. The attempt is made here to tackle a problem, which has for a long time been strangely neglected, with partly new and partly more refined means. To many it may sound surprising if I call a problem neglected about which the present study lists more than two hundred bibliographical references which could easily be doubled and trebled. Probably the word "class" belongs to the most frequently used words of sociology. But I am not concerned here with the word. I should not hesitate to replace it by a better one if I could find such; moreover, it will appear less frequently in the present investigation than might be expected. I am concerned with a problem, namely, with the puzzling fact that social structures as distinct from most other structures are capable of producing within themselves the elements of their supersession and change. Social structures not only are subject to change but create permanently and systematically some of the determinant forces of their change within themselves. Among these forces certain groups are paramount, the conflict of which may lead to modifications of existing values and institutions. I shall attempt to show in the present study how these groups and the processes to which they contribute can be identified theoretically and analyzed empirically.

Perhaps a word of explanation is necessary as to why I have given a study of this problem the title *Class and Class Conflict*. At least one great sociologist, Karl Marx, has used the concept of class in the context intimated by the foregoing remarks. It is undeniable that not very many have followed Marx in this. Little more than a dozen (if important) sociologists who understand Marx's and our problem as one of class will be mentioned in the course of this study. Moreover, we shall have to subject the approaches of Marx and most later sociologists to severe criticism which often leads to the conclusion that they are vague, imprecise, incomplete, or even untenable and erroneous. The overwhelming majority of sociologists since Sombart and Max Weber have associated the concept of class with other types of problems, especially with those of social stratification. A regrettable chain of circumstances seems to have committed both the original meaning of the concept of class and the problem of its first use to oblivion. All these factors can hardly serve to justify the attempts to revive both the problem and the concept of class in their original definition. However, so far as the problem is concerned, no justification is necessary, and with respect to the concept I shall try to point out that the situation is not quite as hopeless as it may seem at first sight. To anticipate but one argument here: There is, in sociological terminology, a useful alternative for the misunderstood concept of class, i.e., the term "stratum," whereas for the well-understood concept of class a substitute has not yet been found.

For two reasons one can predict with some confidence that the present study will be misunderstood. One of these rests with the strict distinction of "class" and "stratum" and their respective heuristic purposes. By stratum I shall understand a category of persons who occupy a similar position on a hierarchical scale of certain situational characteristics such as income, prestige, style of life. "Stratum" is a descriptive category. By contrast, the concept of class is an analytical category which has meaning only in the context of a theory of class. "Classes" are interest groupings emerging from certain structural conditions which operate as such and effect structure changes. The confusion of these two concepts and spheres of analysis is so complete that I cannot hope to eliminate it entirely by this first attempt at clarification, even if I should have succeeded in separating class and stratum convincingly and consistently. I must accept the misunderstanding which is possible, even probable here, just like another one which goes even deeper and touches upon the pathetically preliminary discussion of the possibility of a sociological science. I ask the reader's indulgence if I refrain here from a general consideration of this subject and instead refer to the present study itself as a testimony to my conception of sociology. There is but one aspect of the problem which I should like to mention in advance, even as it is going to increase rather than mitigate misunderstandings: If in this study I speak of "theory," "hypothesis," "empirical test," "refutation," and "science," I use these terms in the strict sense of the methodological characteristics of an empirical discipline. At least logically, physics, physiology, and sociology are subject to the same laws—whatever may render one or the other of these disciplines empirically preferable in terms of exactness. I cannot see why it should not be at least desirable to try to free sociology of the double fetters of an idiographic historical and a meta-empirical philosophical orientation and weld it into an exact social science with precisely—ideally, of course, mathematically—formulated postulates, theoretical models, and testable laws. The attempt must be made; and although the present study remains far removed from its satisfactory completion, I want it to be understood in terms of such an attempt.

Generalizing theoretical formulation and its empirical test are balanced in the present investigation. With R. K. Merton I regard "theories of the middle range" as the immediate task of sociological research: generalizations that are inspired by or oriented towards concrete observations. However, the exposition of the theory of social classes and class conflict stands in the center of this investigation. The résumé of Marx's theory of class, the largely descriptive account of some historical changes of the past century, and the critical examination of some earlier theories of class, including that of Marx, lead up to the central theoretical chapters; with the analysis of post-capitalist society in terms of class theory a first empirical test of my theoretical position is intended. The whole investigation remains in the "middle range" also in that it is, as its title indicates, confined to industrial society.

Many suggestions and stimulations which have gone into the present study originated in discussions in a small informal group of younger sociologists from diverse countries at the London School of Economics in the years 1952-54. This group, which called itself the "Thursday Evening Seminar," although it often continued its discussions until Friday morning and met on other days as well, not only occupied itself with many of the specific questions of this study —such as Marx, Parsons, the whole problem of interest groups— but displayed a conception of sociology and its task which I hope to have upheld throughout this study. Within the "Thursday Evening Seminar" and since, the stimulation of numerous conversations with Dr. D. Lockwood, Lecturer in Sociology at the London School of Economics, has, above all, furthered the progress of my own investigation into class theory. In the hope that the provisional result of these investigations may provide a useful basis for critical discussion I dedicate this study to David Lockwood and with him to our common friends of the London years.

R.D.

Scheidt (Saar)
Spring 1957

Preface to the Revised (English) Edition

In every sense but one, this study is an essay even in its revised version. It is tentative, incomplete, open to criticism at many points, and, I hope, stimulating; but it is also longer than the rules of essay writing would permit. Despite its length, I wish to emphasize the exploratory nature of my attempt to tackle problems of social conflict concerning total societies. By and large, recent developments of sociology have been characterized by two related features. Firstly, there has been a strong concern for the conditions of "equilibrium" in "social systems." Stimulated by anthropological research, an image of society has gained prevalence in sociological thinking which emphasizes the elements of functional coordination, integration, and consensus in units of social organization. The attempt to evolve testable theories and applicable conclusions has led, secondly, to an ever-growing interest in comparatively small "social systems" such as communities, enterprises, and, above all, small groups. Both these concerns of contemporary sociological analysis are, to be sure, important, and have proved fruitful. At the same time, however, they have led many to abandon completely such other subjects of sociological analysis as did not seem to fit in with the general trend. As a result, there is today a considerable need for reorienting sociological analysis to problems of change, conflict, and coercion in social structures, and especially in those of total societies. The interest in total societies, as well as in their historical dimension, is of course as old as sociology itself. Yet their neglect in recent decades makes a study like this one a venture into unmapped areas of inquiry—a venture which is guided not so much by the hope of comprehensive and final results as by the intention of challenging others to follow, criticize, and explore other avenues of discovery.

From the reviews of the original German version of this study I have learned with some pride that it has in fact achieved at least one of its ends: it has stimulated critical discussion. It seems to me that few things are more deadly to the progress of knowledge than the deterioration of book reviews into advertisements. Lack of controversy means lack of interest, of stimulation and advance. I deem myself lucky to have escaped this pathetic fate. Most of the criticism of my study has been concerned with the theory of conflict whose rudiments are presented in the second half of this book. It has converged on five admittedly problematic points: (1) the retention of the term "class" for a theory that dispenses with the historical reference to antagonisms between "bourgeoisie" and "proletariat"; (2) the "definition" of the crucial concepts of power and authority; (3) the separation and, in part, the confrontation of industrial and political class conflict; (4) the application of conflict theory to the analysis of contemporary society, especially to its "ruling classes"; (5) the absence of a grounding of this analysis on "large-scale inquiries of a more 'practical' kind." There have also been misunderstandings and more dogmatic (often Marxian) criticisms of my study; but the five points mentioned indicate comments and objections which seem to me of particular importance. I do not propose to argue with my critics at this point. Instead, I present the revised edition of this essay, in which I have incorporated many suggestions offered by reviewers and other readers, have explicitly rejected others, and have tried to clarify parts that tended to cause misinterpretations. Where the revised version has improved on the original, this is due to no small extent to the critical comments of colleagues reviewing my book.

The revised edition differs from the original in many respects; in fact, the author feels—with what probably is but a sign of lack of detachment from his own work—that it is a completely new book. For the sake of clarity of purpose, I have now divided the whole into two parts. Part One is concerned with a critical examination of facts and theories relating to the problem of class. It deals above all with the doctrine of Marx, its empirical refutation and theoretical supersession. All chapters of this part have been expanded and partly rewritten; one of them—Chapter II—shares with its equivalent in the original little more than the title; otherwise hardly a word has remained the same. Part Two presents my attempt to approach conflict analysis both in terms of abstract considerations (Chapters V and VI) and with reference to post-capitalist society (Chapters VII and VIII). Here, two entirely new chapters have been added, incorporating refinements of the theory as well as extensions of its application, while the remaining two have undergone substantial revision. Careful scrutiny of the emphases in the work of revision would reveal that in the years since this book was originally written my interest has shifted from problems of industry to those of politics. Most of the additions and changes in the present edition have been stimulated by the desire to render conflict theory applicable to the analysis of the political process both in totalitarian and in free societies of the present. A number of new books which either appeared or came to my knowledge since the date of the first publication of this study have been incorporated in the substance of the investigation as well as in its Bibliography.

Finally, an important difference between the original and the revised version of this study consists in the fact that the former was written in German, the latter in English. I should like to emphasize the expression "written in English," for this is not, strictly speaking, a translation. The author translating his own book has the supreme advantage of being free with respect to his text. He can reformulate, change, even leave out at will a phrase that sounds reasonable in one but awkward in the other language. This may be worrying to philologists, but it is gratifying both to the author and —I hope—to his readers. Also, the author translator is not held up by problems of interpretation; presumably he knows what he meant by his statements. (In fact, I found the task of "translation" an acid test for ambiguities of thought and formulation, and therefore a welcome opportunity for rendering many a passage more precise.) I fear, however, that the advantages of "translation" by the author are in this case more than balanced by the considerable disadvantages accruing from the fact that I have "translated" this book into a language other than my mother tongue. If the resulting text is at all readable, this is due in no small extent to the careful and competent editing on the part of the publisher, Mr. Leon Seltzer, and his editors. It is above all due to the assistance of my wife who shares this book with me both in the tangible sense of having put many hours of work into correcting the language (her mother tongue being English), typing, offering suggestions, and listening, and in numerous less tangible yet even more important ways.

I am profoundly grateful also to Mr. G. Fleischmann, my assistant and collaborator at the *Akademie für Gemeinwirtschaft* in Hamburg, for having put aside his own work in order to help me in preparing and editing the manuscript, compiling the Bibliography, checking quotations, preparing the Index, and discussing with me many substantial points and arguments raised in this study.

I had dedicated the original edition of this study to my friend Dr. David Lockwood and to our common friends at the London School of Economics, because it was with and through these that I received the impulses that made me undertake this investigation. Whatever new ideas and analyses there may be in this revised edition are inspired largely by many friendly discussions with fellow fellows at the Center for Advanced Study in the Behavioral Sciences in 1957-58, both inside and outside the "Conflict Seminar." With especial gratitude I record here my debt to Joseph Ben-David, Ph.D., John Bowlby, M.D., Professor Frank Newman, LL.D., Professor Fritz Stern, Ph.D.; and I should like to add Professors R. Bendix and S. M. Lipset of the University of California at Berkeley. As an outward acknowledgment of my indebtedness to these colleagues and friends as well as to many other co-fellows at the Center I have extended to them the dedication of this book.

R.D.

Hamburg
Spring 1959

Contents

PART ONE

The Marxian Doctrine in the Light of Historical Changes and Sociological Insights

I

Karl Marx's Model of the Class Society

THE SOCIAL ETYMOLOGY OF THE CONCEPT OF CLASS

The concept of class has never remained a harmless concept for very long. Particularly when applied to human beings and their social conditions it has invariably displayed a peculiar explosiveness. The logician runs no risk in distinguishing "classes" of judgments or categories; the biologist need not worry about "classifying" the organisms with which he is concerned—but if the sociologist uses the concept of class he not only must carefully explain in which of its many meanings he wants it to be understood, but also must expect objections that are dictated less by scientific insight than by political prejudice. As Lipset and Bendix have stated: "Discussions of different theories of class are often academic substitutes for a real conflict over political orientations" (55, p. 150).[1]

We shall have to show where this impermissible and unfortunate confusion of judgments of fact and value originates in this case, and we shall have to find ways and means to weld the concept and theory of class into useful tools of sociological analysis without evaluative overtones. However, for the time being we have to resign ourselves to the fact that using the concept of class may cause misunderstandings of many kinds.

Evaluative shifts of meaning have accompanied the concept of class throughout its history. When the Roman censors introduced the word *classis* to divide the population into tax groups, they may not have anticipated the eventful future of this category. Yet even their classification implied at least the possibility of evaluative distinctions: on the one end of their classification were the *assidui*, who might well be proud of their 100,000 *as*; on the other end were the *proletarii*, whose only "property" consisted in their numerous offspring—*proles* —and who were outdone only by the *lumpenproletariat* of the *capite censi*, those counted by their heads. Just as the American term "in-

---

[1] Figures in parentheses refer to the corresponding numbers in the bibliography at the end of the volume.

come bracket," although originally no more than a statistical category, touches upon the most vulnerable point of social inequality, it was true for the *classes* of ancient Rome that they divided the population into more than statistical units. "The movie was classy," teen-agers say, meaning "high-class," "first-class." Similarly, to say that some Roman was *classis* or *classicus* meant that he belonged to the *prima classis*, to the upper class—unless he was explicitly described as a "fifth-class" proletarian. Since Gellius we know the adjective *classicus* in its application to "first-class" artists and works of art, a usage which survives in our word "classical" and was eventually related to the authors of the term themselves and their times: they lived in "classical" antiquity.

When more recently sociologists remembered the word, they naturally gave it a slightly different connotation. Initially the word "class" was used—for example, by Ferguson (2) and Millar (15) in the eighteenth century—simply to distinguish social strata, as we should say today, by their rank or wealth. In this sense the word "class" can be found in all European languages in the late eighteenth century. In the nineteenth century the concept of class gradually took on a more definite coloring. Adam Smith had already spoken of the "poor" or "labouring class." In the works of Ricardo and Ure, Saint-Simon and Fourier, and of course in those of Engels and Marx the "class of capitalists" makes its appearance beside the "labouring class," the "rich" beside the "poor class," the "bourgeoisie" beside the "proletariat" (which has accompanied the concept of class from its Roman origins). Since this particular concept of social class was first applied in the middle of the nineteenth century, its history has been as eventful as that of the society for which it was designed. However, before we embark on a critical journey through this history it appears useful to survey the meaning and significance of the "classical" concept of class as it was formulated by Karl Marx.

CONSEQUENCES OF INDUSTRIALIZATION

"The history of the working class in England begins with the last half of the past [eighteenth] century, with the invention of the steam engine and the machines for manufacturing cotton," wrote the young Engels in 1845 (1, p. 31). With the industrial revolution also, the history of the concept of class as a tool of social analysis began. Earlier, the concepts of "class" and "rank" could be interchanged as by Ferguson and Millar; indeed, that of "rank" could be preferred. The superficial observer at least was above all struck by "distinctions of rank" in late feudal society.[2] In the emerging industrial society, however, rank and social position gave way to much cruder distinctions. As capital, property became transformed from a symbol of rank to an instrument of power growing steadily in strength and effectiveness. Much as nobility and small independent peasants might resent it, both became witnesses and victims of the disappearance of an old and the emergence of a new social order, before which all well-tried categories of understanding and explanation failed.

The history of the industrial revolution and its immediate consequences is too well known to be repeated here. However, one aspect of this history appears essential for our discussion. Wealth and poverty, domination and subjection, property and propertylessness, high and low prestige—all these were present before the industrial revolution as afterward. Thus it might appear as if all the industrial revolution effected was to replace old social strata by new ones: landowners and nobility by capitalists, laborers and small peasants by proletarians. This presentation, however, not only is oversimplified but overlooks the revolutionary character of the changes which accompanied industrialization. The difference between the early stages of industrial society in Europe and its historical predecessor was not just due to a change in the personnel of social positions; it was due above all to the simultaneous abolition of the system of norms and values which guaranteed and legitimized the order of preindustrial society. The "distinctions of rank" in preindustrial societies of even the eighteenth century rested as much on a myth of tradition, an intricate system of age-old, often codified rights and duties, as on the comparatively crude gradations of property, power, and prestige. Preindustrial society, of course, had also had its beginnings. Its claim to the legitimacy of the present was also a product of history or, perhaps, an ideology. Yet when it was hit by the revolution of industry, this society had an order endowed by the patina of centuries with a special claim to legitimacy and a special solidity. The power of the landlord was not based on his having money, land, or prestige, but on his being a

---

[2] Of course, Ferguson and Millar understood by "rank" by no means only what we call "prestige" today. In fact, Millar's formulation sounds surprisingly "modern": "According to the accidental differences of wealth possessed by individuals, a subordination of ranks is gradually introduced, and different degrees of power and authority are assumed without opposition, by particular persons, or bestowed upon them by the personal voice of the society." The difference indicated above and caused by the industrial revolution is rather a difference of perspective, which may be expressed by the terms "estate" and "class."

landlord as his fathers had been for time immemorial. The conditions of the master craftsman, his journeymen and apprentices, and even that of the laborer resembled that of the landlord in their legitimation by the authority of tradition. In this sense, preindustrial society was what contemporary sociologists like to call, with a somewhat doubtful expression, a "relatively static social order" (cf. Cox 40, p. 467).

Precisely these features were eliminated by the industrial revolution.[3] Surprisingly soon it created—to begin with, in England—two rapidly growing new strata, those of entrepreneurs and workers. There was no "precedent" for either, even if in England the Poor Laws mixed the old and the new poor in the same way the Crown mixed the old and the new aristocracy. Both these strata, "bourgeoisie" and "proletariat," which had grown up together and were tied to each other, had no tradition of rank, no myth of legitimacy, no "prestige of descent" (to quote Max Weber). They were characterized solely by the crude indices of possession and nonpossession, of domination and subjection. Industrial capitalists and laborers had no "natural," no traditional, unity as strata. In order to gain it, they had to stabilize and create their own traditions. They were, so to speak, *nouveaux riches* and *nouveaux pauvres*, intruders in a system of inherited values and messengers of a new system. And for these strata, bare of all traditions and differentiated merely by external, almost material criteria, the concept of "class" was first used in modern social science. In the analysis of these strata this concept became a sociological category. It is significant that in conversational German the word "class" is even today confined to the two strata of entrepreneurs and workers. Neither the nobility nor the professions nor the older groups of craftsmen and peasants are called classes. They are "estates"—a concept which in the case of the "middle estate" (*Mittelstand*) has been retained even for the newer groups of white-collar workers and civil servants.[4] An estate, however, is something else than a stratum or

---

[3] A schematic sketch like the one attempted here obviously ignores local differences as well as the gradual character of the emergence of industrial societies. All social historians of industrial development—from Weber (189) and Sombart (28), Tawney (187), and the Hammonds (175) to Bendix (138) and Jantke (178) in recent years—emphasize the gradual breakdown of the traditions of agrarian society. Concentration on the imaginary point of an "industrial revolution" can be justified only by the analytical purpose of these introductory remarks.

[4] The significance of this German usage is of course only partly open to generalization. While on the one hand it documents the thesis here advanced about the historical context of the concept of class, it testifies on the other hand to the continued

class, not only in everyday language but for the sociologist as well. "Status position[5] can be based on class position of a definite or indefinite kind. But it is not determined by class position alone: possession of money or the position of entrepreneur are not in themselves status qualifications, although they can become such; propertylessness is not in itself status disqualification, although it can become such" (M. Weber 33*a*, p. 180). "A number of persons forming a social-status stratum more or less clearly delimited from other strata in customary or statutory law constitutes a social estate" (Cox 40, p. 467). An estate, as against a class or—to anticipate the result of later conceptual discussions at this point—an open stratum, is characterized by the very attributes which the bourgeoisie and the proletariat of early industrial societies were lacking: the sacred tie of tradition and the undisputed belief in the historically founded legitimacy of position.

Thus the concept of class in its modern formulation is, if not the result of a definite historical situation, oriented toward and linked with such a situation. How difficult it is to extract the concept from this situation and apply it to other groups than bourgeoisie and proletariat, other societies than the industrializing societies of Europe, is shown most clearly by the long and still unconcluded sociological discussion of the work of Marx. The attempt to generalize the concept of class would of course hardly be worth the effort, if it were merely a name for social units like bourgeoisie or proletariat. In fact it is more. Since Marx, "class," "stratum," "rank," and "position" are no longer interchangeable names for identical groupings. For even if Marx received most of his inspiration and material from the situation of English society half a century after the industrial revolution, this society was in a sense no more than an example for him, an illustration that served to test the usefulness of a more general approach. Since Marx developed, on the basis of the concept of class, at least the rudiments of a theory of class, the model of a class society, his approach stands at the beginning of the considerations of this study.

---

importance of preindustrial strata in German society. The use of the term "middle class" in English is certainly no accident.

[5] In translating Weber's term *Stand*, most translators have used the word "status." This—though not false—is misleading in that it does not convey the double meaning of the German *Stand* as "status" and "estate." In the passage quoted here, Weber undoubtedly meant to describe status in an estate context (rather than, for example, prestige status). This is only one example of the exigencies of translations—and of their creativity. By the very fact of misleading they can create terms that acquire a life of their own.

MARX'S THEORY OF CLASS

There have been many and violent disputes about the interpretation of the work of Marx, but no commentator has seriously doubted the central importance of the theory of class for this work. Indeed, the greatness and fatality of his work become apparent in Marx's theory of class. In this theory, the three roots of his thought are joined. Marx adopted the word from the early British political economists; its application to "capitalists" and "proletarians" stems from the French "utopian" socialists; the conception of the class struggle is based on Hegel's dialectics. The theory of class provides the problematic link between sociological analysis and philosophical speculation in the work of Marx. Both can be separated, and have to be separated, but in this process the theory of class is cut in two; for it is as essential for Marx's philosophy of history as it is for his analysis of the dynamics of capitalist society.

Marx regarded the theory of class as so important that he postponed its systematic exposition time and again in favor of refinements by empirical analysis. As a result we know it only by its application to concrete problems and by the occasional generalizations that occur throughout Marx's works. This may not be the least cause of the many controversies about the real meaning of Marx's concept and theory of class. Only recently the accounts of Geiger (46) and of Bendix and Lipset (36) have concluded these discussions, at least in "Western" sociology. It is not my intention, in presenting my interpretation of Marx's approach, to relight the fires of controversy. The following discussion of the concept and theory of class in the work of Marx, while not materially deviating from either Geiger or Bendix and Lipset, is designed to supplement their works and add some substance to an investigation that is indebted to Marx even in its most radical criticisms of his work.

Marx postponed the systematic presentation of his theory of class until death took the pen from his hand. The irony has often been noted that the last (52nd) chapter of the last (third) volume of *Capital*, which bears the title "The Classes," has remained unfinished. After little more than one page the text ends with the lapidary remark of its editor, Engels: "Here the manuscript breaks off." However, for the thorough reader of Marx this is no reason for despair. If he wants to, he can complete this chapter for Marx—not exactly as Marx would have written it, of course, and not entirely without interpretation either, but in any case without substantially adding to what Marx said himself. In the following section I shall try to do just this. By systematically ordering a number of quotations and connecting them to a coherent text I shall attempt to provide a basis and point of reference for critical discussion without anticipating—beyond the selection and ordering of the quotations—any interpretation.[6]

"THE CLASSES"
The unwritten 52nd chapter of Volume III of Marx's *Capital*

THE PROBLEM

It is the ultimate purpose of this work to reveal the economic laws of development of modern society (12, I, pp. 7 f.). We are therefore not concerned with merely describing, much less regretting, existing conditions, but want to lay bare their revolutionary aspect. We have shown that the capitalist mode of production has become too restricted for its own forces of production. The revolution is near. But this revolution is not the product of economic forces of production or relations of production, but of the people and groups that represent these economic formations. *Of all instruments of production the greatest force of production is the revolutionary class itself* (6, p. 188).

For almost forty years we have emphasized the class struggle as the primary motive force of history, and especially the class struggle between bourgeoisie and proletariat as the great lever of modern social change (11, p. 102). *With the moment in which civilization begins, production begins to be based on the antagonism between accumulated and direct labor. Without conflict, no progress: that is the law which civilization has followed to the present day. Until now the forces of production have developed by virtue of the dominance of class conflict* (6, p. 80). And it always holds that *a change in the relation of classes is a historical change* (5, II, p. 475).

Thus we have to determine in general what constitutes a class and how class conflict emerges and expresses itself. *In a general investigation of this kind it is always assumed that real conditions correspond to their conception, or, which is the same thing, that real conditions are presented only in so far as they express their own general type* (12, III, p. 121). We are therefore not concerned with describing any one society, but with discovering the general laws which determine the trend of social development.

If we observe a given country from the point of view of political economy, we have to start with its population, its distribution into

---

[6] All quotations from Marx in the following section are in italics. Everything else is my text.

classes, town, country, sea, the different industries, export and import,
annual production and consumption, commodity prices, etc. (7,
p. 256). But this method presents difficulties. It leads us astray if in
our abstractions we do not find the way to *the real and concrete, the*
real premise. Population is an abstraction if I ignore, for example, the
classes of which it consists. These classes are again an empty word, if
I do not know the elements on which they are based, e.g., wage labor,
capital, etc. (7, p. 256). Thus our first question concerns the elements
on which classes are based; and since *modern bourgeois society is in*
fact our main subject (7, p. 237), we use it for the time being as an
example.

    The owners of mere labor power, the owners of capital, and the
landowners, whose respective sources of income are wage, profit, and
rent—thus wage laborers, capitalists, and landowners—constitute the
three great classes of modern society based on a capitalist mode of
production.

    In England, modern society has undoubtedly advanced furthest
and most classically in its economic structure. Even there, however,
this class structure is not displayed in a pure form. Intermediate and
transitional stages obliterate the borderlines there as everywhere (al-
though incomparably less in the country than in towns). However,
this does not matter for our investigation. It has been demonstrated
that it is the permanent tendency and law of development of the capi-
talist mode of production to separate the means of production increas-
ingly from labor, and to concentrate the separate means of production
more and more in large groups—in other words, to transform labor
into wage labor, and the means of production into capital. At the same
time, land ownership tends to be separated from capital and labor, and
to be converted into the type of land ownership corresponding to the
capitalist mode of production.

    The question to be answered next is: What constitutes a class?
And this results directly from the answer to the other question: What
makes wage laborers, capitalists, and landowners the constituent forces
of the three great social classes? (12, III, pp. 421 f.)

TWO FALSE APPROACHES

    At first it is the identity of revenues and sources of income. They
are three large social groups, whose components, i.e., the people of
whom they consist, earn their living by wage, profit, and rent, i.e., by
utilizing their labor power, capital, and land ownership. However,
from this point of view, say, doctors and civil servants would also

constitute two classes, for they belong to two different social groups whose members' incomes flow from the same source. The same would hold for the infinite fragmentation of interests and positions which the division of labor produces among workers as among capitalists and landowners (the latter, for example, into vineyard owners, field owners, forest owners, mine owners, fishing ground owners) (12, III, p. 422).

This approach does not therefore lead to a fruitful definition. The same holds for a second approach frequently adopted in explaining class differences and conflicts. *The vulgar mind commutes class differences into "differences in the size of purses" and class conflict into "trade disputes." The size of the purse is a purely quantitative difference, by virtue of which two individuals of the same class can be opposed quite arbitrarily. It is well known that medieval guilds quarreled with each other "according to trade." But it is equally well known that modern class differences are by no means based on "trade." Rather, the division of labor has created very different types of work within the same class* (5, II, pp. 466 f.).

In both cases the essential point is overlooked: property, income, and source of income are themselves a result of the class structure, i.e., of the structure of economic conditions. Income and property are criteria belonging to the realm of distribution and consumption. However, *the use of products is determined by the social relations of the consumers, and these social relations themselves rest on the conflict of classes* (6, p. 81). And since *distribution is itself a product of production, the kind of participation in production* determines *the particular patterns of distribution, the way in which people participate in distribution* (7, p. 250).

There is no property anterior to the relations of domination and subjection which obtain in production and in the political state, and *which are far more concrete relations* (7, p. 258). Therefore we have to look for the elements of classes in production and in the power relations determined by it.

PROPERTY AND ECONOMIC POWER

The essential condition that determines the mode of production of an epoch, and that therefore provides the constituent element of classes as well as the momentum of social change, is property. *The property question, relative to the different stages of development of industry, has always been the life question of any given class* (5, p. 459).

However, this statement is open to misinterpretation. For *the opposition of propertylessness and property as such is indifferent, and not expressed in an active relation to its inner structure, i.e., as a contradiction, so long as it is not comprehended as the opposition between labor and capital* (3, p. 176).

Even in this specification property is still an abstraction, an empty concept. *In every historical epoch property has developed differently and under different social conditions. To define bourgeois property means no less than to describe all the social conditions of bourgeois production. The attempt to define property as an independent relation, a special category, an abstract and eternal idea, can be nothing but an illusion of metaphysics or jurisprudence* (6, p. 169).

Only if we understand property in the particular context of bourgeois society, i.e., as private ownership of the means of production, as the control of a minority over the wealth of a whole nation, do we in fact grasp the core of the antagonism existing in production and creating class conflict. *The power of society thus becomes the private power of a private person* (12, I, p. 138).

The essential *condition of the existence and domination of the bourgeois class is the accumulation of wealth in the hands of private persons, the formation and augmentation of capital; the condition of capital is wage labor* (14, p. 89). Thus the existence of capital as well as wage labor, of the bourgeoisie as well as the proletariat, can be explained in terms of the one condition of the particular form of property in bourgeois society, i.e., ownership of the means of production.

The authority relations within production which are given by the presence or absence of effective property, of control over the means of production, are of course not the class relations themselves. In order to determine these, we have to look for the consequences flowing from the relations of production and for the social antagonisms based on these consequences.

RELATIONS OF PRODUCTION, CLASS SITUATION, AND POLITICAL POWER

One important consequence of the relations of production has already been mentioned. The division of wealth in the sphere of distribution corresponds to the division of property in production. Thus a person's material condition of existence, or class situation, is based on his position in production. *Economic conditions have first converted the mass of the population into workers. The rule of capital has created for this mass a common situation* (6, p. 187). And in a way one can state: *In so far as millions of families live under economic conditions which separate their way of life, their interests, and their education from those of other classes and oppose them to these, they constitute a class* (8, p. 104).

However, these economic conditions of existence are not in themselves sufficient for the formation of classes. They are as such passive, and although they produce the *gap between the life situations of worker and capitalist* (12, I, p. 548), they do not produce a real antagonism. For in so far as there is between people in a common material condition, or life situation, a merely external *contact—in so far as the identity of their interests does not produce a community, national association, and political organization—they do not constitute a class.* Such groups in a common situation *are therefore unable to make their class interest heard in their own name through a parliament or an assembly* (8, p. 104). We shall have to return to this point.

A second and infinitely more important consequence of the distribution of property in production is that it determines the distribution of political power in society. Modern relations of production include the economic power of the owners of private property, the capitalists. And *the political power of the bourgeois class arises from these modern relations of production* (5, p. 455). Indeed it can be said that *the modern state is but an association that administrates the common business of the whole bourgeois class* (14, p. 83).

In this sense, authority relations in production determine the authority relations of society in general. *The specific economic form in which unpaid surplus labor is pumped out of the immediate producers determines the relation of domination and subjection as it grows directly out of and in turn determines production. On this is based the whole structure of the economic community as it comes forth from the relations of production, and thereby at the same time its political structure. It is always the immediate relation of the owners of the conditions of production to the immediate producers— a relation whose specific pattern of course always corresponds to a certain stage in the development of labor and its social force of production—in which we find the final secret, the hidden basis of the whole construction of society, including the political patterns of sovereignty and dependence, in short, of a given specific form of government* (12, III, pp. 324 f.).

Finally, a third and parallel consequence of the distribution of property in production is that it also shapes the ideas that mold the character of a period. *On the different forms of property and the social conditions of existence a whole superstructure of various and peculiarly formed sentiments, illusions, modes of thought, and conceptions of life is built. The whole class creates and forms these out of its material foundations and the corresponding social relations* (8, p. 37).

We can say, therefore, that *the ruling ideas of a period have always been nothing but the ideas of the ruling class* (14, p. 93). *In each epoch, the thoughts of the ruling class are the ruling thoughts; i.e., the class that is the ruling material power of society is at the same time its ruling intellectual power. The class that has the means of material production in its control, controls at the same time the means of intellectual production* (13, II, p. 37).

CLASS INTERESTS

We have seen that relations of property and authority constitute the basis of the formation of social classes. But we have not yet investigated the force that effects this formation. Classes do not exist in isolation, independent of other classes to which they are opposed. *Individuals form a class only in so far as they are engaged in a common struggle with another class* (13, II, p. 59); and the force that effects class formation is class interest. In a sense, class interests precede the formation of classes. *Thus the German bourgeoisie stands in opposition to the proletariat even before it has organized itself as a class in the political sphere* (5, p. 469). The proletariat has, in the beginning of its development, certain *common interests,* but it is nevertheless still an unorganized mass. *Thus this mass is already a class in opposition to capital, but not yet a class for itself* (6, p. 187).

By postulating class interests as preceding the classes themselves, we make it quite clear that class interests are not merely the random personal interests of one person or even many people. *We are not concerned with what this or that proletarian or even the whole proletariat visualizes as a goal for the time being. Its goal and its historical action are obviously and irrevocably predetermined by its own life situation as by the whole organization of contemporary bourgeois society* (4, p. 207). Thus *the shared interest* of a class exists not only *in the imagination, as a generality, but above all in reality as the mutual dependence of the individuals among whom labor is divided* (13, II, p. 23). *As in private life we distinguish between what a man thinks and says of himself and what he really is and does, so in historical struggles we must distinguish even more carefully the catchwords and fantasies of parties from their real organism and their real interests, their conception from their reality* (8, p. 38).

Class interests as "objective" interests subsuming the members of a class under a general force not only can differ from individual, personal interests, but can conflict with these interests. Although, for example, *all members of the modern bourgeoisie have the same interest inasmuch as they form a class vis-à-vis another class,* they have nevertheless *opposite, contradictory interests as soon as they are confronted with each other* (6, p. 140). *This conflict of interests* is not merely a possibility; it arises with a degree of necessity *from the economic conditions of their bourgeois life* (6, p. 140). For example, *the conflict between the interest of the individual capitalist and the class of capitalists makes itself felt* if the problem at hand is not the distribution of profits but that of losses, *just as before the identity of interests found its practical realization through competition* (12, III, p. 235).

The substance of class interests, in so far as they are based on the economic positions of given groups, can be expressed in various ways. To begin with, the immediate interest of the proletariat is the wage, that of the bourgeoisie the profit; and here once again we have to distinguish the *two great categories into which the interest of the bourgeoisie is divided—land ownership and capital* (8, p. 38). From these immediate concerns, confined to the sphere of production, all further interests can be derived. As a society develops to its maturity, the originally divided interests become increasingly united. More and more *it is a specific type of production, and of relations of production, which determines rank and influence of all other activities* (7, p. 264). This means that two particular interests are increasingly articulated: the conservative interest of the ruling class, and the revolutionary interest of the oppressed class. *Of all the classes with which the bourgeoisie is today confronted, only the proletariat is a truly revolutionary class* (14, p. 88). And *a class in which the revolutionary interests of society are concentrated, as soon as it has risen up, finds directly in its own situation the content and the material of its revolutionary activity: foes to be laid low; measures, dictated by the needs of the struggle, to be taken—the consequences of its own deeds drive it on. It makes no theoretical inquiries into its task* (9, p. 42).

On the basis of these class interests, in fighting to realize them or defend them, the groups determined by the distribution of property in production, and by the distribution of political power flowing from it, organize themselves into classes.

CLASS ORGANIZATION AND CLASS STRUGGLE

The organization of classes follows the progress of conflicts within the sphere of production itself. *Increasingly the collisions between the individual worker and the individual bourgeois assume the character of collisions between two classes. The workers start forming coalitions against the bourgeois; they join in order to maintain their wage* (14, p. 87). But the wage is, as we have seen, merely an undeveloped, prerevolutionary interest of the proletariat. This stage of class organization corresponds to a relatively early phase of capitalist development. *As long as the rule of the bourgeois class had not organized itself fully, and had not acquired its pure political expression, the opposition of the other classes could not come forth in its pure form either, and where it did come forth, it could not take that dangerous turn which converts every struggle against government into a struggle against capital* (8, p. 54). The development of the forces of production has to be far advanced for the formation of classes to be possible, because *the organization of the revolutionary elements as a class presupposes the complete existence of all forces of production which could possibly develop in the womb of the old society* (6, p. 188).

The formation of classes always means the organization of common interests in the sphere of politics. This point needs to be emphasized. Classes are political groups united by a common interest. *The struggle between two classes is a political struggle* (6, p. 187). We therefore speak of classes only in the realm of political conflict. Thus *every movement in which the working class as such opposes the ruling class and seeks to destroy its power by pressure from without is a political movement. The attempt, for example, to extort a limitation of working time in a single factory or trade, and from individual capitalists, by strikes, etc., is a purely economic movement; but the movement to enforce legislation stipulating an eight-hour day, etc., is a political movement. And in this manner a political movement grows everywhere out of the isolated economic movements of the workers; i.e., it is a movement of the class in order to realize its interests in a general form, in a form that possesses universal social constraining force* (10, p. 90).

Parallel with the political organization of classes there grows up a *theoretical class-consciousness* (12, I, p. 13), i.e., an awareness on the individual's part of the interests of his class generally. The positive goals of the proletariat become evident and can be formulated by its theoreticians. *As long as the proletariat has not sufficiently developed to organize itself as a class, as long as therefore the struggle of the proletariat with the bourgeoisie as yet has no political character, these theoreticians are merely utopians who invent systems in order to satisfy the needs of the oppressed classes* (6, p. 142).

Thus classes are political forces based on the relations of property and power. But although in principle every individual can be identified as a member of one of the above-named classes according to his share in property and power, it is *quite possible that a man's actions will not always be determined by the class to which he belongs; but these individual cases are as irrelevant to the class struggle as the defection of some noblemen to the Third Estate was to the French revolution* (5, p. 467).

This circulation among the classes or *exchange between them* (7, p. 266) is particularly evident in two stages of the organization of interest groups into classes. We find it in the first place, for example, *in the United States of America, where although classes exist they have not yet become stabilized, but instead exchange and transfer their elements in continuous flux* (8, p. 18). That is to say, we find this exchange in an early stage of class formation when the ruling class is still concerned with consolidating its power. And *the more capable a ruling class is of absorbing the best men of the oppressed class, the more solid and dangerous is its rule* (12, III, p. 140). The second stage in which a certain exchange between the classes takes place is that immediately preceding a revolution. *In times in which the class struggle approaches its decision, the process of disintegration within the ruling class and within the whole old society assumes such a violent and glaring character that a small part of the ruling class renounces it and joins the revolutionary class, the class that carries the future in its hands. Just as earlier a part of the nobility went over to the bourgeoisie, now a part of the bourgeoisie goes over to the proletariat, in particular certain bourgeois ideologists who have achieved a theoretical understanding of the whole historical movement* (14, pp. 87 f.).

This organization of the proletarians as a class, and that means as a political party (14, p. 87), eventually furnishes the basis of the class struggle. To repeat: *Every class struggle is a political struggle* (14, p. 87). It is the deliberate and articulate conflict between two opposed interests, the interests, respectively, of preserving and of revolutionizing the existing institutions and power relations. The formation of classes as organized interest groups, the antagonism between oppressing and oppressed classes, and the resulting revolutionary changes constitute the law of development of all history up to now. *An oppressed class is the condition of existence of every society based on class conflict. Thus the liberation of the oppressed class necessarily involves the creation of a new society* (6, p. 188). *The history of all societies up to the present is the history of class struggles* (14, p. 81).

THE CLASSLESS SOCIETY

Following these laws of development the proletariat has organized itself in the womb of bourgeois society, and has opened its struggle against the bourgeoisie.

Does this mean that after the downfall of the old society there will be a new class rule culminating in a new political authority? No.

The condition of the liberation of the working class is the abolition of every class, just as the condition of the liberation of the Third Estate, i.e., the establishment of the bourgeois order, was the abolition of all estates.

The working class will in the course of development replace the old bourgeois society by an association which excludes classes and their conflict, and there will no longer be any political authority proper, since it is especially the political authority that provides class conflict within bourgeois society with its official expression.

By now the conflict between proletariat and bourgeoisie is a struggle of one class against another, a struggle that means in its highest expression a total revolution. Is there any reason to be surprised that a society based on class conflict leads to brutal opposition, and in the last resort to a clash between individuals?

Nobody should say that society develops independently of politics. There is no political movement which is not at the same time a social movement.

Only in an order of things in which there are no classes and no class conflicts will social evolutions cease to be political revolutions (6, pp. 188 f.).

SOCIOLOGICAL ELEMENTS OF MARX'S THEORY OF CLASS

If Marx himself had written this chapter, it would no doubt have been longer, more polemical, and more directly related to the society of his time.[7] Nevertheless the attempt to present Marx's approach to a theory of class conflict largely in his own words is more than an entertaining game. The result can serve as a fruitful basis for some more general observations which will prove useful for subsequent critical considerations. The following elements of Marx's theory of class appear particularly worth emphasizing for sociological analysis:

1. It is important to realize what Geiger called the "heuristic purpose behind the concept of class" (46, chap. ii). Wherever Marx used the concept in a sociological sense, he was not concerned with describing an existing state of society. He was concerned, rather, with the analysis of certain laws of social development and of the forces involved in this development. To use the misleading terms of modern sociology, the heuristic purpose of the concept of class was for Marx not "static" but "dynamic," not "descriptive" but "analytical." What these terms may mean and what they cannot mean will have to be discussed later in some detail. Here it is sufficient to emphasize that for Marx the theory of class was not a theory of a cross section of society arrested in time, in particular not a theory of social stratification, but a tool for the explanation of changes in total societies. In elaborating and applying his theory of class, Marx was not guided by the question "How does a given society in fact look at a given point of time?" but by the question "How does the structure of a society change?" or, in his own words, "What is the [economic] law of motion of modern society?"

2. This heuristic purpose explains the often criticized two-class model underlying the dynamic theory of Marx. Had Marx wanted to describe his society with photographic accuracy, this model would indeed have been most unsatisfactory. As a matter of fact, Marx does refer occasionally (without always using his concept of class in an entirely unambiguous manner) to a multitude of classes. He refers to the "two great categories into which the interest of the bourgeoisie is divided—land ownership and capital" (8, p. 43), to the petty bourgeoisie as a "transitional class" (8, p. 49), and to the class of small peasants (8, p. 118). But in principle these "intermediate and transitional stages," as Marx significantly calls them, "do not matter for

---

[7] In this sense, Renner's attempt (26, pp. 374 ff.) to reconstruct this chapter of *Capital* is closer to Marx in style and content than the attempt here undertaken to sketch the most general elements of Marx's theory of class. Clearly, the claim that I have written the unwritten last chapter of *Capital* must not be understood literally in the sense of a philological conjecture. My main purpose has been to offer a systematic presentation of the many isolated statements about class in the work of Marx.

our investigation" (12, III, p. 421). Not only are they unstable
entities destined to be drawn sooner or later into the two great whirl-
pools of bourgeoisie and proletariat, but even if this were not the case,
their historical role would be insignificant by comparison with that of
the dominant classes of capitalist society. The concept of class is an
analytical category, or, as Marx says in one of his rare but enlighten-
ing methodological remarks, "real conditions are presented only in
so far as they express their own general type" (12, III, p. 121). The
general type of the real conditions of conflict that generates change,
however, is the opposition of two dominant forces, two prevalent
classes.

Geiger has refuted the unjustified objections to Marx's two-class
model so convincingly that further discussion of them is unnecessary
(46, pp. 37 ff.). But the legitimacy of assuming for analytical purposes the dominance of only two conflicting classes must not blind us
to the fact that Marx has linked with his two-class model a number
of additional postulates whose legitimacy appears rather more dubious. For Marx the category of class defines one side of an antagonism
which entails the dominant issues of conflict in every society as well
as the direction of its development. This means for Marx that (*a*)
every conflict capable of generating structural change is a class conflict, (*b*) the contents of class conflict always represent the dominant
issues of social conflict, and (*c*) the two classes stand in the relation
of Hegel's "thesis" and "antithesis," in the sense that one is characterized by the affirmation (or possession) of those features of which
the other is the complete negation. It is at least open to dispute
whether this last approach recommends itself in social science. The
other two postulates connected with Marx's two-class model, however, are empirical generalizations, the untenability of which will have
to be demonstrated. Only if it is freed of these accessories can the two-
class model be conceived as a feasible principle of knowledge.

3. Marx has tried to argue for the third postulate mentioned
above in the most difficult part of his theory, the part concerned with
the causes and origins of classes. What are the structural conditions
of the formation of social classes? For simplicity's sake I shall treat
this aspect of Marx's theory of class with reference to his analysis of
capitalist society, since the question remains undecided for the time
being whether this theory can be applied to other types of society at all.

Marx states quite clearly that class conflicts do not originate in
differences of income, or of the sources of income. His classes are
not tax classes in the sense of the Roman censors. Rather, the determi-

nant of classes is "property." Property, however, must not be understood in terms of purely passive wealth, but as an effective force of
production, as "ownership of means of production" and its denial to
others. In this sense, the "relations of production," i.e., the authority
relations resulting from the distribution of effective property in the
realm of (industrial) production, constitute the ultimate determinant
of the formation of classes and the development of class conflicts. The
capitalists possess factories and machines, and buy the only property
of the proletarians, their labor power, in order to produce a surplus
value with these means of production and augment their capital.

But our question cannot be answered all that easily. The role of
property in Marx's theory of class poses a problem of interpretation,
and on this interpretation the validity of Marx's theory of class stands
or falls. Does Marx understand, by the relations of property or production, the relations of factual control and subordination in the enterprises of industrial production—or merely the authority relations in
so far as they are based on the legal title of property? Does he conceive of property in a loose (sociological) sense—i.e., in terms of the
exclusiveness of legitimate control (in which the manager also exercises property functions)—or merely as a statutary property right in
connection with such control? Is property for Marx a special case of
authority—or, vice versa, authority a special case of property? These
questions are of considerable significance. If one works with the narrow concept of property, class conflict is the specific characteristic of
a form of production which rests on the union of ownership and control. In this case a society in which control is exercised, for example, by
state functionaries, has by definition neither classes nor class conflicts.
If, on the other hand, one works with the wider concept of property,
class structure is determined by the authority structure of the enterprise, and the category of class becomes at least potentially applicable
to all "relations of production."

Marx does not always make his answer to our questions entirely
clear. But it can be shown that his analyses are essentially based on
the narrow, legal concept of property. This procedure, and this procedure only, enables Marx to link his sociology with his philosophy
of history—a brilliant attempt, but at the same time a fault that robs
his sociological analyses of stringency and conviction, a fault made
no more acceptable by the fact that orthodox Marxists have remained
faithful to their master in this point to the present day.

The most striking evidence for this interpretation can be found in
the preliminary attempts at an analysis of the new form of ownership

characteristic of joint-stock companies which Marx presents in Volume III of *Capital*. Marx is here explicitly concerned with the phenomenon that is commonly described today as the separation of ownership and control. He discusses what he calls the "transformation of the really functioning capitalist into a mere director, an administrator of alien capital, and of the owners of capital into mere owners, mere money capitalists" (12, III, p. 477). "In joint-stock companies, function is separated from capital ownership; thereby labor is entirely separated from ownership of the means of production, and of surplus labor" (p. 478). Now, hard though it is for ordinary minds to see why this change in the size and legal structure of industrial enterprises should end the conflict between entrepreneurs who can command and workers who have to obey (the conflict that Marx postulates for the "pure" capitalist enterprise), Marx ascribes to the joint-stock company a peculiar place in history. Time and again he describes the joint-stock company as "private production without the control of private property" (p. 480), as "the elimination of capital as private property within the capitalist mode of production itself" (p. 477), and even as the "abolition of the capitalist mode of production within the capitalist mode of production itself" (p. 479). For him, the joint-stock company is "a necessary point on the way to reconverting capital into the property of the producers, this no longer being the private property of individual producers but their associated property, i.e., immediate social property" (p. 478). It is a "point on the way to the transformation of all functions in the process of reproduction hitherto connected with capital ownership into mere functions of the associated producers, into social functions" (p. 478). The joint-stock company, in other words, is halfway to the communist—and that means classless—society.

We cannot pursue here the manifold consequences of this strange analysis, which—correct as it may to a certain extent be empirically (if in a sense hardly intended by Marx)—would certainly have exposed Marx, had he lived longer, to many an awkward question from his most orthodox adherents. One point, however, is convincingly demonstrated by this analysis: for Marx, the relations of production as a determinant of class formation were also authority relations, but they were such only because in the first place they were property relations in the narrow sense of the distribution of controlling private ownership. *Qua* property relations they are authority relations, and not vice versa, not *qua* authority relations property relations. If, therefore, the functions of the "director" and the "mere owner," the manager and the stockholder, are separated, this means a first step on the way to the complete abolition not only of effective private property itself, but also of the authority relations dependent on it, and thus a step on the way to the communist society. For Marx, classes were tied to the existence of effective private property. Their formation, existence, and struggle can occur only in a society in which some possess and others are excluded from private ownership and control of the means of production.

4. One of the critical pivots of Marx's theory of class is the undisputed identification of economic and political power and authority. Although classes are founded on the "relations of production," i.e., the distribution of effective property in the narrow sphere of commodity production, they become socially significant only in the political sphere. But both these spheres are inseparable. "The political power" of a class arises for Marx "from the relations of production" (5, p. 455). The relations of production are "the final secret, the hidden basis of the whole construction of society" (12, III, pp. 324 f.); industrial classes are *eo ipso* also social classes, and industrial class conflict is political class conflict. Nowhere has Marx explicitly discussed the basis of this empirical proposition—nor has he seen sufficiently clearly that it is an empirical proposition rather than a postulate or premise. The thesis that political conditions are determined by industrial conditions seems to stem, for him, from the generalized assertion of an absolute and universal primacy of production over all other structures of economy and society. It is evident that a postulate of this kind requires empirical test; how it fares in this test will have to be shown.

5. Relatively thoroughly, if nowhere systematically, Marx has described the steps of the process by which groupings in the form of classes emerge from conditions of social structure. For Marx, the first stage of this process of the formation of classes is given directly by the distribution of effective private property. Possession and nonpossession of effective private property create two peculiar "common situations," "conditions of life," or class situations. These class situations have three complementary aspects: (*a*) that of the mere distribution of effective property, i.e., of possession or nonpossession of means of production and of authority; (*b*) that of the possession or nonpossession of goods and values gratifying personal needs, i.e., the "rewards" of modern sociology; and (*c*) that of the common situationally determined interests of those who share a class situation. By common interest in Marx's sense is not meant a conscious tendency

of individual desires, but a potentially unconscious (or "falsely conscious") tendency of actual behavior shared by people in a common class situation. Common interests exist, as Marx says, "not merely in the imagination, . . . but above all in reality as the mutual dependence of the individuals among whom labor is divided" (13, II, p. 23). This is a difficult notion; for we are used to conceiving of interests above all on a psychological level. For the time being, however, we shall put off considering in what sense a concept of "objective interests" that "exist as" real conditions may be useful. At this point we merely conclude that Marx's theory of class formation starts with the postulate of a common class situation, the main components of which are a common relation to effective private property, a common socio-economic situation, and a common tendency of actual behavior determined by "objective" interests.

In accordance with the premises of the theory of class, we already find, from this point of view, a fundamental dichotomy of class situations in any given society, and of the members of a society by their class situations. Occasionally, Marx refers to the aggregates thus defined as classes. "In so far as millions of families live under economic conditions which separate their way of life, their interests, and their education from those of other classes and oppose them to these, they constitute a class" (8, p. 104). The concept of class as defined so far corresponds to Max Weber's later formulation, " 'Class' shall mean any group of persons in a common class situation" (33a, p. 177).[8] However, this definition has its problems. It has to be asked whether a common situation is sufficient to constitute a group in the strict sense of this term. If—as can be shown—this is not the case, it remains to be asked how an aggregate of people who are merely situated identically, without having any contact or coherence, can become an effective force in social conflict and change. Marx has asked this question, and he therefore emphasizes at many points that the mere "gap between the conditions of life," the mere "identity of interests" and class situations, is a necessary but by no means sufficient condition of the formation of classes. He continues therefore in the passage quoted above: "In so far as there is a merely local contact [among people in a common class situation]—in so far as the identity of their interests does

---

[8] As a matter of fact, Weber is well aware of the problem under discussion. He therefore distinguishes "property classes" (as "not 'dynamic' ") from "income classes" and "social classes." However, since Weber describes all three classes as consisting of all people in a common (if differently defined) class situation, his theory of class lacks the analytical strength of Marx's, which is much more precise on this point.

not produce a community, national association, and political organization—they do not constitute a class. They are therefore unable to make their class interest heard. . . ." (8, p. 104).

6. This may well be the most important step in Marx's theory of class formation: Classes do not constitute themselves as such until they participate in political conflicts as organized groups. Although Marx occasionally uses the concept of class in a less determinate, more comprehensive sense, a multitude of statements leave little doubt that for him class formation and class conflict were phenomena belonging to the sphere of politics. "As long as the proletariat has not sufficiently developed to organize itself as a class, . . . the struggle of the proletariat with the bourgeoisie has not yet assumed a political character" (6, p. 142). This means conversely that the carriers of class conflict have organized themselves as classes, and have become classes, only if class conflict has assumed a political character.

For Marx, this last stage of class formation has two complementary aspects. On the factual level of social structure it involves the association of people who share a class situation in a strict group, party, or political organization. Marx refers to the "organization of the proletarians as a class, and that means as a political party" (14, p. 87). On the normative and ideological level of social structure it involves the articulation of "class-consciousness," i.e., the transformation of "objective" class interests into subjectively conscious, formulated goals of organized action. The complete class is characterized not by a common though unconscious direction of behavior, but by its conscious action toward formulated goals.

7. Marx's theory of class formation is embedded in his work in a wider theory of class conflict as the moving force of social change. However, the elements of this wider theory are only partly of a sociological nature. It contains a number of theses whose validity can no longer be tested by empirical research. In summarizing those elements of Marx's theory of class conflict that are of potential use to the sociologist, we soon reach the point at which Marx the sociologist and Marx the philosopher joined forces:

(*a*) In every society there is possession of and exclusion from effective private property. In every society there is therefore possession of and exclusion from legitimate power. The "relations of production" determine different class situations in the sense indicated above.

(*b*) Differentiation of class situations toward the extremes of possession of and exclusion from property and power increases as a society develops.

(c) As the gap between class situations grows, the conditions of class formation—i.e., of political organization and of the explicit formulation of class interests—mature. The political class struggle between "oppressors" and "oppressed" begins.

(d) At its climax this conflict produces a revolutionary change, in which the hitherto ruling class loses its power position and is replaced by the hitherto oppressed class. A new society emerges, in which a new oppressed class grows up, and the process of class formation and class conflict starts anew.

It will prove necessary to subject this wider theory of Marx to severe criticism from a sociological point of view,[9] even though the most problematical aspects of Marx's theory, such as the notion of a classless society, have so far been left out of consideration. Here we are concerned merely with a résumé of the sociological elements of Marx's theory of class. It is, as we can say now, a theory of structural change by revolutions based on conflicts between antagonistic interest groups. Marx describes in detail the structural conditions and the process of formation of these interest groups. Less elaborately, but clearly enough, he also describes the process of conflict between these groups and its solution in revolutionary changes.

8. Before we leave Marx's sociology one more formal characteristic of his theory of class warrants recognition, since it is not without significance for recent sociological theory. By analyzing the change of social structures in terms of the categories mentioned, Marx introduces at least implicitly a certain image of society. Although an image of society of this kind may not be of immediate empirical relevance for sociological research, it can nevertheless become a measure of the proximity of a theoretical construction to reality, and it serves important functions as a guide to problems of research.[10]

[9] This holds in particular for propositions (a) and (b), which can only be empirical generalizations and are as such untenable even if Marx abandons them arbitrarily for the two societies he invented: the "original society" and the "final society" of history. Proposition (c) is also problematical; see the section on "class conflict and revolution" in Chapter IV. Generally speaking, it is my intention in this chapter—at least in so far as sociological questions are concerned—to indicate the points of departure of criticism, but to postpone the criticism itself.

[10] See Chapter III, pp. 112 ff., and Chapter V, pp. 157 ff., for a more elaborate discussion of "images of society."

For Marx, society is not primarily a smoothly functioning order of the form of a social organism, a social system, or a static social fabric. Its dominant characteristic is, rather, the continuous change of not only its elements, but its very structural form. This change in turn bears witness to the presence of conflicts as an essential feature of every society. Conflicts are not random; they are a systematic product of the structure of society itself. According to this image, there is no order except in the regularity of change. "Without conflict no progress: this is the law which civilization has followed to the present day" (6, p. 80).[11]

This image of society stands in clear contradiction to the images which lie at the basis of the considerations of some recent sociologists. At the same time, it appears considerably more useful for the solution of many problems of sociological analysis than all analogies, explicit or implicit, between society and organism, or society and one or another (essentially "closed") functional system. The reality of society is conflict and flux. Despite our radical criticism of Marx's theory of class, this implication may therefore be retained as a fruitful heuristic principle.

PHILOSOPHICAL ELEMENTS OF MARX'S THEORY OF CLASS

In the imaginary chapter of *Capital* above, I have deliberately emphasized the nonsociological elements of Marx's theory of class rather less than Marx himself would have done. Now, too, I shall discuss them less elaborately than the sociological elements, since this study is intended not as a philosophical discussion or merely as a criticism of Marx, but rather as a means of posing anew the problem of social conflict and its sociological analysis, and furnishing some elements of its solution. Nevertheless, it would hardly be justifiable to represent Marx's theory of class and subject it to critical examination without mentioning its nonsociological elements.

A word of explanation may be in place as to the identification of its nonsociological elements with its "philosophical" elements. It seems to me that it can be shown that the work of Marx falls into two

---

[11] Unfortunately, the clause "to the present day" is meant to imply that one day this law will no longer hold. Here as elsewhere Marx has vitiated the value of his sociology by Hegelian philosophical additions of little plausibility. The image of society indicated in the last paragraph is for Marx an image of historical societies in the period of alienation. Communist society (as well as the early communal society of Marx's philosophical imagination) is different, and indeed in many ways not dissimilar to the constructions of modern sociological theory.

separable parts (cf. 225). On the one hand, there are categories, hypotheses, and theories which permit empirical test, i.e., which either can be falsified themselves by empirical observations, or allow of derivations that can be so falsified. This is true, for example, of the proposition that structural change is a result of class conflicts. If I use the term "sociological" for such elements of the work of Marx, I am well aware that it is too narrow with respect to Marx's strictly economic propositions and theories. In the case of the theory of class, however, it is undoubtedly applicable.

On the other hand, the work of Marx contains postulates and theories utterly removed from the possibility of empirical test. Propositions such as that capitalist society is the last class society of history, or that communist society leads to a complete realization of human freedom, can be disputed and denied, but they cannot be refuted with the tools of science. To be more precise, it is impossible to imagine empirical data which would falsify these postulates or their derivations. For such assertions, which are irrefutable in principle, I use the term "philosophical." This expression is evidently as little exhaustive in terms of the content and method of philosophy as is the term "sociological" in the meaning here proposed for sociology. The attributes "sociological" and "philosophical" signify in this context a difference in the logical status of propositions. Marx's theory of class contains elements of both kinds. Indeed, nowhere has Marx linked both kinds of propositions as cleverly, and hence as deceptively, as in his theory of class.

Marx's conception of the communist society, of its role in history, and of the time of its arrival is the pivotal point of the connection between the philosophical and the sociological elements of his theory of class. Later, we shall have to consider sense and nonsense in the notion of a classless society from a sociological point of view. Here we are concerned with the place of the classless society in Marx's philosophy of history. In an earlier study I have tried to show in detail in what sense the historical process is for Marx a dialectical process of thesis, antithesis, and synthesis (224). Not only does this hold for what is sometimes called the "real dialectics" of history from antique to feudal and further to capitalist society, but it holds above all for the total process of history. For Marx, the supreme meaning and law of historical development lies in the birth of human freedom, or of free man by human labor. In its beginning there is the postulated reality of an original society, in which man is "with himself" and free, though as yet only in a restrained and partial fashion. Private property, classes and class conflict, division of labor, and inequality are absent from this society. But man is still quasi-unborn; he has not developed his talents yet, not recognized his potentialities; his free dom is a dull freedom, without conscious activity and constrained by extraneous purposes. This original society breaks up with the appearance of private property and the division of labor, and is transformed into its antithesis.

Then begins a second stage of human development, which comprises all known history. In this stage, man is alienated from himself. Division of labor and private property create relations of domination and subjection, class formations, and class struggles in ever-changing patterns. Indeed, private property is the specific difference of this second stage of the historical process, as it had been the principle of social inequality and social organization for Locke and Hume, Ferguson and Millar. In this stage man is unfree; but the growth of the forces of production leads him to develop ever new potentialities and talents. He cannot develop these talents to the full so long as he is alienated and enslaved, but they are present now within him. For all men to develop all their talents in all directions by purpose-free activity, all that is needed is regained liberty, de-alienation.

This is realized by the synthesis of classless society. It is classless, because in it there is no private property, and there are therefore— by virtue of Marx's (false) conception of property—no relations of authority, no class conflicts. It is a synthesis, because it combines the dull liberty of original society and the differentiated human potentialities of alienation in the triple sense of the Hegelian concept; it abolishes them as such and yet preserves them on a higher level.[12] In this society man realizes himself as a free being.

Thus formulated, Marx's philosophy of history is little more than Hegel's theory of history as the realization of the spirit of freedom "turned upside down." In this formulation also, Marx's philosophy of history is not directly relevant to the sociological theory of class. However, Marx joins the two by a fascinating trick of definition and thereby manages to give his philosophy the appearance of empirical validity, and his sociology the force of indubitable truth. As long as these two logical bastards were not recognized as such, they could have, singly and combined, that political effect so well known today.

[12] The word Hegel and Marx use most frequently to characterize the synthesis of the dialectical process is *aufheben*. Even as a word, it has three meanings, all of which were intended by Hegel and Marx: (1) to suspend or abolish, (2) to elevate or lift to a higher level, (3) to preserve or maintain.

It might seem that the concept of class is not really necessary for Marx's philosophy of history. In speaking of the transition from the original society to the state of alienation, Marx sees the cause of this "fall of man" in private property. Correspondingly, the central event of the transition from the state of alienation to the realm of liberty is the abolition of effective private property. All other symptoms of alienation, such as classes and power relations, the state and the division of labor,[13] also disappear. But they almost look like empirical trimmings with no particular relation to the argument—unless they are asserted to be dependent on private property.

In a logically independent approach Marx investigates the society of his time. There he notes empirically three factors, among others: (*a*) the presence of a conflict between social groups (classes), (*b*) the presence of effective private property, and (*c*) the presence of relations of domination and subjection. He believes furthermore that he can discern in this society a tendency for private property to be abolished and replaced by communal property—an observation which at least to some extent has proved correct. And what happens if effective private property disappears? It is precisely at this point that Marx jumps from sociology into philosophy and back by introducing his undoubtedly brilliant trick of definition. By asserting the dependence of classes on relations of domination and subjection, and the dependence of these relations on the possession of or exclusion from effective private capital,[14] he makes on the one hand empirically private property, on the other hand philosophically social classes, the central factor of his analyses. One can retrace step by step the thought process to which Marx has succumbed at this point. It is not the thought process of the empirical scientist who seeks only piecemeal knowledge and expects only piecemeal progress, but that of the system builder who suddenly finds that everything fits! For if private property disappears (empirical hypothesis), then there are no longer classes (trick of definition)! If there are no longer any classes, there is no alienation (speculative postulate). The realm of liberty is realized on earth

[13] Marx's considerations are least unambiguous in this question of the division of labor. Thus when Marx and Engels try to prove in their *German Ideology* that there will be no division of labor in communist society, their proof remains understandably unconvincing and is really confined to the thesis that the final society will replace the "specialist," or "detail man," by the "universal man."

[14] An assertion which is of course understandable in view of the factual identity of ownership and control in early industrial capitalism, but which is unpardonable as a generalization. Cf. pp. 41 ff.

(philosophical idea). Had Marx, conversely, defined private property by authority relations, his empirical observation would not have "fitted," and he would have had to drop his philosophy of history. For effective private property may disappear empirically, but authority relations can do so only by the magic trick of the system maniac.[15]

There would be no objection to joining philosophy and sociology, if this were done without consequences detrimental to sociology. This is not, however, the case here. Marx's philosophy has forced him to betray his sociology, and this betrayal forces us to separate the two elements relentlessly. Far-reaching as this assertion may sound, it can easily be justified by reference to Marx's work, as a few examples may show:

1. The dogmatic conjunction of classes and effective private property documents in itself a betrayal of sociology. Perhaps a Marx without the Marxian philosophy of history would have realized that power and authority are not tied to the legal title of property. Marx himself could not realize this, and certainly could not admit it, for had he done so, his philosophical conception of the classless society would have become impossible both empirically and intellectually. In other words, he had either to regard the joint-stock company as a transitional form on the way to the classless society, or to abandon the philosophy according to which private property—and not the possession of or exclusion from authority—is the *differentia specifica* of alienation and the determining factor of classes.

2. In asserting the universality of class conflict in the stage of alienation, Marx has again saved his philosophy and sacrificed his sociology. "The history of all societies up to the present is the history of class struggles." This seemingly empirical sentence is in reality but a reformulation of the philosophical postulate that links alienation (and thereby all known history), private property, and the classes. It becomes a dogma that prevents open, unprejudiced research from developing. There is, moreover, a strange irony in the fact that the same Marx who so often attacked the uncritical assertion that private property is universal, introduces the same assertion in a concealed way but equally uncritically by speaking of the universality of classes, which for him are tied to the presence of private property.

3. Marx's analysis of his own capitalist society is evidently col-

[15] The thesis of this argument was intimated first by Schumpeter. Cf. 73, pp. 19 f. See also below, pp. 84 ff.

ored by his sociologically nonsensical conviction that it is the last class society in history. Thus his assertions of the extraordinary intensity of class conflict in this society and of the messianic role of the proletariat have little to do with empirical knowledge. They invest the concept of class with an importance and a measure of exclusiveness in sociological analysis which is clearly not warranted by historical experience (although it has blinded generations of sociologists).

4. Finally, the application of dialectics as the asserted inherent law of historical development involves a betrayal of sociology in the interests of philosophy. This is especially evident in the misleading and sociologically untenable thesis that structural change is necessarily of a revolutionary character—once again a thesis unfortunately impressive enough to divert the eyes of social scientists away from real changes.

Several further points of lesser importance could be mentioned at which sociological and philosophical elements are linked in Marx's theory of class. However, such points are not our concern here. We are concerned rather with a rough sketch of the nonsociological aspects of Marx's theory of class, and at the same time with finding a point of departure for their radical separation from the sociological aspects. For the sociologist, there can be no doubt that this separation is necessary. But it might be asked: Why all this effort? Why not a completely new and more fruitful approach? There are two answers to these questions: First, it is often useful to start with a critical review of the errors of earlier authors so that one can avoid them oneself. Second, Marx's theory of class, if freed of all speculative trimmings, contains many insights and useful approaches, which we can scarcely afford to ignore.

MARX'S IMAGE OF THE CAPITALIST CLASS SOCIETY

Our discussion has brought out the main lines of Marx's view of the society of his time and its development. To this view some details may be added now which can usefully serve as a point of departure for the analysis of factual changes in industrial societies since Marx, in so far as they relate to the class structure of these societies. Following Marx, we shall use the term "capitalist society" without defining it precisely for the time being. But unlike Marx, we shall ignore the philosophical elements of his analysis and renounce the cheap triumph of "refuting" speculative prophecies by empirical data.

According to Marx, capitalist society is a class society. There is in this society a category of persons who possess effective private property, and another category of those who have no such property. The former is called capital or bourgeoisie, the latter wage labor or proletariat. The typical private property of capitalist society consists of the means of industrial production, i.e., factories, machines, and the like, or capital. The owners or capitalists directly control their means of production; the nonowners or wage laborers are dependent, by the labor contract, on the means of production and their owners. Property and power and the exclusion from both go together; they "correlate." There is also a correlation between these factors on the one hand, and socio-economic position on the other hand: the capitalists are wealthy, secure, and have high status; the wage laborers are lacking a subsistence minimum. This difference in position makes for conflicting interests and conflicting groupings—classes—which fight each other at first on the local level of the individual enterprise, eventually on the political level.

There are, of course, persons in capitalist society—such as landlords, independent craftsmen and small businessmen, peasants, and intellectuals—who stand outside this tension and whose interests are not directly affected by it. These groups, however, not only decrease in numerical importance but increasingly lose their influence on the conflicts determining the structure of society. The capitalist bourgeoisie and its counterpart, the industrial proletariat, move more and more into the center of the social process. Their conflicts dominate the scene of capitalist class society and draw all other groups into their orbit or condemn them to complete insignificance. Society is dominated by the antagonism between the interests of those who defend their possession of effective private property and those who elevate their nonpossession into a demand for a complete change of the property relations.

This sketch of Marx's view of capitalist society is incomplete in one important point. It describes a structure, and not its process of development, whereas it is on the latter count that Marx made his sociologically important contribution to social analysis. Marx tried, at times retrospectively, more often predictively, to determine the tendencies of change that can be derived from this structure. With respect to the development of class structure he emphasized in particular the following four processes:

1. Inherent in capitalist society, there is a tendency for the classes to polarize increasingly. "The whole society breaks up more and more into two great hostile camps, two great, directly antagonistic classes: bourgeoisie and proletariat" (14, p. 7). Here, the model of two domi-

nant classes is no longer merely a heuristic postulate, but describes a factual condition. "The earlier petty bourgeoisie, the small industrialists, the merchants and rentiers, the craftsmen and peasants, all these classes sink down into the proletariat" (14, p. 16). It is really misleading to speak of two "great" classes, since social development, according to Marx, produces a polarized class society with a relatively small ruling class of capitalists and an extraordinarily large oppressed class of wage laborers.

2. As the classes polarize, their class situations become increasingly extreme. On the one hand, the wealth of the bourgeoisie is swelled by larger profits based on increasing productivity as well as by the progressive concentration of capital in the hands of a few individuals. "One capitalist kills many others" (12, I, p. 803). On the other hand, "with the continuously decreasing number of capital magnates who usurp and monopolize all advantages of this process of change . . . [comes an increase in] the mass of poverty, of pressure, of slavery, of perversion, of exploitation, but also of revolt on the part of a working class permanently increasing in size which is skilled, united, and organized by the mechanism of the capitalist mode of production itself" (12, I, p. 803). Here, the so-called theory of pauperization has its place, according to which the poverty of the proletariat grows with the expansion of production by virtue of a law postulated as inherent in a capitalist economy.

3. At the same time, the two classes become more and more homogeneous internally. In the beginning of this process, the classes are clearly delimited from the outside, but rather heterogeneous within. Marx says of the bourgeoisie that its members "have identical interests in so far as they form a class in opposition to another class," but "contradictory and conflicting interests as soon as they are confronted with themselves" (6, p. 140). Analogously, the proletariat is not, in the beginning, a "class for itself." However, a number of processes mold the different constituents of the classes into uniform groups without significant internal differences or conflicts. "More and more the collisions between individual workers and bourgeois assume the character of collisions of two classes" (14, p. 87). This is partly due to pressure from without, such as the growing intensity of the class struggle. Partly it is the effect of social and even technical factors. In the case of the proletariat Marx refers on the one hand to the growing extent of class organization as a unifying factor, on the other hand to the "tendency of equalizing and leveling in work processes" within industry itself (12, I, p. 441), i.e., the reduction of all

workers to unskilled laborers by the technical development of production. Similarly, a combination of economic, and in the narrow sense social, factors unites the bourgeoisie as a class.

4. Once history has carried these tendencies of development to their extremes, the point is reached at which the fabric of the existing social structure breaks and a revolution terminates capitalist society. The hitherto oppressed proletariat assumes power; effective private property is socialized; classes cease to exist; the state is withering away. The proletarian revolution inaugurates the communist, classless society.

Marx's image of capitalist society is the image of a society undergoing a process of radical change. This change culminates in a revolutionary act, into which all earlier developments converge and from which all later developments depart. The executors of this process are structurally generated, organized human interest groups—the classes. One of these—the bourgeoisie—defends with sinking chances of success the existing distribution of property, and with it the whole social status quo. The other one—the proletariat—attacks this status quo with growing success until the day on which its interests become reality, the values of a new society. The capitalist form of economic and social structure is doomed, and the classes are its gravediggers.

At this point in our considerations we shall depart from Marx. His theory of class provides the background of subsequent argument, his analysis of capitalist class society that of later analyses. If we succeed in refuting the sociological theories of Marx or the hypotheses derived from them, we have good reason to rejoice. For science grows by the refutation of accepted propositions and theories, and not by their stubborn retention.

II

Changes in the Structure of Industrial Societies Since Marx

CAPITALISM VERSUS INDUSTRIAL SOCIETY

It is a commonplace today that many of Marx's predictions have been refuted by the social development of industrial societies over the past century. But while commonplaces of this kind can be an excuse for silence, they are also a challenge. If a commonplace is repeated too often, it makes one wonder whether those who repeat it realize what they are saying and are able to substantiate their assertions. In sociological literature, there has been, to my knowledge, but one attempt to present a systematic account of the social changes that molded industrial societies in forms unforeseen by Marx, namely, Theodor Geiger's analysis of the *Class Society in the Melting-Pot*. This account, while useful, is rather less than exhaustive, to say nothing of the fact that Geiger fails to present these changes with a view to formulating a new and better theory of social conflict and change than was provided by Marx.[1] If, therefore, I propose to explore in this chapter some of the important changes in the structure of industrial societies since Marx, I do so with a double purpose. First, I want to indicate certain patterns of social development that justify speaking of Marx's theory of class as being falsified by empirical observations. Second, however, I intend to discuss those features of advanced industrial societies which have to be accounted for by a theory of conflict and change that claims to be applicable not merely to capitalist societies but to industrial societies in general. For both these purposes, and in the context of a study that is largely analytical in nature, it is not necessary to waste much time and space in recounting well-known facts of development. Accordingly, this chapter, although based on observations and empirical generalizations, will be devoted to analyses rather than descriptions of historical trends, and will thus clear the ground for our further considerations.

[1] For an extensive discussion of Geiger's book see below, Chapter III, pp. 97 ff.

Marx dealt with what he called "bourgeois" or "capitalist" society. By contrast, the title of this study and of this chapter refers to "industrial society." In describing modern societies, social scientists have tended to use these concepts either indiscriminately or confusingly. There are several reasons for this confusion. "Whether contemporary Britain, or contemporary America, can properly be described as capitalist societies is partly a question of fact and partly a question of terminology" (T. Bottomore, 37, p. 13 n). In so far as it is a question of terminology, i.e., of an essentially arbitrary decision, political rather than scientific motivations play their part. Some authors—including Bottomore (37) and H. P. Bahrdt (124)—feel that in preferring the concept of industrial society, sociologists have abandoned the impulses of critical detachment from social reality which stood at the origin of social science, and which are even today conveyed by the notion of capitalist society. Those who speak of industrial societies, it is claimed, have accepted the existing state of affairs as unobjectionable in a way in which those who prefer to speak of capitalist societies have not. There is an element of truth in this allegation. Sociologists cannot be said to be free of the suspicion of ideology because they investigate, *inter alia*, such suspicions. However, despite this element of truth I propose to ignore the charge of an ideological bias related to the concepts here in question and concentrate on what Bottomore calls the "question of fact" involved in the terminological dispute. For it seems to me that despite some evidence to the contrary the notions of "capitalist society" and "industrial society" are not different terms for identical concepts, but in fact signify different concepts which we have to disentangle in order to clarify the logical and historical status of our analyses.

"Capitalism" was originally—and still is to some extent—an economic concept. The notion of a capitalist society is an extrapolation from economic to social relations; it assumes some formative power on the part of economic structures if not indeed the thesis that social institutions and values are but a superstructure on the real basis of economic conditions. However, not even economists wholly agreed, or agree, on the characteristics of this "real basis," to say nothing of its social "superstructure." In describing the social and economic order emerging in consequence of the industrial revolution in the late eighteenth and early nineteenth centuries, Marx emphasized private ownership of the means of production, the "free" sale of labor, the production of surplus value, mechanized factory production, and the existence of classes. Sombart and Max Weber later added the rational or rationalist value system, the acquisitive principle, the market character of the economy. According to Weber, it is "one of the fundamental properties of capitalist private economy that it rationalizes on the basis of strict calculation, and that it is structured systematically and soberly by the economic effect intended" (189, p. 61). With deceptive thoroughness, Sombart defines capitalism as "a commercial organization in which two different groups of the population are connected by the market and cooperate regularly: the owners of the means of production, who at the same time have control and are the subjects of the economy, and propertyless mere laborers as objects of the economy; it is an organization which is dominated by the acquisitive principle and by economic rationalism" (28, I, 319). Many further "definitions" of capitalism could be quoted here, but they add little to those of Marx, Weber, and Sombart.[2]

On the other hand, it is evident by definition that—in Heimann's words—"capitalism is a historical concept": "It signifies one economic system among other systems realized in history, and it therefore implies the problem of the origin and, possibly, the transformation and supersedure of capitalism" (177, p. 510). Thus, the derived concept of a capitalist society also signifies a historical pattern of social structure that can change and be replaced by new patterns. Here the question arises which makes all ambiguities of definition apparent: What must change for a capitalist system to cease being capitalist?

Let us take, for example, Sombart's definition quoted above. It contains at least seven elements or determinants of capitalism: (1) the commercial organization, (2) the cooperation of two groups of the population, (3) the fact that one of these groups simultaneously owns and controls the means of production, whereas (4) the other group has no property and is confined to "merely" laboring, (5) their connection by the market, (6) the acquisitive principle, and (7) economic rationalism. What happens—we must ask—if one of these factors changes, but all others remain unchanged? What happens, for example, if ownership and control of the means of production are no

___

[2] Apart from the empirical problem, all these "definitions" also raise a logical problem: Where, in social science, do definitions end and descriptions begin? A more elaborate discussion of this problem would reveal some of the darkest corners of social science. In this study, I shall speak of definitions only with respect to the definition of concepts in terms of their *genus* and *differentia specifica*, and I shall distinguish them as such strictly from statements about objects thus conceptually defined, which will be referred to at times as "definitions" by contrast to definitions proper. What matters in a definition is not that it is "complete" (which is in fact the trouble with Sombart's "definition" quoted above) but that it is precise and unambiguous.

longer simultaneous, but everything else remains as before? Are we then still dealing with a capitalist system or not?

If, like only too many others, we accept the given definition as in some sense "true," then there are two equally nonsensical answers to this question: either a change of one element of the "definition" is seen as "necessarily" involving changes in all the others, so that capitalism is superseded; or a change of one element is neglected as a mere modification, and the concept of capitalism is applied also to systems which do not fulfill all conditions of the "definition." The first of these is Marx's answer. It presupposes a whole series of untenable postulates and becomes a mere trick of definition which may deceive by its brilliance, but which cannot convince. The second and more frequent answer results in an extension of the term "capitalism" beyond the borderline of meaning. Its "definition" is no longer a definition, for it is lacking a *differentia specifica*. One could carry this procedure *ad absurdum* by pointing out the limiting case in which the concept of capitalism becomes identical with the *genus* economic and social system. There can be little doubt that neither method is very fruitful for historical and sociological analysis.

For the concept of a capitalist economy or society to be useful, it is necessary to define it specifically and precisely. If we try to do so, a significant fact becomes apparent. The elements of most of the traditional definitions of capitalism fall into two distinct groups. On the one hand, we encounter factors which can be shown to be connected with industrial production as such, independent of its social, legal, or economic context: for example, the participation in production of a controlling group and a subordinate group, economic rationalism, possibly some form of a market economy, and other factors to be determined presently. On the other hand, there appear in these definitions elements which characterize merely the particular form of industrial production displayed by the industrializing countries of Europe and North America in the nineteenth century: above all the union of ownership and control, but also the poverty of industrial workers, the profit motive, and some other features. It is true that these two groups of factors occurred together in the particular situation of Europe and the United States in the nineteenth century. But after the experience of other types of industrialization we know today that their combination was, from the point of view of industrialization and its social implications, an accident, or rather the result of certain very special historical configurations. If some social scientists claimed, and still claim, that there is a necessary connection between both groups of factors, and that therefore both will disappear at the same time, they are ill-advised; and we shall have to revise this position.

Those factors which can be shown to be generated by the structure of industrial production, and which cannot disappear, therefore, unless industry itself disappears, will be associated in this study with the concept of *industrial society*. Since it appears evident that industrial production is not just a passing guest in history, but will probably be with us forever in one form or another, it follows that the concept of an industrial society is extremely comprehensive. Whenever it is applied to particular societies it will require specification. In general, however, we retain mechanized commodity production in factories and enterprises as the distinguishing feature of industrial societies. The social conditions that correlate with this characteristic can be specified only by way of empirical analysis.

By contrast, *capitalism* merely signifies one form of industrial society. Definitions of terms always contain an element of arbitrariness, and one could certainly define capitalism differently. However, it accords with the definitions of the most acute modern economists to state that the main elements of capitalism are "private property in means of production and regulation of the productive process by private contract (or management or initiative)." Schumpeter adds to this definition of his the factor of "credit creation" (73, p. 167). For purposes of sociological analysis it seems advisable—if we want to retain the concept of a capitalist society at all—to insist on the union of private ownership and factual control of the instruments of production as the distinguishing feature of a capitalist form of society. Thus we follow Sering in expecting the "typical capitalist" to be "at the same time the legal owner of his factory, the practical manager of production, and the supreme commander of his workers" (74, p. 26).

Both terms, "capitalism" and "industrial society," are categories on a high level of generality. In analyzing particular societies they are applicable, but not very useful. They are models describing merely the most general features of social structures.[3] If our aim were a "complete" description or analysis of any given society, we

---

[3] Without here continuing an unconcluded discussion, it may be said for the sake of clarity that "models of structure" in this sense differ from Weber's "ideal types" in that they do not "idealize" existing conditions in a pure form (and thereby assume a goal character, if without explicit evaluation), but indicate merely the common factual skeleton of comparable societies without taking into account their cultural peculiarities.

would have to qualify its classification as a "capitalist" or an "industrial" society, and add many a reference to particular structural variants, cultural traits, and historical traditions of the society in question. If, however, we are concerned merely with the analysis of certain general structural elements, or with that of a multitude of societies that share such elements, the categories of "capitalist" and "industrial" society may be sufficient in themselves. The title of the present study should be understood in this sense. Its subject is not primarily any particular society, but the conditions of class formation and class conflict in industrial society, i.e., in all societies which fulfill the general conditions of this model of structure.

Having separated the two groups of elements of which most of the traditional definitions of capitalism are composed, we are now able to contrast capitalist societies with industrial societies. Following our definitions, this means of course contrasting a whole (industrial society) with one of its parts (capitalist society). It is not our intention here to add another colorful name to the multitude of terms coined for postcapitalist societies in recent years. Faced with the choice between "socialist society," "managerial society," "bureaucratic society," "advanced industrial society," and other such terms, I have no particular preference. In any case no decision is needed here, for the purpose of a confrontation of capitalist and industrial society is evidently one of generalization. In the argument of this section I have deliberately not referred to classes and class conflicts. One of the main questions which the present investigation is supposed to answer is: Do classes and class conflicts belong to that group of phenomena by which only the capitalist type of industrial society is characterized, or is their existence a consequence of industrial production itself, and are they therefore a lasting feature of industrial societies? This question will accompany us throughout the following analysis of changes in the structure of industrial societies since Marx.

OWNERSHIP AND CONTROL, OR THE DECOMPOSITION OF CAPITAL

Marx was right in seeking the root of social change in capitalist society in the sphere of industrial production, but the direction these changes took turned out to be directly contrary to Marx's expectations. With respect to capital, he had, in his later years, at least a vision of what was going to happen, as his brief and somewhat puzzled analysis of joint-stock companies shows. Joint-stock companies were legally recognized in Germany, England, France, and the United States in the second half of the nineteenth century. Laws often indicate the conclusion of social developments, and indeed early forms of joint-stock companies can be traced back at least to the commercial companies and trade societies of the seventeenth century. But it was in the nineteenth and early twentieth centuries that this type of enterprise first gained wide recognition and expanded into all branches of economic activity. Today, more than two-thirds of all companies in advanced industrial societies are joint-stock companies, and their property exceeds four-fifths of the total property in economic enterprises. The enterprise owned and run by an individual, or even a family, has long ceased to be the dominant pattern of economic organization. Moreover, the stock of companies is dispersed fairly widely. Three per cent of the adult population of the Federal Republic of Germany, and approximately 8 per cent of that of the United States, own one or more shares of joint-stock companies. Probably the proportion in other countries is somewhere between these extremes.[4] For purposes of the present analysis, we may add to joint-stock companies the co-operative enterprises and those owned by the state, which command an ever-increasing proportion of the national wealth in contemporary societies. All these together, and their growth in the last decade, leave little doubt about the significance of this change.

It is not surprising that sociologists should have shared, from an early date, the interest of lawyers and economists in these new and rapidly expanding types of organization. There is, moreover, on the whole an astonishing degree of consensus among sociologists on the implications of joint-stock companies for the structure of industrial enterprises, and for the wider structure of society. If one wants to distinguish between points of view, one might contrast a rather more radical with a somewhat conservative interpretation of this phenomenon. Marx was, in this sense, the founder of the radical school; surprisingly enough, however, most of his later adherents took the more conservative view.

According to the radical view, joint-stock companies involve a complete break with earlier capitalist traditions. By separating what has come to be called ownership and control, they give rise to a new group of managers who are utterly different from their capitalist predecessors. Thus for Marx, the joint-stock company involves a complete alienation of capital "from the real producers, and its opposition as alien property to all individuals really participating in pro-

---

[4] For the data presented or implied in this paragraph, and in this section in general, see, among other sources, Berle and Means (173), Parkinson (180), Rosenstiel (183), Schwantag (184), and the Yearbook of the Institut für Demoskopie (229).

duction, from the manager down to the last day-laborer" (12, III, p. 478). In other words, by separating ownership and control, the joint-stock company reduces the distance between manager and worker while at the same time removing the owners altogether from the sphere of production and thereby isolating their function as exploiters of others. It is merely a step from this kind of analysis to the thesis that, as Renner has it, the "capitalists without function" yield to the "functionaries without capital," and that this new ruling group of industry bears little resemblance to the old "full capitalists" (71, pp. 182, 198). Burnham, Geiger, Sering, and others followed Marx (and Renner) in this radical interpretation of the social effects of joint-stock companies.

The conservative view, on the other hand, holds that the consequences of the apparent separation of ownership and control have been vastly overrated. It is argued that in fact owners and controllers, i.e., stockholders and managers, are a fairly homogeneous group. There are often direct connections between them, and where this is not the case, their outlook is sufficiently similar to justify insisting on the old assumption of a homogeneous class of capitalists opposed to an equally homogeneous class of laborers. This view is not often heard in the West nowadays, although traces of it are evident in the work of C. Wright Mills (62, 63). It may be added that this conservative view is clearly contrary to Marx's own analysis.

We cannot here exhaust the complex subject of ownership and control, but it seems desirable not to leave the subject without considering which of these two views seems more plausible and appropriate. There can be little doubt that the social structure of joint-stock companies as well as cooperative and state-owned enterprises differs from that of the classical capitalist enterprise, and that therefore a transition from the latter to the former is a process of social change. However, what type of change are we dealing with in this problem? Is it a change involving the transference of certain rights and duties attached to social positions from an old to a new group? Or is it a change that involves some rearrangement of the positions endowed with rights and duties themselves? These questions are not quite as rhetorical as they may sound. In fact, I would claim that the separation of ownership and control involved both a change in the structure of social positions and a change in the recruitment of personnel to these positions. But it is evident that, in the first place, joint-stock companies differ from capitalist enterprises in the structure of their leading positions. In the sphere with which we are here concerned, the process of transition from capitalist enterprises to joint-stock companies can be described as a process of role differentiation. The roles of owner and manager, originally combined in the position of the capitalist, have been separated and distributed over two positions, those of stockholder and executive.[5]

At the very least, this process of differentiation means that two physical entities occupy the positions formerly occupied by one. But this is not all. Apart from its manifest effects, the separation of ownership and control has a number of latent effects of even greater importance; i.e., it seems clear that the resulting positions, those of stockholder and executive, differ not only with respect to the obvious rights and duties of their incumbents, but also in other respects. Generally, the "capitalist without function" is indeed, as Marx emphasized, alienated from production, i.e., largely removed from the enterprise whose stock he owns. He does not participate in the day-to-day life of the enterprise, and above all he does not have a defined place in the formal hierarchy of authority in the enterprise. The "functionary without capital," on the other hand, has this place, although he typically has no property in the enterprise which he runs.[6]

From the point of view of the social structure of industrial enterprises, this means a significant change in the basis of legitimacy of entrepreneurial authority. The old-style capitalist exercised authority because he owned the instruments of production. The exercise of authority was part and parcel of his property rights, as indeed property may always be regarded from one point of view as simply an institutionalized form of authority over others. By contrast to this legitimation by property, the authority of the manager resembles in many ways that of the heads of political institutions. It is true that even for the manager property has not ceased to function as a basis of authority. The right of the manager to command and expect obedience accrues in part from the property rights delegated to him by the shareholders, acting either as a group or through an elected board of direc-

[5] In a more extensive analysis, it would have to be recognized that this process of differentiation involved not only two, but at least three, roles and positions: the third being that of investor or "finance capitalist" (Hilferding). Renner would add even more: "Three capitalist character masks have stepped into the place of the one full capitalist: the producer owning the capital of production in the mask of the entrepreneur, the commercial capitalist in the character mask of the businessman, and the financial capitalist" (71, p. 175).

[6] In 1935, members of management in 155 of the 200 largest American corporations had on the average no more than 1.74 per cent of the ordinary shares of their enterprises (cf. 159, p. 135).

tors. But besides these delegated property rights, the manager, by virtue of his more immediate contact with the participants of production, has to seek a second, and often more important, basis of legitimacy for his authority, namely, some kind of consensus among those who are bound to obey his commands. Typically, this consensus merely takes the form of an absence of dissensus. However, the manager, unlike the "full capitalist," can ill afford to exercise his authority in direct and deliberate contravention to the wishes and interests of his subordinates. The mechanisms by which manual and clerical workers who object to a member of top management can make their interests felt are complex and largely unregulated.[7] But there are such mechanisms, and managers have ways and means to forestall their being brought to bear. In this sense, the "human relations" movement is nothing but a symptom of the changing basis of legitimacy of entrepreneurial authority once ownership and control are separated.[8]

With the differentiation of capitalist roles, the composition of the entrepreneurial class—if it is a class—changes too. This is probably a gradual development, but one that is far advanced in most of the highly industrialized societies today. If we follow Bendix (138, p. 228) in distinguishing capitalists, heirs, and bureaucrats as three types of entrepreneurs, it is evident that three significantly different patterns of recruitment correspond to these types. The capitalist in this sense is a man who owns and manages an enterprise which he has founded himself. From having been perhaps a skilled craftsman or a shopkeeper at the beginning of his career, he has built up, "from scratch," a sizable firm or factory and one that continues to grow in scope, size, and production. The heir, by contrast, is born into the ownership of an enterprise, and apart from perhaps a few years' experience in some of its departments he has known nothing but the property he has inherited. Both the capitalist and the heir are owner-managers.

[7] They extend from direct pressure aimed at forcing the manager to resign or change his attitudes to indirect means of disturbing the operation of the enterprise which may result in the manager's being reprimanded or deposed by the directors, who, in this case, act in a sense on behalf of the employees.

[8] Bendix has impressively demonstrated that this change was accompanied by a change in "managerial ideologies," i.e., in attempts to justify theoretically the authority of the entrepreneur (cf. 138). He asserts an ideological change from basing unlimited authority on the interests of a ruling class to presuming, on the part of modern management, an identity of interests among all participants of production. Bendix's argument lends considerable support to my thesis that the separation of ownership and control involved a change in the basis of legitimacy of authority.

For mere managers, however, there are two typical patterns of recruitment, and both of them differ radically from those of capitalists and heirs. One of these patterns is the bureaucratic career. In the early joint-stock companies in particular, executives were often chosen from among the firm's leading employees, both technical and clerical. They had worked their way up from the ranks. More recently, a different pattern has gained increasing importance. Today, a majority of top management officials in industrial enterprises have acquired their positions on the strength of some specialized education, and of university degrees. Lawyers, economists, and engineers often enter management almost immediately after they have completed their education, and gradually rise to the top positions. There can be little doubt that both these patterns of recruitment—but in particular the latter—distinguish managerial groups significantly from those of old-style owner-managers as well as new-style mere owners. Their social background and experience place these groups into different fields of reference, and it seems at least likely that the group of professionally trained managers "increasingly develops its own functionally determined character traits and modes of thought" (Sering, 74, p. 205). For this is, in our context, the crucial effect of the separation of ownership and control in industry: that it produces two sets of roles the incumbents of which increasingly move apart in their outlook on and attitudes toward society in general and toward the enterprise in particular. Their reference groups differ, and different reference groups make for different values. Among classical capitalists, the "organization man" is an unthinkable absurdity. Yet the manager is "not the individualist but the man who works through others for others" (Whyte, 169, p. 21). Never has the imputation of a profit motive been further from the real motives of men than it is for modern bureaucratic managers.[9] Economically, managers are interested in such things as rentability, efficiency, and productivity. But all these are indissolubly linked with the imponderables of what has been called the social "climate of the enterprise" (*Betriebsklima*). The manager shares with the capitalist two important social reference groups: his peers and his subordinates. But his attitude toward these differs considerably from that of the capitalist (as does consequently, the atti-

---

[9] Which is not to say that this "imputation" may not be useful as an assumption in economic theory. There is no need for theoretical assumptions to be altogether realistic. However, it may be advisable even for economists to try and extend their models by including in their assumptions some of the social factors characteristic of entrepreneurial roles.

tude expected from him by his peers). For him, to be successful means to be liked, and to be liked means, in many ways, to be alike. The manager is an involuntary ruler, and his attitudes betray his feelings.

Before concluding this analysis it would perhaps be well to point out briefly what it does not mean or imply. Despite many differences, there are without doubt considerable similarities in the positions, roles, and attitudes of both the capitalist and the manager. Both are entrepreneurial roles, and both are therefore subject to certain expectations which no social context can remove. Moreover, there are numerous personal and social ties between owners and managers in all industrial societies. If anything, the unpropertied managers are more active in political affairs, both as individuals and through their associations and lobbies. Also, while the joint-stock company has conquered the sphere of industrial production (i.e., of secondary industries), it is still of only minor importance in the tertiary industries of trade and commerce and in the services. Thus, the separation of ownership and control is not as fundamental a change as, say, the industrial revolution. But it is a change, and one with very definite, if restricted, implications for class structure and conflict.

There is little reason to follow Marx and describe the condition of separation of ownership and control as a transitional form of historical development. It is no more transitional than any other stage of history, and it has already proven quite a vital pattern of social and economic structure. But I think that we can follow Marx in his radical interpretation of this phenomenon. The separation of ownership and control has replaced one group by two whose positions, roles, and outlooks are far from identical. In taking this view, one does of course agree with Marx against himself. For it follows from this that the homogeneous capitalist class predicted by Marx has in fact not developed. Capital—and thereby capitalism—has dissolved and given way, in the economic sphere, to a plurality of partly agreed, partly competing, and partly simply different groups. The effect of this development on class conflict is threefold: first, the replacement of capitalists by managers involves a change in the composition of the groups participating in conflict; second, and as a consequence of this change in recruitment and composition, there is a change in the nature of the issues that cause conflicts, for the interests of the functionaries without capital differ from those of full-blown capitalists, and so therefore do the interests of labor vis-à-vis their new opponents; and third, the decomposition of capital involves a change in the patterns of conflict. One might question whether this new conflict, in which labor is no longer opposed to a homogeneous capitalist class, can still be described as a class conflict at all. In any case, it is different from the division of the whole society into two great and homogeneous hostile camps with which Marx was concerned. While I would follow the radical view of the separation of ownership and control in industry to this point, there is one thing to be said in favor of the conservative view. Changes in the composition of conflict groups, of the issues, and of patterns of conflict do not imply the abolition of conflict or even of the specific conflict between management and labor in industry. Despite the effects of the decomposition of capital on class structure, we have no reason to believe that antagonisms and clashes of interest have now been banned from industrial enterprises.

SKILL AND STRATIFICATION, OR THE DECOMPOSITION OF LABOR

While Marx had at least a premonition of things to come with respect to capital, he remained unaware of developments affecting the unity and homogeneity of labor. Yet in this respect, too, the sphere of production which loomed so large in Marx's analyses became the starting point of changes that clearly refute his predictions. The working class of today, far from being a homogeneous group of equally unskilled and impoverished people, is in fact a stratum differentiated by numerous subtle and not-so-subtle distinctions. Here, too, history has dissolved one position, or role, and has substituted for it a plurality of roles that are endowed with diverging and often conflicting expectations.

In trying to derive his prediction of the growing homogeneity of labor from the assumption that the technical development of industry would tend to abolish all differences of skill and qualification, Marx was a genuine child of his century. Only the earliest political economists had believed that the division of labor in manufacturing would make for an "increase of dexterity in every particular workman" (Adam Smith, 185, p. 7) by allowing him to refine the "skill acquired by frequent repetition of the same process" (Babbage, 172, p. 134). Already in the following generation, social scientists were quite unanimous in believing that the processes of industrial production "effect a substitution of labor comparatively unskilled, for that which is more skilled" (Ure, 188, p. 30), and that the division of labor had reached a phase "in which we have seen the skill of the worker decrease at the rate at which industry becomes more perfect" (Proudhon, 181, p. 153). Marx was only too glad to adopt this view which tallied so well with his general theories of class structure: "The interests and life situations of the proletariat are more and more equalized, since the machinery increasingly obliterates the differences of labor and depresses the wage almost everywhere to an equally low level" (14, p. 17). "The hierarchy of specialized workmen that characterizes manufacture is replaced, in the automatic factory, by a tendency to equalize and reduce to one and the same level every kind of work that has to be done" (12, I, p. 490).

Indeed, so far as we can tell from available evidence, there was, up to the end of the nineteenth century, a tendency for most industrial workers to become unskilled, i.e., to be reduced to the same low level of skill. But since then, two new patterns have emerged which are closely related on the one hand to technical innovations in production, on the other hand to a new philosophy of industrial organization as symbolized by the works of F. W. Taylor (167) and H. Fayol (145). First, there emerged, around the turn of the century, a new category of workers which today is usually described as semiskilled. As early as 1905, Max Weber referred to the growing importance of "the semiskilled workers trained directly on the job" (32, p. 502). By the 1930's, the theory had become almost commonplace that "there is a tendency for all manual laborers to become semiskilled machine minders, and for highly skilled as well as unskilled workers to become relatively less important" (Carr-Saunders and Jones, 89, p. 61). The semiskilled differ from the unskilled not so much in the technical qualifications required from them for their work, as in certain less easily defined extrafunctional skills which relate to their capacity to accept responsibility, to adapt to difficult conditions, and to perform a job intelligently. These extrafunctional skills are acquired not by formal training (although many semiskilled workers receive this also), but by experience on the job; yet these "skills of responsibility" constitute a clear line of demarcation between those who have them and the unskilled who lack both training and experience. Apart from the semiskilled, there appeared, more recently, a new and ever-growing demand for highly skilled workers of the engineer type in industry. Carr-Saunders and Jones, in their statement above, still expected the simultaneous reduction of unskilled as well as skilled labor. Today we know—as Friedmann (146), Geiger (46), Moore (157), and others have pointed out—that the second half of this expectation has not come true. Increasingly complex machines require increasingly qualified designers, builders, maintenance and repair men, and even minders, so that Drucker extrapolates only slightly when he says: "Within the working class a new shift from unskilled to skilled labor has begun—reversing the trend of the last fifty years. The unskilled worker is actually an engineering imperfection, as unskilled work, at least in theory, can always be done better, faster and cheaper by machines" (144, pp. 42-43).

Because of changing classifications, it is a little difficult to document this development statistically. As for the unskilled, a slight decrease in their proportion can be shown for England where, in 1951, they amounted to 12.5 per cent of the occupied male population, as against 16.5 per cent in 1931. In the United States, an even sharper decrease has been noted, from 36 per cent of the labor force in 1910 to just over 28 per cent in 1930 and, further, to less than 20 per cent in 1950 (see Caplow, 141, p. 299). But statistics are here neither very reliable nor even indispensable evidence. Analysis of industrial conditions suggests quite clearly that within the labor force of advanced industry we have to distinguish at least three skill groups: a growing stratum of highly skilled workmen who increasingly merge with both engineers and white-collar employees, a relatively stable stratum of semiskilled workers with a high degree of diffuse as well as specific industrial experience, and a dwindling stratum of totally unskilled laborers who are characteristically either newcomers to industry (beginners, former agricultural laborers, immigrants) or semi-unemployables. It appears, furthermore, that these three groups differ not only in their level of skill, but also in other attributes and determinants of social status. The semiskilled almost invariably earn a higher wage than the unskilled, whereas the skilled are often salaried and thereby participate in white-collar status. The hierarchy of skill corresponds exactly to the hierarchy of responsibility and delegated authority within the working class. From numerous studies it would seem beyond doubt that it also correlates with the hierarchy of prestige, at the top of which we find the skilled man whose prolonged training, salary, and security convey special status, and at the bottom of which stands the unskilled man who is, according to a recent German investigation into workers' opinions, merely "working" without having an "occupation" proper (see Kluth, 150, p. 67). Here as elsewhere Marx was evidently mistaken. "Everywhere, the working class differentiates itself more and more, on the one hand into occupational groups, on the other hand into three large categories with different, if not contradictory, interests: the skilled craftsmen, the unskilled laborers, and the semiskilled specialist workers" (Philip, 161, p. 2).[10]

In trying to assess the consequences of this development, it is well

---

[10] In argument and evidence, the preceding account is based on two more elaborate studies of mine, one of unskilled labor (143), and one of skill and social stratification (142). For further references as well as data I must refer to these studies.

to remember that, for Marx, the increasing uniformity of the working class was an indispensable condition of that intensification of the class struggle which was to lead, eventually, to its climax in a revolution. The underlying argument of what for Marx became a prediction appears quite plausible. For there to be a revolution, the conflicts within a society have to become extremely intense. For conflicts to be intense, one would indeed expect its participants to be highly unified and homogeneous groups. But neither capital nor labor have developed along these lines. Capital has dissolved into at least two, in many ways distinct, elements, and so has labor. The proletarian, the impoverished slave of industry who is indistinguishable from his peers in terms of his work, his skill, his wage, and his prestige, has left the scene. What is more, it appears that by now he has been followed by his less depraved, but equally alienated successor, the worker. In modern industry, "the worker" has become precisely the kind of abstraction which Marx quite justly resented so much. In his place, we find a plurality of status and skill groups whose interests often diverge. Demands of the skilled for security may injure the semiskilled; wage claims of the semiskilled may raise objections by the skilled; and any interest on the part of the unskilled is bound to set their more highly skilled fellow workmen worrying about differentials.

Again, as in the case of capital, it does not follow from the decomposition of labor that there is no bond left that unites most workers —at least for specific goals; nor does it follow that industrial conflict has lost its edge. But here, too, a change of the issues and, above all, of the patterns of conflict is indicated. As with the capitalist class, it has become doubtful whether speaking of the working class still makes much sense. Probably Marx would have agreed that class "is a force that unites into groups people who differ from one another, by overriding the differences between them" (Marshall, 57, p. 114), but he certainly did not expect the differences to be so great, and the uniting force so precarious as it has turned out to be in the case both of capital and of labor.

THE "NEW MIDDLE CLASS"

Along with the decomposition of both capital and labor a new stratum emerged within, as well as outside, the industry of modern societies, which was, so to speak, born decomposed. Since Lederer and Marschak first published their essay on this group, and coined for it the name "new middle class" (*neuer Mittelstand*), so much has been written by sociologists about the origin, development, position, and function of white-collar or black-coated employees that whatever one says is bound to be repetitive. However, only one conclusion is borne out quite clearly by all these studies of salaried employees in industry, trade, commerce, and public administration: that there is no word in any modern language to describe this group that is no group, class that is no class, and stratum that is no stratum. To be sure, there have been attempts to describe it. In fact, we are here in the comparatively fortunate position of having to decide between two or, perhaps, three conflicting theories. But none of these attempts has been free of innumerable qualifications to the effect that it is impossible to generalize. Although the following brief discussion will not distinguish itself in this respect, it could not be avoided in an account of social changes of the past century that have a bearing on the problem of class.

By the time Marx died, about one out of every twenty members of the labor force was in what might roughly be described a clerical occupation; today, it is one out of every five and, in the tertiary industries, one out of every three. More accurate figures of size and growth of the "new middle class" could be given,[11] but even these are surprisingly precise in view of the fact that it is virtually impossible to delimit the "group" which they count. For, technically, the "occupational salad" (Mills) of salaried employees includes post-office clerks as well as senior executives, shop supervisors as well as hospital doctors, typists as well as prime ministers. Presumably, a "middle class" is located somewhere between at least two other classes, one above it and one below it. Yet the "new middle class" has stubbornly resisted all attempts to define its upper and lower limits. In fact, it is obvious that the questions where salaried employees begin to be members of an upper stratum or ruling class and where they "really" still belong in the working class cannot in general be answered. Our questions will have to be rather more specific.

If one is, as we are, concerned not with patterns of social stratification but with lines of conflict, then one thing is certain: however we may choose to delimit the aggregate of salaried employees, they are not a "middle class," because from the point of view of a theory of conflict there can be no such entity as a middle class. Evident as it is, this statement is bound to be misunderstood—but, then, much of this study is an attempt to elucidate it. It is true that in terms of prestige and income many salaried employees occupy a position somewhere

[11] For data used in the following section, see, apart from the early work by Lederer and Marschak (133), above all the studies of Lockwood (135), Geiger (91), Croner (129), Lewis and Maude (134), and C. Wright Mills (137). Some interesting figures are given by Bendix (138, p. 214).

between the very wealthy and the very poor, somewhere in the middle of the scale of social stratification. But in a situation of conflict, whether defined in a Marxian way or in some other way, this kind of intermediate position just does not exist, or, at least, exists only as a negative position of nonparticipation. This point might be illuminated by a slightly misleading example: an election in which there is a choice between two parties; while it is possible to abstain, only those who make up their minds one way or the other participate actively in the contest. Similarly, our problem here is to determine in which way the so-called new middle class has made up its mind or is likely to make up its mind. And the answer we shall give corresponds—to remain within the metaphor for a moment—to the findings of Bonham in England (127) and Von der Heydte in Germany (196), according to which two-thirds of the "new middle class" tend to vote for conservative, and one-third for radical parties.

I have claimed above that there are two or, perhaps, three competing theories about the position of the "new middle class." From the point of view of our problem, these are soon reduced to what at best amounts to two-and-a-half theories. For the third theory I had in mind is in fact little more than a description, and an inconclusive one at that. It is embodied in Crozier's "working hypothesis" of an empirical investigation conducted in France: "The situation of the salaried employee is one that makes possible an identification with the world of the ruling class and promises considerable rewards if this succeeds. But at the same time it is a working-class situation and therefore suffers from most of those limitations to which all other workers are subjected—limited income as well as lack of autonomy and a position of subordination" (130, pp. 311–12). Statements of this kind are as frequent as they are useless for purposes of conflict analysis. We can therefore dismiss at the outset any theory that confines itself to statements with clauses like "partly this . . . partly that" or "on the one hand this . . . on the other hand that."

There are two theories which do not suffer from this indecision, and they are directly contradictory. According to the first of these, the "new middle class" constitutes in fact an extension of the old, capitalist or bourgeois, ruling class, and is in this sense part of the ruling class. Croner—who, apart from Renner (71), Bendix (138, chap. iv), and others, recently espoused this theory—argues that "the explanation of the special social position of salaried employees can be found in the fact that their work tasks have once been entrepreneurial tasks" (129, p. 36). This statement is meant by Croner both in a historical and in a structural sense. Historically, most clerical occupations were differentiated out of the leading positions in industry, commerce, and the state. Structurally they are, according to this view, characterized by the exercise of delegated authority—delegated, that is, from the real seat of authority in social organizations, from, in other words, their leading positions. In contrast to this view, Geiger, C. Wright Mills, and others claim that the "new middle class" is, if not exactly an extension of the proletariat, at any rate closer to the working class than to the ruling class, whether capitalist or managerial. "Objectively, . . . the structural position of the white-collar mass is becoming more and more similar to that of the wage-workers. Both are, of course, propertyless, and their incomes draw closer and closer together. All the factors of their status position, which have enabled white-collar workers to set themselves apart from wage-workers, are now subject to definite decline" (137, p. 297). Mills does not say so, but he would probably have no quarrel with Geiger's conclusion that "from the point of view of class structure in Marx's sense the salaried employee is undoubtedly closer to the worker than to any other figure of modern society" (46, p. 167).

The two views are clearly in conflict, and it seems desirable to come to a decision as to their relative merits.[12] Fortunate as it is, from a methodological point of view, to have to decide between two conflicting theories, our situation here does not, upon closer inspection, turn out to be quite so simple. In fact, Mills may well be right when he suspects that because of the vastly different "definitions" of the "new middle class" the two theories not only may peacefully co-exist but even both be correct (137, pp. 291 ff.). Clearly the theory that salaried employees have delegated authority and are therefore part of the ruling class cannot have meant the office boy, the salesgirl, or even the skilled worker who has been granted the status symbol of a salary; equally clearly, the theory that salaried employees resemble the working class does not apply to senior executives, higher civil servants, and

---

[12] C. Wright Mills, in his very balanced account of views about the "new middle class" (137, chap. 13), enumerates four competing theories (pp. 290 ff.). To the two mentioned he adds the theories that (1) the middle class is destined to be the ruling class of the future, and (2) the growth of the "new middle class" operates as a force to stabilize the old, and eventually to abolish all class conflicts. The latter view will be discussed at a later stage, since it presupposes some consideration of the significance of social conflict in general. As to the former view, it simply betrays an unpardonable confusion of terms on the part of the authors Mills refers to. It seems obvious that so long as the middle class is a middle class there must be a class above it, and once it is the ruling class it is no longer the middle class.

professional people. However, there is more than a question of definition involved in this difficulty.

Instead of asking which of two apparently conflicting theories applies to the "new middle class," we can, so to speak, reverse our question and ask whether there is any criterion that would allow us to distinguish between those sectors of the "new middle class" to which one theory applies and those to which the other theory applies. I think that there is such a criterion, and that its application provides at least a preliminary solution to our wider problem of the effects of the growth of a "new middle class" on class structure and class conflict. It seems to me that a fairly clear as well as significant line can be drawn between salaried employees who occupy positions that are part of a bureaucratic hierarchy and salaried employees in positions that are not. The occupations of the post-office clerk, the accountant, and, of course, the senior executive are rungs on a ladder of bureaucratic positions; those of the salesgirl and the craftsman are not. There may be barriers in bureaucratic hierarchies which are insurmountable for people who started in low positions; salaried employees outside such hierarchies may earn more than those within, and they may also change occupations and enter upon a bureaucratic career; but these and similar facts are irrelevant to the distinction between bureaucrats and white-collar workers proposed here. Despite these facts I suggest that the ruling-class theory applies without exception to the social position of bureaucrats, and the working-class theory equally generally to the social position of white-collar workers.

There is, in other words, one section of the "new middle class" the condition of which, from the point of view of class conflict, closely resembles that of industrial workers. This section includes many of the salaried employees in the tertiary industries, in shops and restaurants, in cinemas, and in commercial firms, as well as those highly skilled workers and foremen who have acquired salaried status. It is hard to estimate, from available evidence, the numerical size of this group, but it probably does not at present exceed one-third of the whole "new middle class"—although it may do so in the future, since the introduction of office machinery tends to reduce the number of bureaucrats while increasing the demand for salaried office technicians.[13] Although some white-collar workers earn rather more than

[13] It is still too early to make any definite statements about this important development, which Bahrdt described as the "industrialization of bureaucracy" (cf. 124); but the automation of office work is sure to have consequences for the class structure of contemporary societies.

industrial workers, and most of them enjoy a somewhat higher prestige, their class situation appears sufficiently similar to that of workers to expect them to act alike. In general, it is among white-collar workers that one would expect trade unions as well as radical political parties to be successful.

The bureaucrats, on the other hand, share, if often in a minor way, the requisites of a ruling class. Although many of them earn less than white-collar and even industrial workers, they participate in the exercise of authority and thereby occupy a position vis-à-vis rather than inside the working class. The otherwise surprising fact that many salaried employees identify themselves with the interests, attitudes, and styles of life of the higher-ups can be accounted for in these terms. For the bureaucrats, the supreme social reality is their career that provides, at least in theory, a direct link between every one of them and the top positions which may be described as the ultimate seat of authority. It would be false to say that the bureaucrats are a ruling class, but in any case they are part of it, and one would therefore expect them to act accordingly in industrial, social, and political conflicts.[14]

The decomposition of labor and capital has been the result of social developments that have occurred since Marx, but the "new middle class" was born decomposed. It neither has been nor is it ever likely to be a class in any sense of this term. But while there is no "new middle class," there are, of course, white-collar workers and bureaucrats, and the growth of these groups is one of the striking features of historical development in the past century. What is their effect on class structure and class conflict, if it is not that of adding a new class to the older ones Marx described? It follows from our analysis that the emergence of salaried employees means in the first place an extension of the older classes of bourgeoisie and proletariat. The bureaucrats add to the bourgeoisie, as the white-collar workers add to the proletariat. Both classes have become, by these extensions, even more complex and heterogeneous than their decomposition has made them in any case. By gaining new elements, their unity has become a highly doubtful and precarious feature. White-collar workers, like industrial workers, have neither property nor authority, yet they display many social characteristics that are quite unlike those of the old work-

---

[14] Evidently, rather more will have to be said to make a convincing case for what I have sketched very briefly and somewhat dogmatically at this point. In so far as the structural position of bureaucrats has a bearing on the problem of class conflict in the present and future, these remarks will in fact be extended and supplemented below in Chapter VIII.

ing class. Similarly, bureaucrats differ from the older ruling class despite their share in the exercise of authority. Even more than the decomposition of capital and labor, these facts make it highly doubtful whether the concept of class is still applicable to the conflict groups of post-capitalist societies. In any case, the participants, issues, and patterns of conflict have changed, and the pleasing simplicity of Marx's view of society has become a nonsensical construction. If ever there have been two large, homogeneous, polarized, and identically situated social classes, these have certainly ceased to exist today, so that an unmodified Marxian theory is bound to fail in explaining the structure and conflicts of advanced industrial societies.

SOCIAL MOBILITY

The decomposition of capital and labor as well as their extension by sections of the "new middle class" are phenomena which have an obvious and direct bearing on class structure. But they are neither the only changes that have occurred since Marx nor, perhaps, the most significant ones from the point of view of class. Apart from such political and economic forces as totalitarianism and socialism, it was in particular the institutionalization of the two great social forces of mobility and equality that has steered class structures and conflicts in directions unforeseen by Marx. Marx was not, in fact, unaware of the importance of these forces. In explaining the absence of stable classes in the United States in terms of what he called the "exchange between classes" (cf. 8, p. 18), he anticipated the cardinal thesis of Sombart's brilliant essay, *Why is there no Socialism in the United States?* (204). But for Marx, mobility was a symptom of short-lived transitional periods of history, i.e., of either the emergence or the impending breakdown of a society. Today, we would tend to take the opposite view. Social mobility has become one of the crucial elements of the structure of industrial societies, and one would be tempted to predict its "breakdown" if the process of mobility were ever seriously impeded. Marx believed that the strength of a ruling class documents itself in its ability to absorb the ablest elements of other classes. In a manner of speaking, this is permanently the case in advanced industrial societies, yet we should hesitate to infer from a steady increase in the upward mobility of the talented that the present ruling class is particularly strong or homogeneous.

Social mobility represents one of the most studied and, at the same time, least understood areas of sociological inquiry. Today, we know a great deal about social mobility in various countries, and yet we do

not really know what we know. Not only do we not have any satisfactory answer to the question about the causes and consequences of
social mobility that was recently put by Lipset and Zetterberg (116,
p. 158), but we cannot even be sure about the so-called facts of the
case. The evidence we have is most conclusive with respect to mobility
between generations, although even here generalizations rest on extrapolation as much as on interpretation. It appears that in countries like
the United States, Great Britain, and Germany the rate of intergeneration mobility is generally fairly high. Only in the highest and, in
some countries, in the lowest ranges of the occupational scale do we
still find a considerable amount of self-recruitment. Moreover, the
rate of mobility seems to correspond roughly to the degree of industrialization in a country. It is higher in Britain than in France, higher
in the United States than in Italy. This correlation between industrial
development and social mobility seems to hold also in the historical
dimension. For Britain and Germany, investigations suggest a considerable increase in mobility rates over the last three generations.[15]

However, even if these generalizations are taken as suggestions
rather than conclusions, they have a high degree of verisimilitude.
For with respect to intergeneration mobility we have at our disposal
another kind of evidence which, although not quantitative, is quite
conclusive. When Marx wrote his books, he assumed that the position
an individual occupies in society is determined by his family origin and
the position of his parents. The sons of workers have no other choice
but to become workers themselves, and the sons of capitalists stay in

---

[15] The first of these generalizations is really little more than a guess based on the
interpretation of mobility studies by Glass and others in Britain (107), Bolte in Germany (102, 103), Rogoff in the United States (121), the Japan Sociological Society
(115), and the data included in the article by Lipset and Zetterberg (116). Some
comparative data have been brought together in this article also, as well as in the volume
edited by Glass (111, p. 263). Historical studies of mobility suffer from the fact that
they have to rely on people's memories; some tentative findings have been presented
by Mukherjee (119, p. 284) and Bolte (104, p. 186). Despite my qualifications,
this evidence is not, after all, unimpressive. However, all the studies mentioned do
not really stand up to a thorough methodological inspection. This is almost obvious
in comparative analyses based on vastly different occupational classifications which nobody so far has taken the trouble to reclassify. But it is also true for studies in one
country. They have usually employed the index of association for measuring mobility
rates, and, as Professor John W. Tukey has pointed out to me, this index is neither
formally sound nor empirically useful. Formally, the index of association would have
to be weighted by the size of status categories to be of any use at all. Empirically, it
fails to describe the most important aspect of social mobility: the existence of barriers
between strata. These and other objections to existing studies make great caution
imperative in the use of their findings.

the class of their fathers. At the time, this assumption was probably not far from the truth. But since then a new pattern of role allocation has become institutionalized in industrial societies. Today, the allocation of social positions is increasingly the task of the educational system. Even a hundred years ago, "the attendance of a certain type of school meant a confirmation of a certain social status or rank, and not its acquisition" (Schelsky, 122, p. 3). Today, the school has become the "first and thereby decisive point of social placement with respect to future social security, social rank and the extent of future consumption chances" (122, p. 6). In post-capitalist society, it is "the process of socialization itself, especially as found in the educational system, that is serving as the proving ground for ability and hence the selective agency for placing people in different statuses according to their capacities" (Davis, 208, p. 219). To be sure, there still are numerous obstacles and barriers in the way of complete equality of educational opportunity, but it is the stubborn tendency of modern societies to institutionalize intergeneration mobility by making a person's social position dependent on his educational achievement. Where this is the case, no social stratum, group, or class can remain completely stable for more than one generation. Social mobility, which, for Marx, was the exception that confirmed the rule of class closure, is built into the structure of post-capitalist society and has therefore become a factor to be reckoned with in all analyses of conflict and change.

There are forms of mobility other than that between generations, but about these we know even less. Thomas' study of intrageneration mobility in Britain (123) suggests a truly extraordinary degree of exchange between occupational groups. According to this study, there is not in contemporary Britain a single status category the majority of the members of which have never been in higher or lower strata (123, p. 30). But while it seems probable that there is a considerable amount of movement between occupations in various spheres of work, findings like those of Thomas's would require a more thorough analysis than the data published so far permit. There are sure to be even higher barriers for intrageneration mobility than for mobility between generations, so that all we can infer from what patchy data we have is what anybody living in a modern society can observe for himself: in post-capitalist societies there is a great deal of movement, upwards and downwards as well as on one social level, between generations as well as within them, so that the individual who stays at his place of birth and in the occupation of his father throughout his life has become a rare exception.

When Marx dealt with the "exchange between classes" in the

United States, he assumed that a high degree of exchange would be detrimental to the formation of powerful classes and therefore inconducive to the fomentation of violent conflicts. This assumption is plausible. A class composed of individuals whose social position is not an inherited and inescapable fate, but merely one of a plurality of social roles, is not likely to be as powerful a historical force as the closed class Marx had in mind. Where mobility within and between generations is a regular occurrence, and therefore a legitimate expectation of many people, conflict groups are not likely to have either the permanence or the dead seriousness of caste-like classes composed of hopelessly alienated men. And as the instability of classes grows, the intensity of class conflict is bound to diminish. Instead of advancing their claims as members of homogeneous groups, people are more likely to compete with each other as individuals for a place in the sun. Where such competition is not possible, or not successful, group conflicts assume a somewhat milder and looser character than class struggles of a Marxian type. Again, the question arises whether such conflict groups of mobile individuals can still be described as classes. In any case, the institutionalization of social mobility through both the educational and the occupational systems contradicts quite clearly the prediction of a continuous increase in the intensity of class conflicts.

In a study of the effects of social mobility on group relations, Janowitz arrived at two interesting conclusions: "One, social mobility generally has been found to have disruptive implications for the structure of primary group relations and on related social psychological states, and thereby to carry socially maladjustive consequences. . . . Second [with respect to the consequences of social mobility for secondary group structures], markedly different order of inferences can be made. Upward social mobility, especially in the middle class, tends to orient and incorporate mobile groups into many types of secondary structures with relative effectiveness. On the other hand, . . . downward mobility does not produce effective involvement in secondary group structures in pursuit of self-interest" (114, p. 193). This finding (which evidently applies to intergeneration mobility only) is a welcome reminder of the fact that although mobility diminishes the coherence of groups as well as the intensity of class conflict, it does not eliminate either. While civil wars and revolutions may be unlikely in a highly mobile society, there is no a priori reason to believe that conflicts of interests will not find their expression in other ways. Marx's theory of class fails to account for such other types of conflict, and it will be our task in this study to find an approach that accounts for group conflicts in mobile as well as in relatively immobile industrial societies.

EQUALITY IN THEORY AND PRACTICE

In the preceding sections two of the three predictions that Marx made about the future development of classes in capitalist society have been discussed in the light of the social history of the last decades. We have seen that neither of them has come true. Contrary to Marx's expectations, the increasing differentiation as well as homogeneity of classes was checked by the decomposition of labor and capital, the emergence of white-collar workers and bureaucrats, and the institutionalization of social mobility. But none of Marx's hopes—for such they were—has been refuted more dramatically in social development than his prediction that the class situations of bourgeoisie and proletariat would tend toward extremes of wealth and poverty, possession and deprivation. Here, too, Marx had a simple theory. He believed in a direct and unfailing correlation between the extremity of class situations and the intensity of class conflict. It is quite possible that this theory contains an element of truth, but if it does, then the remarkable spread of social equality in the past century has rendered class struggles and revolutionary changes utterly impossible.

T. H. Marshall has shown that much of modern social history can be understood in terms of what he calls the "war" between "citizenship rights" (which, by definition, are equal rights) and the "capitalist class system" (cf. 57). In successive periods, three types of citizenship rights have been adopted by most industrial societies, and they have increasingly affected the processes of class differentiation and class conflict. The first of these rights, that of the generalization of legal equality, was still quite compatible with class conflict and even with class war. Indeed, Marx used his most mocking and cynical style when he referred to legal equality in capitalist society: "Liberty! For buyers and sellers of a commodity, e.g., labor power, are determined by their free will alone. They enter into contracts as free, legally equal persons. . . . Equality! For they are related merely as owners of commodities, and exchange equivalent for equivalent. Property! For everybody controls merely what is his" (12, I, p. 184). But Marx overlooked what Tocqueville (whose work he probably knew) had observed before him, namely, that equality is a highly dynamic force, and that men, once they are equal in some respects, "must come in the end to be equal upon all" (232, p. 55).

A considerable step towards complete equality was taken when citizenship rights were, in the nineteenth century, extended to the political sphere. Universal suffrage and the right to form political parties and associations involved the removal of political conflicts from the factory floor and the street to negotiating bodies and parliaments. On a different level, it opened up the possibility for Marx's followers to convert their master's theories into political realities— but it is as well that they did not fail as miserably in this process as Marx did himself. By virtue of freedom of association and political equality, the early trade-union movement as well as socialist parties grown out of it achieved considerable success in improving the lot of the working class, although this progress was still restricted by many an obstacle. "Civil rights gave legal powers whose use was drastically curtailed by class prejudice and lack of economic opportunity. Political rights gave potential power whose exercise demanded experience, organization, and a change of ideas as to the proper functions of government" (57, p. 46). Only when, in our own century, legal and political citizenship rights were supplemented by certain social rights, did the process of equalization of status really reach a point where the differences and antagonisms of class are affected.

The social rights of citizenship which are widely recognized in contemporary societies include old-age pensions, unemployment benefits, public health insurance, and legal aid, as well as a minimum wage and, indeed, a minimum standard of living. "Equal participation in the material and intellectual comforts of civilization . . . is the undisputed basic material right of our social constitution" (Schelsky, 122, p. 5). Where established rights guarantee this kind of equality for every citizen, conflicts and differences of class are, at the very least, no longer based on inequalities of status in a strict sense of this term. From the point of view of legal privileges and deprivations, every citizen of advanced industrial societies has an equal status, and what social differences there are arise on the undisputed basis of this fundamental equality. The "absolute" privilege of the bourgeoisie, and the equally "absolute" alienation of the proletariat which Marx with a characteristic Hegelian figure of thought predicted, has not only not come true, but, by institutionalizing certain citizenship rights, postcapitalist society has developed a type of social structure that excludes both "absolute" and many milder forms of privilege and deprivation. If equality before the law was for most people in the early phases of capitalist society but a cynical fiction, the extended citizenship rights of post-capitalist society represent a reality that forcefully counteracts all remaining forms of social inequality and differentiation.

This is a fortiori the case, since along with the spread of citizenship rights, the social situation of people became increasingly similar. The completeness of this leveling tendency can be, and has been, exaggerated. There are of course even today considerable differences in income, prestige, spending habits, and styles of life. But as a tendency the process of leveling social differences cannot be denied. By the simultaneous rise of the real wages of workers and the taxation of top earnings, a redistribution of incomes has taken place—a redistribution that some believe today has gone so far as to remove every incentive for work requiring special training or skill. Many of the technical comforts and status symbols of modern life are increasingly available to everybody. The mass-produced commodities of the "culture industry" (Horkheimer and Adorno, 227) unite distant people and areas in nearly identical leisure-time activities. Schelsky gives voice to the impression of many when he summarizes this development as a process of "social leveling with predominantly petty-bourgeois or middle-class patterns of behavior and ideals" (231, p. 349).[16]

Social stratification and class structure are two distinct aspects of social organization, but they both refer to inequalities in the social life of individuals. If, therefore, the legal and social status of people undergoes a process of leveling which apparently tends towards complete equality of status, the concepts of social stratification and class structure tend to lose their meaning. In so far as social stratification is concerned, there is evidence and argument to contest this inference. For one thing there is some doubt as to whether one can really extrapolate from developments of the past century and infer a further leveling of socioeconomic status. For another thing, it seems far more likely from the point of view of a functioning social structure that there is a certain minimum of inequalities which will not be touched by egalitarian trends under any condition.[17] With respect to class structure, the answer is not as simple. There can be little doubt that

[16] There is a host of literature on problems of equality and social class. Apart from the works of Marshall and Schelsky (which are discussed more extensively in Chapter III, below), see especially Tawney's classic (187), and Bottomore's recent discussion of the problem (37).

[17] The argument of Davis and Moore (90) to this effect is not, in my opinion, wholly convincing, but many of the considerations relevant to the problem of the function of inequality have come out in their argument and the controversy following it.

the equalization of status resulting from social developments of the past century has contributed greatly to changing the issues and diminishing the intensity of class conflict. By way of extrapolation—fairly wild extrapolation, I may say—some authors have visualized a state in which there are no classes and no class conflicts, because there is simply nothing to quarrel about. I do not think that such a state is ever likely to occur. But in order to substantiate this opinion, it is necessary to explore the structural limits of equality, i.e., to find the points at which even the most fanatic egalitarian comes up against insurmountable realities of social structure. One of these is surely the variety of human desires, ideas, and interests, the elimination of which is neither desirable nor likely. But while this is important, it is not as such an element of social structure. I shall suggest in this study that the fundamental inequality of social structure, and the lasting determinant of social conflict, is the inequality of power and authority which inevitably accompanies social organization. But this is an anticipation about which much more will have to be said. In so far as the theory and practice of equality in post-capitalist societies are concerned, it seems certain that they have changed the issues and patterns of class conflict, and possible that they have rendered the concept of class inapplicable, but they have not removed all significant inequalities, and they have not, therefore, eliminated the causes of social conflict.

THE INSTITUTIONALIZATION OF CLASS CONFLICT

A historian might argue that all the tendencies of change here described as changes in the structure of industrial societies since Marx had in fact begun before and in some cases long before Marx died in 1883. Joint-stock companies existed even before the industrial revolution; there have always been workers of varying degrees of skill; bureaucrats and white-collar workers are not an invention of capitalism, nor is social mobility; and the spread of social equality began at least with the French Revolution, if not earlier. The historian is of course right, but so is, strangely enough, the sociologist (and while the latter usually admits the former, the historian is rather less likely to admit the latter). The sociologist is generally interested not so much in the origin of social phenomena as in their spread and rise to wider significance. There is, however, one line of social development in industrial societies which has both originated and spread since about the time of Marx's death, and which is directly relevant to our problem. Geiger, who has described this change as the "institutionalization of class conflict," says: "The tension between capital and labor is recognized as a principle of the structure of the labor market and has become a legal institution of society. . . . The methods, weapons, and techniques of the class struggle are recognized—and are thereby brought under control. The struggle evolves according to certain rules of the game. Thereby the class struggle has lost its worst sting, it is converted into a legitimate tension between power factors which balance each other. Capital and labor struggle with each other, conclude compromises, negotiate solutions, and thereby determine wage levels, hours of work, and other conditions of work" (46, p. 184).

Marx displayed a certain sociological naïveté when he expressed his belief that capitalist society would be entirely unable to cope with the class conflict generated by its structure. In fact, every society is capable of coping with whatever new phenomena arise in it, if only by the simple yet effective inertia which can be described, a little pretentiously, as the process of institutionalization. In the case of class conflict, institutionalization assumed a number of successive and complementary forms. It began with the painful process of recognition of the contending parties as legitimate interest groups. Within industry, a "secondary system of industrial citizenship" (Marshall, 57, p. 68) enabled both workers and entrepreneurs to associate and defend their interests collectively. Outside industry, the primary system of political citizenship had the same effect. And while, in the stage of organization, conflict may develop a greater visible intensity, organization has at least two side effects which operate in the opposite direction. Organization presupposes the legitimacy of conflict groups, and it thereby removes the permanent and incalculable threat of guerrilla warfare. At the same time, it makes systematic regulation of conflicts possible. Organization is institutionalization, and whereas its manifest function is usually an increasingly articulate and outspoken defense of interests, it invariably has the latent function also of inaugurating routines of conflict which contribute to reducing the violence of clashes of interest.

These are generalizations derived from the experience of class conflict in capitalist and post-capitalist societies. Here, the organization of capital and labor, bourgeoisie and proletariat, was soon followed by several further patterns of conflict regulation. On the one hand, the contending parties in industry and politics agreed on certain rules of the game and created institutions which provided a framework for the routinization of the process of conflict. In industry, these include collective-bargaining bodies of many kinds as well as systems of conciliation, mediation, and arbitration. In politics, legislative bodies and courts of law serve similar functions.[18] All these forms help to convert strikes and civil wars from an exclusive weapon of conflict to an *ultima ratio* of the contending parties.

Such forms of conflict regulation proper have been supplemented, in most industrial societies, by changes in the structure of the industrial enterprise and of the state which aim at reducing the intensity of conflict. The establishment of shop stewards and factory committees, and the participation of workers in industrial management, as well as certain rules and customs relating to the rights of opposition parties,[19] are changes of this kind. There is an element of ideological misconception in many of these institutions. That is, though these new institutions may be designed to eliminate conflict, they may, indeed, actually increase the violence of conflict by redirecting it. In any case, these structural changes in those social organizations that generate conflict show the acceptance by society of conflicting interests, with which society has attempted to cope by institutionalizing them.

The institutionalization of class conflict implies its continued existence. But institutionalized class conflict is nevertheless far removed from the ruthless and absolute class struggle visualized by Marx. It is quite probable that most contemporary industrial societies have ceased to be capitalist societies. If this is true, it has happened not because they were unable to cope with the contradictions and conflicts generated by the structure of capitalist society, but, more likely, precisely because they were able to cope with their conflicts. Like many of his contemporaries—if with rather different evaluative accents— Marx was so struck by the dynamics of early industrial conflict that he believed its satisfactory settlement utterly impossible except by a revolution. However, also like many of his contemporaries, Marx was mistaken. Some feared and others wanted the revolution, but both fear and hope were equally unfounded. Nobody can, of course, ever

---

[18] For some discussion of the sociological aspects of these types of conflict regulation, and of the institutionalization of class conflict in general, see, apart from Geiger's work, the book by W. E. Moore (157) and the articles by Lockwood (86) and Kerr (84). A systematic, though more abstract, exposition of the regulation of social conflict will be given below, in Chapter VI.

[19] By contrast to changes in the structure of the enterprise, those in political institutions are very varied in different countries. They include, however, the participation of opposition members in decision-making bodies, especially in matters of defense, the rights of higher civil servants to be retained even if they are not in the majority party, the custom to appoint a member of the opposition as speaker of parliament, and the like.

be sure that a given pattern of conflict regulation will always prove successful. There are still strikes, and for all we know they will continue to occur. But it has proved possible for industrial society to get along with the clashes of interest arising from its industrial and political structure—and it has proved possible for interest groups to get along with industrial society. Instead of a battlefield, the scene of group conflict has become a kind of market in which relatively autonomous forces contend according to certain rules of the game, by virtue of which nobody is a permanent winner or loser. This course of development must naturally be bitter for the orthodox and the dogmatic, but theirs is the kind of bitterness which makes liberal minds rejoice.

CAPITALISM *cum* INDUSTRIAL SOCIETY

Not every industrial society is a capitalist society, and one of the differences between the time of Marx and ours might be described as the supersedence of capitalism. But while there are a number of significant differences between industrial societies of a hundred years ago and today, there are also similarities. Some of these are obvious. There are machines and factories, workers and entrepreneurs, wages and profits today as there were a hundred years ago. The historical traditions of the countries with which we are here concerned have been added to, but not changed. Many of the specific cultural and social features of capitalist societies in Europe and North America have survived the changes of the last century almost untouched. However, we are not concerned here with a general and comprehensive account of industrial societies and their development. Within the more limited scope of the present study, the culture and history of societies is but a background before which specific structures and conflicts unfold, and in turning to those elements of social structure that remained unchanged in the past century we shall again confine our discussion to aspects relevant to the problem of class.

Every society has a structure of institutions, groups, and roles. But every society is also, as Durkheim put it, a "moral society," that is, it entails a set of norms and values which live both in the minds of its citizens and in the patterns of their social relations. One of the paradoxes of the social history of industrial societies is that the structure of their institutions has in the past century changed in many respects, while their values have merely advanced, but not changed. This is but a seeming contradiction, because one can show that most of the changes discussed in this chapter occurred within a framework which remained intact, and that the values of rationality, achievement, and equality belong to this framework rather than to its changing details.

Thus, "economic rationalism," the value of purposeful economic activity oriented toward the maximization of gains, has never left industrial societies. As Max Weber has shown, this value preceded capitalism and, indeed, constitutes one of the factors which account for the emergence of capitalism. But its dynamics were not exhausted once capitalism was under way. Within capitalism, the impulse to organize economic activity more "rationally" remained a stubborn tendency. When, towards the end of the nineteenth century, many countries experienced what has sometimes been called a "second industrial revolution," the value of rationality stood behind it: at about this time, the "extensive" increase of industrial production was replaced by an "intensive" increase, i.e., by a "more rational" organization of existing resources. "Scientific management" and even "social engineering" were part of this trend. It was in the course of this development that ever larger concentrations of production enterprises proved imperative—enterprises so large that few individuals could provide the capital to establish them, so that some new form of ownership became desirable. At the same time, the usefulness of human skills in terms of the maximization of gains was rediscovered. It proved more "rational" to carry on production with experienced and well-trained workers than with mere "hands." Finally, rationality and bureaucracy are never very far apart; in one sense the rapidly growing demand for clerks and office employees, accountants and supervisors, statisticians and submanagers is but a concomitant of the "rational" organization of enterprises. Thus, the changes that led to the supersedence of capitalist society were the reflection of values on which this type of social and economic organization was based. Economic "rationalism" seems a value characteristic of all industrial societies, not merely of their capitalist variant.[20]

Essentially the same holds for the value of achievement, i.e., the central place accorded to individual capacity, effort, and success in industrial societies. As with gains and profits, the content of success may change in the course of history, but achievement has remained,

---

[20] I do not think that the replacement of the "protestant ethic" by a "social ethic" (Whyte) contradicts this argument. If by "rationalism" we understand purposeful activity oriented to maximizing gains, it remains open whether these gains are entirely monetary in nature, or whether they include certain less tangible gains well compatible with a "social ethic." The opposite of "rationalism" is "traditionalism," and I see no evidence for a return of the latter.

so far, the cardinal social virtue of the citizens of industrial societies. If anything, the recognition of achievement has progressed in the past century. Ever since the industrial revolution, ascriptive criteria of status have proved an obstacle to the systematic exploitation of resources, material and human. An industrial enterprise cannot afford to rely on the social origin of its members in the sphere either of management or of labor; to carry on its tasks it needs above all capable, well-trained people. From the enterprise, this premium on achievement has spread to the whole society. For this reason, industrial societies need a minimum—if not a maximum—of social mobility; and for this reason also, the educational institutions have grown, in industrial societies, into the place of agents of role allocation.

Like rationality and achievement, equality is also a value which characterizes all industrial societies, capitalist or otherwise. We have seen that legal equality is not merely compatible with, but conditional for the capitalist class system. Even Marx realized, despite his scorn for the "purely formal" ideology of equality, that "this one condition comprehends a world history" (12, I, p. 178). But we have also seen that "this one condition" has not remained confined to equality before the law, and its extension to other spheres was probably no accident. Inequalities of status, legal and social, obstruct the formation of rational organizations in which the place of individuals is determined by achievement. Although the realization of equality remained pitifully imperfect in capitalist societies, it was a part of the program of these as it is of their successors.

There is only one point at which the changes in the structure of industrial societies since Marx might appear to have affected the values of these societies. It is often said that modern societies are always "open" (Weber) or "adaptive" (Mayo). And in seeking for an explanation of such terms one may encounter statements like: "We have in fact passed beyond that stage of human organization in which effective communication and collaboration were secured by established routines of relationship" (154, p. 12).[21] But, then, this kind of statement is simply a misunderstanding of social reality. As I have pointed out before, post-capitalist societies do in fact display effective routines of human cooperation (e.g., the institutionalization of class conflict), but this is not a reason for assuming a change in values. The fact that the values of industrial societies were realized incompletely in their

[21] This formulation, by the way, is a typical example of a statement which, in its logical status, is not sociological in that it does not permit of empirical test. This in itself would be sufficient reason to be skeptical about its validity.

earliest, capitalist, forms is not surprising, nor does it affect the importance of these values for both capitalist and post-capitalist phases of development. We can conclude with some confidence that the social changes discussed in this chapter have all been compatible with, and to some extent consequent of, certain social values which advanced industrial societies share with their capitalist precursors.[22]

Apart from these social values, certain other elements of the social structure of industrial societies have also survived the changes of the past century and are therefore characteristic of capitalist and industrial societies alike. These structural features are so formal and general in nature that they may well be elements not only of industrial but also of all human societies. Yet, while this general problem need not concern us here, they have to be mentioned, for they both have a special bearing on class structure and conflict. I mean, here, the existence of social stratification and of authority relations.

Although, as the preceding discussion has incidentally brought out, patterns of social stratification have undergone considerable changes in the course of the last hundred years, these changes have not affected the existence of a hierarchical differentiation of status, and there is no indication that hierarchies of socioeconomic status will disappear in the foreseeable future. There still are rewards to be distributed by society, these are still desired by individuals, and the distribution of desired rewards is still unequal. I think one can go one step further and add that, by and large, the criterion by which rewards are unequally distributed is still that of occupation. Many contemporary sociologists believe that we have left the age of work and production and entered an era of leisure and consumption. But to the present day the extent of a person's leisure, as well as the level of his consumption, is entirely determined by his occupation and the rewards associated with it. Whatever criterion of social stratification one prefers, prestige or income, spending habits or styles of life, education or independence, they all lead back to occupation. Social stratification based on occupation is as such neither the whole nor a part of class structure, but it does constitute an element of inequality which has

---

[22] A second conclusion that can and must be drawn from this analysis of changing structures within unchanged values has to do with the usefulness of the value concept for the analysis of social change. Despite their boundaries, the changes discussed in this chapter are by no means unimportant; yet it would be hard if not impossible to retrace them on the level of values. Thus it would appear that only long-term changes (like the emergence of industrial society) can be fruitfully analyzed in terms of values; for the other changes, it seems best to analyze them in terms of structural elements.

persisted and which continues to influence the issues and patterns of social conflict.

This is even more clearly the case with respect to relations of domination and subordination as they exist in social organizations of both capitalist and post-capitalist industrial societies. The assertion that there still are authority relations in industry, in the state, and in many other forms of social organization does not go unchallenged in contemporary sociology. In surveying recent theories of conflict in the following chapter, we shall encounter a number of authors who believe that power is a thing of the past. Short of anticipating this discussion and giving a precise definition of what is meant by power and authority, I would here merely assert this: in post-capitalist as in capitalist industrial enterprises there are some whose task it is to control the actions of others and issue commands, and others who have to allow themselves to be controlled and who have to obey. Today as a hundred years ago there are governments, parliaments, and courts the members of which are entitled to make decisions that affect the lives of many citizens, and there are citizens who can protest and shift their vote but who have to abide by the law. Insofar as either of these relations can be described as one of authority, I would claim that relations of domination and subordination have persisted throughout the changes of the past century. Again, I believe that we can go even further. The authority exercised in both capitalist and post-capitalist society is of the same type; it is, in Weber's terms, "rational authority" based "on the belief in the legality of institutionalized norms and the right of command on the part of those invested with authority by these norms" (33*b*, p. 124). From this condition many others, including the necessity of bureaucratic administration, follow. But these are based above all on the fundamental social inequality of authority which may be mitigated by its "rational" character, but that nevertheless pervades the structure of all industrial societies and provides both the determinant and the substance of most conflicts and clashes.

III

Some Recent Theories of Class Conflict in Modern Societies

REFUTATION IS NOT ENOUGH

Our account of changes in the structure of industrial societies since Marx has been largely descriptive, although I have tried to weave a number of threads of development into some main cords. Description, however, is but the basis of scientific knowledge, not its proper substance. I am not sure whether Merton's statement that ". . . in building the mansion of sociology during the last decades, theorists and empiricists have learned to work together" (214, p. 102) was not a little premature when he made it in 1948. Merton may well be right in his claim that empirical research can serve to inspire, transform, redirect, and clarify theories, apart from testing them. But it is still necessary to emphasize that fact-finding is not in itself explanation, and that therefore "empirical research" cannot replace "theoretical insight."[1]

With respect to Marx's theories of class formation and class conflict the overwhelming majority of social scientists have failed to proceed beyond the level of description. There is a growing number of studies about occupational prestige and social mobility. A library of social psychological and sociological monographs has been written about the "new middle class." There are numerous investigations into trends of social stratification, egalitarian or otherwise. Research in industrial sociology often touches upon problems of industrial conflict and the authority structure of the enterprise. But the authors of all these studies would do well to call them sociographic rather than sociological investigations. There is no lack of data, but *cui bono?* Of what use is the remark found in many a research report that its results refute one thesis or another thesis of Marx's? What is the use of re-

---

[1] Of course, the reverse must also be emphasized: theoretical insight cannot replace empirical research; but then, this misconception is very much rarer today than the one alluded to in the text.

futing one or the other thesis, if the progress of science stops at this early point? It is certainly of some moment to refute theories and hypotheses derived from them. But it is more important to supersede, on the basis of such refutations, the theories themselves, and to put better and more satisfactory ones in their place. From this point of view all the authors whose approaches we shall discuss in this chapter have advanced far beyond the so-called pure empiricists.

Theory is "the net which we throw out in order to catch 'the world'—to rationalize, explain, and dominate it" (Popper, 218, p. 26). In this sense, a theory is "more" than a particular hypothesis, and a hypothesis is "more" than a concept or category. For Marx, "class" is a category. Its substance can be found by observation and described by the category. Thus the statement that "the proletariat is a class" is descriptive in that it subsumes an empirical datum under a concept. But the statement that the proletariat is involved in a conflict with the bourgeoisie which can only be solved by a revolution is a hypothesis. It is derived from a theory, from which other hypotheses are also derived; we have called it Marx's theory of class conflict. According to this theory, every society generates in its structure conflicting classes which develop in a certain way and the conflict of which eventually leads to structural upheavals. Thus a theory is a general "point of view" which structures an area of facts and transforms it into an ordered context. As scientists, it is not our task to "select only such facts as confirm the theory and, as it were, repeat it; the method of science is rather to look out for facts which refute the theory" (Popper, 219, II, p. 260). Facts refute theories by proving false one or several hypotheses necessarily following from them.[2] In this sense, we can conclude that Marx's theory of class conflict—insofar as it is a scientific theory and not untestable speculation—has been refuted by the "facts" discussed in the preceding chapter.

But the refutation of theories, although "the vehicle of scientific progress" (Popper), is not its substance. Refutation of old theories makes sense only if it becomes the point of departure for the development of new theories. This is what is meant here by the supersedence of a theory. Such supersedence may assume several different forms. In the case of Marx's theory of class it may mean that we restrict the validity of this theory to a single, limited type of social organization, such as capitalism. Alternatively, it may involve reformulating

[2] Properly speaking it is not "facts," but "statements of fact" that refute hypotheses. For a more detailed discussion of these methodological problems, see the quoted works of Popper.

Marx's theory by modifying some of its elements. Finally, we may decide to dismiss this theory altogether and replace it by an entirely new theory of social conflict. However, one of these paths will have to be chosen if we want to advance our knowledge of social conflict and change. In the present chapter, we shall discuss some recent attempts to supersede Marx's theory in the light of historical facts and sociological insights. It will emerge from this discussion that none of these approaches has substituted a satisfactory new theory for that of Marx—that is, a theory which survives the test of observed data. It will then be our task to explore new paths and to hope that this exploration will contribute to the development of a useful theory of social conflict. But before we embark on this long and at times somewhat tedious journey, it is unfortunately necessary to free the central category of our analysis, the concept of class, of the jumble of misconceptions which obscures its meaning today, and to try and reinstate it in its proper place.

THE DILUTION OF THE CONCEPT OF CLASS

The history of the concept of class in sociology is surely one of the most extreme illustrations of the inability of sociologists to achieve a minimum of consensus even in the modest business of terminological decisions.[3] Only recently, Geiger, Lipset and Bendix, and some others have unraveled the conceptual confusion a little and begun to inaugurate a rather more rigid use of the category of class. It is not our intention here to discuss all the versions and perversions of the concept of class. That would be a task for the sociologist of knowledge; indeed, it has been done, with varying success and often not without additional confusion, since Mombert (23) and Sorokin (30), who counted thirty-two variations of the concept as early as thirty years ago, by Geiger (91, 46), Marshall (58), Cox (40), Pfautz (97), Lipset and Bendix (55), Croner (129), and others. For curiosity's sake, then, rather than in order to attempt a comprehensive survey, I shall quote here a small selection of definitions of the much abused concept of class:

Class "is a force that unites into groups people who differ from one another, by overriding the differences between them" (Marshall, 57, p. 114).

"Class, as distinguished from stratum, can well be regarded as a psy-

---

[3] I have discussed the conceptual problems raised here more extensively in an essay (41).

chological phenomenon in the fullest sense of the term. That is, a man's class is a part of his ego, a feeling on his part of belongingness to something; an identification with something larger than himself" (Centers, 38, p. 27).

"We shall then mean by a social class any portion of a community which is marked off from the rest, not by limitations arising out of language, locality, function, or specialization, but primarily by social status" (MacIver, 211, p. 167).

"According to the point of view here advanced, social classes . . . are social groups determined by three factors, namely, (1) similar social conditions, (2) similar social status, (3) similar social values" (Croner, 129, p. 185).

"By class is meant two or more orders of people who are believed to be, and are accordingly ranked by the members of the community, in socially superior and inferior positions" (Warner and Lunt, 100, p. 82).

Whoever reads these definitions may well be tempted to regard sociology as rather a frivolous discipline. Indeed, theories can neither be formulated nor refuted on the basis of these definitions, some of which are plainly bare of substance, others too profuse, and all far removed from the original purpose of the concept of class. Attempts have been made to classify the multitude of existing concepts of class itself. Usually, "objective" and "subjective" definitions of class are distinguished; Pfautz has added to this the distinction between "external objective," and "internal objective" approaches (97). But such attempts achieve the opposite of their purpose, if this may be suspected in a clarification of the concept. We are indeed faced with an alternative: either we renounce the discredited term "class" altogether and endeavor to find a less ambiguous set of terms, or we reject radically all definitions which depart from the original, i.e., Marxian heuristic purpose, and return to this source.

In a historical discipline it is always difficult to take a "protestant" view and ignore traditions. While the attempt to reinstate the concept of class in its original meaning is methodologically unobjectionable, we must also ask whether it is pragmatically feasible. There are legitimate doubts about the latter aspect, and to some extent I share these doubts. As a tentative and reversible decision, however, I propose to retain the term "class" and contrast it with others for which alternative terms have already begun to become accepted. The criterion by which this distinction seems possible is the heuristic purpose of the categories in question. From this point of view, we shall have to reject all definitions of class as a category of social stratification whether they be "internal objective," "external objective," or "subjective." Wherever classes are defined by factors which permit the construction of a hierarchical continuum, they are wrongly defined; i.e., the term has been applied wrongly. Status, ranking by others, self-ranking, style of life, similar economic conditions, and income level are all factors which define social strata but not social classes. However one may interpret, extend, or improve Marx, classes in his sense are clearly not layers in a hierarchical system of strata differentiated by gradual distinctions. Rather, "the analysis of social class is concerned with an assessment of the chances that common economic conditions and common experiences of a group will lead to organized action" (Lipset and Bendix, 55, p. 248).[4] *Class* is always a category for purposes of the analysis of the dynamics of social conflict and its structural roots, and as such it has to be separated strictly from *stratum* as a category for purposes of describing hierarchical systems at a given point of time.

This statement of the meaning of the concept of class (or, rather, of what it cannot properly mean) automatically excludes from the present investigation a large number of sociological works which overtly deal with "classes." For example, Warner's six-"class" theory (75, 100)—if it deserves the name of theory at all—constitutes neither a refutation nor a supersession of Marx's theory of class. It cannot be conceived as such, for, using the terms correctly, Warner should have referred to his groups of equal rank not as "upper-upper *class*," "lower-upper *class*," etc., but as "upper-upper *stratum*," "lower-upper *stratum*," etc. In the following discussion of recent theories, we shall therefore confine ourselves to three types of approaches: those which are explicitly based on what, with a deliberate overstatement, I shall now call the correct concept of class; those whose authors assert that they are based on the correct concept of class; and those which, although they are not based on this concept, are formulated in such a way as to suggest that they might genuinely supersede Marx's theory of class. Obviously, even those post-Marxian theories of class which conform with these standards are too numerous all to be included in a brief discussion. A comprehensive summary and critique of these theories would require a lengthy book in itself. I have therefore selected, from a multitude of works, those which are comparatively recent and which are consequently not them-

---

[4] At a later stage, I shall raise some objections to the exclusive reference to "economic conditions" in statements of this kind; they are nevertheless true to the heuristic purpose of the concept of class.

selves accompanied by a host of interpretations and critiques.[5] Furthermore, I have tried to choose examples which are characteristic of entire schools of thought. In this chapter, I have also left out purely conceptual discussions, some of which will be mentioned later, and I have concentrated on analyses of modern societies in terms of class structure and class conflict. Finally, my selection has been guided by the fruitfulness of approaches for a new sociological theory of conflict, the formulation of which constitutes the ultimate aim of the present study.

ON AND OFF THE PARTY LINE
(Nemchinov, Djilas)

Evidently, those are faced by the most difficult problems of analysis who, by a philosophical or political decision, are bound to maintain Marx's theory in all essential features as an instrument of sociological explanation. One need hardly mention that this kind of decision makes fruitful scientific research and analysis impossible. Dogmatic insistence on scientific theories always mars the progress of knowledge. Quite possibly, this is one of the reasons why many of the analyses presented by Soviet scholars are so sterile and naïve that in non-Communist countries they would hardly be acceptable for publication in scholarly journals or by serious publishers. Thus the brief study by Nemchinov (64), a member of the Soviet Academy of Sciences, is distinguished from the mass of these analyses not by its profoundness or thoroughness, but by its subject matter which Marxist social scientists[6] have been extremely hesitant to deal with, namely "changes in the class structure of the population of the Soviet Union."

To begin with, Nemchinov recalls the original definition of class and distinguishes it from the notion of social stratification, with which the analysis of class has in his opinion been confused in the West in an impermissible manner. "Thus, the objective criteria for the determination of social classes are the position of the society member in the occupation and the character of his income, determined by the pre-

[5] This criterion excludes the whole Marxist literature. While a discussion of Marxist thinking on class from Kautsky to Lukacs and further would certainly promise many a useful result, it seemed to me an unnecessary ballast in a book that is primarily concerned not with Marx but with social conflict.

[6] Perhaps it would be more precise to speak here of "Marxist-Leninist" or "orthodox Marxist" authors, for among Marxians, i.e., scholars who profess a scientific (which means last, not least, critical) relation to Marx, there have been many serious studies of class. See, e.g., the work of Djilas discussed below.

vailing form of property and the type of productive relations in which individual members stand to other members under the particular system of social labor" (p. 14).[7] There is but one interesting and potentially consequential point at which Nemchinov supplements Marx's theory. He separates, both conceptually and empirically, property and power, and he states that in bourgeois society "it is beyond any doubt that to a greatest extent property relations provide an all-round control over the living conditions of the workers," whereas "common ownership of the means of production in the USSR makes it impossible to transform private income into a source of power" (p. 13). This does not, of course, contradict the position of Marx, for whom effective private property, and not property in general, was the determinant of class structure, but it nevertheless opens up unexpected vistas. If property can, but must not, convey power, a curious alternative emerges of which Nemchinov has chosen the dogmatic, untenable side, whereas Djilas, as we shall presently see, chose to apply Marx's theory plausibly, although critically. Nemchinov does not hesitate to state his "theoretical position" quite unambiguously. "The great historical changes of the twentieth century and those of the past centuries [!] have confirmed the scientific objectivity, truth and validity of the theory of social classes formulated by Marx and later developed and worked out by Lenin" (p. 3). It is nice to know that Lenin's "objectivity, truth and validity" was assured even before he was born. But if we ignore for the moment the fact that this statement is a confession rather than a proposition, we must ask: In what sense could it possibly be valid? How does a theory based on such beliefs cope with the changes which industrial societies have undergone since Marx?

Nemchinov takes a stand only with respect to two of the changes we discussed in the preceding chapter: to the problems of property and of the "middle class." Moreover as to the first of these, he has no more to offer than a few dogmatic assertions. "The material basis of bourgeois hegemony lies in the private ownership of the means of production. . . . The workers in a capitalist society do not possess the means of production and are obliged to sell their labour to the employer, the owner of the means of production" (p. 12). This is but an inferior repetition of Marx and ignores completely the

---

[7] Nemchinov's essay, as well as the paper by his colleague P. N. Fedoseyev quoted below, was originally submitted to the Third World Congress of Sociology in English. All quotations are from these English texts. It is evident, however, that the translators at the disposal of the Soviet Academy of Sciences are rather inferior to those employed by the Soviet government and the Politbureau.

phenomenon of the separation of ownership and control. However, Nemchinov's colleague Fedoseyev (45) settled this problem in accordance with the party line, although I have to confess that I find his approach more amusing than impressive. Fedoseyev thinks that "it is not difficult to understand that the replacement of the individual capitalist owners by corporative monopolistic capital does not mean at all that the capitalist class disappears. The place of the individual owners of the capitalist enterprises is taken by the participants of the monopolistic unions, by the magnates of financial capital, millionaires and multimillionaires, who exploit the working people through the system of trusts, joint-stock companies, banks and state-capitalist enterprises" (45, p. 267). Had Fedoseyev read his Marx more thoroughly, he would have known that "the place of the individual owners" has been taken by at least two sets of people, of which one, the managers, can hardly be described as magnates and multimillionaires. But perhaps such plain facts are too insignificant for the imagination of Soviet thinkers.

Not unexpectedly, Nemchinov and Fedoseyev are essentially agreed with respect to the "middle class." "The problem of the so-called middle classes plays a great role in the theory of social classes. Bourgeois sociologists assume that homogeneous societies can be achieved as a result of the growth and development of the middle classes" (64, p. 6). So far so good. But what is the "true" place of the middle class? "History has, however, shown," says Nemchinov (p. 6), "that this social group is economically unstable and subject to class disintegration." Fedoseyev goes even further. According to him, the middle strata "have declined not only in their specific share in production, but also in their numbers" (p. 268). Evidently, both authors refer here to the "old middle classes" of peasants, artisans, and shopkeepers. As to the "new middle class," Nemchinov confines himself to criticizing Clark's distinction of "primary," "secondary," and "tertiary" industries and asserting that the latter are "undoubtedly the continuation of the process of production and must come under social production" (p. 8), and that therefore the old classes exist in these as in older forms of production.[8]

There is, however, one aspect of Nemchinov's analysis which leads

---

[8] Nemchinov's disinclination to accept Clark's distinctions seems to me a characteristic illustration of the "sterility" and "naïveté" of orthodox Marxist analyses: many concepts which are both useful and necessary for descriptive purposes are simply denied, as if such denials could conjure away the realities described by such concepts. This kind of deliberate primitiveness of the scientific instrumentarium makes communication difficult and differentiated insights virtually impossible.

beyond such stereotyped repetitions of dogma. He deals at some length with the position of specialists, professional people, and higher technical and administrative employees. Nemchinov refers to this group as the "intelligentsia," or "intellectuals." "The intellectuals are an intermediate social group, the class character of which is determined by the prevailing method of social production. Under capitalism, intellectuals stem mostly from the propertied classes and are closely connected with their own class. Among them there are also representatives of the workers' intelligentsia, closely connected with the peasantry and the working class. In socialist society intellectuals are mostly drafted from the workers and collective farmers and are closely connected with the working masses. Nevertheless the intelligentsia cannot be considered, under capitalism as well as under communism, as a special middle class. They are only an intermediate social group, existing along with the basic social classes" (pp. 9–10). Elsewhere, Nemchinov describes this group as an "intermediate social stratum."

Here we find indeed something like a precarious theoretical attempt to explain a new phenomenon of social development with the categories of the old theory of class. However, this attempt is, in the first place, based on erroneous statements of fact. With respect to the Soviet Union, we still know comparatively little about the social origin of the "intelligentsia." But in "capitalist societies" of the present, this group is by no means solely, or even mainly, recruited from the "propertied classes." If we look at contemporary England (1949) as an example, we find that of all men in the status categories 1, 2, and 3 of D. V. Glass's study (107)—i.e., all higher salaried employees, and people in managerial and professional occupations— 24.3 per cent (category 1), 40.9 per cent (category 2), and 62.1 per cent (category 3), respectively, were recruited from strata which Nemchinov would count among the "working class" (108, p. 183). Nemchinov has bracketed out the phenomenon of social mobility in advanced industrial societies, and his theory therefore explains at best one aspect of the social changes that have occurred since Marx.

But does it really explain this aspect? It is Nemchinov's thesis that the "intelligentsia" is in principle a stratum which is neutral from the point of view of class, and which does not therefore constitute an autonomous force in class conflicts. Were it not for Nemchinov's definition of this group, this might sound rather like A. Weber's and Mannheim's theory of the "free-floating" or "socially unattached intelligentsia." But we must remember that Nemchinov includes in the "intelligentsia" apart from "intellectuals" proper the "technicians employed in various branches of industry" as well as "administrative workers," which latter groups presumably constitute the majority of this strange stratum. It includes, indeed—as soon as Nemchinov refers to Soviet society—government ministers, party functionaries, and the managers of industrial enterprises. In other words, Nemchinov claims that the incumbents of positions of authority in state and industry, and their bureaucracies, neither are a social class themselves nor provide a reason to modify Marx's theory of class at any point. We shall see presently that the first of these claims is a matter of dogma rather than of Marxian analysis; for on this point Djilas's analysis seems perfectly convincing. The second of Nemchinov's claims, however, is manifestly false and leads its author into interesting contradictions. If it is true that the bureaucratic managers of state and industry do not form a class, and if it is further true that contemporary Western societies are still class societies in Marx's sense, then it follows that mere property (of shares, for example) without control can be the basis and determinant of a class. This consequence would undoubtedly modify Marx's theory, and it would reveal Nemchinov as a representative of the "vulgar mind" which "commutes class differences into 'differences in the size of the purse'" (Marx, 5, p. 466). If, on the other hand, the incumbents of leading bureaucratic positions do form a class in Western societies, it is hard to see why in the Soviet Union they should be a mere "stratum," an outgrowth of the working class. Nemchinov's venture in social theory manages to repeat Marx's theory up to a point, but it falls victim also to the changed patterns of advanced industrial society.

Where Soviet social science refers to the West, it is almost invariably unconvincing, but also often colorful and amusing. "The abyss between labour and capital, between working people and exploiters is not filled, but deepened, for the profits of the monopolists grow, whereas the share of the masses of the population in the national income steadily falls. The growth of technology leads to the intensification of labour and to greater exploitation of workers. This is the source of the aggravation of social contradictions and the basis of continuous class struggle in the capitalist countries" (Fedoseyev, 45, p. 268). However, where Soviet social science refers to Communist countries, it is not only unconvincing but also remarkably barren and boring. Nemchinov reiterates in detail Stalin's theory of "nonantagonistic classes"—without of course mentioning, in 1956, its author. "The modern class structure of Soviet society has been reflected in the Soviet Constitution of 1936. At present Soviet society consists of two basic classes, the working class and the collective farmers,[9] as well as a social stratum, the intelligentsia" (p. 22). That the mere attempt to extend the concept of class in this fashion bears witness to the "inadequacy of the classical Marxist-Leninist conception of class," Nemchinov could have learned from his less dogmatic Polish colleague Ossowski (66, p. 24). That it conceals rather than reveals and explains the realities of Soviet society seems evident, and has been convincingly demonstrated by Djilas's analysis of the "new class" (44).

Djilas's work is of interest in our discussion, because its author applies a fairly strict Marxian approach to the analysis of Communist societies. Its subject matter is precisely that odd "intelligentsia" of managers, party secretaries, and bureaucrats which—if Nemchinov's study is at all symptomatic—appears to have puzzled Soviet scholars for some time. Only, Djilas cuts deeper than Nemchinov. He is not content with the problematic construction of an "intermediate social stratum" which belongs neither here nor there, but instead explicitly calls this "intelligentsia" a new ruling class with its own very special social characteristics. "It is the bureaucracy which formally uses, administers, and controls both nationalized and socialized property as well as the entire life of society. The role of the bureaucracy in society, i.e., monopolistic administration and control of national income and national goods, consigns it to a special privileged position. . . . Ownership is nothing other than the right of profit and control. If one defines class benefits by this right, the Communist states have seen, in the final analysis, the origin of a new form of ownership or of a new ruling and exploiting class" (44, p. 35).

The main peculiarity of the bureaucratic ruling class of Communist societies is, according to Djilas, that it has not grown spontaneously like other classes in history, but has been the deliberate creation of a party elite. It follows from this fact that the rule of the new class is more brutal and all-embracing than that of any other class in history. But otherwise this "new class of owners and exploiters" (p. 54) resembles earlier classes in many ways. Its domination is based on ownership, for, as Djilas argues at great length, "collective ownership" is but a façade behind which "this new class, the bureaucracy, or more accurately the political bureaucracy" (p. 38), exercises

[9] See 64, p. 15. "The workers and collective farmers are friendly classes in the USSR, as their material interests are not opposed. . . ."

its control. Coupled with its "monopolistic ownership" the new class has "totalitarian authority," that is, its power extends over all spheres of life. Like earlier classes, it tries to legitimize its rule by an elaborate ideology. Finally, Djilas hopes and predicts that, like other classes in history, this new class will also be overthrown and displaced in a revolutionary action of the oppressed.

Djilas naturally does not include the contemporary Western scene in his analysis, so that we cannot infer from his work how he would try to modify Marx's theory to fit the Western case. But it is an important fact to remember that his analysis shows that a fairly strict Marxian analysis might still be applicable to Communist countries. This conclusion may mean either of two things. It is conceivable that a Marxian theory of class conflict applies fully only to countries undergoing the process of industrialization. But it is also possible that we can infer from Djilas's analysis that some kind of Marxian theory is of more general usefulness and applicability. I have deliberately referred to Djilas's approach as a *fairly* strict Marxian analysis, and as *some kind of* Marxian theory. There is, in this approach, a slight shift of emphasis at a crucial juncture of Marx's theory which may prove essential to the problem of the applicability of this theory. This shift of emphasis concerns the relation between ownership, or property, and power.

I think it can be shown that Djilas is not unambiguous when he speaks of the determinants of the new class. On the one hand, he says, "As in other owning classes, the proof that it is a special class lies in its ownership and its special relations to other classes" (p. 44), or, "The specific characteristic of this new class is its collective ownership" (p. 54). On the other hand, one can find a statement like, "Today power is both the means and the goal of Communists, in order that they may maintain their privileges and ownership. But since these are special forms of power and ownership, it is only through power itself that ownership can be exercised. Power is an end in itself and the essence of contemporary Communism" (p. 169). There is at least a hint here that it is ultimately not the ownership of the means of production that determines a class, but that this very ownership is only a special case of a more general social force, power. While Marx, as we saw, subordinates relations of authority to those of property, Djilas seems inclined to subordinate ownership to power. The problem of the relationship of these two factors will recur time and again in the considerations of this study; and it will, I hope, become increasingly clear that in explaining social conflicts and changes, there is greater promise in an approach that follows Djilas than follows Marx.

CAPITALISM, SOCIALISM, AND SOCIAL CLASSES
(Schumpeter)

It was of course not merely by Nemchinov, and not only in Communist countries, that the attempt has been made to save Marx's theory of class as a principle of explanation for advanced industrial societies. Two lines of argument are characteristic of such attempts at rescue. On the one hand, certain new facts of social development, such as the separation of ownership and control or social mobility, are either denied or explained away. This was done, for example, by Kuczynski, whose attempts to "prove" the "pauperization" of the proletariat in "capitalist" societies despite a continued rise in real wages (152) has been exposed by Geiger in all its untenability and even ridiculousness (46, pp. 60 ff.). Obviously, a dogmatic approach of this kind does not advance our knowledge of society. On the other hand, seemingly unimportant elements of Marx's theory are modified by such "revisionists" without their realizing how the original theory is being transformed in their hands. Thus, Renner introduced in his early attempt at a systematic formulation of Marx's theories (26) an interesting additional distinction. He argues that recent social development has complicated class structure, especially the bourgeoisie. "It puts alongside the capitalist who owns and functions the other one who owns but does not function. . . . What is more: It also produces the non-capitalist who exercises capitalist functions, who therefore does not own but functions as a capitalist" (26, p. 375). For us this is by now a familiar line of argument. But if one regards in this way the merely controlling manager as a "capitalist," i.e., as the founder of a class, then class conflict is separated from its Marxian root, private property. The assertion loses its meaning that a ["socialist"] society based on communal property is a classless society. Thus, an argument of this kind cannot save Marx's theory either. Saving Marx's theories is of course in any case a highly doubtful undertaking, in which a social science should take good care not to become involved. But in his early writings Renner has neither wanted nor clearly seen the necessity of superseding Marx's theory of property and social class[10]; it was Schumpeter who first carried through

---

[10] By contrast to the later Renner, whose work will be discussed below. The attempt to supersede Marx on the basis of his own principles and yet retain the political impetus of "scientific socialism" expresses itself even more clearly in the work of Renner than in that of Bernstein.

the conscious separation of Marx's theory of the development of property from his theory of class conflict.

Schumpeter poses Marx's question of the "economic law of development of capitalist society" anew. Can capitalism survive? And, can socialism work? Both "capitalism" and "socialism" are for Schumpeter categories that describe economic systems—in particular, property relations. In this sense, Schumpeter agrees with Marx's conclusion that the economic order of capitalism is bound to break down and give rise to a new economic constitution which is socialist in that it is based on communal or, as Schumpeter prefers to say, state ownership. This is a "necessary" process—not, however, in a Marx-Hegelian sense of immanent laws of historical development, but as a scientific "statement about the tendencies present in an observable pattern," which does not "tell us what *will* happen to the pattern but only what would happen if they continued to act as they have been acting in the time interval covered by our observation and if no other factors intruded" (73, p. 61).

If, up to this point, his analysis is quite compatible with that of Marx, Schumpeter now goes his own way. Socialism is, as he says, "culturally indeterminate; . . . in fact, . . . a society may be fully and truly socialist and yet be led by an absolute ruler or be organized in the most democratic of all possible ways; it may be aristocratic or proletarian; it may be a theocracy and hierarchic or atheist or indifferent as to religion; it may be much more strictly disciplined than men are in a modern army or completely lacking in discipline" (73, pp. 170–71). It may be—Schumpeter does not say so at this point, but it corresponds to his conception—a class society or not. Although this, too, has to be inferred from Schumpeter's text, it would seem that for him socialism betrays many traits of a class society; for the work of workers "would remain substantially what it is" (p. 203); "there will be plenty to fight about in socialist society" (p. 213), for which "the problem of bureaucratic management" is not the least cause (pp. 205 ff.).

For Schumpeter, this kind of analysis becomes possible by a complete and deliberate departure from Marx's theory of class. "Marx wished to define capitalism by the same trait that also defines his class division. A little reflection will convince the reader that this is not a necessary or natural thing to do. In fact it was a bold stroke of analytic strategy which linked the fate of the class phenomenon with the fate of capitalism in such a way that socialism, which in reality has nothing to do with the presence or absence of social classes, became, by definition, the only possible kind of classless society, excepting primitive groups. This ingenious tautology could not equally well have been secured by any definitions of classes *and* of capitalism other than those chosen by Marx—the definition by private ownership of means of production" (p. 19).

It is evident from this passage that although Schumpeter would like to retain the concept of class as an instrument of analysis, he considers it a useful instrument only if it is freed of its Marxian connection with private property. Thus we must ask: What kind of a theory of class promises, in the opinion of Schumpeter, a more satisfactory analysis of the processes of development of industrial societies? The answer is, Schumpeter presents neither a theory nor an analysis of class of his own. One might almost be tempted to believe that his (potentially correct) thesis of the "cultural indeterminateness" of economic systems has led him to the (false) conclusion that cultural and social processes cannot be explained systematically and therefore do not permit scientific theories. However, this assumption is contradicted by the fact that in an earlier work (27) Schumpeter has in fact dealt extensively with the phenomenon of class and developed the rudiments of an original theory. Unfortunately—and I suspect that this is the ultimate root of the uselessness of Schumpeter's analysis for the explanation of class conflict and its development—this theory was based on a concept of class which we have explicitly dismissed above, namely, that "class structure is an arrangement of individuals according to their social rank as it varies by groups, ultimately according to differences of ability; even more, it is based on the fact of the institutionalization of such rank once achieved" (27, p. 205). Schumpeter himself defines the area of problems to which his "classes" belong when elsewhere he refers to "social strata or groups" and adds, "As is known, we call them social classes" (99, p. 216). Schumpeter's classes are indeed not classes but strata.

At one point of his analysis Schumpeter has begun to approach a genuine supersedence of Marx's theory of class. He has shown that the necessary connection between the existence of classes and the existence of private property asserted by Marx is empirically untenable. Thus he has opened up the possibility—later seized by Djilas—of analyzing also, with the instrument of class theory, societies in which private property no longer functions or exists. But Schumpeter has, by diluting the concept of class into that of stratum, made it impossible for himself to make use of this critical decision. Sering, who follows Schumpeter in dissociating the concepts of class and private property, goes further here, if he states with respect to the transition from capitalist to modern industrial societies that "the new social order does not emerge without classes" (74, p. 205). However, Sering's analysis (which is not, on the whole, very original) pre- supposes another theory which under the name of the "managerial revolution" has become a widely used slogan.

THE MANAGERIAL AND THE CLERICAL REVOLUTIONS
(Burnham, Croner)

Although James Burnham refers with suspicious frequency to science in general and the scientific nature of his analyses in particu- lar, his theories are not very clear and his analyses not very acute.[11] He wants to establish the fact of a social revolution, and yet he says (140, p. 7), "I am going to *assume* further . . . that the present is in fact a period of social revolution." At one point, the managers, *dramatis personae* of his revolution, are described rather specifically as "the operating executives, production managers, plant superintend- ents, and their associates" (p. 82); but later this concept suddenly includes not merely "production executives" and "directing engi- neers," but also quite generally "administrators," "propaganda spe- cialists," and "technocrats" (p. 281). He proposes to demonstrate that the managers are everywhere about to assume power, but many of his formulations lend support to the suspicion that he simply calls managers those who are powerful. It would not be difficult to dis- miss Burnham's theory almost offhand if all we wanted to prove was that it is formulated in a most unsatisfactory manner and therefore not, as such, a useful instrument of sociological analysis. However, I propose to avoid this simple path and try to explicate in the work of Burnham the elements of a theory that might supersede Marx's.

Burnham, too, starts off by discussing the tendency to supersede capitalism which is inherent in modern economic and social develop- ment. The new fact which he is trying to explain is the phenomenon described above as the separation of ownership and control. Burn- ham does not like this expression. "The truth is that, whatever its legal merits, the concept of 'the separation of ownership and control' has no sociological or historical meaning. Ownership *means* control; if there is no control, then there is no ownership. . . . If ownership and control are in reality separated, then ownership has changed hands

---

[11] He is also not the first author to present a theory of managerial rule, as Schel- sky has pointed out with reference to Veblen, Rathenau, and others (cf. 164).

to the 'control,' and the separated ownership is a meaningless fiction"
(p. 92). Terminological (and confused) as this argument may
appear, it is nevertheless basic for Burnham's theory. Because he
defines property ownership[12] by control, he can describe the transition of control over industrial means of production from owner-
managers to mere managers as a process which leads to the supersedence of capitalism without affecting class conflict in its Marxian
definition as relating to property ownership.

   "In all complex societies so far, there is a particular, and relatively small, group of men that controls the chief instruments of
production" (p. 59). In capitalist society this was the capitalist class.
But in the society toward which we tend today "the managers will,
in fact, have achieved social dominance, will be the ruling class in
society" (p. 72). In this society, legal property lies with the state,
but factual control over the means of production is exercised by the
managers who, in this sense, are their owners. And "the instruments
of production are the seat of social domination; who controls them,
in fact not in name, controls society, for they are the means whereby
society lives" (p. 125). Like their capitalist predecessors, the new
"owners" of the means of production, the managers, are confronted
with the propertyless class of workers. "The managerial economy is
in actuality the basis for a new kind of exploiting, class society" (p.
122). Indeed, exploitation is worse here than in capitalist society.
On the one hand, the working class becomes increasingly homogeneous, for "in comparison with the organization of industry in the period
prior to modern mass production, the individual tasks . . . require
relatively less skill and training on the part of the individual worker"
(p. 77). There is a wide gap between largely unskilled workers and
highly specialized managers. On the other hand, in bureaucratized
managerial societies, even the dubious liberty to sell his labor is taken
from the worker and he is forced to work (cf. p. 130). We are still
in a "transition period," but before long all industrial societies will
be managerial class societies.

   Clearly, Burnham's theory, even if it proves useful, can at best
only partially supersede Marx's theory of class. It is based on one

---

   [12] An accident of language has probably contributed to no small extent to make
Burnham's theory possible. The German word *Eigentum* comprises both the passive
"property" and the active "ownership," and whereas a separation of property and control is a plausible occurrence, one of ownership and control seems indeed somewhat
doubtful, i.e., the element of control is indeed somewhere implied in the term ownership, though not in property.

new fact, the separation of ownership and control. We can therefore trace it back to Renner's somewhat liberal interpretation of Marx, or even to Marx's own analysis of the phenomenon of joint-stock companies. (Incidentally, Burnham's identification of the managerial rule with state property in the means of production indicates an important limiting case, but it is really quite unnecessary; the separation of legal and effective ownership would be fully sufficient for his theory.) Other tendencies of development of industrial societies, such as the growth of social mobility, do not contradict Burnham's theory but remain unexplained by it. The theory of managers merely modifies one aspect of Marx's approach.

There are, moreover, a number of tendencies which directly contradict Burnham's theory. Burnham follows Marx in asserting the increasing homogeneity of the working class, brought about by virtue of the leveling of their skills and qualifications. We have seen that this thesis is false. The working class has not in fact become more uniform with respect either to its skill structure or to differentiations of income and prestige; there are, rather, tendencies to the opposite. Burnham further refers to an increase in the intensity of class conflict in managerial society. This assertion, too, is hardly compatible with what we have described as the institutionalization of class conflict, nor, for that matter, does it agree with the fact that the legitimacy of managerial authority rests to a considerable extent on the consensus of those subjected to this authority. Also, as we have seen, there are many tendencies toward decreasing the intensity of class conflict and toward enlarging the sphere of institutionally regulated clashes. Here, too, Burnham is in error.

However, the crucial and most problematic aspect of Burnham's theory is that he blindly follows Marx in identifying economic with political power and domination. "The sources of wealth and power are the basic instruments of production, these are to be directed by the managers; and the managers are, then, to be the ruling class" (pp. 158 f.). Not surprisingly, Burnham's critics pounced on this observation. "The real question is," states Bendix (126, pp. 119 f.), "whether (1) men who control the policies of industries, government, labor unions, farm groups, etc., constitute a cohesive group owing to this common characteristic; or (2) the ideas and policies of the so-called managerial group differ in any respect from those of the older type of entrepreneur." These are both empirical questions which cannot be answered by dogmas or definitions. But Burnham neither proved nor could he prove that in real societies the propertyless managers of industry are in any sense identical with the ruling groups of the state. Instead it appears that "either by violating the principle of identity or by taking the term 'manager' as an emblematic slogan to mean those in power, Burnham exploits the facts concerning the growth of bureaucratic structures for his own thesis" (Gerth and Mills, 148, p. 173).

Burnham tried to abridge the pedestrian process of scientific discovery, and for this he had to pay. The facts which he wants to connect systematically in his theory originate in the sphere of industrial production. But the theory which he presents claims to be a valid explanation of the development of the entire society. Between its claim and its basis there gapes an abyss of implicit assumptions and dogmatic assertions. The value of Burnham's theory lies in its consequence that the class structure of the industrial enterprise is based on control and not on legal ownership of the means of production.[13] With this hypothesis, the separation of ownership and control becomes a phenomenon which is fundamentally irrelevant for class conflict. But the problem of political conflicts in advanced industrial societies is logically and empirically independent of that of the class structure of the enterprise and must therefore be investigated separately. The simple assertion that the means of production are the "seat of social domination" explains little, even if it is repeated a hundred times.

In fact, many sociologists have tried for more than thirty years to find an answer to the second, more comprehensive question of the political structure of advanced industrial societies and its class basis. Usually, approaches to this problem are focused on the phenomenon of bureaucracy, i.e., on those parts of the "new middle class" which are more or less intimately connected with public administration. Burnham tries in vain to ridicule what he calls the "theory of the bureaucratic revolution," and to dismiss it with a few superficial arguments (pp. 278 ff.). No great effort is needed to realize that the analyses of Max Weber and Michels, Bendix and Merton, and many others[14] have contributed more to our knowledge of the structure of contemporary societies than Burnham with his theory of the managerial revolution. Yet neither Weber nor most of the subsequent

[13] Although I would doubt whether it is sensible to express this approach with Burnham by an extension of the definition of property ownership and to hide thereby a substantial difference behind the verbal agreement with Marx.

[14] For a good collection of the most important texts of the authors mentioned and of others, see the reader edited by Merton and others (136).

analysts of bureaucracy were explicitly concerned with developing a theory which might lead to the supersedure of Marx's theory of class in the light of new facts. Rudiments of such a theory can first be found in the work of Geiger to which we shall turn presently, and, if on a much less ambitious level, in that of Fritz Croner (129).

Like Burnham, Croner believes he is able to perceive in the development of industrial societies in the twentieth century a "social revolution." "Everywhere the social revolution with which we are dealing here has changed the face of society fundamentally. . . . Its product and its bearer is a new social class: white collar" (p. 9). "Capitalist order created in its beginning the social space for a new class, the existence of which rests on individual economic effort. The age of rationalization has also created the social space for a new class: the class of salaried employees. . . . This process is the real cause why society today appears in an entirely different light than society fifty years ago: this social process is the real substance of the 'social revolution' of our time" (p. 246). If Croner speaks of a "real cause" and of the "bearers" of a social revolution, he evidently aims at an explanation of the changed structures of advanced industrial societies. However, he does not regard himself as an opponent or superseder of Marx. For him, "there is no systematic theory of class in the work of Marx" (p. 169), because Croner does not see, and much less realizes, the heuristic purpose of the analysis of social conflict or the analytical departure from antagonisms based on the distribution of property or power. Thus, he says "class" but he means "stratum" when he refers to "similar economic conditions," "similar social status," and "similar social values" as determinants (p. 185). On the strength of this fact, we should have to exclude Croner's contribution from this survey as being outside its scope. Yet Croner has presented—perhaps unwillingly— with his "theory of delegation" and his account of the functions of white collar, an approach which might be understood as a contribution to our discussion and which I shall regard as such.

The "new" fact with which Croner is concerned is the spectacular growth of the "new middle class" since 1890. Croner explains this fact as a subdivision of entrepreneurial functions in industry and of leading positions in the state, which had become necessary in the course of rationalization. "The explanation for the special social position of salaried employees can be found in the fact that their work tasks used to be entrepreneurial tasks" (p. 36). "What we . . . have said about the division of entrepreneurial 'power' and the resulting emergence of certain 'services' in the economy, can be applied also to the emergence of the civil 'service.' Here of course it is not the entrepreneur, but the highest chief of state, e.g., the king, who delegates certain tasks which he has so far carried out himself to men of his confidence who then 'represent' the king in their fields" (p. 37). Croner does not mention the separation of ownership and control, but his "theory of delegation" presupposes this process to a certain extent. His approach also includes the explanation of one aspect of social mobility,[15] if he says: "The salaried employees are a class with considerable variations of income, influence and prestige. . . . When the salaried employee enters his first job, he may have a host of superordinates. . . . At the end of his career he may have hundreds and thousands of subordinates. . . . But this whole career occurs within one and the same class" (p. 195).

One could derive from these statements a theory which would argue approximately as follows. By the separation of ownership and control and the rationalization of industrial and political administration, a new class of bureaucrats has emerged, the functions of which are subdivided authority functions. In this sense, the new class is a ruling class, and even the only ruling class. It is mobile; there is within it a continuous upward movement; and the class is by no means uniform as a social stratum. But by virtue of its share in (delegated) authority it is in conflict with all other groups in society.

To repeat this, Croner himself does not formulate a theory of this kind. The concept of ruling class plays no part in his investigation. Yet Croner's analysis contains certain elements of such a theory —elements which can of course also be found in the works of Burnham and of Weber and Michels, and which deserve our attention. The historical trends which we have emphasized may suggest certain restrictions of this theory (such as of the notions of salaried employee or bureaucracy), but they do not refute it. However, it is evident that in speaking of bureaucracy as a ruling class one implies a concept of class which has little to do with that of Marx. Whether some extension or modification of managerial and bureaucratic theories might be considered a useful explanation of post-capitalist societies and their conflicts, we cannot decide before we have settled the problem of method, substance, and limits of class analysis in sociological research.

[15] Namely, intrageneration mobility. The formulation quoted here might, however, also be thought to account for the multitude of social origins of members of a class in a society in which intergeneration mobility is institutionalized.

CLASS SOCIETY WITHOUT CLASS CONFLICT

(Renner)

Both Burnham's and Croner's works suffer from the peculiar inconsequence of books that were quite obviously written to be bestsellers. In profoundness of thought and significance of analysis they compare badly with two late, posthumously published essays of the Austrian Karl Renner (71), whose sociological work—if it is known at all—is often underestimated. Renner refers to himself as a "Marxist." But this epithet means for him that although he wants to retain the "Marxian method" he is quite prepared to apply this "method"[16] in a critical and unprejudiced fashion to the new realities of postcapitalist industrial society. For it is for Renner "crystal-clear that the factual substratum, the social substructure, has changed completely in the last hundred years" (p. 214). In fact, Renner begins his analysis of class structure in the essays under discussion, contrary to his program, with a critique of Marx's "method," of the theory of class itself. He adds to the statement that for Marx private property was the basis of class formation. "But obviously there have been domination and exploitation of other kinds in history, and in my opinion the Marxian school, although it has not overlooked and has in fact occasionally analyzed these, has failed to investigate systematically and balance with each other all historical and possible relations of authority" (p. 89). This sentence implies more than its cautious formulation betrays. It indicates that Renner—much like Djilas, Schumpeter, Burnham, and others—is trying to free the concept of class from its definitional tie with private property and to apply it more generally to all relations of domination and subjection. Renner's further considerations confirm this conclusion. His catalogue of possible forms of domination—"stratocracy," "capitalism," "theocracy," "graphocracy," "bureaucracy," etc.—is at the same time supposed to be a catalogue of possible forms of class conflict.

By this modification of Marx's approach, Renner can, following Burnham, analyze the separation of ownership and control without assuming that it involves the elimination of class conflict. "Besides the capitalist who has lost his function, there stands . . . the functionary who has lost his capital: a social character mask of great future

---

[16] Renner makes nowhere quite clear what he means by this "method." But his use of the notions of a "factual substratum" and a "normative superstructure" occasionally suggests that he subscribes to a considerably modified "historical materialism" which for him probably represents the "Marxian method."

significance" (p. 182). Contrary to Burnham, however, Renner regards the managers as "a stratum which, at least for the time being, is politically anonymous," and for which "a general solidarity of interest and ideology . . . is no longer given" (p. 215). This conclusion is made possible for Renner because he regards neither the "managerial revolution" nor the "white-collar revolution" as an isolated phenomenon which in itself characterizes advanced industrial society; these two social changes he consistently connects. For Renner the emergence of a managerial stratum is merely part of a general development in the course of which a new class emerges—the "service class."

Before Croner, Renner developed a kind of "theory of delegation." In post-capitalist society, "the functions of capitalists appear subdivided in a steadily growing number of salaried employees of the very highest and of high and of lower rank. . . . These new aids are neither capitalists nor workers, they are not owners of capital, they do not create value by their work, but they do control values created by others" (p. 119). Renner calls this stratum the "service class." It has fashioned itself on the model of public civil service and has been transformed from a caste into a class. Although it participates in authority, it does not exercise absolute authority but is subject to the norms and laws of society.

There is a further point at which Renner goes beyond Burnham and Croner. He does not confine himself to the analysis of changes of the ruling class; he also deals with changes in the position of the working class. By its political and industrial achievements, the working class has today become a constituent element of society. "Today, the working class is no longer that incoherent sum of helpless individuals who are exposed to the storms of economic crises and the arbitrary rule of rulers as the desert sand is exposed to the elements. It is no longer the proletariat of 1848, but a powerful, confident, well-organized member of society. It is this member position which gives it power, and often more power and security than the possession of private wealth" (p. 211). By virtue of security thus guaranteed, the wage system based on effort and output has been replaced by a "livelihood system" based on needs. "Thus the working class and the service class have moved closer together" (p. 123). Capital is "controlled by a service class which obviously amalgamates more and more with the working class" (p. 226).

For Renner, industrial society after the disappearance of the "full capitalist" is characterized by two classes: the service class and the working class. There still are, of course, the "finance capitalists," shareholders, and bankers, but Renner prophesies their impending end. Thus the basic question of class analysis has to be asked anew (p. 102), "Who or what has the real power today?" The "what" in the formulation of this question already betrays Renner's unorthodox answer: working class and service class gradually amalgamate. Neither is really a ruling class. The ruling force is, rather, a "something," something "objective" which Renner expresses by the notions of "norms" or "law." "As in a democratic state the citizen does not obey the person of the monarch but complies with the laws, as he does not serve the official but the office as the bearer of lawful mandates, so every employee now works according to the plan of the enterprise" (p. 102). The "general will of society" has replaced the "rule of a minority." "This general will defines the aim for society and thereby for the economy, and all functionaries pass over from the service of a master to the service of the whole. This general will is the law. . . . The exclusive rule of the law makes all forms of political illiberty impossible. The law creates the general order. Adaptation and subordination by law do not create a state of illiberty." Nor does the execution of legal norms create a ruling class, for it is "a matter of institutions which are organized exclusively under economic and technical aspects." "Economic democracy supplements political democracy (p. 227).

This is, of course, Rousseau versus Marx—a contest that produces some fascinating results. But fascinating as they are, these results are not, perhaps, altogether convincing. Renner does not always make it quite clear whether his analysis refers to the present or to tendencies of the future. Yet he is evidently not concerned with long-term predictions, much less with dreams of a classless society à la Marx. From the separation of ownership and control, the extension of citizenship rights and equality, the institutionalization of class conflict, and the emergence of the "new middle class," Renner infers the formation of two large classes. But these are "nonantagonistic classes" or, rather, they blend into each other and tend to amalgamate. Renner's theory of class structure has many traits which appear well compatible with the changed realities of post-capitalist society and which it will therefore be useful to bear in mind. But this cannot be said of the final step and climax of Renner's analysis, the postulate of a class society without class conflict.

That classes can exist without entering into violent relations of conflict is a thesis not permitted by Marx's theory of class; nevertheless, it might well be correct. It is at least conceivable that it corresponds to observable conditions. There is no reason to contest Renner's analysis merely because he asserts a class society without class *struggle*. What we have to reject, however, is the idea of a class society without class *conflict*, because this notion is incompatible with the heuristic purpose of concept and theory of class. In arriving at his conclusion, Renner makes two significant mistakes. He confuses, first, the aspects of integration and conflict, and, second, the levels of institutions and norms. Instead of applying both to all societies, he looks at capitalist society in terms of conflict and institutions and at post-capitalist society in terms of integration and norms. Throughout his work, Renner recognizes a dualism of "factual substratum" and "normative superstructure" and considers both in any given society. Then, as he comes to deal with the new society of the present, he suddenly forgets this dualism and concentrates on the "normative superstructure" alone. "Who or what has the real power today?" he asks. He answers the "what" and neglects the "who." In fact, Renner should have asked in the beginning: "Who *and* what have the real power today?" For it is always its institutional structures *and* its values that characterize a society—just as every society may and must be regarded from the point of view of its unity and coherence as well as from that of its inherent contradictions and conflicts. By forgetting the dichotomies of his earlier approach, Renner has been misled into an almost Stalinist notion of "nonantagonistic classes" in a happily integrated society. Yet his is an interesting mistake which will occupy us a great deal more in the present study.

There is an empirical point also which must be held against Renner's strange conclusion. Every society has its norms and laws, including what might be called ruling norms and laws. Norm is a very general category. Its relevance for class conflicts begins only when we ask which particular norms and laws are prevalent in a given society and which groups or aggregates of people either tend to enjoy privileges or suffer deprivations by virtue of the prevalent norms. The statement that the rule of the capitalists has been replaced by that of "the law" or "the general will" is remarkably meaningless, unless Renner wants to imply that in post-capitalist society power and its unequal distribution no longer exist. If, however, this is what he intended to say, there is little evidence to support his guess. There are many useful elements in Renner's analysis, including the assumption of the emergence of a service class vis-à-vis the working class, but his conclusions are disappointing in the light of general theoretical considerations as well as empirical evidence.

CLASS SOCIETY IN THE MELTING-POT

(Geiger)

All authors mentioned so far insist on the possibility of describing post-capitalist society, like its precursor, as a class society in an unmodified or restricted Marxian sense. This premise is abandoned by Geiger in his study of the *Class Society in the Melting-Pot* (46). For Geiger, the old class society stands on the threshold of a new type of order, the structure of which can no longer be adequately comprehended in the notion of class conflict. Significantly, the phenomenon of the "new middle class"—the "experts" and "bureaucrats"—is one of the major facts leading Geiger to this conclusion. Conceptually, Geiger prepares his conclusion by distinguishing "social stratum" as a general category from "class" as a "special case of social stratum," the case, namely, of a grouping "determined by the relations of production" (p. 35). This distinction is not purely terminological, and we shall have to question it; but this conceptual discussion will be postponed for the time being in favor of empirical critique. In any case, it is easy to renounce conceptual polemics against Geiger, since he himself has repeatedly stated his position with great clarity (20, 46, 91), and has based his considerations on a fairly precise and insightful account of Marx's concept and theory of class.

Geiger's "penetrating essay" (Marshall, 95, p. 13) is, despite its essayistic features and its restriction in evidence and argument, in its plan and execution perhaps the most ambitious attempt so far undertaken by a sociologist to master the changed reality of advanced industrial society in terms of a theory that is critically inspired by Marx. Geiger begins his study with a fairly elaborate critical account of Marx's concept of class and his "doctrine of the class society." He strongly emphasizes the "dynamic" purpose of class analysis and rejects objections against the model of two "dominant" classes resulting from this purpose as "unfounded." There are, for him, well-founded objections against the application of the Marxian class model to post-capitalist society: the pauperization of the working class has not come true; the working class has neither become more uniform nor grown proportionately; the "old middle class" is still in evidence and has not become "proletarianized"; the capitalists are dying out; class consciousness has not increased. Before this background Geiger develops his central thesis. "The Marxist model of the industrial class society was presumably not inappropriate for the period of high capitalism" (p. 156). But even before this class structure "was able to penetrate the whole society, many other structural trends broke into the picture, deflected the stratification of 'capital and labor' and obscured it" (p. 157). Today, we are living in a process of transition from class "stratification" to a new type of "stratification." "The transition of society from one type of stratification to another one means . . . that hitherto subordinate lines of stratification become dominant, and hitherto dominant ones fade into the background" (p. 153 f.). In this sense, the class conflict based on relations of production has given way in advanced industrial societies to certain "new lines."

Evidently, the proof of Geiger's theories lies in what he calls "new lines" and, furthermore, in the method that leads him to discover these trends. Geiger proceeds cautiously and empirically. "The class society of Marxist coloring is obviously in retreat. Nobody can tell as yet with assurance which direction development will take. But we can today point out a number of competing trends and, with due caution, venture some suggestions as to the weight and force with which these will contribute to the future formation of society" (p. 158). Geiger discusses in some detail five such tendencies. If we neglect the conflict between town and country (which presumably figures so largely in Geiger's book because it was first published in and for Denmark), four remain: the tendency of independent political action on the part of the "old" and "new" middle strata, that of the increasing importance of the consumer status, that of a conflict between all participants of production and the "mere consumers," and that of what Geiger calls the "rule of the experts." Geiger does not deal with the phenomenon of social mobility. But otherwise he explains the majority of conflicts arising out of new developments so convincingly that one is inclined to forgive him his unjust and superfluous conclusion, "Thus the doctrine of Karl Marx is nothing but the anti-ideology corresponding to the liberal social reality of his time" (p. 228).

Geiger's account of the four significant "new lines" of development is not without interest for our discussion. (1) As to the position of the middle strata in advanced industrial societies he notes a strange paradox. The "old middle stratum" of independent artisans and shopkeepers was engaged simultaneously in an economic struggle with large-scale capitalism and in an ideological struggle with the proletariat. In this two-sided conflict it is today supported by the "new middle stratum." Both resent the notion of class structure itself; they fight it in the name of an estate ideology which, in Germany, led them to support national socialism. "A class denies indignantly that it is a class, and it carries on a bitter class struggle against reality and idea of the class struggle" (p. 168). (2) The redistribution and equalization of income has cut through the class fronts. Besides the social status based on a man's "position as consumer," "the Marxian relation of production fades" (p. 175). "Most workers have become petty bourgeois in their purchasing power and spending habits" (p. 176). (3) Thanks to the "institutionalization of class conflict," the social partners of industry have come closer to one another. Both derive a profit from every increase in production; in that sense one can "speak of a proximity of interest among capital and labor within urban industrial society. . . . The victims are those strata of society which one could describe as mere consumers, i.e., those who have no immediate share in the production and sale of material goods. . . . Poverty increases with the distance of an income-earner from commodity production" (p. 194). (4) Which is the new "ruling stratum"? According to Geiger, Burnham has to some extent correctly diagnosed a tendency of development. But his assertion of the political rule of the economic managers is nonsensical; rather, "political bureaucratism absorbs the economy itself" (p. 217). "Thus the rule of the managers of private economy has not come about. In a centrally planned economic and social order power belongs to the economic officials, and if the name bureaucracy sounds too forbidding, one may replace it by 'rule of the experts' " (p. 220).

The empirical references of Geiger's analyses are as plausible as most of his arguments. But the question remains to be asked, What is the theoretical position that has enabled Geiger to supersede Marx? In what sense do Geiger's "new lines" provide an analysis of advanced industrial societies that is equivalent to Marx's analysis of the capitalist class society? Once again, the answer is disappointing. Geiger has not superseded Marx. His theoretical position is restricted to what is really just the formal statement that some societies display a kind of "stratification" different from that based on relations of production.[17] His analysis can be condensed to the single statement that the transition from early to advanced industrial societies puts hitherto subordinate lines of "stratification" in the place of class conflict.

[17] Although Geiger always speaks of "stratification," he is in fact dealing with social conflicts. Yet he cannot be spared the charge of having obscured the essentially sound distinction between "stratum" and "class" by not distinguishing sufficiently strictly the different "heuristic purposes" (this, too, one of Geiger's concepts!) associated with "stratum" and "class" and by falsely subordinating that of the concept of class to that of the concept of stratum.

Popper has described scientific theories by the metaphor of the "searchlight." "What the searchlight makes visible will depend upon its position, upon our way of directing it, and upon its intensity, color, etc.; although it will, of course, also depend very largely upon the things illuminated by it" (219, II, p. 260). But always the searchlight illuminates only a sector of reality, i.e., every theory is, as such, selective. It guides analysis to facts which are relevant for a particular context and excludes others. This is precisely what Geiger's "theory" does not achieve, and could not achieve, because it is not really a theory. For this reason, Geiger's "new lines" consist in fact of a number of barely connected descriptions concerned partly with elements of social conflict (mere consumers against participants of industry), partly with changing relations of domination (rule of experts), partly simply with general social trends (consumer status). There is no point at which these lines converge; they have not emerged in the selective beam of the searchlight of a theory but have instead been chosen arbitrarily from the infinite number of actual lines and trends of development. If they are nevertheless not without significance, this is a tribute to the good sense of a sociologist of Geiger's stature. Of the two aims of his investigation Geiger has achieved only one. He has shown that the model of a class society based on the relations of production is no longer applicable to the analysis of postcapitalist society. But he has not been able to show what must be substituted for this model in order to render the new society accessible to sociological analysis.

CITIZENSHIP, EQUALITY, AND SOCIAL CLASS
(Marshall, Schelsky)

By several authors, one of Geiger's "new lines" has recently been made the point of departure of the attempt to penetrate the changed structure of post-capitalist society by means of sociological analysis: the increasing equalization of the social status of incumbents of different social positions, and in particular of the old classes. T. H. Marshall, for whom status emphasizes, in analogy to the legal meaning of the term, "the fact that expectations (of a normative kind) exist in the relevant social groups" (94, p. 13), has investigated this tendency at the example of the extension of the citizenship status. According to his theory, the main features of which we have summarized above, the basic rights common to all citizens have been extended, during the last two centuries, to ever new spheres of social life. At first, legal status lost its differentiating force; later, political status followed suit; and recent social development is characterized by a tendency to equalize the social position of all citizens with respect to the rights and privileges associated with this status. There are many indications of this trend, including equality of educational and occupational opportunity, and the generalized right to a minimum income, to sickness benefits, and to old-age pensions, etc. "The basic human equality of membership . . . has been enriched with new substance and invested with a formidable array of rights. . . . It has been clearly identified with the status of citizenship" (57, p. 9). Marshall does not confine himself, however, to an account of processes of social history, but goes on to pose the sociological problem, "Is it still true that basic equality, when enriched in substance and embodied in the formal rights of citizenship, is consistent with the inequalities of social class?" (57, p. 9). His attempt to answer this question makes Marshall's analysis an essential contribution to our problem.

To all appearances, equality rights associated with citizenship and class antagonisms are incompatible quantities. "Citizenship is a status bestowed on those who are full members of a community. All who possess the status are equal with respect to the rights and duties with which the status is endowed. . . . Social class, on the other hand, is a system of inequality. . . . It is therefore reasonable to expect that the impact of citizenship on social class should take the form of a conflict between opposing principles" (57, pp. 28 f.). In capitalist class society, however, this was the case only if one conceives of classes as groups endowed with different rights and privileges that are completely closed off from each other. For classes in the Marxian sense, the principle of equal civil rights was, "on the contrary, necessary to the maintenance of that particular form of inequality" (p. 33): legal equality was the basis of the (labor) contract, on which at the time inequalities of class were founded. Even the extension of citizenship rights to the political sphere did not seriously affect inequalities of class. It is only when the principle of universal basic rights is extended to the social sphere that the existence of classes becomes problematical. Of course, there still are inequalities. In a way, these are even caused by equal rights: "Through education in its relations with occupational structure, citizenship operates as an instrument of social stratification" (p. 67). But in a society in which these differences are not only reduced to a minimum but also stripped of their ascriptive character, they cease to be productive of conflicts. "It may be that the inequalities permitted, and even molded, by citizenship do not any longer constitute class distinctions in the sense in which that term is used of past societies" (p. 75). In so far as class distinctions survive—and

Marshall seems to believe that there is a limit beyond which inequalities cannot be abolished—they become "socially acceptable," lose their "economic function," and thereby their force as determinants of classes (see pp. 77 ff.).

In a later essay (95), Marshall has supplemented this thesis by the assertion that classes may not have disappeared altogether, but have changed their character: they are no longer homogeneous interest groups whose unity is based on a common position in production and molded by common behavior patterns and ideologies, but "associations" formed temporarily in the occupational sphere "for the pursuit of . . . common interests whenever they arise and with such degree of combination of groups as they demand" (p. 12). Such associations are not as permanent and comprehensive as classes. "This might be described as a weakening of class in the Marxian sense, on the grounds that the operative interest groups are no longer determined by the social relationship within the system of production, that is, primarily by property" (p. 13).

Marshall refers at this point to Geiger's study. But by contrast to those of Geiger his theses do contain elements of a theory that might be thought to supersede that of Marx. Geiger has merely demonstrated that Marx's theory of class conflict is *de facto* insufficient for the analysis of post-capitalist societies, because it fails to account for certain new lines of social structure. Marshall suggests that the extension of citizenship rights has penetrated the social sphere, and that these rights gradually lead to the elimination of all relevant inequalities, so that only such "class distinctions may survive . . . which have no appropriate economic function" (57, p. 77). If these suggestions are correct (which is open to dispute), then Marshall has shown that there *can* be no class conflicts in the Marxian sense in advanced industrial societies, because the structure of these societies is subject to a different law of development. If Marshall's theses are valid, the theory of an increasing institutionalization of an equal basic status of all citizens represents a genuine supersedure of Marx's theory. It explains both why capitalist society was a class society and why there are no classes in post-capitalist society. Before we examine the theoretical and empirical basis of this theory, I shall supplement its formulation by an independently developed variant which places the emphasis on slightly different evidence: Helmut Schelsky's thesis of the leveling of class society.

So far, Schelsky's approach must be inferred from a number of scattered papers (cf. 72, 98, 164). In one of these, he explicitly poses what he calls (72, p. 62) the "naïve, but nevertheless frequently heard question": "Have we still got a class society today?" "Class theory," the Marxian version of which Schelsky correctly describes (p. 63) as concerned with the "decisive law of development and the dominant structure of society" was "a legitimate explanation of social reality. But is it still that?" To begin with, Schelsky replies rather cautiously, "Sociology will not be able to answer this general question with a plain Yes or No" (p. 62). In so far as "something which existed once never disappears entirely in history, the question whether today there are still class structures has of course to be answered in the affirmative" (p. 63). But the answer is different if we ask whether class relations are still the dominant force in the structure and development of advanced industrial societies. Is, in other words, this society still characterized by one conflict of interests towering above all others and creating an "abyss between the classes"? "As a social scientist, one would have to answer this question today clearly in the negative: in this sense we are at present no longer a class society. Why? Since the time which Marx had in mind, several social processes have occurred which have leveled-in and mitigated that abyss of class tension, and at the same time new social structures and patterns have emerged which, more than the remnants of class conflict, must be regarded as the dominant structures of contemporary society that determine its course" (p. 64). In support of his thesis, Schelsky refers to the consequences of three parallel processes: (1) social mobility, (2) the leveling of styles of life, and (3) the inadequacy of surviving "ideologies" for the explanation of contemporary society.

"Comprehensive and structurally far-reaching processes of upward and downward social mobility" have, according to Schelsky, "diminished class conflicts and leveled society into a very wide, comparatively uniform social stratum" (72, p. 64). By these processes of mobility Schelsky seems to mean above all collective processes, such as the "collective rise of industrial labor," the "rise of . . . salaried employees into the new middle stratum," and the *declassement* particularly of the "strata of the former bourgeoisie by property and education." Elsewhere, however, Schelsky also refers to the increase in the "mobility of single families," i.e., social mobility in the proper sense of the sociological concept, "which has broken up collective ties and solidarities of stratification to a large extent and has created an egoism of small groups and families as one of the essential social forces of our social constitution," so that "this highly mobile society cannot provide a lasting social status consciousness" (122, p. 5).

The growth of collective and individual mobility is accompanied by a process of "leveling" social differences in the realm of income and prestige and above all in patterns of behavior and styles of life. This latter process, although emphasized also by Marshall, is central for Schelsky's conception. One could call this new and uniform "pattern of life . . . 'petty bourgeois' or 'middle class,' if it were not for the fact that these terms lead to too many misunderstandings on account of their class character" (72, p. 65). As a less ambiguous term Schelsky proposes that of the "leveled middle class society." "This comparative leveling of formerly class- or stratum-determined patterns of behavior with respect to family life, occupational and educational aspirations of children, the functions of living, consumption and support—indeed, of the cultural, political, and economic patterns of reaction in general—is perhaps at present the most dominating process in the dynamics of our modern society" (72, p. 65). "It appears that in place of class status the consumer position is becoming the central determinant of all patterns of behavior . . . so that the negative process of leveling the class society would have to be described positively as the emergence of the highly industrialized leisure and consumer society" (pp. 65 f.).

At first sight, the trend of social mobility—which, after all, presupposes differences of position—and the leveling of styles of life appear to contradict each other. Indeed, "the paradox of our social change consists in the fact that the urge to rise on the social ladder has become universal at a time at which this 'ladder' has been completely abolished or at least severely shortened. By reaching an extent that converts it into the fluid structure of society itself, social mobility contradicts the motives of individuals which are effective in it" (p. 71). For this reason a sort of "false self-consciousness" emerges or, as Schelsky calls it, a "constitutional irreality of social self-consciousness" (98, p. 4): because other explanations are lacking, men experience society in categories which no longer hold. The need for security effects the "retention of antiquated notions of social status inherited from class or estate society" (72, p. 71).

Schelsky does not assert that in advanced industrial societies there are no tensions or conflicts; indeed, he strongly objects to what he calls a "utopian 'bourgeois' idea or hope of social harmony" (p. 66). However, the tensions peculiar to the new society are no longer class conflicts. They are, rather, typically tensions "between the abstract orders of society and little primary groups" (231, p. 350), conflicts "of the individual or the immediate 'We' with the anonymous system of every kind of bureaucracy, on which one depends and by which one feels controlled, and even exploited" (72, p. 67). Elsewhere Schelsky claims in almost literal agreement with Marshall that "the conflict of organized representations of interests" has "replaced the conflict of the large, diffuse blocs of classes" (p. 68).

This summary gives a rough outline of a kind of social theory the influence of which seems to grow steadily today in sociology as well as in public opinion. Marshall has formulated it in terms of an analysis of English social development, Schelsky with reference to (West) German society. We shall presently turn to American studies which resemble those of Marshall and Schelsky in many points. Thus it seems permissible to infer that a conception claims validity for all advanced industrial societies when its main arguments are as follows: (1) the dynamics of post-capitalist society can no longer reasonably be described by a Marxian notion of class conflict; (2) the equalization of basic rights, conditions of life, and patterns of behavior has removed the basis of class differentiation; (3) moreover, an extraordinary intensification of social mobility makes the formation of lasting solidary groups impossible; (4) the (Marxian) theory of class has therefore lost its value as an instrument of explanation and must be replaced by a fundamentally different theory of social tensions on the basis of equal positions and situations. It will now be our task to consider whether these theses, and especially the second and the third of them, stand up to a critical examination in the light of empirical evidence.

It can indeed be shown, as has been indicated in the previous chapter, that a certain equalization of aspects of the situation of various social groups has taken place in the course of social development during the past century. Marshall and Schelsky plausibly emphasize two aspects of this development: the extension of equal basic rights and the leveling of differences of social status. On the other hand, there can be no doubt that this egalitarian trend has by no means advanced to the point of equality. It is certainly true that equal opportunity of education and upward mobility is a characteristic value orientation of industrial societies. But has this principle been realized yet? As D. V. Glass summarizes an empirical investigation, "Though between the two World Wars there was an unprecedented expansion in the opportunities for secondary and university education, the discrepancies in educational opportunity as between individuals of different social origins had by no means been eliminated" (107, p. 16).

The same holds for Germany, the United States, and other socie-

ties on a similar level of development. Even today legal and political
citizenship rights are often restricted by social deprivations and disadvantages. The right to proceed against others is of little moment for
him who has not got the money to loose his case or even engage a
lawyer. Differences not only of income and prestige, but also of the
"consumer position" are even more apparent. The "comforts of civilization" are still distributed quite unequally, at least in the European
countries to which Marshall's and Schelsky's analyses refer. Although in 1955 nine out of ten German households possessed an
electric iron, only one out of ten had a washing machine or a refrig-
erator, and only two out of ten a motor vehicle (229, pp. 27 f.). Although the cinema is open to everybody in his leisure time, there are
considerable differences between those who make use of this possibility
quite regularly (Germany, 1955: 46 per cent), rarely (30 per cent),
or never (24 per cent). Although almost everybody listens to the
radio (Germany, 1955: 92 per cent), not everybody listens to the
same programs (cf. 229, pp. 59, 62, 67, etc.). Of course, neither Marshall nor Schelsky claimed that "equality" or "leveling" are as yet
completely realized; both refer to "tendencies" of social development; but, trivial as it may sound, it is necessary to emphasize time
and again that so far the realization of these tendencies is extremely
incomplete, and that the empirical validity of any theory based on
these tendencies alone is therefore severely restricted. We have raised
the question before, whether there might not be structural limits beyond which the leveling of status symbols, rights, and situations cannot advance. It may well be that Marshall and Schelsky have been
too fascinated with the leveling of traditional statuses and status symbols to realize that *new*, more subtle criteria are already taking their
place.[18]

However, this kind of objection in terms of empirical evidence
cannot as such be regarded as a refutation of Marshall's and Schelsky's
theories. There is no point in disputing the existence of leveling elements of social status in modern societies. The really important questions which we have to ask are of a different order: which spheres
have been affected by this tendency? Are there any areas of social
structure in which a tendency of this kind is not discernible? If we
examine the theories of Marshall and Schelsky from the point of view
of these questions, a peculiar fact becomes apparent. Schelsky's claim

[18] I am thinking here of makes of cars, kinds of leisure time activity, patterns of
participation in culture, etc., in the sphere of statuses and their symbols, and of merely
customary privileges of attendance and belongingness in the sphere of rights.

of a tendency of leveling statuses, styles of life, and patterns of behavior indicates above all a factual assimilation of status differences
and their symbols. Marshall's notion of equal citizenship rights emphasizes beyond that a shrinking of the sphere of possible social differences and, thereby, a lessening of possible sources of conflict. Both
tendencies have certain obvious consequences for class conflict, in particular for the substance of the opposing interests. But both tendencies leave entirely untouched one problem which is of crucial importance for Marx's as for any other theory of class, namely, the problem
of power or authority and its social distribution.

Earlier we found that with respect to the social distribution of
positions invested with authority a leveling tendency is hard to imagine and has certainly not occurred in modern societies. Probably, differences of legitimate authority are a basic fact of social structure; in
any case, they are a fact systematically overlooked by Marshall and
Schelsky. Their theories do not contain an answer to the problem of
the position of the manager or bureaucrat, and, what is more, this
problem is not even raised. The theory of leveling does not supersede
Marx's theory of class but redirects analysis to different problems and
different aspects of social structure on the silent or explicit assumption
that in advanced industrial societies these aspects are in some sense
more important and more dominating. Why they should be more important, and above all why the distribution of authority should no
longer be important—these are questions to which Marshall and
Schelsky give no answer. For them, turning away from the problem
of power is a thematic decision and not a result of analysis. The theory
of leveling may not be wrong; but it is ultimately simply irrelevant
for the problem of class. It deals with a different subject, that of
social stratification, and it becomes objectionable, therefore, if the
misleading attempt is made to pretend that it supersedes Marx or
represents a comprehensive account of the dynamics of post-capitalist
society.[19]

This objection of ours requires one slight modification. As we
have seen, Marshall and Schelsky do not deny the existence of conflicts and tensions in post-capitalist society. Schelsky in particular

---

[19] Marshall and Schelsky can be accused of illegitimately applying a theory of
social stratification to class analysis only in so far as both *implicitly* pass by the proper
area of class analysis. But this charge applies in full to some authors who have recently
tried to prove that contemporary Western society is classless, whereas Eastern society
is a quasi-capitalist class society, and who have developed this argument by using two
entirely different conceptual schemes for these two types of social order.

speaks of the "bureaucracy, on which one depends and by which one feels controlled, and even exploited." Elsewhere he refers to the "rule of the managers" (164) and even abandons the term "leveled middle-class society" in favor of "industrial-bureaucratic society" (163, pp. 275 ff.). But these conflicts and tensions have no systematic place in his theory. If one excludes the problem of power and authority from social analysis, one abandons the possibility to trace social conflicts back to structural conditions. They become essentially random phenomena, carried on by unpredictable chance groupings and related to fundamentally uncertain issues. For this is precisely what Marx's theory had achieved: to demonstrate the structural determinateness of social conflicts. An approach that throws overboard the intention and formal achievement of a theory with its particular, if empirically refuted, formulation does not supersede this theory but withdraws a sphere of knowledge from science in order to hand it over to the randomness of arbitrary opinion.

Thus the theory under discussion is by no means what it purports to be, a supersedure of Marx's theory of class. Yet there is one element of it, the relevance of which for the problem of class we have to examine briefly. Marshall and particularly Schelsky place great emphasis on the phenomenon of social mobility in the sense of individual movements up and down the status scale within and between generations. Schelsky asserts that mobility has become "the fluid structure of society itself" and "has broken up collective ties and solidarities of stratification to a large extent." This assertion implies the hypothesis that classes lose their *raison d'être* in a society in which belongingness to all nonprimary groupings assumes a merely temporary character. We shall have to return to this complex problem repeatedly. But the hypothesis of the impossibility of class formation in highly mobile societies contain an error which must be exposed at this point.

In analyzing social structures of entire societies or individual institutions, associations, and groups, a clear distinction is necessary between social positions or roles and their agglomerations on the one hand, and the personnel of these units, the incumbents of such positions, on the other hand. Social mobility constitutes in the first place a type of recruitment of the personnel of given positions. Social classes, however, are phenomena which at least potentially exist independent of the mode of recruitment and rate of fluctuation of their members. An industrial enterprise does not cease to exist if the annual rate of turnover of its workers amounts to 100 per cent or even 200 per cent and more. In this sense, the degree of social mobility is as such irrelevant to the problem of the existence of classes. "Every class," Schumpeter remarks with a plausible metaphor, "resembles for the duration of its collective life . . . a hotel or a bus which is always occupied, but always by different people" (27, p. 171). It is therefore false to assume that social classes and social mobility are as such incompatible. This is not to say, of course, that the increasing institutionalization of upward and downward mobility does not require certain modifications of the theory of class.

THE NEW SOCIETY

(Drucker, Mayo)

It might appear strange if we conclude this survey of some recent theories of class conflict with a discussion of the work of two sociologists in the analyses of whom the concept of class plays no part at all.[20] Yet there is a certain logic in the sequence of theories discussed in this chapter. We began with a conception which at least pretends to be based on a strictly Marxian model. The theories of Djilas, Schumpeter, Burnham, Croner, and Renner involve increasingly consequential modifications of Marx's approach. From these modifications it is only a step to Geiger's thesis that class structures have lost their dominant character, and further to Marshall's and Schelsky's assumption of the leveling of inequalities in post-capitalist society. The analyses of Drucker and Mayo—which, more than the others, may be regarded as arbitrarily selected examples for a widespread conception—perfect this line of analytical development by working with entirely different categories. The problem of class conflict was at least touched upon by all other authors mentioned in this survey; for Drucker and Mayo it no longer seems to exist. We shall have to find out what Drucker and Mayo have to offer instead of the Marxian theory of class, in so far as they deal with this aspect of social structure at all.

The books by Drucker (144) and Mayo (154) with which we are here concerned have many features in common. Both authors believe—like Burnham and Croner—that modern social development involved a "revolution." "The world revolution of our time

---

[20] Both authors occasionally use the word "class" in the sense of "stratum." Even this is rare, however, and furthermore it remains without the slightest analytical significance for the theories of Drucker and Mayo.

is 'made in USA.' . . . The true revolutionary principle is the idea
of mass-production" (Drucker, p. 1). For both authors the industrial enterprise of production is "the decisive, the representative and
the constitutive institution" of the new order (Drucker, p. 27). Both
have similar names for this "new order": "industrial order," "industrial society" (Drucker), "industrial civilization," "modern industrial
society" (Mayo). However, neither for Drucker nor for Mayo are
these categories mere sociological concepts; rather, they indicate a
model in the sense of a desirable ideal. Thus both authors share an
inclination to profess values and social policies which cuts through
their analyses of reality at many points.

Drucker's and Mayo's line of argument—neither of them likes
the term "theory," because they identify it with practical uselessness,
and thus we shall refrain from applying it to their conceptions—
can be summarized in three main points. First, they begin their
analyses with the model of an industrial society. Cooperation of individuals and groups is the supreme principle of such a society. It is
"a general principle for organizing people to work together" (Drucker, p. 3), "a balanced relation between various parts of the organization, so that the avowed purpose for which the whole exists may
be conveniently and continuously fulfilled" (Mayo, p. 45). The
structure of this society does not generate any conflicts that cannot
be completely solved; in it, "split allegiance" is converted into "twin
allegiance" (Drucker, pp. 146 f.), and a "common interest" combines
all (Mayo, p. 127). There still are different group interests, even
certain conflicts—an aspect emphasized rather more by Drucker than
by Mayo—but their elimination is merely a matter of "intelligent
organization that takes careful account of all the group interests
involved" (Mayo, p. 128). "The proper study of mankind is organization" (Drucker, p. 263).

Second, both Drucker and Mayo admit that industrial societies
were in an early stage, before the "revolution of mass-production,"
far removed from this model. Capitalist society had marked elements
of a closed (Mayo: "established," Drucker: "traditional") society,
dominated by permanent (class) conflicts, "a confused struggle of
pressure groups, power blocs" (Mayo, p. 7), and many other disturbances. A number of historical trends have already largely abolished this state of affairs. Drucker mentions the separation of ownership and control, the emergence of the "new middle class," the leveling of status, the extension of citizenship rights, the institutionali-

zation of class conflict. But as yet the model—an ideal for both, but a realizable ideal—has not been realized properly. One element is still lacking, the absence of which at the same time explains all disturbances and conflicts of industrial societies to the present day; and this element is psychological in nature.

For, third, the central thesis which overshadows all other considerations for Mayo, but is little less important for Drucker, can be summarized in the statement that conflicts and tensions such as those which class analysis is supposed to explain constitute but a "deviation" from a normal state of human attitudes and actions, and can and must therefore be eliminated by "education." Mayo thinks that "Marx detested 'the bourgeoisie' on grounds that will some day probably be shown to have been personal" (p. 120). The same holds for the labor leaders whom Mayo encountered. "These men had no friends. . . . They had no capacity for conversation. . . . They regarded the world as a hostile place. . . . In every instance the personal history was one of social privation—a childhood devoid of normal and happy association in work and play with other children" (p. 24). Thus, class conflict was but a relapse into barbarian conditions, an expression of human imperfections, and it is necessary to render it impossible by the formation of "social skills," i.e., the education of cooperative and peace-loving men. "Where cooperation is maintained between the individual and his group, the group and the union, the union and management, the personal sense of security and absence of discontent in the individual run high" (p. 128). Drucker, who, by contrast with Mayo, is not a university professor, is a little more careful in his formulations. But he, too, works with Mayo's concept of "social skills" (p. 23); for him, too, social conflict and its elimination is largely a matter of "managerial attitude" (pp. 158 ff.), a problem of "communication" and mutual understanding (pp. 191 ff.). "The individual" must obtain "status and function in the industrial enterprise" (p. 165), must learn to understand its goals and purposes as his goals and purposes, and must be induced to "responsible participation as a citizen" (p. 156) for the "industrial order" to function properly. What Drucker calls "integration" and Mayo "cooperation" is based for both "on understanding and the will to work together rather than on force" (Mayo, p. 115).

The "right attitude" of individuals, or "force"—an intermediate reality, such as social structure, does not exist at all for Mayo and evaporates for Drucker wherever its patterns might disturb his policy recommendations. But I shall refrain here from a comprehensive critique of the conceptions of Drucker and Mayo, and those who followed them.[21] Instead, I shall confine myself to those aspects of this conception the critical examination of which may advance my own investigation. The first question will therefore have to be, Does this "conception" contain a theory which at any point affects the problem of class conflict in industrial societies? The answer to this question depends on how strict a concept of theory we employ.

Expressed in a formula, it is Drucker's and Mayo's thesis that the class conflict of capitalist society was an (almost psychological) phenomenon of "deviance" from a normal state of integration and cooperation. Post-capitalist society tends toward this "normal state," although a number of educational measures are still required to bring it about. This thesis barely conceals a value judgment; it is not really a hypothesis that permits of empirical test, but a philosophical observation about the immanent goal of social history or, more likely, an expression of certain political aims and desires. In either case I should hesitate to call this conception a theory. But if not a theory, something else is implied by Drucker's and Mayo's conception which justifies its discussion here. It is based on a notion of society which Mayo makes explicit when he says, "A society is a cooperative system" (p. 115). The two essential ingredients of this notion are the assumptions that social conflict is not an essential and necessary feature of social structure, and that the variables which explain conflict, and consequently "order" and "integration," are psychological in nature. This basic theoretical attitude, from which a variety of analytical consequences follow, is by no means confined to Drucker and Mayo. In fact it dominates, if in sometimes rather more complex and subtle forms, much of contemporary American sociology, including the work of its most eminent theorist, Talcott Parsons. If, however, a basic attitude of this type proves sensible, then there is indeed no point in a theory of class conflict, and we should have to search for new tools of analysis.

It is difficult to examine "basic attitudes" of scientific analysis with respect to their usefulness. The question of empirical rightness or wrongness does not apply to them. That "society is a cooperative system" is a statement which can neither be confirmed nor refuted by empirical propositions. We are dealing here with "meta-theoreti-

---

[21] Especially in Mayo's case, this critique has been carried out several times, for which see as the most recent, and best, example the essay by H. L. Sheppard (87).

cal"[22] decisions which determine the direction of analysis with respect to specific problems without being part of this analysis themselves. Their test is their analytical fruitfulness and not their empirical correctness or logical soundness. We have to ask whether an image of society as an integrated system in which destructive conflicts occur only as deviations of a psychological nature from a normal state of order can be an appropriate background for the analysis of sociological problems. It is one of the themes of this study to reject and supersede this image of society, and the works of Drucker and Mayo provide a welcome opportunity to substantiate the point of view which underlies our considerations.

If it is true that we have to regard society as an integrated "cooperative system," and that deviations from this integration must be explained in terms of psychological variables, it would follow, for example, that all socialists in a capitalist society are in some sense psychologically deficient, that they are "deviants." Mayo has seen this extreme implication; he tries therefore to explain the work of Marx as well as the actions of the labor leaders he met by reference to their "case history." There is little doubt that some recent studies of social psychologists with their attempt of a correlation between political attitudes and personality types[23] have lent themselves to the support of this conclusion. However, the hypothesis seems reasonable and has not so far been refuted, that there is no significant correlation between, say, a voting decision for a conservative or progressive party and neurotic dispositions. Moreover, even if there was such a correlation, one would have to find out whether its causes are purely a matter of individual history or of social conditions. For this is the image of society which we want to oppose to that of Drucker and Mayo: that societies create out of their structure with predictable certainty the conditions of social antagonisms, and that therefore society is not an integrated cooperative system but at best a relatively integrated system of conflicting structural forces, even more, a permanently changing structure of integrative and disruptive factors.

[22] An expression which in its specific meaning intended here I have taken from an unpublished essay of U. Torgersen (Oslo), and which indeed seems a plausible description of attitudes that guide empirical research without themselves permitting of empirical test.

[23] I am referring here, e.g., to research on the subject of "authoritarian personalities" and on national, political, and ethnic stereotypes. It would seem to be an important task of scientific criticism to examine such studies from the point of view here advanced and to ask in what sense their very design excludes the assumption of conflicts generated by social structure.

Another extreme implication of the integration image of society is that "social problems" can in principle be solved only by influencing, "improving," and "normalizing" individuals. Elton Mayo has realized this implication, too, both in theory and in practice, in the context of the Hawthorne experiment in the 1920's and early 1930's. But it seems to me that H. L. Sheppard was right in accusing Mayo of systematically underestimating "economic and political determinants" and problems of the distribution of power, and of reducing all conflicts to "person-to-person relations" (87, p. 327). In so far as refutation is possible here, it appears sufficient to recall the causes and consequences of numerous institutional changes of recent social development in the spheres of economy, state, education, etc.

It is neither possible nor perhaps desirable to arrive at a final decision about which image of society is "better" or "more correct." But examples such as those mentioned here suggest that we reject the integration model as insufficient and deal with problems of conflict on the basis of a different, more appropriate model. According to this new model, conflict is an essential element of the structure of every society. It grows out of this structure and can be eliminated only very temporarily, and only by structural changes. The carriers of conflict are of course individuals, but these only in so far as the impact of their action is directed by structural conditions to larger aggregates of individuals. Psychological factors are a secondary characteristic, not the cause of social conflict. Society is process; its order lies solely in the lawfulness of its change.

It would not have been difficult to expose the insufficiencies and defects of Drucker's and Mayo's analyses on the level of empirical criticism. But the deepest shortcoming of their works and those of others becomes apparent only if we examine their meta-theoretical conception of society. If Drucker and Mayo are right, then not only are there no classes, but there never have been such systematic conflict groups in history. The phenomenon of structural conflict itself loses its reality and, indeed, its potentiality. However, the theorists of integration would find it hard to hold on to this assertion in their analyses. There are too many problems for which it fails to account, and we shall therefore be well advised to operate with a more dynamic image of society.

UNSOLVED PROBLEMS·

None of the theoretical approaches of modern sociology which we have examined in this chapter appears to provide an entirely satisfactory solution of our problem. Although every one of them tries to incorporate one or another element of the new reality of an advanced industrial society as it emerged since Marx's time, although therefore all of them go beyond the Marxian theory of class, none of them succeeds in superseding Marx's theory by a new and similarly comprehensive formulation. Four main reasons for this failure have emerged. (1) Some sociologists confine themselves to demonstrating that Marx's predictions have not come true and that, therefore, his theory has not been confirmed. If they indicate certain "new lines," as Geiger does, these remain unconnected and merely confirm the uselessness of Marx's theory without replacing it by a new approach. (2) The trend of sociological analysis founded on meta-theoretical assumptions that deny the possibility of analyzing social conflict as a structural phenomenon intrinsically rejects, of course, the very idea of a theory to replace Marx's. Thus, for Drucker and Mayo there is no point in any theory of conflict, since systematic antagonisms have no place in their image of society. (3) Some prominent sociological theories of post-capitalist society remove the subject matter of analysis to aspects of social structure other than those dealt with by Marx in his class theory. For this reason T. H. Marshall's and H. Schelsky's contributions remain marginal to our problem and cannot be considered as superseding the old theory. (4) Finally, there are some theoretical approaches which retain the heuristic intention of Marx's theory but fail to account for more than one or two changes that have occurred since. Thus Burnham's thesis is, contrary to the claim of its author, in fact confined to the realm of industrial production and ignores problems of political structure as well as changes in the skill structure of labor, the institutionalization of class conflict, etc. Djilas restricts himself to the analysis of contemporary Communist societies, and his model cannot easily be applied to other countries. Renner's approach is, even apart from its untenable conclusion, merely an indication that wants elaboration and completion.

Without doubt, every one of the theories discussed in this chapter contributes something to our knowledge of contemporary society and, more particularly, to our understanding of social conflict in post-capitalist societies. But with respect to the precise formulation of a theory of social class or its equivalent, we can learn more from their weaknesses and mistakes than from their substance. Our problem is the explanation of systematic social conflicts in industrial societies. In order to solve this problem, we shall have to find a formulation that passes beyond the mere statement of facts. It appears advisable to base this formulation on an image of society that permits the explanation of conflicts in terms of structural, not individual, conditions. For the theory to be useful, it will be necessary to define with utmost precision the area of problems for which it holds and for which it does not hold. Finally, the theory will have to be capable of accounting for the society with which Marx was concerned as well as for contemporary society and for the changes that have transformed the former into the latter.

IV

A Sociological Critique of Marx

SOCIOLOGY AND THE WORK OF MARX

"The relation of succeeding generations to the phenomenon of class society has been determined," or so Geiger thinks, "to the present day by the doctrine of Marx" (46, p. 10). Lipset and Bendix are of the opposite opinion: "The study of social classes has suffered in the past from the proclivity of social scientists to react against the influence of Karl Marx" (55, p. 151). There is probably an element of truth in both of these statements. Only too long has discussion in social science been dominated by the attempt either to reject the doctrine of Marx altogether or to sustain it without qualification.[1] Implicitly, if not explicitly, this attempt underlies the endless disputes about "what Marx really meant" (as G. D. H. Cole called one of his books). It is not difficult to see why this has happened. There is, for one thing, the political attractiveness, or repulsiveness, as the case may be, of Marx's work; there is, secondly, the prophetical promise of his predictions; and there is, above all, what Schumpeter called the "imposing synthesis" of Marx's doctrine. "Our time revolts against the inexorable necessity of specialization and therefore cries out for synthesis, nowhere more loudly than in the social sciences, in which the nonprofessional element counts for so much. But," Schumpeter adds with equal right at this point, "Marx's system illustrates well that, though synthesis may mean new light, it also means new fetters" (73, p. 45). Schumpeter does not hesitate to free himself and his discipline, economics, from these fetters at the expense of the "imposing synthesis." In this we shall have to follow him for sociology.

To ignore Marx is convenient, but it is also naïve and irrespon-

[1] And the two statements quoted bear witness not only to opposing attitudes to be found among sociologists in general, but in particular to the differences in approach between European and American sociologists. To the present day the reaction against Marx (often coupled with complete ignorance of his work) is as widespread in the United States as the uncritical acceptance of Marx's theories in Europe.

sible. No physicist — if this analogy be pardoned — would ignore Einstein because he does not approve of his political attitude or of some aspects of his theories. To accept Marx *toto coelo* may testify to an honorable faithfulness but is scientifically fruitless and dangerous. No physicist would abstain from attacking Einstein just because he happened to like the man and his work as a whole. We have started our investigation with an examination of the work of Marx, because his formulation of class theory is both the first and, as we know now, the only one of its kind. Today this theory is refuted, but it has not been superseded. Now we have to draw from Marx what is still useful, or, more precisely, we have to separate the problem of class theory from Marx's class theory itself. We are concerned with the theory of class as a sociological instrument; from this point of view, the Marxian theory of class is in principle a matter of indifference, i.e., it interests us only as a historical background or an object of critique.

At an early point, we have distinguished Marx's "philosophy" from his "sociology." In doing this we have not meant, of course, to sustain Marx's "sociology" in its entirety. In an empirical discipline, that kind of intention can only lead to disaster. We shall now go about the business of dissecting Marx's "sociology," of sustaining what is useful in his approach and rejecting what is useless. There is no place for sentimental regard or even undue respect in a critical process of this kind. If, for example, the exclusive connection of the concept of class with economic conditions or structures ("relations of production") should turn out to be a "fetter," a useless assumption, it must be rejected, no matter what Marx said, meant, or wanted. If, conversely, certain elements of Marx's theory of class formation stand up to the test of empirical evidence, they must be sustained; but, again, it is essentially a matter of indifference that it was Marx who formulated these elements.

The charge of eclecticism might be leveled against a procedure of this kind. If this is so, the notion of eclecticism is used with some justice, but it does not constitute a charge. Eclecticism may be considered a sin in philosophy, but science is essentially eclectic. In fact, a scientist who is not as such an eclectic is no scientist or at least a bad one. The unqualified acceptance of a "doctrine"—dogmatism—is the cardinal sin of science.

The unbiased reader may grow weary of so many words about so obvious a matter, but unfortunately they are, in the case of Marx, still necessary. There still are many who do not see that the epithets "Marxist" or "anti-Marxist" have no meaning and place in a science.

In fact, this is not the least reason why the vast literature about the subject of class (or at least about the word "class") has brought so little real advance. It appears as if sociology has hardly progressed at all in this respect since Marx—surely an astonishing fact in view of its extraordinary development in other fields!

However, it would be false to say that the attempt to reformulate the theory of class is entirely lacking in precedents and points of contact in recent sociology. We shall have opportunity to refer to numerous connections and suggestions in the course of our considerations. Without injuring the originality and individuality of the scholars concerned, one might even construct a certain convergence of the conceptual and theoretical discussion of class in recent sociology. The works of Schumpeter, Renner, Geiger, Lipset, Bendix, and even Parsons mark some of the milestones on this road towards a sociological theory of conflict in industrial societies. Other contributions will be added to this list as we go along. Thus the present investigation does not claim particular originality (which in any case is a dangerous virtue in scholarship). It is rather an attempt to connect many loose threads into a net with which we can "catch" an important sector of social reality.

In the present chapter we shall be concerned with elucidating the prerequisites of the fruitful use of something like a concept and theory of class in sociological analysis. Although we shall in every case build our discussion around a critical examination of Marx's position, our assumptions will increasingly depart from those of Marx and his theory of class. Having ascertained the conditions and main categories of a class theory of social conflict, we can then proceed (in the following two chapters) to an attempt to outline the main features of this theory. In the last two chapters of this study the analytical usefulness of the reformulated theory of class conflict will be subjected to a test by its application to the structure of post-capitalist societies.

SOCIAL STRUCTURE AND SOCIAL CHANGE: MARX SUSTAINED

In the last decades, considerable progress has been made in the development of a theoretical instrumentarium for analyzing the structure of total societies and their parts. The credit for codifying the elements of this analysis is principally due to American sociologists, although their most eminent representative, Talcott Parsons, has rightly referred (see 216) to earlier impulses in the work of the Englishman Alfred Marshall, the Frenchman Emile Durkheim, the Italian Vilfredo Pareto, and the German Max Weber. It is too early yet to speak of a complete theory that is at our disposal in structural analysis; all we have is a theoretical instrumentarium. The notions of a "functional" or "structural-functional theory" are in many ways premature, if one does not want to extend the term "theory" beyond its strict meaning. These notions refer to what is above all a set of interconnected categories (partly linked by generalizing assumptions), whose application to empirical problems permits the general description of social structures as well as the determination of the place of specific elements in them. Societies and organized units within societies (groups, associations, institutions)[2] have a structure or can be regarded as units displaying a structure. "To exhibit the structure of an object is to mention its parts and the ways in which they are interrelated. . . . Every account of structure is relative to certain units which are, for the time being, treated as if they were devoid of structure, but it must never be assumed that these units will not, in another context, have a structure which it is important to recognize" (Russell, 222, pp. 267, 269). The basic unit of structural analysis in sociology to which this statement obviously applies, is that of role, i.e., of a complex of behavior expectations which are associated with a given social position or status. In structural analysis, the human individual in the fullness of his expressions figures only as an incumbent of such positions, and "player" of roles. The relations between roles and their agglomerations around certain institutional spheres (occupation, education, family, politics, etc.) are expressed by the concept of function, i.e., by their latent or manifest consequences for the "functioning" of the total structure. Thus, the structure of a society presents itself in its most formal aspect as a functional system the units of which are social roles and role sets.[3]

But by contrast with the structure of other objects of knowledge, especially of organisms with which they are frequently compared, social structures have one important peculiarity. They are not as such "given," they cannot in principle be analyzed independent of their

---

[2] "Structural-functional" theorists like to refer to both with the term "social system." Reasonable as this link by a general category is, it is nevertheless dangerous because of the possible implications of the concept of system from the point of view of conflict and change: systems might appear as closed units which do not permit of change. This is, to be sure, a misunderstanding; but in order to forestall it I would propose to avoid the term "system."

[3] I neither intend nor can attempt here to give even the barest outline of the categories and assumptions of the "structural-functional" approach. For that, see the works of Parsons, Merton, Levy, and others; see also my essay on Parsons (206). Here we are concerned merely with certain formal aspects of this approach, in so far as they are relevant for the theory of class.

historical context, but they are themselves subject to continuous change. By change in this sense we do not mean the occurrence of certain processes within a given structural pattern, for this is accounted for by the category of structure in any case. Regular processes within objects that have a structure—such as the processes of role allocation, or of the socialization of new members of society—are indeed an essential element of every structure; structural analysis is essentially the analysis of such processes. What is meant here is, rather, that the entire structural arrangement of so-called forms of society can change. Function and functional importance of the heart or liver in an organism do not change; function and functional importance of religious or economic institutions in society not only can change but also are subject to a continuous process of change in all known societies. The functioning of medieval European society would evidently be strongly endangered if in an experiment of imagination we removed all religious institutions from this society; were we, however, to remove these institutions from today's secularized industrial societies the effect would be considerably milder. An analogous argument could not be made for organisms. Should we remove the heart from the human organism, the consequences would be the same at all times. Radcliffe-Brown has realized this peculiarity of social structures more clearly than many of the later "structural-functionalists" when he states, "that an animal organism does not, in the course of its life, change its structural type. A pig does not become a hippopotamus. . . . On the other hand a society in the course of its history can and does change its structural type without any breach of continuity" (220, p. 181).

Russell remarks in his logical analysis of the concept of structure, "An analysis of structure, however complete, does not tell you all that you may wish to know about an object. It tells you only what are the parts of the object and how they are related to each other; it tells you nothing about the relations of the object to objects that are not parts or components of it" (222, p. 268). In the case of organic structures, this involves a limitation of structural analysis, not an objection against it. Anatomy and physiology have heuristic value and scientific validity even without a social psychology of relations between organisms. Social structures, however, carry within them the seed of other structures that lie beyond their (fictitious) borderlines. They reach, so to speak, beyond themselves; at any given point of time they either are no longer or not yet what they appear to be. Process and change are their very nature and indicate therefore superordinate categories of analysis. Although in biology the analysis of the evolutionary process can rest on structural analysis, such analysis must, in sociology, be subordinated to the analysis of processes of change of structural patterns.

Time and again, structural-functional theory has been accused of not recognizing this basic fact of social reality. With respect to the intention of most of its advocates at least, this accusation is unjustified. Not merely, but especially, in sociology the analysis of changes of structural patterns creates almost insuperable problems. "We reason about movement," so Bergson laments on behalf of philosophy, "as if it were composed of immobilities, and if we consider it, we compose it of immobilities. Movement for us is a position"—such as a structure—"and then a new position, etc., *ad infinitum*" (223, p. 165). The statement is justified, but not the lament. It appears, rather, as if processes are accessible to our analysis only, if we dissect them into their static elements; more precisely, if we try to reconstruct them from a static basis (which changes) and from certain forces (which cause change).[4] Talcott Parsons has been acutely aware of this problem of knowledge. For him, the concept of structure is therefore no more than an inevitable expedient, no more than this constructed "static basis": "Structure does not refer to any ontological stability in phenomena but only to a relative stability—to sufficiently stable uniformities in the results of underlying processes so that their constancy within certain limits is a workable pragmatic assumption" (217, p. 217). Parsons and many other sociologists have also seen that the next step of analysis must lie in the designation of the dynamic elements of social structures. But in carrying out this designation they make that central mistake which renders a large part of their categories useless for the analysis of structural change, and which therefore justifies the charge of a "static bias" in their approach.

Parsons continues the statement quoted above by saying: "Once resort is made to the structure of a system as a positive constituent of dynamic analysis there must be a way of linking these 'static' structural categories . . . to the dynamically variable elements in the system. This link is supplied by the all-important concept of *function*. Its crucial role is to provide criteria of the *importance* of dynamic factors and processes within the system. They are important in so far as they have functional significance to the system." The consequential mis-

---

[4] There is another way of looking at the same logical situation, and one that in the long run may prove more appropriate. In a Galilean sense, one might assume movement as the normal state of affairs, and instead of looking for forces that inaugurate change one might concentrate on forces which arrest movement or slow it down. In Chapter VI below we shall explore the applicability of this kind of approach to problems of social change.

take of this step of analysis already lies in its intention to find the dynamically variable elements "in the system." The category of function is indeed subordinated to that of structure. Parts of a structure have a function in relation to this structure as a whole. In this sense the category is certainly important. However, it is not "all-important": it is rather the first requisite of a dynamic analysis of structure to find variables which are not subordinated to the category of structure (and are in this sense "within the system") but which operate as forces or factors changing the structure. That Parsons, and with him many other recent "theorists," have overlooked this fact may be due to a more or less deliberate identification of organic and social structures or "systems." For this is the most difficult problem of the analysis of structural change: by contrast to organic structures, the "dynamically variable elements" which influence the construction of social structures do not necessarily originate outside the "system" but may be generated by the structure itself. There are, in other words, within social structures certain elements or forces which are at the same time their constituent parts (and therefore "function" within them) and impulses operating toward their supersedence and change. As we shall see, social classes are elements of this kind.

It is neither necessary nor possible here to examine the implications of this critique in detail. Moreover, we shall have to confine ourselves to these few and necessarily abstract remarks, the empirical relevance of which will emerge more clearly when we turn to the discussion of class or role interests. Structural-functional analysis as it stands today fails to explain problems of change because it does not account for the peculiar character of social as opposed to organic structures. It does not look for the dynamic variables that, though operating within given structures, are in principle independent of their (constructed) functional integration. If, as is the undisputed premise of all sociological inquiry, we are ultimately concerned with the scientific description and explanation of structural change, then we must find, apart from the undoubtedly important construction of functionally integrated structures, elements which are independent of these without being necessarily external to them and which determine relative stability as well as kind and degree of change of structural patterns. In identifying such factors we shall have to be careful not to abandon the gain in systematic analysis achieved by the structural-functional approach to the randomness of factors adduced *ad hoc*. The emergence and operation of forces that change social structure are also subject to laws which we may want to recognize.

Even the careful reader of Marx may ask himself, in vain, in what sense the rather abstract discussion of this section sustains Marx's position (as the heading of it promises). Indeed, this discussion shows how far sociology has advanced since Marx. In the place of undifferentiated and often implicit premises and assumptions we have today almost too elaborate categories and theoretical standpoints. Yet implicit and perhaps not even conceived with full clarity as it may be, the right approach to dynamic social analysis can be discerned in the works of Marx. Throughout his works, Marx displayed a strong conviction of the primacy of the analysis of structural change. He, too, had to construct the model of a society ("capitalism") for this purpose. But he did not stop there. Being intensely concerned with discovering pattern in history, he searched for factors and forces that promise to explain the process of social change. As we shall presently see, Marx overstated his case, to say nothing of making numerous mistakes in details of his theory. But in so far as historical societies are concerned, Marx never fell into the trap of abandoning the problem of change out of fascination with the beauty of his structural model. His subject was social change, and the category of social structure was no more than a tool with which to tackle this elusive and intricate problem.

SOCIAL CHANGE AND CLASS CONFLICT (I): MARX SUSTAINED

Many aspects of Marx's theory of class have to be rejected in the light of sociological knowledge. These do not include, however, the heuristic purpose of Marx's sociological work and its immediate consequences. It is without doubt important to develop categories to describe social changes. Concepts like "role differentiation," "transference of functions," "leveling of statuses," and the like serve this purpose. But it is clearly more important to find ways and means to explain change. It is of course most unlikely that any one hypothesis will be capable of accounting for all types of change that can be observed in the course of history, and in so far as Marx advances an absolutist claim for his own theory we shall have to depart from him radically. At the same time, Marx has explored one of the most interesting, and perhaps the most significant, relationship between social structure and social change by postulating conflict groups and their clashes as forces that make for change. Obvious as it may seem that social conflicts often result in the modification of accepted patterns of organization and behavior, it has neither been seen by all nor been explored as systematically by anybody as by Marx.

Throughout his life, Marx was clearly influenced by the memory of two events which overshadowed the consciousness of the nineteenth century, although they were its heritage rather than its product: the French Revolution and the Industrial Revolution. There were obvious explanations for both of them, and these were widely held. One might summarize them by the phrases that "men make history" and that "inventions make history." Even today, historians find it hard to free themselves from the conception that at the turning points of history there stood outstanding and powerful individuals or important and consequential inventions. Indeed, it would be nonsensical to try and deny the effect of these forces. But, as Marx well knew, in the French Revolution and the Industrial Revolution another kind of force had also become apparent. Apart from powerful individuals and revolutionary inventions, larger and more anonymous aggregations of men had played a visible part in bringing about these events. Nor had they been unanimous in purpose and action. It was, rather, the conflict between aggregates of differing (but considerable) size, and the changing fortunes of this conflict, that had effected a restructuring of society so far-reaching that it could only be called revolutionary. As we shall see, the revolutionary tradition of the eighteenth century not only inspired Marx but misled him as well. He tended to believe that the only way in which social conflicts could produce structural changes was by revolutionary upheavals. But despite such errors he did discover the formative force of conflicting social groups or classes. This "discovery"[5] is accompanied, in the work of Marx, by two steps of analysis which, although rather formal, are nevertheless worth mentioning and sustaining.

Firstly, Marx succeeded in tracing conflicts that effect change back to patterns of social structure. For him, social conflicts were not random occurrences which forbid explanation and therefore prediction. Rather, he believed these conflicts to be necessary outgrowths of the structure of any given society and, in particular, of capitalist society. It is doubtful whether Marx, by assuming property relations to be the structural origin of conflict, was right in the substance of his analysis. But this does not diminish the analytical achievement of tracing in the structure of a given society the seeds of its supersedure. The idea of a society which produces in its structure the antagonisms that lead to

[5] Like all discoveries, it is not, strictly speaking, original. It would not be difficult to find, throughout the history of pre-Marxian philosophy from Heraclitus to Hegel, numerous thinkers who regarded "conflict as the father of all things." But it is Marx's merit to have embodied this approach in a fairly systematic theory of the generation and course of social conflict in modern societies.

its modification appears an appropriate model for the analysis of change in general.[6]

Secondly, Marx properly assumed the dominance of one particular conflict in any given situation. Whatever criticism may be required of the Marxian theory, any theory of conflict has to operate with something like a two-class model. There are but two contending parties—this is implied in the very concept of conflict. There may be coalitions, of course, as there may be conflicts internal to either of the contenders, and there may be groups that are not drawn into a given dispute; but from the point of view of a given clash of interests, there are never more than two positions that struggle for domination. We can follow Marx in this argument (which, for him, is often more implicit than explicit) even further. If social conflicts effect change, and if they are generated by social structure, then it is reasonable to assume that of the two interests involved in any one conflict, one will be pressing for change, the other one for the *status quo*. This assumption, again, is based on logic as much as on empirical observation. In every conflict, one party attacks and another defends. The defending party wants to retain and secure its position, while the attacking party has to fight it in order to improve its own condition. Once again, it is clear that these statements remain on a high level of formality. They imply no reference to the substance or the origin of conflicting interests. But, again, it will prove useful to have articulated the formal prerequisites of Marx's and, indeed, of any theory of conflict.

With these formal points, however, our agreement with Marx ends. Although the heuristic purpose and general approach of his theory of class can and must be sustained, this is not the case with respect to most other features of this theory. Only by rejecting these can we hope to clear the way for a more useful theory of class conflict in industrial societies.

SOCIAL CHANGE AND CLASS CONFLICT (II): MARX REJECTED

Since Talcott Parsons wrote his *Structure of Social Action* the neglect of a systematic analysis of the dynamics of social action by sociologists has become increasingly conspicuous. Only very recently have a number of scholars set out to explore and map this white spot in the

[6] Parsons justly emphasizes, in an essay on Marx that is surprising in more than one sense, this achievement of Marx and states that Marx "did . . . unlike the utilitarians, see and emphasize the massive fact of the structuring of interests rather than treating them at random" (67, p. 323).

atlas of sociological knowledge. If only for this reason, it is of some importance to determine the logical status and limits of dynamic analysis rather more precisely than is necessary today with respect to problems of, say, social stratification. We have tried to reduce the spongy concept of social change to that of structural change. This constitutes a gain, but it is not in itself sufficient. At a later point we shall have to return to the dangerous question "When does a structure begin to change or, conversely, up to what point does it remain unchanged?"— a dangerous question because it implies an essentially static concept of structure. So far we have merely touched upon the two cardinal requirements of a theory of change, i.e., the construction of the model of a functionally integrated structure, and the discovery of certain factors or forces the effect of which leads to a modification of this structural model. As to the first of these requirements we have, in the structural-functional approach, a considerable instrumentarium at our disposal today. But with respect to the codification of forces that effect structural change everything is still to be done. *Ad hoc* and at random factors are introduced wherever necessary, and all too often these factors are afterwards generalized in an impermissible manner. Thus we get so-called theories of the primacy of the economy, of race, of elites, of cultural diffusion—or of classes. We cannot hope to remedy the obvious lack of a systematic treatment of this subject by preliminary classifications and delimitations as will be proposed here; but we can try to avoid the most obvious errors of one-sided theories. In order to do so, however, it will be inevitable that—as T. H. Marshall says with pleasant irony of his own investigation (57, p. 10)—"I shall be running true to type as a sociologist" by proposing to divide our subject into several distinct parts.

Among the forces that are capable of changing elements of social structure, two large groups must evidently be distinguished—those that originate outside a given structure and those that are generated by the structure itself. We shall use for the former the concept of exogenous structure change, or exogenous factors, and for the latter that of endogenous structure change, or endogenous factors.[7]

---

[7] M. J. Levy has introduced a similar distinction (209, p. 114). "The strategic factors for change (i.e., the factors necessary and sufficient for a change given the initial stage) may be internal factors (i.e., factors produced by the operation of the unit without any new influences from other units), or external factors (i.e., factors newly introduced to the system from other units), or some combination of the two." Unlike us, however, Levy is above all concerned "with cases of strategic external factors."

If the invasion of an African territory by European conquerors causes the abolition or modification of the chieftain system in certain tribes, we are faced with exogenous structure change. But the separation of ownership and control or the institutionalization of class conflict in post-capitalist society are endogenous, whichever factors one may identify as responsible for these changes. It is clear that this distinction is strictly possible only in analytical and not in empirical contexts. In conspicuous structure changes in particular, such as the industrial revolution, exogenous and endogenous forces usually combine to produce the change. It is an important task of the empirical analysis of specific problems to disentangle the two and assess their respective weights.

Within each of these fields of factors further distinctions are required. Thus, exogenous change can result from military conquest and deliberate intervention with existing structures; but it can also result from the diffusion of culture patterns unaccompanied by political or military force. In past decades, many efforts have been made, above all by social anthropologists, to bring the different forms of exogenous change into an ordered context by introducing such concepts as "diffusion," later "acculturation," "culture contact," and "culture change." Empirical instances of some of these forms have been studied in great detail. But despite Malinowski's attempt to systematize such approaches (213), this effort has not yet advanced beyond a loose catalogue of possible factors. The sociology of war and of contacts between advanced societies (until now an utterly neglected field of study) could also contribute to closing this gap in theory.

However, we are not only no further, but possibly less advanced, with respect to the classification of forces operative in endogenous structure change, although many seem to think that this is the proper subject matter of sociological inquiry. Although the number of such factors proposed by sociologists to fulfill requirements of research (and sometimes demands of philosophical or political convictions) grows steadily, a systematic examination of these factors and their interrelations has not even been attempted. The matter is further complicated by the fact that in some cases, such as the differentiation of roles or functions and of technological processes, we can hardly venture a guess as to which factors contribute to their emergence, to say nothing of certain knowledge about them. Marx's attempt to connect the development of productive forces with that of classes marks one of the weakest points in his sociology. It appears most improbable that the complication of the social division of labor, or technological processes that have social consequences, can be explained in terms of group conflicts. In any case, structure changes resulting from social conflicts between organized groups or between the representatives of unorganized masses constitute but one form of endogenous change.

Even within this considerably restricted sphere of social conflicts affecting structure change it is not only possible but necessary to distinguish a plurality of different forms. It obliterates the precision of analysis if, with one and the same set of categories, we try to analyze conflicts between slaves and freemen in ancient Rome, Negroes and whites in the United States, Catholics andProtestants in contemporary Holland, capital and labor in capitalist society—to mention only a few possibilities. All these conflicts can result in structure changes; they are in this sense factors of endogenous change. Moreover, several of these types of conflict may be superimposed on each other, and may thus constitute a single conflict front in a given country and situation. For purposes of analysis, however, it is necessary to introduce distinctions if one wants to master reality with the tools of science.[8] Endogenous change is but one kind of social structure change; social conflict is but one of the causes of endogenous change; and class conflict is but one type of social conflict. Endogenous change may be of great, even dominant, significance in a given society; but that is a matter for empirical research. In principle a theory of class illuminates only a small segment of the wide field which can be described by the vague concept of structure change. We can neither expect nor, above all, assume that a theory of class will cast a glimmer of its light on other aspects of structure change as well.

It is apparent that from this point of view Marx is in a sense guilty of the same mistake of which, in a different context, we have accused those who have endeavored to supersede the theory of class with a theory of stratification. They, too, have illegitimately transposed a theory from its legitimate place to other areas of inquiry. The assertion that the history of all past society is the history of class struggles is either meaningless or false. It is meaningless if it is merely intended to say that, *inter alia*, there were also class conflicts in every society. But Marx did not mean this. He believed that the dominant conflicts of every society were class conflicts, and indeed that all social conflicts and all structure changes can be explained in terms of antagonisms of class. This generalization is as impermissible as it is untenable. The

---

[8] In an earlier article I have indicated a classification of types of endogenous conflicts, distinguishing "partial conflicts" (minorities), "sectional conflicts" (town–country), and class conflicts (41, p. 175); but this is only a beginning.

place to which we have assigned the theory of class may appear modest. In fact, this reduced significance of class analysis will be corrected to a certain extent with respect to the particular historical constellations of industrial societies. This does not alter the fact, however, that social analysis in terms of class—as Gurvitch remarks quite rightly (50, p. 290)—"does not by any means provide a key which opens all doors to the solution of problems of social change." I would claim that only by restricting the theory of class to one, if one major, aspect of structural change, can we hope to weld it into a useful tool of sociological analysis.

CLASS CONFLICT AND REVOLUTION: MARX REJECTED

"The conflict between proletariat and bourgeoisie" is, according to Marx, "a conflict of one class against another, a struggle which in its highest expression means a total revolution" (6, pp.188 f.). More generally, the revolutionary character of social change is for Marx a central feature of his theory of class. Indeed, it appears to be Marx's conviction that wherever classes exist structure change has always and "necessarily" a revolutionary character. "Only in an order of things where there are no classes and no class conflicts will the social evolutions cease to be political revolutions" (6, p. 189). It emerges clearly from Marx's writings, and has never been doubted by his interpreters, that the concept of revolution meant for him the sudden and rapid upheaval of a social structure; Marx did not speak of revolutions in the extended sense of a "managerial revolution" and the like.[9] This conception, according to which social change occurs suddenly and by widely visible explosions, has not been confined to Marx and his faithful followers. Even Brinkmann betrays a trace of the conviction that social changes are always revolutionary if they result from class conflict, when he observes an "evolutionary moderation of revolutionary forces and patterns" in recent social development (192, p. 12). Yet, here again we find one of those untenable generalizations which bar the path to our knowledge of reality and which have to be replaced by more reasonable, if not empirically confirmed, assumptions. The error that changes of social structure are generally of a revolutionary nature is especially interesting for two reasons which are worth pursuing. In

[9] It is however true that Lassalle and, following him, Renner have in the course of their revision of Marx replaced the notion of the "revolution in the hay-fork sense" (Lassalle) with the notion of gradual social changes. But in doing so, these men were aware of the fact that they had abandoned a central tenet of Marx's theory.

the first place this very assumption might, despite its dynamic appearance, induce us to join in with Bergson's lament about dissolving change into "immobilities." In the thesis that a given structure can be changed and transformed into a new one only by radical upheavals, there is ultimately an assumption that social structures are basically static entities. Of course, Marx spoke of the "law of development," that is, of the dynamics of capitalist society. But this law of development was for him little more than the law of development of an organism: the gradual unfolding of a "system" to its inherent image. The structure, or "system," is as such immutable. If it changes, it is destroyed entirely. It changes in one stroke (or at least by one "stroke") in all its parts and thus becomes a new "system." This is a point at which Marx and Parsons meet in a curious fashion: both of them freeze the flow of the historical process in the idea of a "system." If we accept this, either structure change can be nonexistent (which, by an extreme interpretation, might be called the Parsonian "solution"), or it exists only as revolutionary change (the Marxian "solution"). Both those solutions are equally unsatisfactory and untenable. They testify, moreover, to the insufficiency of all conscious or unconscious analogies between organic and social "systems."

If changes of social structure are invariably revolutionary in character, there can be no change without revolutions. It is easy to see how at this point the sophistic argument offers itself that Western industrial societies have remained unchanged since Marx because they have not experienced revolutions. But it is also easy to see how miserably an assertion of this kind fails to account for the processes of reality. We have seen that many recent sociological theories of class conflict refer to a "revolution" in the social development of past decades. The use of the term "revolution" for processes which are neither sudden nor explosive bears witness to the extent to which "revolution" and "change" are interlaced in general opinion. Quite contrary to such ill-considered formulations, it is the decisive characteristic of the development of industrial societies since Marx that profound structure changes have occurred without sudden, widely visible upheavals. In this sense, social development of the past decades furnishes evidence for the ubiquity and gradualness of social change and for the untenability of the assertion that change must always be revolutionary.

For Marx, the assertion of the revolutionary nature of social change has another aspect which appears no less untenable in the light of empirical knowledge. Before Marx, Hegel had, when analyzing the dialectics of "wealth" and "poverty" in his *Phenomenology of*

Mind, identified the "deepest depravation," "purest inequality," and "absolute insignificance of the absolutely significant" with the "deepest rebellion" (226, p. 368). Insignificantly changed, this idea reappears when Marx says that the proletariat "is forced, by the irrejectable, indefensible, absolutely commanding need—the practical expression of necessity—to rebel against this inhumanity" (4, p. 207). It is only a step from here to Marx's assertion that the class struggle will become more intense as the life situation of the proletariat deteriorates and will culminate in a revolution when the point is reached at which this situation has attained its extreme. Even from the point of view of a sociology of revolution, this assumption can be regarded as disproved today. Revolutions and revolts do not occur when need and oppression have reached an extreme point; they occur rather once this extreme has been passed and the lethargy given with it superseded.[10] Beyond this empirical inadequacy, Marx's notion of a linear increase of the violence of class conflict to the breaking-point of the revolution proves a Hegelian heritage which contributes little to our understanding of reality. Plausible as the application of dialectics to history may appear, its schematized and simplified consequences rarely survive empirical test.

If in this study I refer to structure change, I do not therefore mean revolutions. If I refer to class conflict, I do not imply an assumption that it is subject to an "inevitable" process of intensification leading up to a revolutionary explosion. Although the construction of a structural model is a prerequisite of the systematic analysis of change, this structural model must not be viewed as a monolithic entity which in some unknown sense can only change "as a whole." Rather, structure change has to be assumed as a permanent aspect of every society. It can begin in one sphere of a structure, such as industry, and propagate to other spheres, such as political society; but it can also remain confined to one sphere. Even if, for example, it could be shown that the separation of ownership and control in industry has no consequence for the political structure of society, such a separation would nevertheless constitute a structural change. Only if we view structure change as a ubiquitous and constituent element of social structure do we free ourselves of the fetters of the assumption that social change is always of a revolutionary character. At the same time we can thus avoid the in-

---

[10] The revolts and revolutions in the recent history of Eastern Europe (June 17, 1953; Poznan, Hungary) have confirmed this hypothesis quite convincingly. In general, these events provide many an illustration for the theses advanced in this and the following chapters of this study.

soluble task of determining when and where processes of change "begin" and "end."

Regarding class conflict, one important assumption follows from this decision. If social change is not confined to revolutionary explosions but is a constituent element of every structure as such, it is no longer necessary to assert a linear development of classes and class conflicts toward the point of revolution. For Marx, the classes themselves were within a given system something like "organisms" with a predetermined course of development leading to their perfection. It follows from this that, among other things, organized classes begin to affect the structure within which they have grown only in the moment of revolution, and that their changing force is indeed confined to this moment. All that happens before the revolution happens merely in preparation for this event; afterwards, the classes of the old society dissolve. Again, this simplifying assumption robs the concept of class of its empirical value for nonrevolutionary processes, and that means for the majority of social processes. Again, we have to depart radically from Marx. The "necessity" of a linear intensification of class conflict is in any case a nonsociological postulate which has to be rejected. Moreover, it will prove reasonable to view the interrelations of classes as potentially a process of permanent readjustment. Periods of violent conflict can be succeeded by others of relative harmony, and vice versa. There is no general law that determines the course of clashes and struggles between classes; and no revolutionary upheaval can be postulated as a "normal" goal and climax of class conflict. The course of conflicts between classes presents a problem which cannot be solved by arbitrarily introducing assumptions or premises but has to be determined on the basis of empirical investigations into particular historical constellations in particular societies.

SOCIAL CLASSES AND CLASS CONFLICT: MARX REJECTED

In rejecting the premise of a predetermined course of class conflict, we implicitly deny the validity of a further assertion that is part and parcel of Marx's theory of class, namely, that classes are always manifestly antagonistic groups or tend toward manifest conflicts. The assumptions rejected so far were more or less peripheral for Marx's theory of class, but here we come to its core. This cannot prevent us from rejecting untenable assumptions without hesitation, but it makes caution imperative, if we do not want to run the risk of disputing the heuristic value of any theory of class together with the problematic aspects of its Marxian formulation. "Individuals," Marx says at one place, "form a class only in so far as they are engaged in a common struggle against another class" (13, II, p. 59). This statement contains, if it is interpreted in the light of other statements of Marx about the same matter, a necessary assumption and a false empirical generalization. In the interest of an analytically useful theory of class we shall have to separate the two.

The theory of class aims at a systematic analysis of one of the causes of the endogenous structure change of societies. It has its place within the wider context of the analysis of structural changes caused by social conflicts. From this it is evident that, however one may choose to define classes, they must always be regarded as groupings related to each other in such a way that their interplay is determined by a structurally conditioned conflict of interests. In this sense, one class alone is a *contradictio in adiecto*; there must always be two classes. In this sense, also, Stalin's concept of "nonantagonistic classes" is meaningless; where there are classes, there is conflict. Inasmuch as any theory of class is a theory of structure change by social conflict, the assumption of a conflict between classes is part of the definition of classes. There can thus be no reason to reject Marx's formulation on this point.

But beyond this formal statement, Marx postulated acute and violent conflict ("class struggle") as part of the definition of classes; and we cannot follow him in this step. That class conflict invariably assumes violent forms and becomes civil war is an assumption the empirical character of which Marx could not abolish by joining it to his definition of the concept of class. "Exactly how serious the element of conflict is becomes a matter of empirical investigation" (Parsons, 67, p. 324). What evidence we have permits at least the negative conclusion that class conflict does not always assume the form of civil war. Instead, a phenomenon like the institutionalization of class conflict shows that an "oppressed" class may well be capable of effecting structure changes by discussion and negotiation. Here, as elsewhere, more acute analysis reveals that the overly simple assumptions of Marx tend to obliterate rather than illuminate the intricacies of the problem of class.

Parsons introduced for purposes of a subtler analysis of class relations the useful concept of "potential" or "latent conflicts" (67, p. 329). Apart from the actual or manifest clashes between classes it seems reasonable to distinguish at least two kinds of latent conflicts. Marx has himself dealt with one of these, namely, with what one might call the immature conflicts between classes which are still in the process of formation and organization. But a second form of latent class conflict seems even more important. It appears that conflicting classes can, for several reasons, co-exist for shorter or longer periods of time in a kind of "armistice" without engaging in open struggles. Some of the symptoms of this reduction of manifest to latent conflicts are well known and confirmed by considerable evidence: common interests, such as national interests in emergency situations, can be superimposed on group antagonisms for certain (limited) periods; conflicts can be formalized to the extent of being transformed into discussions between plenipotentiaries or representatives in parliaments or industrial negotiation bodies. At this point, too, sociological analysis has to turn away from the sterile magic of definitional premises to the investigation of empirical conditions under which latent conflicts become manifest or manifest conflicts fade into the background.

Some authors prefer to describe antagonisms and tensions which are not expressed in manifest struggles in terms other than conflict. Thus, they distinguish conflicts and tensions, conflicts and disputes, conflicts and contests, or—most frequently—conflict and competition. Such terminological distinctions are in fact in keeping with common usage. We do, indeed, tend to associate with the word "conflict" visible clashes between forces, i.e., antagonisms which are manifest as such. A football game, a competition between applicants for a job, a parliamentary debate, or a legal contest are not usually called conflicts. However, it will be evident from the preceding discussion that I am using the term "conflict" in this study for contests, competitions, disputes, and tensions as well as for manifest clashes between social forces. All relations between sets of individuals that involve an incompatible difference of objective—i.e., in its most general form, a desire on the part of both contestants to attain what is available only to one, or only in part—are, in this sense, relations of social conflict. The general concept of conflict does not as such imply any judgment as to the intensity or violence of relations caused by differences of objective. Conflict may assume the form of civil war, or of parliamentary debate, of a strike, or of a well-regulated negotiation.

It is important to realize that this conceptual decision is not merely of terminological significance. It implies, and is supposed to imply, that civil war and parliamentary debate, strike and negotiation are essentially motivated by the same type of social relationship and are therefore but different manifestations of an identical force. In what sense this definition of conflict makes possible a fruitful reformulation of problems will become apparent in our subsequent considerations. We have already seen, however, that by identifying conflict and revolution, or conflict and civil war, Marx has obscured more problems than he solved. Whoever uses the category of class without assuming the presence of class conflict abuses this category. It is the declared aim of class theory to explain one type of constitutional group conflict in social structures. But the empirical hypothesis is false that insists that this class conflict must always assume the form of violent civil war and "class struggle." Indeed, it seems plausible that under certain conditions (which it is possible to determine) class antagonism becomes latent or is reactivated from a state of latency. Social classes and class conflict are categories connected inseparably; but type and intensity of the conflicts in which particular classes are involved in a particular situation can be discovered only by studying empirical conditions.

PROPERTY AND SOCIAL CLASS: MARX REJECTED

For Marx, the determinant of social classes was effective private property in the means of production. In all essential elements, his theory of class is based on this definition of the concept of class. We have seen, meanwhile, that precisely this tie between the concept of class and the possession of, or exclusion from, effective private property limits the applicability of class theory to a relatively short period of European social history. A theory of class based on the division of society into owners and nonowners of means of production loses its analytical value as soon as legal ownership and factual control are separated. For this reason, any effective supersedure of Marx's theory of class has to start at this point. Now, it is one of the central theses of this study that such a supersedure is possible if we replace the possession, or nonpossession, of effective private property by the exercise of, or exclusion from, authority as the criterion of class formation. Renner, Schumpeter, Burnham, Djilas, and others have prepared the ground for this decision; by contrast to most of these we shall not confine the notion of authority to the control of the means of production, but consider it as a type of social relations analytically independent of economic conditions. The authority structure of entire societies as well as particular institutional orders within societies (such as industry) is, in terms of the theory here advanced, the structural determinant of class formation and class conflict. The specific type of change of social structures caused by social classes and their conflicts is ultimately the result of the differential distribution of positions of authority in societies and their institutional orders. Control over the means of production is but a special case of authority, and the connection of control with legal property an incidental phenomenon of the industrializing societies of Europe and the United States. Classes are tied neither to private property nor to industry or economic structures in general, but as an element of social structure and a factor effecting change they are as universal as their determinant, namely, authority and its distribution itself. On the basis of a concept of class defined by relations of authority, a theory can be formulated which accounts for the facts described by Marx as well as for the changed reality of post-capitalist society.

At several points of our investigation it has become apparent how many doubts and objections can be raised against Marx's treatment of the relationship between property and social class. In presenting Marx's theory, in describing the phenomenon of the separation of ownership and control, and in discussing Burnham's inferences from this phenomenon and Djilas's analysis of Communist totalitarianism, we have seen how, by connecting the concept of class with private property (and thereby capitalism), Marx renders this concept fit for inclusion in his philosophical conception of history but unfit for the sociological analysis even of the conflicts with which he was concerned. Marx, too, is concerned with relations of authority; indeed, he explicitly refers to these when he describes class conflicts generated by the structure of the industrial enterprise. But Marx believed that authority and power are factors which can be traced back to a man's share in effective private property. In reality, the opposite is the case. Power and authority are irreducible factors from which the social relations associated with legal private property as well as those associated with communal property can be derived. Burnham, and above all Geiger, have rightly stressed that property is in its sociological aspect in the first place a permission to exclude others from control over an object. It is therefore (Weber, 33, p. 28) a "chance to find obedience with defined persons for an order" (in this case a prohibition), i.e., a form of authority. But property is by no means the only form of authority; it is but one of its numerous types. Whoever tries, therefore, to define authority by property defines the general by the particular—an obvious logical fallacy. Wherever there is property there is authority, but not every form of authority implies property. Authority is the more general social relation.

This formal argument is not, however, the only reason for substituting for Marx's definition of classes by private property one by a man's share in authority; this generalization is necessary, also, for the sake of the empirical applicability of the theory of class. For this purpose, it is moreover necessary to separate radically the concept of authority from its narrow application to the control over economic means of production. Just as property is formally, thus control over the means of production is empirically but a special case of those general relations of authority which, according to our conception, lie at the base of class formation and class conflict. Why this extension is empirically necessary will be shown in detail in the following section of this chapter, where we deal with the relation between industrial and social authority structures. However, this much can be stated even without a more detailed discussion: that a theory of group conflict the central category of which is defined by a man's share in the control of the means of production can apply only to the sphere of industrial production. In any case, its significance for structure change would be even more restricted than is the significance of the theory of class.

To say that classes are based on a man's share in legitimate power is not to formulate an empirical hypothesis. If this were so, it would presuppose an independent definition of the concept of class. It is rather a definition which, in a preliminary way, we can state as follows: classes are social conflict groups the determinant (or *differentia specifica*) of which can be found in the participation in or exclusion from the exercise of authority within any imperatively coordinated association. In this sense, classes differ from other conflict groups which rest on religious, ethnic, or legal differences. In principle, a definition is of course an arbitrary decision. If it is logically unassailable, it cannot be refuted by empirical facts. Yet the definition proposed here is more than a terminological decision without empirical consequences. We shall see that this decision alone opens up many new possibilities for the analysis of social conflicts.

At the same time, the definition of classes by people's participation in or exclusion from the exercise of authority distinguishes this category clearly from many earlier definitions.[11] The concept of class proposed here as promising an effective supersedure of Marx's concept is not based on the level or source of income. Even those sociologists who rightly sought the analytical place of a theory of class in the study of social conflict have tended to retain two aspects of the Marxian concept of class which I propose to abandon. Most of them

[11] It is perhaps necessary to emphasize at this point that our definition, as formulated so far, contains many ambiguities and is bound to raise doubts. In this chapter, I confine myself to statements required by the critical dissociation from Marx. A more detailed discussion of power and authority as determinants of social class will be found in the subsequent chapter; in the course of this discussion the definition proposed here will become rather more specific and, I hope, unambiguous.

maintained (1) that classes are in some sense "economic" groupings and (2) that the lines of class structure run parallel to those of social stratification. So far as I can see, neither Marshall nor Geiger, neither Schumpeter nor Lipset and Bendix have renounced these two stipulations. "To us," Lipset and Bendix state (55, pp. 244, 248), "the purpose of research in this field is an analysis of the incessant interplay between the *factors of stratification* which make for social change and those which tend to arrest it." And: "The analysis of social class is concerned with an assessment of the chances that common *economic conditions* . . . will lead to organized action." Geiger similarly views social classes as "a special case of *social strata*," namely, strata "determined by the *relations of production*" (46, p. 35). Although Marshall goes one step further by trying to dissociate the concept of class from economic conditions and extend it to a notion of "social class," he, too, insists that the phenomenon of class "represents a hierarchical *social stratification*" (58, p. 90).[12] Both the stipulation that class is a phenomenon of stratification and that it is associated with economic conditions are fetters from which we have to free this category in order to transform it into a useful tool of social analysis.

If we define classes by relations of authority, it is *ipso facto* evident that "economic classes," i.e., classes within economic organizations, are but a special case of the phenomenon of class. Furthermore, even within the sphere of industrial production it is not really economic factors that give rise to class formation, but a certain type of social relations which we have tried to comprehend in the notion of authority. Classes are neither primarily nor at all economic groupings.

It is less easy to determine the relation between classes as authority groups and the system of social stratification. In the first place, it is important to realize that there is no one-to-one correlation between class structure and social stratification in the sense that classes result from people's place in the hierarchy of stratification. The analyses of class and of social stratification are essentially independent subjects of sociological inquiry. On the other hand, there is between them a significant indirect connection which results from the fact that authority, the determinant of class, is at the same time one of the determinants of social status. It can be demonstrated that there is an empirical tendency for the possession of authority to be accompanied, within certain limits and with significant exceptions, by high income and high prestige, and, conversely, for the exclusion from authority

---

[12] All italics in this paragraph are mine.

to be accompanied by relatively low income and prestige. Indeed, it is one of the distinguishing features of authority that it can become an instrument for the satisfaction of other desires and needs and for the attainment of directly gratifying social rewards. Thus, there is in most societies a tendential, if not unequivocal, correlation between the distribution of authority and the system of social rewards that underlies stratification.[18] In this sense, but only in this sense, the partial parallelism between the lines of class division and those of social stratification may be an empirical fact. One might go further and regard this parallelism as probable, as it could be argued that a certain correspondence between people's share in authority and in social rewards in general is a functional imperative of relatively stable societies. But no parallelism between structures of class and stratification can be postulated. Classes can be identical with strata, they can unite several strata within them, and their structure can cut right through the hierarchy of stratification.

For purposes of clarity it seemed advisable to state, in the strongest possible terms, the way in which class is independent of property, economic conditions, and social stratification. In the abstract, no qualification need be made to this statement. Fortunately, however, empirical conditions do not usually reproduce the simplicity of our assumptions and theories. Although the idea of property, of the relationships that have to do with production, and of the hierarchy of social stratification is, in each instance, clearly distinct from the idea of class, these factors have a great deal to do with the realities of social class and class conflict. Without doubt, the fact that at the time Marx wrote there were capitalists who simultaneously owned and controlled their enterprises contributed greatly to the formation of classes and the antagonism between them. Similarly, the fact that it is possible to identify the powerful with the wealthy cannot be overlooked in class analysis. While the connection between property and social class is not one of definition or mutual dependence, it is one that affects the empirical course of class conflict. If distinctions of property are superimposed on distinctions of class, class conflict is likely to be more violent than if these two lines of social differentiation diverge. An analogous argument could be made for class and social stratification. In fact, this is one of many points at which Marx has transformed a

---

[18] We can leave open, here, whether this correlation can be explained in terms of a common basic factor, such as a "value system" (Parsons), or whether it is due to the direct effect of authority. I doubt that a final answer to this problem is methodologically possible.

correct empirical observation into a false and useless assumption by arbitrarily generalizing what was characteristic only of the comparatively short historical period which he lived to see.

INDUSTRY AND SOCIETY: MARX REJECTED

The substitution of relations of authority for those of production in defining class is but a radical interpretation of some of the theories discussed in the preceding chapter. Djilas, Schumpeter, Renner, Geiger, and, above all, Burnham in his theory of managerial power, have paved the way for this step. But Burnham makes a curious mistake which is worth examining in some detail. There is an interesting nuance peculiar to his approach which rapidly turns into a consequential fallacy and renders his theory empirically nonsensical and analytically useless. Burnham tries to supersede Marx's theory by replacing the narrow legal concept of property by a wider sociological concept. Quite rightly he defines property relations (the particular) by authority relations (the general). But with a theoretical inaccuracy which is characteristic of his work he now reverses this definition and declares authority relations (the general) to be property relations (the particular). The managers have property ownership because they have factual control. At best, this reversal results in a nonsensical extension of the concept of property to all forms of authority, in which case the head of state would have property in "his" state. At worst, however, and this is Burnham's case, the logical somersault is followed by an empirical *salto mortale* consisting in the assertion that authority can exist only where there is property, or, as Burnham says himself, that "the instruments of production are the seat of social domination" (140, p. 125). Marx and Burnham meet in the premise that economic power is *eo ipso* political power, because there is no power except that based on ownership in the means of production. But both of them are wrong, and their error makes it necessary to pose the problem of the relation between economic and social power anew.

It must be emphasized, in the first place, that the relations between industry and society can be established only by empirical investigation. There is no axiomatic identity between the managers or capitalists of industry and the ministers or highest civil servants of the state, just as the exclusion of industrial workers from top political positions is by no means an unchangeable element in the structure of industrial societies. Again, it was true in Marx's own time, and in English society, that the captains of industry or their relatives tended to monopolize many of the leading political positions. The same is still true in several countries, including the United States and Germany. But this particular observation does not legitimize the formulation of a general law. Should this law nevertheless be advanced as a hypothesis, then it was refuted by the first government of a labor party in an industrial country. The political state and industrial production are two essentially independent associations in which power is exercised; and their interrelations are a subject for empirical research.

Once again, we must supplement, if not correct, an unequivocal analytical distinction by empirical facts. A number of empirical generalizations about the particular—and especially close—relation between the organizations of industrial production and the state are in fact possible for modern societies. Among all imperatively coordinated associations apart from the state, those of industry occupy, indeed, a place which endows them with particular significance in connection with conflicts in industrial societies. This is above all because of three factors which distinguish industry from all other institutional orders of society, with the exception of the state itself: the mere size of industrial production, its significance for the lives of those who participate in it, and the severity of the sanctions at the disposal of the rulers of industry.

If in this context we refer to industry, we always mean primarily that sector of the economy of advanced societies which is concerned with commodity production in enterprises (factories), and in which "means of production" exist in the strict sense of the term. By industry we mean, in other words, what C. Clark would call "secondary production." This delimitation seems justified by the fact that the enterprise of industrial production displays with particular clarity the traits of an association coordinated by relations of authority. In industrial societies, the sector of secondary production is prominent even in terms of its purely physical extent. Nearly one out of every two citizens of such societies earns his living in industrial enterprises of production. Their position in the national economy exceeds that of all other branches of activity. Moreover, the enterprises of production themselves grow into mammoth organizations with a hundred thousand employees or more. Without doubt, Drucker is right in emphasizing the special place of the modern large corporation.

The particular significance of large-scale industry is further emphasized by the fact that those who earn their living in industrial enterprises spend a large part of their lives there and for an even larger part are under the influence of the social relations characteristic of industry. Sociologists have often emphasized the importance of occupational roles in industrial societies; these roles also have their ramifications in problems of class conflict. Since the authority relations of industrial production occupy so large a space in the lives of so many people, they tend to overshadow the authority relations of most, if not all, other associations. Except for the political society—the state —no other imperatively coordinated organization can compare with industrial production in the number of persons affected by its structure and in the intensity of this influence. Finally, the special position of industrial production is due to the type of sanction inflicted by it. Weber defined the state in terms of the monopoly of physical force in a given territory. But even in recent times there are examples where the managers of industrial enterprises of production have broken this monopoly and used their own police force to try to enforce the obedience of their workers.[14] Even apart from extreme cases of this kind, dismissal and even removal to a worse-paid position constitutes infringements on the lives of people so severe that one could call them at least quasi-physical sanctions. The severity of sanctions is not the least cause of the fact that under certain conditions conflicts within industrial organizations may transcend their limits and dominate the scene of social conflict.

These are empirical generalizations. Although they underline the significance of industry for industrial societies, no universal law of connection or interrelation between industrial and political power can be derived from them. On the contrary, we shall argue at a later point that the validity even of these generalizations can be restricted by social changes and has been restricted by recent developments. Nevertheless, we can conclude from the considerations of this section that the organizations of industrial production play a prominent part in modern societies. While in principle the problem of the relation of particular associations to the political state has to be posed anew for each association, that of the relation between industry and society has *de facto* a certain primacy in industrial societies. The state is an association coordinated by authority relations, and so is industrial production. The questions whether the structures of the one are also those of the other, whether the rulers of industry are also directly or indirectly those of the state, and whether the powerless of industry are also powerless politically stand in the center of any analysis of

[14] Examples are the cases revealed by the La Follette Committee on Civil Liberties in the United States of the 1930's, where some industrialists controlled arsenals of arms larger than that of the Chicago City Police.

industrial societies in terms of class. Although we have to reject as untenable or, perhaps, as a refuted empirical generalization Marx's assertion that political power follows "necessarily" from industrial power, his premise reveals—as is so often the case in his work—a correct feeling, an instinct, even, for empirically significant relations. Even today it is one of the essential tasks of class analysis to explain industrial conflict with the model of a class theory and to examine the ramifications of industrial conflict for the political process in terms of specific hypotheses. As to the result of such an examination, we can but suspect that it will bring out more complex and less one-sided relations than Burnham or Marx believed existed.

SOCIAL ROLES AND THEIR PERSONNEL: MARX SUPPLEMENTED

The problem of the relation between individuals and classes has been as conspicuously neglected by Marx as it has been overemphasized by modern sociologists. It is not surprising that neglect cannot solve the problem, but it is unfortunately true that neither has overemphasis. Despite many a treatment of the problem, there is as yet no clear formulation of its several dimensions. "For the individual," Schumpeter says, "his belonging to a certain class is a given fact"; he is "born into a certain class position." More accurately, this does not hold for the individual *qua* individual: "The family, and not the physical person, is the true individual of class theory" (27, p. 158). Marshall refers to this statement of Schumpeter's but contrasts it with the latter's other thesis, according to which "classes which by their character and relative position might be called identical social individuals never consist of the same family individuals for any length of time, but always of different ones" (27, p. 170). Against this, Marshall postulates "some permanence in the grouping, so that a man who belongs to a certain class remains in it unless—to use a colloquialism—'something is done about it'" (58, p. 91). Again, we encounter the problem in Renner's analysis, which goes even further than Marshall's: "Like its causes, class position is almost without exception lasting, comprising the whole life and sequence of generations. . . . Every class develops in its members a uniform type" (70, p. 103). Parsons lays less stress on the time aspect but, like Schumpeter, defines the "class position of an individual" as the position "which he shares with other members in an effective kinship unit," i.e., as a family position (67, p. 328). These quotations are selected at random; it would not be difficult to supplement them with others. I quote them only to indicate a general problem about which some agreement will have to be reached in order for concept and theory of class to become useful tools of sociological analysis.

So far, we have referred to classes only in connection with social positions or roles. Authority structures as well as the associations in which they prevail can in principle be analyzed independent of the actions and motives of their specific human representatives. They are facts of structure which, like the parts of a play or an organization chart, can be analyzed without reference to the specific individuals who occupy the positions. It seems to me one of the most important discoveries of modern sociology that in analyzing class structure—as of course most other phenomena of social structure—we can and must concentrate on such quasi-objective facts, on roles and role structures. Here, again, Marx displayed an admirable instinct. "We are concerned here," he says in the preface to his *Capital*, "with persons only in so far as they are the personifications of economic categories, carriers of certain class relations and interests" (12, p. 8). However, today we should substitute for the "only" in Marx's statement an "in the first place," for the second and equally important step of structural analysis is concerned with the relation between social roles and their personnel. Marx deliberately avoided this step; he confined himself to introducing, wherever necessary, certain *ad hoc* assumptions which bear on this relation. Here, the traditional theory of class requires not so much criticism or supersedence as supplementation.

The problem of the relation between social roles and the persons who occupy them appears in more recent literature on the theory of class under four main aspects which it is useful to distinguish: (1) the problem of the determinant of class, (2) the problem of class behavior, (3) the problem of stability, and (4) the problem of recruitment to classes. The first of these problems results, as we shall see, from an erroneous conception of the subject matter of class analysis; it is in this sense a false problem. The substance of the solution of the second and third problems is a matter of class theory itself and will therefore be postponed to subsequent chapters; these preliminary considerations aim only at the precise formulation of questions relating to these problems. The solution of the fourth problem follows from our earlier discussions and can therefore be formulated here.

(1) For more than thirty years the distinction between "subjective" or "subjectivist" and "objective" or "objectivist" concepts and even theories of class—a distinction that is as unclear as it is superfluous—has deflected sociological discussion from the proper field of

class analysis. It is little surprising that in this discussion the rubber terms "objective" and "subjective" were themselves subject to many a fluctuation of meaning. If we return here briefly to this question, we do so only because it might appear to have something to do with the relation between (subjective?) individuals and (objective?) social classes.

By "subjective" theories of class most classifiers mean conceptions which are in some sense "social psychological" (Geiger), according to which "a man belongs to the class that he feels he belongs to" (Marshall, 58, p. 93) and which "seek the cause of social classes entirely 'within' the members of a class, in their psyche and values" (Croner, 129, p. 154). Analogously, "objective" theories try "to determine the basis of class exclusively by 'objective' data, i.e., by data which are given in the environment, the conditions of existence, etc., of the members of classes" (Croner, 129, p. 148); such theories "represent class as automatically determined by definite criteria, especially wealth and occupation" (Marshall, 58, p. 93). Thus, this is supposed to be a classification of theories of class according to the determinant of social class; it is asserted that this determinant can be found either within the individual class members or in conditions outside them. At first sight, this distinction may appear plausible, but upon closer inspection it turns out to be both meaningless and misleading.

Let us look first at the so-called "subjective" theories. Here, classes are based on the psyche of individuals. Croner quotes Centers, for whom "class . . . can well be regarded as a psychological phenomenon in the fullest sense of the term" (38, p. 27). If, therefore, a class exists anywhere, this means that people with common or similar "psyches" and "values" have found each other. But why do they have common "values"? Why do they have a common "class consciousness"? There are two possible answers to these questions: either this individual disposition is in fact an ultimate determinant—in which case classes are, from a sociological point of view, random phenomena, and there cannot be any theory of class; or the class consciousness, the "psychology," is in itself a phenomenon generated by and explainable in terms of social structure—in which case there can be a theory of class, but it is not "subjective." It is only fair to add that for most scholars classified as "subjectivists" psychic phenomena are in fact secondary or, which is the same thing, socially structured. Their determinant of class is in reality not the individual but the social relations in which he and others are involved.

Are, then, all theories of class "objective"? If by "objectivists" we mean people who operate with factors like "wealth" or "conditions of existence," we are dealing, as we know by now, not with theorists of class but with theorists of stratification. But if "objective" means no more than that class analysis is based on the study of conditions of social structure, such as relations of authority, then the epithet is meaningless for two reasons: first, it is hard to see what, if anything, one says about social structure by calling it "objective"; second, there never has been, and never can be, a theory of class which does not proceed from extra-individual conditions of social structure to their individual bearers.

Indeed, many of the classifiers formulate triumphantly what they call "subjective-objective" concepts of class (thus Geiger, Marshall, Croner, and others). Theirs is a cheap triumph, for it constitutes no more than the solution of a self-made task. They could have saved themselves, and us, many words by simply stating that, being sociologists, they proposed to deal with their subject matter both in its structure and in the personnel of this structure. This statement might have been a commonplace but it would have done less harm than the endless discussion of the spurious problem of "subjectivism" and "objectivism."[15]

(2) The alternative problem whether classes are generated "primarily" by the structure of social roles or by the psyche of their incumbents reveals itself as a senseless construction. If classes are a legitimate subject of sociological analysis, their determinant must be structural. But there is a genetic problem or, to be more careful, a problem of correlation with respect to the relation between social classes and the individual personalities of their members. Class consciousness, community of values, attitudes, "cultures," and behavior patterns are no less important for the theory of class just because they are assumed to be structured. We have to differentiate, here, between the determinant of classes and their empirical character. Empirically, of course, classes consist of human individuals. Even if individuals are members of classes only as incumbents of certain roles—i.e., with a sector of their personalities—problems of attitude and behavior must be raised. No theory of class can ignore them. In particular it will

---

[15] By way of qualification of this polemical conclusion it is only fair to add that there is in fact a difference of emphasis among different theories of class. Thus, it is undoubtedly true that Marx has put less emphasis on the psychological aspects of class action than Centers. But this differential distribution of emphasis cannot justify any inference as to the nature of class theory.

be necessary to include in the formulation of such a theory certain generalizations regarding the questions: (*a*) which motivational directives follow quasi-automatically from the incumbency of social roles relevant for class conflict (class interests), (*b*) under which conditions these structured directives become conscious motives recognized by the individual (class consciousness), and (*c*) by which additional common features of primarily psychological reality social classes or some of their forms are characterized (class culture). All these problems are closely allied with the systematic formulation of class theory. We shall therefore have to deal with them in some detail in the subsequent chapters.

(3) The problems of motivation and class behavior are evidently closely connected with a further problem which we have encountered repeatedly, most recently in the quotations at the beginning of this section. I mean the question: how permanent is an individual's membership in a class, and how permanent has it to be in order for classes to persist and operate as such? Here, sociologists hold widely divergent opinions. Whereas for Renner "class position is almost without exception lasting, comprising the whole life and the sequence of generations," for Schumpeter classes "never consist of the same family individuals for any length of time." This, too, is a problem in the personnel of social classes, the solution of which does not by any means follow from the analysis of the structural determinant of class but requires, instead, an independent investigation. It touches on the problem of social mobility of individuals within and between generations. However, as with the psychology of social classes, their stability and solidarity can adequately be dealt with only in the context of the systematic exposition of class theory. We shall return to this problem in the subsequent chapters of this study.

(4) However, the problem of the relation between individuals and classes that underlies all others can be solved with the elements assembled so far. On the one hand, classes are somehow based on a structural arrangement of social roles; on the other hand, they consist of persons. How do these two get together? How are social classes recruited? How does the individual become a member of a class? Are people born into classes, or do they acquire membership by achievement? These questions, which appear without fail in any analysis of social structure, refer to the problem of role allocation or of the recruitment of the personnel for social roles. They can be answered by analogy to general sociological procedure. Class conflict results ultimately from the distribution of authority in social organizations.

Classes are based on the differences in legitimate power associated with certain positions, i.e., on the structure of social roles with respect to their authority expectations. It follows from this that an individual becomes a member of a class by playing a social role relevant from the point of view of authority.[16] Since any role in any social organization coordinated by authority is relevant in this sense, and since, further, every individual belongs at least to political society, every individual belongs by virtue of such membership to at least one class. He belongs to a class because he occupies a position in a social organization; i.e., class membership is derived from the incumbency of a social role. In this sense the criterion of allocation of individuals and classes is subordinated to the criterion of the allocation of individuals and authority roles. The question "How does the individual become a member of the working class?" can be reduced to "How does he become a worker?"

If Schumpeter states in general that the individual "is born into a certain class position," this statement is as a general proposition false. The individual is born into a class position only in societies in which he is born into a position endowed with or deprived of authority. If participation in governmental functions, or exclusion from these, is hereditary, class membership, too, is hereditary. If, on the other hand, admission to positions of authority is based on individual ability or achievement, class membership, too, is achieved. The industrial worker who, by virtue of a law, is elected an executive of an industrial enterprise thereby changes both his authority position and his (industrial) class membership. The principle of recruitment to social classes must respond to the relevant social structures. The determination of class is therefore a task of empirical inquiry and cannot be made in general; it can be made only for specific societies.

With some qualifications, this conclusion also holds for the question whether the "physical person" or the family (the "effective kinship unit") is the "true individual" of a social class. This question cannot be decided in general either; it is meaningful only in the context of specific arrangements of social structure. In a society in which the wife, children, and possibly even other relatives of an entrepreneur "borrow" their entire social position from him, can replace him in it, and share his social position in this sense at least potentially, the (extended) family is indeed the "individual" of a class. But if social

[16] In the next chapter, this statement will be qualified by the distinction between quasi-groups and interest groups. Properly speaking, the present analysis holds for quasi-groups only; interest groups presuppose additional factors.

positions are fundamentally individualized, if wife and children of a manager can make no claim to his position when he retires or dies, then the "physical person" is also the individual of the class, and it is therefore possible for members of the same family to belong not only to different classes (classes generated by different imperatively coordinated associations) but, indeed, to opposing classes (classes opposed within the same association). The manifold empirical types of class will become more apparent in the course of our investigation; criteria of recruitment give an indication of their possible differentiation.

THE CONCEPT AND THEORY OF CLASS

Several early German sociologists have carried on a passionate debate about a problem which is not dissimilar to that of "subjectivist" and "objectivist" theories of class and has in fact explicitly been identified with this problem by Geiger. This problem, too, relates to the concept of class and was always formulated as an alternative: Are classes a "real phenomenon" (*Realphänomen*) or a "theoretical phenomenon" (*Ordnungsphänomen*)? Are they realities or constructions of science? "The term class," Geiger says (91, p. 2), "occurs on the one hand as the abstract of men of one *type*, and on the other hand as the concept of a *collectivity*. . . . In the first case men are classified on the basis of certain characteristics or sets of characteristics ['theoretical phenomenon'—R.D.]. . . . The concept of class as a collectivity has a different origin. . . . Class in this sense is the concept of a social entity which as such involves a specific goal and intention, is the concept of a specific totality" ['real phenomenon'—R.D.]. Even before Geiger, Schumpeter had introduced a similar distinction between class as a "particular social creature which acts and suffers as such and wants to be understood as such" ['real phenomenon'] and class in the sense of "orders of pluralities according to certain characteristics. Understood in this sense class is a creature of the scientist and owes its existence to his ordering hand" ['theoretical phenomenon'] (27, pp. 149 f.).[17] Both Geiger and Schumpeter emphatically decide in favor of an understanding of class as a "real phenomenon" and relegate the "theoretical phenomenon" to a lower level of analysis. But both have overlooked the fact that they have fallen victim, here, to a false problem much like the classifiers of "subjectivism" and "objectivism."

The concept of class as described so far in this study has, indeed,

---

[17] The same "problem" reappears in some recent American discussions of the sociology of class, for which cf. Lenski (54).

two distinct aspects. On the one hand, we have dealt with classes as effective forces in social conflicts, even as organized groupings carrying on such conflicts. As such, classes are obviously "real phenomena," i.e., empirically identifiable "social entities" or "creatures." On the other hand, we have derived classes from positions in associations coordinated by authority and defined them by the "characteristic" of participation in or exclusion from the exercise of authority. In this sense, classes are evidently "theoretical phenomena," "creatures of the scientist," and not organized groupings. There can be no doubt that there is a difference between these two "definitions." But is it necessary to decide in favor of one or the other of these "definitions"? Are they really mutually exclusive alternatives? These questions can be answered in the affirmative only if one is concerned not with a theory of class but merely with the formulation of a descriptive category. Whoever answers it in the affirmative thereby explicitly renounces the development of a theory of class.

As with the case of alternative "subjective" or "objective" concepts, the fallacy of the problem derives from the fact that what is basically an analytical or genetic problem is projected, so to speak, from the third into the second dimension and thereby falsely creates what appears to be a logical alternative. One can contrast a caterpillar and a butterfly and state triumphantly that they are different, but then one must not be surprised to find that a "two-dimensional" treatment of this kind does not permit the question as to whether the one may have developed out of the other. In the case of classes, no problem of genesis in this real sense is involved, but we do find an analogous situation on the level of analysis. One may of course confine oneself to describing the "real phenomenon" and the "theoretical phenomenon" of class as an "alternative of formal-logical possibilities" (Geiger, 91, p. 2). But if one does so, it is no longer possible to ask whether the structural analysis of the one requires the assumption of the other. Analyses, explanations, theories are always "creatures of the scientist," and this holds for their elements, too. But can this be regarded as an objection? Is it not rather the very point and substance of all science to explain "real phenomena" in terms of "theoretical phenomena" by dissecting the living richness of the one with the tools of the other and reconstructing it on the level of theory?

Schumpeter and Geiger were indeed on doubtful ground not only in constructing an artificial alternative, but also in deciding unconditionally for one of its sides. Their choice can at best be accepted and considered as a methodological principle, but even as such it is not justifiable. It may be useful to start the formulation of theories by considering real problems instead of by constructing "reality" out of the skies of theory; it may be sensible to derive the general from the particular, instead of starting with the general. However, reasonable as this procedure may be from the point of view of the psychology of scientific discovery, it is erroneous to derive from it a principle of the logic of scientific discovery. Logically, at least, a theory takes precedence over a hypothesis, a hypothesis over a descriptive statement. Moreover, it is empirically of no consequence for the validity of a theory whether it be formulated with a view to one, ten, or a hundred "real phenomena" or, indeed, independent of these *in abstracto*. What matters, rather, is whether and how a theory illuminates its proper area of reality, and whether empirical processes refute the hypothesis derived from the theory.

Many of the considerations of this chapter were concerned with the determinant and context of the concept of class. It was necessary, first of all, to clarify the most important prerequisites of a sociological theory of class. But as an isolated category the concept of class is meaningless even for purely descriptive purposes. The statement that the managers or bureaucrats of industry constitute an industrial class is more than a mere designation, an empty *quid pro quo*, only if "class" is not merely a defined term but a category embedded in a theory. Concept and theory of class are inseparably connected. For this reason, the considerations of this chapter have been more than a mere discussion or definition of the concept of class; at every stage they pointed beyond the category of class into the field of class theory. Before we embark on a systematic discussion of this theory, it seems appropriate to try and delimit its field a little.

Class theory is concerned with the systematic explanation of that particular form of structure-changing conflict which is carried on by aggregates or groups growing out of the authority structure of social organizations. The general theory of class precedes the empirical analysis of given societies in terms of class in that it states the underlying regularities of class conflict in a form that in principle allows application to all societies. But the following formulation of the theory of class does not claim universal applicability, for such applicability is always subject to the test of empirical research; it is confined, instead, to that type of society which we have described as industrial society. Its extension to other types of society may be possible and will in fact be suggested at several points; but a thorough discussion of class theory on this most general level falls outside the limits of the present investigation.

The general theory of class consists of two analytically separable elements: the theory of class formation and the theory of class action, or class conflict. Schumpeter does not sufficiently recognize this distinction if he differentiates between the problems of the "essence of the phenomenon," "class association," "class formation," and the "concrete causes and conditions of an individually specific, historically given class structure" (27, p. 151). By the "problem of essence" he seems to understand, above all, the problem of definition, which is preliminary from the point of view of class theory. The problems of "class association" ("How and why do classes hang together?") and "class formation" ("How do classes originate?") belong together and will here be dealt with under the one heading of class formation. The problem of concrete empirical conditions of given class structures is part of the theory of class only by privation: the theory must make clear where its general propositions must be supplemented with empirical observations and where only empirical generalizations, not "laws" or postulates, are possible. Schumpeter does not even formulate the important problem of the regularities of class conflict and the relations between classes.[18]

The *theory of class formation*—which will be dealt with in Chapter V—is concerned with the question of analyzing the "genesis" of social classes. The theory must establish relations which connect the specific "real phenomenon" class by way of the "theoretical phenomenon" class with patterns of social structure, and in this sense derive social classes from social structure. This is evidently a problem of genesis, but it will prove useful to use this word in quotes. The analytical reduction ("explanation") of social classes to structural conditions cannot be understood as an empirical generalization of what actually happens in the emergence and formation of classes. In making a structural analysis of the class phenomenon we do not assert that a given arrangement of structure "necessarily" results in the full formation of organized classes, or that every step of analysis reflects a factual stage of development in the history of given classes. In so far as the theory of class formation is a scientific theory, it can neither presuppose, nor imply, nor give rise to empirical generalizations that are usually of doubtful logical status.

The *theory of class action*, or class conflict—which will be dealt with in Chapter VI—is based on the theory of class formation. Its subject matter consists in the general analytical elements of the inter-

[18] Evidently the reason for this omission is that Schumpeter's concept of class is in fact—as we found above—a concept of social stratum.

relations between classes conceived as structural phenomena. It is concerned in particular with patterns of class conflict and the regulation of class conflict. This aspect of the theory of class appears to come close to the limits of the possibility of theoretical analysis. It will indeed be our task, here, to determine, in the light of class theory, the area and types of variability of empirical classes, class conflicts, and changes caused by class conflict, and to define the points at which the theory of class has to be supplemented by empirical generalizations.

PART TWO

Toward a Sociological Theory of Conflict in Industrial Society

V

Social Structure, Group Interests, and Conflict Groups

Throughout the history of Western political thought, two views of society have stood in conflict. Both these views are intended to explain what has been, and will probably continue to be, the most puzzling problem of social philosophy: how is it that human societies cohere? There is one large and distinguished school of thought according to which social order results from a general agreement of values, a *consensus omnium* or *volonté générale* which outweighs all possible or actual differences of opinion and interest. There is another equally distinguished school of thought which holds that coherence and order in society are founded on force and constraint, on the domination of some and the subjection of others. To be sure, these views are not at all points mutually exclusive. The Utopian (as we shall call those who insist on coherence by consensus) does not deny the existence of differences of interest; nor does the Rationalist (who believes in coherence by constraint and domination) ignore such agreements of value as are required for the very establishment of force. But Utopian and Rationalist alike advance claims of primacy for their respective standpoints. For the Utopian, differences of interest are subordinated to agreements of value, and for the Rationalist these agreements are but a thin, and as such ineffective, coating of the primary reality of differences that have to be precariously reconciled by constraint. Both Utopians and Rationalists have shown much ingenuity and imagination in arguing for their respective points of view. This has not, however, led them more closely together. There is a genuine conflict of approach between Aristotle and Plato, Hobbes and Rousseau, Hegel and Kant, and this conflict has grown in intensity as the history of thought has advanced. Unless one believes that all philosophical disputes are spurious and ultimately irrelevant, the long history of the particular dispute about the problem of social order has exposed—if not solved—what appear to be fundamental alternatives of knowledge, moral decision, and political orientation.

Conflicting philosophical positions must inevitably, it seems to me, reappear constantly in theories of science. Even if this should not generally be the case, I would claim that the philosophical alternative of a Utopian or a Rational solution of the problem of order pervades modern sociological thinking even in its remotest manifestations. Here, as elsewhere, philosophical positions do not enter into scientific theories unchanged. Here, as elsewhere, they pass through the filter of logical supposition before they become relevant for testable explanations of problems of experience. The sociological Utopian does not claim that order *is based on* a general consensus of values, but that it *can be conceived of in terms of* such consensus, and that, if it is conceived of in these terms, certain propositions follow which are subject to the test of specific observations. Analogously, for the sociological Rationalist the assumption of the coercive nature of social order is a heuristic principle rather than a judgment of fact. But this obvious reservation does not prevent the Utopians and the Rationalists of sociology from engaging in disputes which are hardly less intense (if often rather less imaginative and ingenious) than those of their philosophical antecedents. The subject matter of our concern in this study demands that we take a stand with respect to this dispute.

Twice in our earlier considerations we have been faced with differences in the image of society—as I then called it—which correspond very closely to the conflicting views of Utopians and Rationalists. I have tried to show that, at least in so far as historical societies are concerned, Marx subscribed to an image of society of the Rational variety. He assumed the ubiquity of change and conflict as well as domination and subjection, and I suggest that this view seems particularly appropriate for the analysis of problems of conflict. In any case, it seems more appropriate than the Utopian view implicit in the works of Drucker and Mayo, according to which happy cooperation is the normal state of social life. Marx, or Drucker and Mayo, may not be especially convincing representatives of these views,[1] but the distinction with which we are concerned here is, in

---

[1] This would be true, of course, for rather different reasons. Drucker and Mayo are rather lacking in subtlety, and it is therefore too easy to polemicize against their positions. Marx, on the other hand, is certainly subtle, but his notions of the "original" and the "terminal" societies of (imaginary) history demonstrate that he was but a limited Rationalist with strong Utopian leanings. Such mixtures of views really quite incompatible are in fact not rare in the history of social thought.

any case, not tied to their names. Generally speaking, it seems to me that two (meta-)theories can and must be distinguished in contemporary sociology. One of these, the *integration theory of society*, conceives of social structure in terms of a functionally integrated system held in equilibrium by certain patterned and recurrent processes. The other one, the *coercion theory of society*, views social structure as a form of organization held together by force and constraint and reaching continuously beyond itself in the sense of producing within itself the forces that maintain it in an unending process of change. Like their philosophical counterparts, these theories are mutually exclusive. But—if I may be permitted a paradoxical formulation that will be explained presently—in sociology (as opposed to philosophy) a decision which accepts one of these theories and rejects the other is neither necessary nor desirable. There are sociological problems for the explanation of which the integration theory of society provides adequate assumptions; there are other problems which can be explained only in terms of the coercion theory of society; there are, finally, problems for which both theories appear adequate. For sociological analysis, society is Janus-headed, and its two faces are equivalent aspects of the same reality.

In recent years, the integration theory of society has clearly dominated sociological thinking. In my opinion, this prevalence of one partial view has had many unfortunate consequences. However, it has also had at least one agreeable consequence, in that the very onesidedness of this theory gave rise to critical objections which enable us today to put this theory in its proper place. Such objections have been stimulated with increasing frequency by the works of the most eminent sociological theorist of integration, Talcott Parsons. It is not necessary here to attempt a comprehensive exposition of Parsons' position; nor do we have to survey the sizable literature concerned with a critical appraisal of this position. To be sure, much of this criticism is inferior in subtlety and insight to Parsons' work, so that it is hardly surprising that the sociological climate of opinion has remained almost unaffected by Parsons' critics. There is one objection to Parsons' position, however, which we have to examine if we are to make a systematic presentation of a theory of group conflict. In a remarkable essay, D. Lockwood claims "that Parsons' array of concepts is heavily weighted by assumptions and categories which relate to the role of *normative* elements in social action, and especially to the processes whereby motives are structured normatively to ensure social stability. On the other hand, what may be called the *substratum* of social action, especially as it conditions interests which are productive of social conflict and instability, tends to be ignored as a general determinant of the dynamics of social systems" (210, p. 136). Lockwood's claim touches on the core of our problem of the two faces of society—although his formulation does not, perhaps, succeed in exposing the problem with sufficient clarity.

It is certainly true that the work of Parsons displays a conspicuous bias in favor of analysis in terms of values and norms. It is equally true that many of those who have been concerned with problems of conflict rather than of stability have tended to emphasize not the normative but the institutional aspects of social structure. The work of Marx is a case in point. Probably, this difference in emphasis is no accident. It is nevertheless as such irrelevant to an understanding of or adoption of the alternative images of society which pervade political thought and sociological theory. The alternative between "normative elements in social action" and a factual "substratum of social action," which Lockwood takes over from the work of Renner, in fact indicates two levels of the analysis of social structure which are in no way contradictory. There is no theoretical reason why Talcott Parsons should not have supplemented (as indeed he occasionally does) his analysis of normative integration by an analysis of the integration of social systems in terms of their institutional substratum. However we look at social structure, it always presents itself as composed of a moral and a factual, a normative and an institutional, level or, in the doubtful terms of Marx, a superstructure and a substratum. The investigator is free to choose which of these levels he wants to emphasize more strongly—although he may be well-advised, in the interest of clarity as well as of comprehensiveness of his analysis, not to stress one of these levels to the exclusion of the other.

At the same time, there is an important element of genuine critique in Lockwood's objection to Parsons. When Lockwood contrasts stability and instability, integration and conflict, equilibrium and disequilibrium, values and interests, he puts his finger on a real alternative of thought, and one of which Parsons has apparently not been sufficiently aware. For of two equivalent models of society, Parsons has throughout his work recognized only one, the Utopian or integration theory of society. His "array of concepts" is therefore incapable of coping with those problems with which Lockwood is concerned in his critical essay, and which constitute the subject matter of the present study.

For purposes of exposition it seems useful to reduce each of the two faces of society to a small number of basic tenets, even if this involves some degree of oversimplification as well as overstatement. The integration theory of society, as displayed by the work of Parsons and other structural-functionalists, is founded on a number of assumptions of the following type:

(1) Every society is a relatively persistent, stable structure of elements.

(2) Every society is a well-integrated structure of elements.

(3) Every element in a society has a function, i.e., renders a contribution to its maintenance as a system.

(4) Every functioning social structure is based on a consensus of values among its members.

In varying forms, these elements of (1) stability, (2) integration, (3) functional coordination, and (4) consensus recur in all structural-functional approaches to the study of social structure. They are, to be sure, usually accompanied by protestations to the effect that stability, integration, functional coordination, and consensus are only "relatively" generalized. Moreover, these assumptions are not metaphysical propositions about the essence of society; they are merely assumptions for purposes of scientific analysis. As such, however, they constitute a coherent view of the social process[2] which enables us to comprehend many problems of social reality.

However, it is abundantly clear that the integration approach to social analysis does not enable us to comprehend all problems of social reality. Let us look at two undeniably sociological problems of the contemporary world which demand explanation. (1) In recent years, an increasing number of industrial and commercial enterprises have introduced the position of personnel manager to cope with matters of hiring and firing, advice to employees, etc. Why? And: what are the consequences of the introduction of this new position? (2) On the 17th of June, 1953, the building workers of East Berlin put down their tools and went on a strike that soon led to a generalized revolt against the Communist regime of East Germany. Why? And: what are the consequences of this uprising? From the point of view of the integration model of society, the first of these problems is susceptible

---

[2] It is important to emphasize that "stability" as a tenet of the integration theory of society does not mean that societies are "static." It means, rather, that such processes as do occur (and the structural-functional approach is essentially concerned with processes) serve to maintain the patterns of the system as a whole. Whatever criticism I have of this approach, I do not want to be misunderstood as attributing to it a "static bias" (which has often been held against this approach without full consideration of its merits).

of a satisfactory solution. A special position to cope with personnel questions is functionally required by large enterprises in an age of rationalization and "social ethic"; the introduction of this position adapts the enterprise to the values of the surrounding society; its consequence is therefore of an integrative and stabilizing nature. But what about the second problem? Evidently, the uprising of the 17th of June is neither due to nor productive of integration in East German society. It documents and produces not stability, but instability. It contributes to the disruption, not the maintenance, of the existing system. It testifies to dissensus rather than consensus. The integration model tells us little more than that there are certain "strains" in the "system." In fact, in order to cope with problems of this kind we have to replace the integration theory of society by a different and, in many ways, contradictory model.

What I have called the coercion theory of society can also be reduced to a small number of basic tenets, although here again these assumptions oversimplify and overstate the case:

(1) Every society is at every point subject to processes of change; social change is ubiquitous.

(2) Every society displays at every point dissensus and conflict; social conflict is ubiquitous.

(3) Every element in a society renders a contribution to its disintegration and change.

(4) Every society is based on the coercion of some of its members by others.

If we return to the problem of the German workers' strike, it will become clear that this latter model enables us to deal rather more satisfactorily with its causes and consequences. The revolt of the building workers and their fellows in other industries can be explained in terms of coercion.[3] The revolting groups are engaged in a conflict which "functions" as an agent of change by disintegration. A ubiquitous phenomenon is expressed, in this case, in an exceptionally intense and violent way, and further explanation will have to account for this violence on the basis of the acceptance of conflict and change as universal features of social life. I need hardly add that, like the integration model, the coercion theory of society constitutes but a set of assumptions for purposes of scientific analysis and implies no claim

[3] For purposes of clarity, I have deliberately chosen an example from a totalitarian state. But coercion is meant here in a very general sense, and the coercion model is applicable to all societies, independent of their specific political structure.

for philosophical validity—although, like its counterpart, this model also provides a coherent image of social organization.

Now, I would claim that, in a sociological context, neither of these models can be conceived as exclusively valid or applicable. They constitute complementary, rather than alternative, aspects of the structure of total societies as well as of every element of this structure. We have to choose between them only for the explanation of specific problems; but in the conceptual arsenal of sociological analysis they exist side by side. Whatever criticism one may have of the advocates of one or the other of these models can therefore be directed only against claims for the exclusive validity of either.[4] Strictly speaking, both models are "valid" or, rather, useful and necessary for sociological analysis. We cannot conceive of society unless we realize the dialectics of stability and change, integration and conflict, function and motive force, consensus and coercion. In the context of this study, I regard this point as demonstrated by the analysis of the exemplary problems sketched above.

It is perhaps worth emphasizing that the thesis of the two faces of social structure does not require a complete, or even partial, revision of the conceptual apparatus that by now has become more or less generally accepted by sociologists in all countries. Categories like role, institution, norm, structure, even function are as useful in terms of the coercion model as they are for the analysis of social integration. In fact, the dichotomy of aspects can be carried through all levels of sociological analysis; that is, it can be shown that, like social structure itself, the notions of role and institution, integration and function, norm and substratum have two faces which may be expressed by two terms, but which may also in many cases be indicated by an extension of concepts already in use. "Interest and value," Radcliffe-Brown once remarked, "are correlative terms, which refer to the two sides of an asymmetrical relation" (221, p. 199). The notions of interest and value indeed seem to describe very well the two faces of the normative superstructure of society: what appears as a consensus of values on the basis of the integration theory can be regarded as a conflict of interests in terms of the coercion theory. Similarly, what

[4] This, it seems to me, is the only—if fundamental—legitimate criticism that can be raised against Parsons' work on this general level. In *The Social System*, Parsons repeatedly advances, for the integration theory of society, a claim that it is the nucleus of "the general" sociological theory—a claim which I regard as utterly unjustified. It is Lockwood's main concern also, in the essay quoted above, to reject this claim to universal validity.

appears on the level of the factual substratum as integration from the point of view of the former model presents itself as coercion or constraint from the point of view of the latter. We shall presently have occasion to explore these two faces of societies and their elements rather more thoroughly with reference to the two categories of power and of role.

While logically feasible,[5] the solution of the dilemma of political thought which we have offered here for the more restricted field of sociological analysis nevertheless raises a number of serious problems. It is evidently virtually impossible to think of society in terms of either model without positing its opposite number at the same time. There can be no conflict, unless this conflict occurs within a context of meaning, i.e., some kind of coherent "system." No conflict is conceivable between French housewives and Chilean chess players, because these groups are not united by, or perhaps "integrated into," a common frame of reference. Analogously, the notion of integration makes little sense unless it presupposes the existence of different elements that are integrated. Even Rousseau derived his *volonté générale* from a modified *bellum omnium contra omnes*. Using one or the other model is therefore a matter of emphasis rather than of fundamental difference; and there are, as we shall see, many points at which a theory of group conflict has to have recourse to the integration theory of social structure.

Inevitably, the question will be raised, also, whether a unified theory of society that includes the tenets of both the integration and the coercion models of society is not at least conceivable—for as to its desirability there can be little doubt. Is there, or can there be, a general point of view that synthesizes the unsolved dialectics of integration and coercion? So far as I can see, there is no such general model; as to its possibility, I have to reserve judgment. It seems at least conceivable that unification of theory is not feasible at a point which has puzzled thinkers ever since the beginning of Western philosophy.

For the explanation of the formation of conflict groups out of conditions of social structure, we shall employ a model that emphasizes the ugly face of society. In the following sections of this chap-

---

[5] As is demonstrated most clearly by the fact that a similar situation can be encountered in physics with respect to the theory of light. Here, too, there are two seemingly incompatible theories which nevertheless exist side by side, and each of which has its proper realm of empirical phenomena: the wave theory and the quantum theory of light.

ter I shall try to show how, on the assumption of the coercive nature of social structure, relations of authority become productive of clashes of role interest which under certain conditions lead to the formation of organized antagonistic groups within limited social organizations as well as within total societies. By proceeding step by step along these lines, we shall eventually be in a position to contrast the rudiments of a sociological theory of group conflict with such earlier approaches as have been discussed in the first part of this study, and to decide whether the category of class is still a useful tool of sociological analysis.

POWER AND AUTHORITY

From the point of view of the integration theory of social structure, units of social analysis ("social systems") are essentially voluntary associations of people who share certain values and set up institutions in order to ensure the smooth functioning of cooperation. From the point of view of coercion theory, however, the units of social analysis present an altogether different picture. Here, it is not voluntary cooperation or general consensus but enforced constraint that makes social organizations cohere. In institutional terms, this means that in every social organization some positions are entrusted with a right to exercise control over other positions in order to ensure effective coercion; it means, in other words, that there is a differential distribution of power and authority. One of the central theses of this study consists in the assumption that this differential distribution of authority invariably becomes the determining factor of systematic social conflicts of a type that is germane to class conflicts in the traditional (Marxian) sense of this term. The structural origin of such group conflicts must be sought in the arrangement of social roles endowed with expectations of domination or subjection. Wherever there are such roles, group conflicts of the type in question are to be expected. Differentiation of groups engaged in such conflicts follows the lines of differentiation of roles that are relevant from the point of view of the exercise of authority. Identification of variously equipped authority roles is the first task of conflict analysis;[6] concep-

---

[6] To facilitate communication, I shall employ in this study a number of abbreviations. These must not however be misunderstood. Thus, "conflict analysis" in this context stands for "analysis of group conflicts of the class type, class being understood in the traditional sense." At no point do I want to imply a claim for a generalized theory of social conflict.

tually and empirically all further steps of analysis follow from the investigation of distributions of power and authority.

"Unfortunately, the concept of power is not a settled one in the social sciences, either in political science or in sociology" (Parsons, 201, p. 139). Max Weber (33), Pareto (25), Mosca (24), later Russell (203), Bendix (126), Lasswell (200), and others have explored some of the dimensions of this category; they have not, however, reached such a degree of consensus as would enable us to employ the categories of power and authority without at least brief conceptual preliminaries. So far as the terms "power" and "authority" and their distinction are concerned, I shall follow in this study the useful and well-considered definitions of Max Weber. For Weber, power is the "probability that one actor within a social relationship will be in a position to carry out his own will despite resistance, regardless of the basis on which this probability rests"; whereas authority (*Herrschaft*) is the "probability that a command with a given specific content will be obeyed by a given group of persons" (33*b*, p. 28). The important difference between power and authority consists in the fact that whereas power is essentially tied to the personality of individuals, authority is always associated with social positions or roles. The demagogue has power over the masses to whom he speaks or whose actions he controls; but the control of the officer over his men, the manager over his workers, the civil servant over his clientele is authority, because it exists as an expectation independent of the specific person occupying the position of officer, manager, civil servant. It is only another way of putting this difference if we say—as does Max Weber—that while power is merely a factual relation, authority is a legitimate relation of domination and subjection. In this sense, authority can be described as legitimate power.

In the present study we are concerned exclusively with relations of authority, for these alone are part of social structure and therefore permit the systematic derivation of group conflicts from the organization of total societies and associations within them. The significance of such group conflicts rests with the fact that they are not the product of structurally fortuitous relations of power but come forth wherever authority is exercised—and that means in all societies under all historical conditions. (1) Authority relations are always relations of super- and subordination. (2) Where there are authority relations, the superordinate element is socially expected to control, by orders and commands, warnings and prohibitions, the behavior of the subordinate element. (3) Such expectations attach to relatively permanent social positions rather than to the character of individuals; they are in this sense legitimate. (4) By virtue of this fact, they always involve specification of the persons subject to control and of the spheres within which control is permissible.[7] Authority, as distinct from power, is never a relation of generalized control over others. (5) Authority being a legitimate relation, noncompliance with authoritative commands can be sanctioned; it is indeed one of the functions of the legal system (and of course of quasi-legal customs and norms) to support the effective exercise of legitimate authority.

Alongside the term "authority," we shall employ (and have employed) in this study the terms "domination" and "subjection." These will be used synonymously with the rather clumsy expressions "endowed with authority" or "participating in the exercise of authority" (domination), and "deprived of authority" or "excluded from the exercise of authority" (subjection).

It seems desirable for purposes of conflict analysis to specify the relevant unit of social organization in analogy to the concept of social system in the analysis of integration. To speak of specification here is perhaps misleading. "Social system" is a very general concept applicable to all types of organization; and we shall want to employ an equally general concept which differs from that of social system by emphasizing a different aspect of the same organizations. It seems to me that Max Weber's category "imperatively coordinated association" (*Herrschaftsverband*) serves this purpose despite its clumsiness.[8]

In conflict analysis we are concerned *inter alia* with the generation of conflict groups by the authority relations obtaining in imperatively coordinated associations. Since imperative coordination, or authority, is a type of social relation present in every conceivable social

[7] This element of the definition of authority is crucial. It implies that the manager who tries to control people outside his firm, or the private lives of people inside his firm, trespasses the borderline between authority and power. Although he has authority over people in his firm, his control assumes the form of power as soon as it goes beyond the specified persons and spheres of legitimate control. This type of trespassing is of course frequent in every authority relation; and an empirical phenomenon well worth investigating is to what extent the fusion of authority and power tends to intensify group conflicts.

[8] Parsons, in his translation of Weber's *Wirtschaft und Gesellschaft*, suggests "imperatively coordinated group." Any translation of Weber's term is bound to be somewhat awkward, but it seems to me that the word "group" in Parsons' translation is false. Weber uses *Verband*, e.g., to describe the state, or a church—units of organization which can hardly be called "groups." "Association" is probably as precise an English equivalent of *Verband* as is likely to be found.

organization, it will be sufficient to describe such organizations simply as associations. Despite prolonged terminological discussions, no general agreement has been attained by sociologists on the precise meaning of the categories "organization," "association," and "institution." If I am not mistaken in my interpretation of the trend of terminological disputes, it appears justifiable to use the term "association" in such a way as to imply the coordination of organized aggregates of roles by domination and subjection. The state, a church, an enterprise, but also a political party, a trade union, and a chess club are associations in this sense. In all of them, authority relations exist; for all of them, conflict analysis is therefore applicable. If at a later stage we shall suggest restriction to the two great associations of the state and the industrial enterprise, this suggestion is dictated merely by considerations of empirical significance, not logical (or definitional) difference. In looking at social organizations not in terms of their integration and coherence but from the point of view of their structure of coercion and constraint, we regard them as (imperatively coordinated) associations rather than as social systems. Because social organizations are also associations, they generate conflicts of interest and become the birthplace of conflict groups.

I have assumed in the preceding remarks that authority is a characteristic of social organizations as general as society itself. Despite the assertion of Renner—and other modern sociologists—that in some contemporary societies the exercise of authority has been eliminated and replaced by the more anonymous "rule of the law" or other non-authoritative relations, I should indeed maintain that authority is a universal element of social structure. It is in this sense more general than, for example, property, or even status. With respect to post-capitalist industrial society, I hope to establish this position more unambiguously in the final chapters of this study. Generally speaking, however, the universality of authority relations would seem evident as soon as we describe these relations in a "passive" rather than in an "active" sense. Authority relations exist wherever there are people whose actions are subject to legitimate and sanctioned prescriptions that originate outside them but within social structure. This formulation, by leaving open who exercises what kind of authority, leaves little doubt as to the omnipresence of some kind of authority somehow exercised. For it is evident that there are many forms and types of authority in historical societies. There are differences of a considerable order of magnitude between the relations of the citizen of classical Athens and his slaves, the feudal landlord and his villeins and serfs, the nineteenth-century capitalist and his workers, the secretary of a totalitarian state party and its members, the appointed manager of a modern enterprise and its employees, or the elected prime minister of a democratic country and the electorate. No attempt will be made in this study to develop a typology of authority. But it is assumed throughout that the existence of domination and subjection is a common feature of all possible types of authority and, indeed, of all possible types of association and organization.

The notion of power and authority employed in the present study represents what Parsons in a critical review of C. W. Mills's book on the American power elite (63) calls the "zero-sum" concept of authority. Parsons objects to this concept, and his argument provides a welcome opportunity to clarify our notion somewhat further and relate it to the two models distinguished above. "The essential point at present is that, to Mills [and of course to us in this study—R.D.], power is not a facility for the performance of function in and on behalf of the society as a system, but is interpreted exclusively as a facility for getting what one group, the holders of power, wants by preventing another group, the 'outs,' from getting what it wants" (201, p. 139). This statement is unobjectionable, and in so far as Mills really uses power "exclusively" in the "zero-sum" sense, I should tend to agree also with Parsons' critique. But then Parsons continues, in the same passage, to make the same mistake in the opposite direction, and to make it deliberately and consideredly: "What this conception does is to elevate *a secondary and derived aspect of a total phenomenon* into the central place" [italics mine]. Not surprisingly, Parsons continues to point out what is presumably the primary and original aspect of the total phenomenon: "It is the capacity to mobilize the resources of the society for the attainment of goals for which a general 'public' commitment has been made, or may be made. It is mobilization, above all, of the action of persons and groups, which is binding on them by virtue of their position in the society" (201, p. 140). A clearer exposition of the two faces of society, and of the untenable and dangerous one-sidedness of Parsons' position, is hardly conceivable.

It is certainly true that for many purposes of analysis, power or—as I should prefer to say—authority, both realizes and symbolizes the functional integration of social systems. To use a pertinent illustration: in many contexts, the elected president or prime minister of democratic countries[9] represents his country as a whole; his position

---

[9] This illustration is unambiguous with respect to the president of the United States. Elsewhere, the representative and the governmental functions are usually separated; in these cases I mean not the head of state (king, president), but the chief of government (prime minister, chancellor).

expresses therefore the unity and integration of a nation. In other contexts, however, the chief of government is but the representative of the majority party, and therefore exponent of sectional interests. I suggest that as in the position of the prime minister neither of these elements is primary or secondary, thus neither the integrative nor the disruptive aspect of authority in social analysis is primary or secondary. Like all other elements of social structure, authority has two faces— those, so to speak, of Mills and of Parsons—and on the highest level of abstraction it is illegitimate to emphasize either of these to the exclusion of the other. Authority is certainly not *only* productive of conflict; but neither is it *only* (or even primarily) "a facility for the performance of function in and on behalf of the society as a system." If we are concentrating in this study on what Parsons would call the "negative functions" of authority, we do so because this aspect is more appropriate and useful for the analysis of structurally generated systematic social conflicts.

In referring to the ugly face of authority as a "zero-sum" concept, Parsons brings out one further aspect of this category which is essential for our considerations. By zero-sum, Parsons evidently means that from the point of view of the disruptive "functions" of authority there are two groups or aggregates of persons, of which one possesses authority to the extent to which the other one is deprived of it.[10] This implies—for us, if not for Parsons—that in terms of the coercion theory of society we can always observe a dichotomy of positions in imperatively coordinated associations with respect to the distribution of authority. Parsons, in his critique of Mills, compares the distribution of authority to the distribution of wealth. It seems to me that this comparison is misleading. However unequally wealth may be distributed, there always is a continuum of possession ranging from the lowest to the highest rank. Wealth is not and cannot be conceived as a zero-sum concept. With respect to authority, however, a clear line can at least in theory be drawn between those who participate in its exercise in given associations and those who are subject to the authoritative commands of others. Our analysis of modern societies in later chapters will show that empirically it is not always easy to identify the

[10] There is one implication of the expression "zero-sum" which would be contrary to my thesis. Mathematically, it would be possible for both groups to have no authority in the sense of a complete absence of authority. I have argued above that under all conditions the authority of one aggregate is, so to speak, greater than zero, and that of the other aggregate correspondingly smaller than zero. The presence of authority, and its unequal distribution, are universal features of social structure.

border line between domination and subjection. Authority has not remained unaffected by the modern process of division of labor. But even here, groups or aggregates can be identified which do not participate in the exercise of authority other than by complying with given commands or prohibitions. Contrary to all criteria of social stratification, authority does not permit the construction of a scale. So-called hierarchies of authority (as displayed, for example, in organization charts) are in fact hierarchies of the "plus-side" of authority, i.e., of the differentiation of domination; but there is, in every association, also a "minus-side" consisting of those who are subjected to authority rather than participate in its exercise.

In two respects this analysis has to be specified, if not supplemented. First, for the individual incumbent of roles, domination in one association does not necessarily involve domination in all others to which he belongs, and subjection, conversely, in one association does not mean subjection in all. The dichotomy of positions of authority holds for specific associations only. In a democratic state, there are both mere voters and incumbents of positions of authority such as cabinet ministers, representatives, and higher civil servants. But this does not mean that the "mere voter" cannot be incumbent of a position of authority in a different context, say, in an industrial enterprise; conversely, a cabinet minister may be, in his church, a mere member, i.e., subject to the authority of others. Although empirically a certain correlation of the authority positions of individuals in different associations seems likely, it is by no means general and is in any case a matter of specific empirical conditions. It is at least possible, if not probable, that if individuals in a given society are ranked according to the sum total of their authority positions in all associations, the resulting pattern will not be a dichotomy but rather like scales of stratification according to income or prestige. For this reason it is necessary to emphasize that in the sociological analysis of group conflict the unit of analysis is always a specific association and the dichotomy of positions within it.

As with respect to the set of roles associated with an individual, total societies, also, do not usually present an unambiguously dichotomic authority structure. There are a large number of imperatively coordinated associations in any given society. Within every one of them we can distinguish the aggregates of those who dominate and those who are subjected. But since domination in industry does not necessarily involve domination in the state, or a church, or other associations, total societies can present the picture of a plurality of competing dominant (and, conversely, subjected) aggregates. This, again, is a problem for the analysis of specific historical societies and must not be confounded with the clearer lines of differentiation within any one association. Within the latter, the distribution of authority always sums up to zero, i.e., there always is a division involving domination and subjection.[11]

I need hardly emphasize that from the point of view of "settling" the concepts of power and authority, the preceding discussion has raised more problems than it has solved. I believe, however, that for the purposes of this study, and of a sociological theory of conflict, little needs to be added to what has been stated here. In order somewhat to substantiate this perhaps rather bold assertion, it seems useful to recapitulate briefly the heuristic purpose and logical status of the considerations of this section.

I have introduced, as a structural determinant of conflict groups, the category of authority as exercised in imperatively coordinated associations. While agreeing with Marx that source and level of income —even socioeconomic status—cannot usefully be conceived as determinants of conflict groups, I have added to this list of erroneous approaches Marx's own in terms of property in the means of production. Authority is both a more general and a more significant social relation. The former has been shown in our critique of Marx; the latter will have to be demonstrated by subsequent considerations and analyses. The concept of authority is used, in this context, in a specific sense. It is differentiated from power by what may roughly be referred to as the element of legitimacy; and it has to be understood throughout in the restricted sense of authority as distributed and exercised in imperatively coordinated associations. While its "disruptive" or conflict-generating consequences are not the only aspect of authority, they are the one relevant in terms of the coercion model of society. Within the frame of reference of this model, (1) the distribution of authority in associations is the ultimate "cause" of the formation of conflict groups,

---

[11] Inevitably, the qualifications introduced in the two preceding paragraphs are rather vague if stated merely in the abstract. They are, however, of the utmost importance for empirical analysis. By strictly postulating imperatively coordinated associations as units of conflict analysis, we are able to consider, e.g., the relations between industry and society as an empirical problem which allows of varying solutions in different historical contexts. Similarly we can, by this emphasis, regard subjection (and consequent deprivation) in several associations as a condition strengthening and intensifying conflict, but by no means necessary in historical situations. These and similar problems will become increasingly crucial as our investigation proceeds.

and (2), being dichotomous, it is, in any given association, the cause of the formation of two, and only two, conflict groups.

The first of these statements is logically an assumption, since it underlies scientific theories. It cannot as such be tested by observation; its validity is proven, rather, by its usefulness for purposes of explanation. We shall derive from this assumption certain more specific hypotheses which, if refuted, would take the assumption with them into the waste-paper basket of scientific theories. We assume in this sense that if we manage to identify the incumbents of positions of domination and subjection in any given association, we have identified the contenders of one significant type of conflicts—conflicts which occur in this association at all times.

As to the second statement, the one concerned with the dichotomy of authority positions in imperatively coordinated associations, it is not, I suggest, either an assumption or an empirical hypothesis, but an analytical statement. It follows from and is implicit in the very concept of authority that within specified contexts some have authority and others not. If either nobody or everybody had authority, the concept would lose its meaning. Authority implies both domination and subjection, and it therefore implies the existence of two distinct sets of positions or persons. This is not to say, of course, that there is no difference between those who have a great deal and those who have merely a little authority. Among the positions of domination there may be, and often is, considerable differentiation. But such differentiation, while important for empirical analysis, leaves unaffected the existence of a border line somewhere between those who have whatever little authority and the "outs." Strictly speaking, an analytical statement which states that there is a dichotomy of authority positions is tautological; but as this example shows, there are tautologies which are worth stating.

Having thus established the frame of reference and basic assumptions of a sociological theory of conflict, we now turn to its more specific elements—first with respect to the formation of conflict groups, then with respect to patterns of conflicts between these groups.

LATENT AND MANIFEST INTERESTS

The analytical process of conflict group formation can be described in terms of a model. Throughout, the categories employed in this model will be used in terms of the coercion theory of social structure. With this restriction in mind, the thesis that conflict groups are based on the dichotomous distribution of authority in imperatively coordinated associations can be conceived of as the basic assumption of the model. To this assumption we now add the proposition that differentially equipped authority positions in associations involve, for their incumbents, conflicting interests. The occupants of positions of domination and the occupants of positions of subjection hold, by virtue of these positions, certain interests which are contradictory in substance and direction. In the case of incumbents of ruling positions, these interests, being "ruling interests" themselves, might also be described as values; however, in the present context I propose to retain the category of interest as a general term for the orientation of dominating and subjected aggregates.

By postulating interests that are given and conditioned by positions, we encounter once again a problem which we must now face squarely. In everyday language, the word "interest" signifies intentions or directions of behavior associated with individuals rather than with their positions. It is not the position, but the individual who "is interested in something," "has an interest in something," and "finds something interesting." It might indeed appear that the notion of interest is not meaningfully conceivable other than in relation to human individuals. Interests would seem to be psychological in the strictest sense. Yet the proposition of certain antagonistic interests conditioned by, even inherent in, social positions contains precisely this apparently meaningless assertion that there can be interests which are, so to say, impressed on the individual from outside without his participation.

"As in private life we distinguish," says Marx, "between what a man thinks and says of himself and what he really is and does, so must we distinguish even more carefully in historical struggles the catchwords and fantasies of parties from their real organism and their real interests, their conception from their reality" (8, p. 38). Elsewhere, Marx equates a "common situation" with "common interests" (see 6, p. 187) and thereby shows that—as we do here—he bases his theory on a quasi-"objective," nonpsychological concept of interest. Geiger was the most extreme critic of such a concept. He regards it as "questionable whether one can speak at all of interest in an objective sense. Interest is above all something subjective . . ." (46, pp. 127 f.). He believes that the (Marxian) postulate of interests existing independently of individuals conceals a judgment "about the true advantage of others," for which "one would evidently have to possess an objective and universally valid scale of values" (p. 129). Since such a scale "plainly does not exist," it is not science that has guided Marx's pen here, but pure speculation. He imputes, according to Geiger, "true interests" to the proletariat which are independent of the wishes and goals of its members. But here "the proper analysis of the interest structure of social classes ends—religious mania alone speaks here" (p. 133).

I would agree that the postulate of nonindividual class interests in its Marxian formulation requires criticism. But such criticism need not be directed against the possibility of a nonpsychological concept of interest. A concept of this kind responds, in fact, to a genuine need of sociological analysis. It is no accident that it appears and reappears frequently in the history of sociology—after Marx, in the works of Ratzenhofer, Small, Sumner, and many others. For L. Robbins, the distinction between "subjective" and "objective communities of interest" is the starting point of a critique of Marx; yet Robbins never doubts the usefulness of the category of "objective community of interest" (182, p. 112). M. Ginsberg refers to "aggregates . . . whose members have certain interests or modes of behavior in common" without being "definite groups" (47, p. 40). Even Parsons not only frequently uses the clearly "objective" category of "vested interests," but also explicitly emphasizes the existence of common "ideologies" or "attitude systems" among those "who are structurally placed at notably different points in a differentiated social structure," i.e., occupy identical or similar social positions (67, p. 330).

For purposes of the sociological analysis of conflict groups and group conflicts, it is necessary to assume certain structurally generated orientations of the actions of incumbents of defined positions. By analogy to conscious ("subjective") orientations of action, it appears justifiable to describe these as "interests." It has to be emphasized, however, that by so doing no assumption is implied about the substance of these interests or the consciousness and articulate orientation of the occupants of the positions in question.[12] The assumption of "objective" interests associated with social positions has no psychological implications or ramifications; it belongs to the level of sociological analysis proper.

In saying that the Marxian notion of class interest requires criticism, I mean that Marx fuses, in this notion, generalization and specific empirical observation in an impermissible manner. This becomes apparent if we look at the substance of socially structured interests. What is it that the occupants of positions of domination or subjection

---

[12] This statement will be qualified below by the distinction of "latent" and "manifest interests." Strictly speaking, it holds for latent interests only.

are "interested in" by virtue of their positions? Geiger is right in rejecting Marx's attempt to answer this question in terms of material value conceptions. That "the realization of a socialist society" constitutes "the true interest of labor" is indeed an assertion for the (empirical) premises of which "the proof is missing" (46, pp. 130 f.). An assumption of this kind cannot be introduced by way of a postulate. The substance of socially structured "objective" interests can be described only in highly formal terms: they are interests in the maintenance or modification of a *status quo*. Our model of conflict group formation involves the proposition that of the two aggregates of authority positions to be distinguished in every association, one—that of domination—is characterized by an interest in the maintenance of a social structure that for them conveys authority, whereas the other— that of subjection—involves an interest in changing a social condition that deprives its incumbents of authority. The two interests are in conflict.

Max Weber has convincingly demonstrated that the problem of maintaining or changing given structures of authority can be expressed, both conceptually and empirically, in terms of the basis of legitimacy of relations of authority. From our assumption of an at least latent conflict of interests in every imperatively coordinated association, it follows that the legitimacy of authority must always be precarious. There always is one aggregate of positions and their incumbents which represents the institutionalized doubt in the legitimacy of the *status quo* of the distribution of authority. In this sense, the proposition that there are "objective" interests in changing any given structure of authority might also be expressed in terms of the potential illegitimacy of all relations of authority. Empirically, group conflict is probably most easily accessible to analysis if it be understood as a conflict about the legitimacy of relations of authority. In every association, the interests of the ruling group are the values that constitute the ideology of the legitimacy of its rule, whereas the interests of the subjected group constitute a threat to this ideology and the social relations it covers.

There are two further ways of elucidating the important notion of socially structured conflicts of interest. One of these has recourse to what is, if not a general "psychological law," at least an assumption implicit in many theories of economics, psychology, and sociology. In a word, this "law" might be described as the pleasure principle. It might be argued that the assumption of a fundamental human tendency to improve the balance of pleasure and pain, or gratification and deprivation, implies *inter alia* that wherever there is authority those in positions of domination would tend to defend their gratification, whereas those in positions of subjection are forced to attack existing conditions in order to remedy their deprivation.[13]

Plausible as this argument may sound, it is both unnecessary and somewhat misleading. It is unnecessary because the proposition that a conflict of interests is associated with authority positions in any association requires no recourse to more general assumptions. At the same time, the argument is misleading not only because (since Freud) we know that the pleasure principle is at best of restricted applicability, but above all because it might suggest that the "objective" interests of our model are after all psychological realities. Our proposition does not imply that the incumbents of positions equipped with "objective" interests will necessarily become conscious of these interests and act accordingly. While this may be probable, it is not as such required by the model of conflict group formation.[14]

I suggest, therefore, that a second line of argument is rather more appropriate for elucidating the notion of "objective" interests. This has the additional advantage of enabling us to abandon the awkward concept of "objective" interests in favor of more unambiguous and precise notions. In terms of the integration theory of society, social positions, with which we are here concerned, are significant, above all, as social roles. By roles are understood sets of role expectations, "patterned expectations defining the *proper* behavior of persons playing certain roles" (Parsons, 217, pp. 61 f.). "Proper" means, of course, within the frame of reference of integration theory, appropriate for the functioning of the social system and contributing to its integration. The notion of role expectations ascribes an orientation of behavior to social positions or roles. The individual "player" of roles may or may not internalize these role expectations and make them conscious orientations of action. If he does so, he is in terms of integration theory "adapted" or "adjusted"; if he does not do so, he is a "deviant." In any case, the assumption of certain "objective" expectations of behavior proves analytically useful. I suggest that the category of

---

[13] In several earlier essays (cf. 42, p. 42; 206, p. 512 and note 81), I have in fact argued along these lines. However, today I would regard this argument, if not as false, then as misleading, and prefer the second approach indicated below.

[14] Thus, the model does not prejudice the (empirical) problem of whether in any given case those in subjection want to attack those in domination or not. Conscious motivations are, from the point of view of conflict theory, largely a matter of empirical research.

interest in the coercion theory of society must be understood in strict analogy to that of role expectation. The "objective" interests under discussion are in fact role interests, i.e., expected orientations of behavior associated with authority roles in imperatively coordinated associations. Again, the individual incumbent of roles may or may not internalize these expectations. But in our context he behaves in an "adapted" or "adjusted" manner if he contributes to the conflict of contradictory interests rather than to the integration of a social system. The individual who assumes a position in an association finds these role interests with his position, just as he finds certain role expectations from the point of view of the social system. For different purposes of sociological analysis, different aspects of its basic unit—the position-role—are relevant; roles, too, have two faces. In our context they figure primarily as sets of expected interests within imperatively coordinated associations.[15]

For certain purposes of the theory of conflict group formation, it will prove useful to replace the concept of role interests by another one which makes its relation to the incumbents of authority positions even more apparent. Role interests are, from the point of view of the "player" of roles, *latent interests*, i.e., undercurrents of his behavior which are predetermined for him for the duration of his incumbency of a role, and which are independent of his conscious orientations. As such they can, under conditions to be specified presently, become conscious goals which we shall correspondingly call *manifest interests*.[16] By contrast to latent interests, manifest interests are psychological realities. They describe—as Geiger demands for all interests—"the fact that emotion, will, and desire of a person are directed toward some goal" (although we presuppose that this goal is "some goal" only in a substantial, not in a formal, sense). The specific substance of manifest interests can be determined only in the context of given social conditions; but they always constitute a formulation of the issues of structurally generated group conflicts of the type in question. In this sense, manifest interests are the program of organized groups.

---

[15] The fruitfulness of this necessarily rather abstract analysis can be demonstrated only by empirical analysis. For some indication of the potentialities of the position here suggested, cf. the discussion of codetermination in industry in Chapter VII.

[16] These two terms which—apart from their evident meaning as words—refer back to Merton's distinction of "manifest" and "latent functions" and further to Freud's categories of "manifest" and "latent dream contents," were first proposed by me in an essay on class (42, pp. 11 f.). Some of the purely conceptual problems are discussed at somewhat greater length in that essay.

The psychological formations which we have called "manifest interests" are evidently similar to what in Marxian, and more generally in sociological, literature is usually referred to as "class consciousness." However, it is necessary to distinguish strictly the philosophical and speculative elements of this concept as used, for example, by Marx and Lukacs (21), from the observable articulate interests of organized groups. Class consciousness in the sense of manifest interests is a "real category." Its existence and substance can in principle be discovered by interviews. The conception of a "false consciousness" can, in the context of the categories here employed, be meaningful only for manifest interests which are not adapted to the latent interests underlying them; even then, it is a highly problematical conception. In terms of a scientific theory which is supposed to explain problems of reality, the statement that a large group of people thinks "falsely" is plainly meaningless. "One has to be a philosopher of real dialectics to be serious about such nonsense" (Geiger, 46, p. 114). While latent interests are, in a psychological sense, "nonexistent," manifest interests are always realities in the heads of the occupants of positions of domination or subjection in associations. It is the task of the theory of class formation to establish a systematic connection between the two categories of latent and manifest interests.

QUASI-GROUPS AND INTEREST GROUPS
(1): THEORETICAL CONDITIONS OF CONFLICT GROUP FORMATION

So far our discussion has left undecided the question as to what kind of aggregates conflict groups are. We have established the determinant of group conflicts in the sense of this study; we have also established the categories characteristic of conflict groups on the normative level of analysis; but conflict groups are evidently not normative phenomena but real groupings which as such form part of the substratum of society. In describing these groupings, the categories of quasi-group and interest group are essential.

We have postulated two conflicting orientations of latent interests as characteristic of the role structure of imperatively coordinated associations. By implication, this means, of course, that the authority positions equipped with expected interests as well as their incumbents have at least one attribute in common. In a significant sense, the occupants of identical authority positions, i.e., either of positions of domination or of positions of subjection, find themselves in a common situation. Being united by a common, potentially permanent, characteristic, they are more than mere masses or incoherent quantities.

At the same time, the incumbents of like authority positions in an association do not in any sociologically tenable sense constitute a group. Just as all doctors, or all inhabitants of Berlin, do not as such constitute social groups, the occupants of positions with identical latent interests are not a group. For groups, a feeling of belongingness is as constitutive as a minimum of organization; but both are explicitly not demanded by the concept of latent interests. The aggregates of incumbents of positions with identical role interests are at best a potential group. Following M. Ginsberg we shall use for this particular type of social grouping the term *quasi-group*. "Not all collectivities or aggregates form groups. Groups are masses of people in regular contact or communication, and possessing a recognizable structure. There are other aggregates or portions of the community which have no recognizable structure, but whose members have certain interests or modes of behavior in common, which may at any time lead them to form themselves into definite groups. To this category of quasi-groups belong such entities as social classes, which, without being groups, are a recruiting field for groups, and whose members have certain characteristic modes of behavior in common" (47, p. 40).

A note of caution is required with respect to the "modes of behavior" included by Ginsberg in his definition of quasi-groups. The constituent element of the type of quasi-groups with which we are here concerned is the community of certain latent interests. Latent interests are not psychological phenomena; quasi-groups based on them might therefore be called a mere theoretical construction. They are "theoretical phenomena," i.e., units constructed for the purpose of explaining problems of social conflict. They are, as Ginsberg plausibly states, "recruiting fields for groups." For purposes of a sociological theory of group conflict it is useful to reduce the actual conflict groups of empirical associations to larger aggregates which form part of their structure and consist of the incumbents of roles endowed with like expectations of interest. Only by doubtful analogy can we speak of "members" of such aggregates or quasi-groups. Thus it transcends the legitimate possibilities of theory construction to postulate common modes of behavior for these "members."

On the other hand, common modes of behavior are characteristic of *interest groups* recruited from larger quasi-groups. Interest groups are groups in the strict sense of the sociological term; and they are the real agents of group conflict. They have a structure, a form of organization, a program or goal, and a personnel of members. If Ginsberg demands for such groups "regular contact or communication," however, this applies only in an indirect sense. Interest groups are always "secondary groups"; their members are in contact with each other only by virtue of their membership or by way of their elected or appointed representatives. One might emphasize the difference between interest groups and primary groupings such as family or friendship by calling them with MacIver "associations" or with Malinowski "institutions." However, it seems to me that the concept of interest group is sufficiently unambiguous if, apart from terminological considerations, we keep the modern political party in mind as an example of such organizations.

It is perhaps necessary to emphasize that the groupings with which we are here concerned are by no means satisfactorily described by the concepts of quasi-group and interest group. This is especially evident in the case of interest groups. The statement that conflict groups are interest groups is meaningful, but incomplete. The category of interest group is a general category; virtually any secondary group can be regarded as an interest group—a chess club as well as an occupational association, a football team as well as a political party or a trade union. The specific difference of the quasi-groups and interest groups with which we are concerned in this study accrues from their origin in the authority structure of associations or, to put it differently, from the formal characteristic of their underlying (latent or manifest) interests as interests related to the legitimacy of relations of domination and subjection. This limitation clearly excludes the chess club, the football team, and the occupational association, while it leaves us to consider groupings such as trade unions and political parties. Whenever we refer in the subsequent analysis to quasi-groups and interest groups without specifically stating this limitation, this is merely an abbreviated way of referring to conflict groups as they emerge from the authority structure of associations.

The empirical problem of the genesis of interest groups constitutes the subject matter of the following section of this chapter. On a more formal level, however, the problem of the relation between quasi-groups and interest groups may be raised here. In what sense are interest groups, such as political parties, to be regarded as representative of the quasi-groups that can be inferred behind them? Can the same quasi-group become a recruiting field for several interest groups? In principle, the possibility intimated by the latter question has to be answered in the affirmative. From the point of view of conflict theory, competing trade unions of, say, Christian and Socialist description originate from the same quasi-group. Empirically, interest groups are always smaller than their recruiting fields, the quasi-groups. They are subsets of the sets constituted by quasi-groups; and the identity of set and subset remains a limiting case. One might compare the relation of the two with that of the members and the voters of one political party. Furthermore, a number of specific intervening variables may disturb the immediacy of the relation between given quasi-groups and interest groups. While quasi-groups, being in the nature of a theoretical construction, are unequivocally defined, organized interest groups may supplement the interests accruing from authority structures by a multitude of other and independent goals and orientations. This is merely another expression for the fact that interest groups are "real phenomena," and that, like all such phenomena, they cannot be completely described by one attribute. Thus, the theory of group conflict involves no statement about the empirical variety of interest groups. It concentrates on one of their aspects: on their function in social conflicts as units of manifest interests which can be explained in terms of latent role interests and their aggregation in quasi-groups.[17]

QUASI-GROUPS AND INTEREST GROUPS
(II): EMPIRICAL CONDITIONS OF CONFLICT GROUP FORMATION

"It is a matter of no small interest," Ginsberg adds to his definition of quasi-groups, "to determine at what point these looser configurations crystallize into associations" (47, p. 41). The categories of quasi-group and interest group mark the two foci of the analysis of conflict group formation, but they do not describe the connecting lines between them. It will now be our task to examine the conditions under which a "class in itself" becomes a "class for itself." Perhaps the negative side of this problem is of even greater importance. We shall want to ascertain the conditions under which the organization of interest groups does not take place despite the presence of quasi-groups of latent interests in an imperatively coordinated association. This is evidently a matter of ascertaining possible intervening variables which we shall comprehend under the collective term of "structural conditions of organization."

In dealing with the empirical process of development of classes

---

[17] To illustrate this rather abstract formulation: for the theory of conflict, socialist parties are of interest not as instruments of workers' education or as clublike associations, but merely as forces in social conflicts. The same party may function in many ways other than as an interest group, but only the latter aspect is in question in the present analysis.

Marx has touched upon this problem at many points. Among these there is one which is particularly illuminating for our present context. At the end of his essay on the 18th of Brumaire of Louis Bonaparte, Marx is dealing with "the most numerous class of French society, the small independent peasants" (8, p. 104). Marx states, to begin with, that these peasants, by virtue of their situation, their conditions of existence, their way of life, and their (latent) interests, constitute a "class," namely, a quasi-group. One would therefore expect a political organization or interest group to grow out of their midst. However, precisely this did not happen. In so far as the identity of the (latent) interests of the peasants "does not produce a community, national association and political organization, they do not constitute a class" (p. 105). In explaining this surprising fact, Marx refers to conditions of the kind of the intervening variables in question here: "The small independent peasants constitute an enormous mass, the members of which live in the same situation but do not enter into manifold relations with each other. Their mode of production isolates them from each other instead of bringing them into mutual intercourse. This isolation is strengthened by the bad state of French means of communication and by the poverty of the peasants. . . . Every single peasant family is almost self-sufficient . . . and thus gains its material of life more in exchange with nature than in intercourse with society" (p. 104). The brilliant conclusion Marx draws from this analysis—namely, that Louis Bonaparte is trying to justify his claim for power by reference to this quasi-group of peasants whose interests are condemned to latency—will concern us less here than the problem impressively demonstrated by it. Under certain conditions, quasi-groups may persist as such without interest groups emerging from them. What are these conditions, and under which conditions do interest groups come to be formed?

It may be useful to begin by clarifying the logical status of a generalizing answer to this question. The categories of latent and manifest interest, quasi-group and interest group, constitute the elements of a model of conflict group formation. Under ideal conditions, i.e., if no variables not contained in this model intervene, the analytical[18] process of conflict group formation can be represented as follows. In every imperatively coordinated association, two quasi-

---

[18] This needs to be emphasized. We are not here concerned with the chronological development of conflict groups. Marx commits at this point an error of hypostasis. By asserting the analytical sequence as a chronological one, he transforms the "theoretical phenomenon" quasi-group into a "real phenomenon" in an impermissible manner.

groups united by common latent interests can be distinguished. Their orientations of interest are determined by possession of or exclusion from authority. From these quasi-groups, interest groups are recruited, the articulate programs of which defend or attack the legitimacy of existing authority structures. In any given association, two such groupings are in conflict. This model of conflict group formation is as such complete and suffices for all purposes of theoretical analysis. In principle, little need be added to it, and what additions are required are in the nature of refinements. However, for purposes of empirical analysis the model may—as the example of Marx's "18th of Brumaire" shows—be useful as a guide to relevant problems, but it is as such incomplete. As soon as we pass from the level of model construction to that of the explanation of empirical problems, the premise of ideal conditions is no longer given. We encounter intervening variables the identification of which is our concern at this point.

Determination of the structural conditions of organization requires the formulation of empirical generalizations. Here, the security of theoretical postulates and constructions gives way to the precarious attempt to expose general facts of social life, to classify them, and to formulate them hypothetically. It might be argued that this step transcends the limits of theory and need not therefore be taken here. It passes, indeed, beyond the limits of model construction. Nevertheless, it has to be taken in order for the model to be freed of the suspicion of analytical uselessness. The attempt to classify intervening variables in a generalizing manner is all the more important, since without it *ad hoc* hypotheses and additions have free reign.[19] For the sake of the empirical applicability of the model proposed here it is necessary to indicate in general the structural conditions of the organization of conflict groups. Completeness is intended but of course not by any means guaranteed.

Malinowski endeavored, in his attempt to classify the characteristics of what he calls "institutions" (and what might equally well be called "associations" or simply "organized groups"), to render, as he puts it, this category "more serviceable in field-work" (212, pp. 52 ff.). Malinowski lists at this point six features which are of importance also for interest groups of the kind discussed here: such groups require a charter, a personnel, certain norms, a material in-

---

[19] In this sense, Marx's explanation in the "18th Brumaire" is of course also an *ad hoc* addition, if a brilliant one. All subsequent considerations in this chapter are on the level of supplementing a theoretical model by empirical generalizations.

strumentarium, certain regular activities, and an "objective" function. The latter characteristic is in our case part of the underlying model. Otherwise, however, Malinowski's list contains an important sector of the empirical conditions of organization of interest groups. I shall call these conditions the *technical conditions of organization*. Without a charter, certain norms, a personnel, and certain material requisites, interest groups cannot be formed, even if it is justified to assume that quasi-groups exist. Obvious as these conditions may appear, at least two of them—"charter" and "personnel"—are of considerable significance, as will become apparent if we specify them a little.

It is a commonplace that groups cannot exist without members and, in that sense, without a personnel. Moreover, since we have postulated the presence of a personnel in the quasi-groups from which interest groups emerge, this condition does not at first sight appear to be a genuine intervening variable. It is, indeed, not the total membership of an interest group which is in question here, but that sector of the membership which can be described as the leading group or cadre. For an organized interest group to emerge from a quasi-group, there have to be certain persons who make this organization their business, who carry it out practically and take the lead. Every party needs its founders. The availability of founders in this sense, however, is by no means given in our model nor can it be. It is an additional empirical condition of conflict group formation. As such it is a necessary, although not sufficient, condition of organization. To stipulate a leading group as a prerequisite of the organization of interest groups must not be misunderstood to mean that conflict groups are based on the goals and actions of a handful of leaders. The availability of possible organizers, founders, and leaders is essentially a technical prerequisite which must be satisfied for unorganized quasi-groups to be transformed into organized interest groups. The organizers are one of the ferments, not the starting point or cause of organization. That without them organization is impossible has been demonstrated convincingly—in so far as it is not self-evident—by Marx at the place in the "18th Brumaire" quoted above, and above all in the "Communist Manifesto."

Marx has realized, also, that the creation of a charter is not an automatic process. Malinowski defines the charter of an organization as the "system of values for the pursuit of which human beings organize" (212, p. 52). In the particular case of conflict groups these values consist of what we have called "manifest interests." While latent interests are nonpsychological orientations implicit in the social structure of roles and positions, manifest interests are articulate, formulated (or at least formulable) programs. They entail specific claims related to given structures of authority. The articulation and codification of such interests is again a process that presupposes certain conditions. Either there must be a person or circle of persons who take on themselves the task of articulation and codification, or, alternatively, an "ideology," a system of ideas, must be available which in a given case is capable of serving as a program or charter of groups. As evidence for the first, it seems sufficient to refer to the role of the political ideologist Marx for the organization of the socialist movement; as evidence of the latter alternative, to the role of a certain interpretation of Calvinism for early English capitalists. Ideologies understood as articulated and codified manifest interests are again but a technical condition of organization. Ideologies do not create conflict groups or cause conflict groups to emerge. Yet they are indispensable as obstetricians of conflict groups, and in this sense as an intervening variable.

Even if we are given not only quasi-groups with common latent interests, but leaders and ideologies as well—if, in other words, the technical conditions of organization are present—it is still not justified to make the empirical inference that interest groups will be formed. A second category of prerequisites which have to be satisfied for organization to be possible will be described here as the *political conditions of organization.* The totalitarian state is probably the most unambiguous illustration of a social situation in which these conditions are not fulfilled, and in which therefore at least oppositional interest groups cannot emerge despite the presence of quasi-groups and latent interests.[20] Where a plurality of conflicting parties is not permitted and their emergence suppressed by the absence of freedom of coalition and by police force, conflict groups cannot organize themselves even if all other conditions of their organization are present. The study of the possibilities and actual types of group conflict under such conditions is a problem of sociological analysis of the highest

[20] Technically similar conditions obtain in many preindustrial societies. In terms of the political conditions of organization the restriction of this study to industrial societies can be well illustrated. In all preindustrial societies group conflict is seriously impeded by the absence of certain political conditions (the political "citizenship rights"). It would be a matter for separate analysis to investigate forms of group conflict in these societies.

importance. There is a starting point, here, of the analysis not only of "underground movements" and the development of revolutions, but more generally of structure and dynamics of totalitarian states. But this type of problem can be merely intimated here, since we are for the time being concerned with formulating the general structural conditions of organization. We can maintain that the political permissibility of organization is one of the additional intervening prerequisites of conflict group formation.

Apart from technical and political conditions, some, in the narrow sense, *social conditions of organization* are of importance for the formation of interest groups. Among these we find the condition of communication between the "members" of quasi-groups emphasized by Marx in the case of French peasants. If an aggregate within an association can be described as a community of latent interests, is also provided with the technical and political possibilities of organization, but is so scattered topologically or ecologically that a regular connection among the members of the aggregate does not exist and can be established only with great difficulty, then the formation of an organized interest group is empirically most unlikely. However, important as this premise of organization is, the generalization seems tenable that its significance is steadily diminishing in industrial societies with a highly developed system of means of communication. In advanced industrial societies this condition may be assumed to be generally given; it enters, therefore, into the analysis of conflict group formation as a constant.

This is not the case, however, with another social condition of organization the implications of which will occupy us a good deal more. Empirically, the formation of organized interest groups is possible only if recruitment to quasi-groups follows a structural pattern rather than chance. By this condition, the group described by Marx as *lumpenproletariat* is excluded from conflict group formation.[21] Persons who attain positions relevant for conflict analysis not by the normal process of the allocation of social positions in a social structure, but by peculiar, structurally random personal circumstances, appear generally unsuited for the organization of conflict groups. Thus the lowest stratum of industrial societies is frequently recruited in manifold but structurally irrelevant ways: by delinquency, ex-

[21] In my study of unskilled industrial workers in England (143) I have tried to show in detail how this one condition is capable of excluding a large group of people from political activity.

treme lack of talent, personal mishaps, physical or psychological instability, etc. In this case, the condition of structural recruitment is not satisfied, and conflict group formation cannot be expected.

From the empirical conditions of the organization of conflict groups thus briefly sketched, we can, by way of generalization, derive a number of social constellations which are unfavorable if not prohibitive for conflict group formation and group conflict. Here, again, I shall confine myself to giving an indication. One constellation resisting conflict group formation, namely, that of the totalitarian state, is directly given in the formulated conditions. A second important constellation can be defined by combining several of the factors mentioned. If imperatively coordinated associations are either themselves just emerging or subject to radical change, the probability is small that the quasi-groups derived from their authority structure will lead to coherent forms of organization. Examples for this may be seen in the early stages of industrial development, or in societies immediately after social revolutions (such as the Soviet Union in the 1920's).[22] In both cases authority structures, latent interests, and quasi-groups are present. But in both cases it seems reasonable to assume that the absence of leaders and ideologies as well as the still unpatterned and unnormalized recruitment to the relevant positions stand in the way of conflict group formation. In this sense, it seems feasible to attempt to reformulate Marx's problem of the gradual formation of classes in the course of industrialization.

The empirical conditions of organization have been described here as prerequisites of conflict group formation. However, their effect goes beyond the process of emergence of conflict groups. These factors are relevant, also, as variables affecting organized interest groups. They must then be understood, of course, as continua which permit gradations. A relative lack of technical, political, and social conditions of organization can hamper organized interest groups in their operation, and it can, indeed—which is apparent in the case of the political conditions—result in their disintegration. Ideologies may lose their value as programs and their validity, especially if significant structure changes have occurred since their formulation. Parties may go through a "leaderless" period. Modes of recruitment to quasi-groups may change. Some of the problems of this type we shall encounter again in the empirical analyses of the final chapters

---

[22] Here, the absence of the political conditions of organization is of course an added obstacle to interest group formation.

of this study. First of all, I propose to look a little more closely into the social and psychological characteristics of the conflict groups stipulated by our model.

A NOTE ON THE PSYCHOLOGY OF CONFLICT GROUPS

Conflict groups are certainly also psychological phenomena. We have defined organized interest groups by manifest interests, i.e., a characteristic of clearly psychological reality. Beyond that it is probable that the formation of interest groups presupposes certain psychological conditions apart from its technical, political, and social prerequisites. For example, identification with the expectations associated with authority roles is a condition of conflict group formation which has been mentioned already. It seems questionable, however, whether we comprehend this or any other problem of the psychology of conflict groups any better by following Warner (75, 100) and many other predominantly American social scientists in restricting our questions to an investigation of how people rank themselves or each other in society. From the point of view of a theory of social conflict, an approach of this kind is meaningless because it seeks to establish the notion of conflict groups empirically by deriving it from the opinions of a (more or less) representative sample of people. Although investigations concerned with people's self-evaluation and ranking of others are not entirely without interest for the sociologist, they are useless for our problem. They substitute for the effort of a theoretical derivation of significant problems of research the skills of drawing up questionnaires and interpreting interview findings. This is not to say, of course, that there are no social psychological studies at all which might be helpful for conflict theory. Four independent yet substantially similar studies—those of Centers (38), Hoggart (52), Popitz (69), and Willener (76)—are of considerable significance here, and will occupy us in some detail as we come to analyze post-capitalist society in terms of conflict theory. At this point, however, we are concerned not with empirical findings but with the type of problem suggested by conflict group formation on the level of psychological research. A note on this may facilitate our further considerations.

We can maintain, to begin with, that the model of group formation formulated in this chapter does not presuppose or imply any psychological assumption. In this model, individual behavior figures —as indeed it should in sociological analysis—as a constant. However, in applying this model to specific empirical conditions, we inevitably encounter factors and variables of a psychological as well as a sociological nature. The attempt to present a general formulation of the three most important types of problems which come up here cannot of course relieve us of testing the validity of such generalizations anew in every specific instance.

(1) In exploring the emergence of interest groups from quasi-groups we encounter a problem which is logically equivalent to that of "deviant behavior" in the integration theory of social structure. Our model postulates quasi-groups and interest groups on the basis of the position of roles in imperatively coordinated associations. Thus, his "class situation" is forced upon the individual with the position he assumes in an association. On the level of interest groups, conscious and intentional participation of individuals is moreover assumed by definition. Manifest interests are psychological realities. Evidently, their presence can be neither simply assumed nor inferred from the presence of the technical, political, and social conditions of organization. Rather, we have to ask under which psychological conditions individuals may orient themselves in accordance with or in contradiction to the expected interests of their position. The worker who behaves as if he is not in a position of subjection is like the entrepreneur who acts as if he is not in a position of domination, a "deviant" within the association of industry whose behavior requires a psychological explanation. I shall refrain from offering vague suggestions about possible causes of such behavior; evidently this is a matter of social psychological research.[23] It may be added that if any patterns of deviance from postulated norms or expectations in this sphere of social action are discovered, these patterns would by implication constitute the psychological conditions of organization which would thus supplement the three types of conditions distinguished in the preceding section.

(2) A second aspect of the psychology of conflict groups would seem to be of a phenomenological character. It is worth exploring the psychic determinants and features of manifest interests and of the solidarity of interest groups based on these. The sociological aspect of manifest interests is defined by the model of conflict group formation; moreover, this model permits the discovery of the substance of manifest interests in given social situations. However, it is a matter of psychological research to examine in given cases whether

---

[23] The theory of reference group behavior might here be helpful. It could account for the weight of conflict groupings in the minds and actions of individuals by comparison to other types of relation.

specific manifest interests correlate with certain types or characteristics of personality, and to what extent role interests mold and penetrate the personalities of their carriers.[24] For this purpose it would
be desirable to have an operational definition of manifest interests
which establishes, in general, indices and methods of measuring the
presence as well as the intensity of manifest interests.

(3) The hypothesis seems plausible that weight and intensity of
manifest group interests within the individual personality decrease
as social mobility and the openness of conflict groups increase. The
easier it is for the individual to leave his conflict group, the less likely
is he to engage his whole personality in group conflicts and the more
marginal is his authority role likely to remain. But the degree of
openness of conflict groups is probably not the only determinant of
the intensity of identification with conflict groups. According to our
theory, an individual can belong to several conflict groups simultaneously, in so far as he may play roles in several associations (e.g.,
industry and political society) simultaneously. It appears that the
factual weight of an individual's belongingness to different associations within the ensemble of his social personality also influences the
intensity of his solidarity with any one conflict group to which he
belongs.

The problem indicated by these hypotheses is at least in part
psychological. It is related to the problem of "class culture" which
frequently appears in sociological literature. "One of the significant
properties . . . of the phenomenon of class consists in the fact that
the members of a class behave towards each other in a way characteristically different from that towards members of other classes, that
they stand in a closer relation to each other, understand each other
better, cooperate more easily, join together and close themselves off
from the outside, look at the same sector of the world with equally
disposed eyes and from like points of view" (Schumpeter, 27, p.
152). "Subjectively regarded, class differences rest upon the development of sentiments or groups of emotional dispositions. These
are of three sorts. There is, first, a feeling of equality in relation to
members of one's own class, a feeling of being at ease with them, a
consciousness that one's mode of behavior will harmonize with the
behavior of the others. There is, secondly, a feeling of inferiority
to those above in the social hierarchy, and, thirdly, a feeling of su-

---

[24] This is rather a delicate task, since it is necessary to avoid the error of correlating
group belongingness and personality type in a linear fashion, or even by way of assumption. See the discussion of Mayo's work in Chapter III above.

periority to those below" (Ginsberg, 47, pp. 160 f.). "Social class is a derivative of the whole social personality of the individual, not of a mere facet of it, such as some technical equipment and the interests it may create. Social class is a human aggregation which has not been submitted to that splitting of individuality into its associative elements so subtly analyzed by Simmel. Each member mirrors in the microcosm of his personality the many featured image of his class" (Marshall, 58, p. 100). These assertions and assumptions—which are representative for a large number of authors—had to be quoted here in some detail, because they constitute a potential limitation of conflict theory to particular historical situations. They raise once again the problem of the feasibility of the concept of class. While postponing this aspect for a little while, we must emphasize here that conflict groups in the sense of this study differ radically from classes as described by Schumpeter, Ginsberg, and Marshall in the passages quoted.

Conflict groups in the sense of our model describe primarily groupings based on positions in imperatively coordinated associations. Just as, from the point of view of the individual, his position in an association constitutes but one potentially very small sector of his social personality, his membership in a conflict group refers merely to a small segment of his personality. His conflict group claims—to use an illustration—the entrepreneur as an occupant of a position of domination in the enterprise, while leaving his behavior as husband, father, member of a church, a club, even as voter in principle undecided. If there is a connection between the behavior of an individual by virtue of his membership in a conflict group and his total social behavior, this signifies a special case and cannot be postulated in general, just as the connection between industry and society is not determined a priori. The connection or correlation between conflict behavior and total social behavior is empirically variable and a matter for specific investigation. We have rejected Marx's and Burnham's alleged postulate of an identity of the authority structures of industry and the state, because it has revealed itself as a speculative dogma. Analogously, we must also reject the general correlation asserted by Schumpeter, Marshall, and Ginsberg between conflict group membership and social personality; again, this is no more than a generalization derived from a single observation.[25] If we take this step, we

[25] It may be suspected that all three authors are talking of social strata rather than conflict groups; and for strata their criteria may indeed hold. But the effort of the distinction between the analysis of social stratification and that of conflict must be sustained on all levels.

have reduced the problem of "class culture" (i.e., of the connection between membership in conflict groups and general social behavior) to a problem of empirical psychology. A continuous scale might be constructed, ranging from complete identity (a correlation of $+1$) of conflict behavior and general social behavior to complete irrelevance (a correlation of o) of conflict behavior for other social behavior. At a later stage, the importance of this step for the analysis of conflict in advanced industrial societies will become apparent. The authority role of the individual and such patterns of behavior as can be inferred from it are an independent variable the connection of which with other aspects of social behavior is theoretically indeterminate and can be established only by empirical observation. Whether the whole personality of the individual is molded by his belonging to a conflict group, or whether the individual acts as a member of a conflict group only for limited periods of time (such as during his working time) and in limited social relations (such as in his capacity as trade unionist) while being guided by entirely different norms at other times and in other relations—this is a problem the solution of which suggests types of conflict groups and degrees of intensity of conflicts but has nothing to do with the existence of such groups and conflicts. At least in part, this solution is evidently a task of psychological research.

"ELITES" AND "RULING CLASSES"

Our model of conflict group formation stipulates the existence of two opposed groupings in any given association. Each of these groups shares certain features, and each differs from the other by contradictory orientations of interest. Before concluding the abstract discussion of the model and the examination of some of its empirical consequences we may ask what, if anything, can be stated in general about the two groups thus distinguished. Independent of particular empirical conditions, are there any features that characterize or otherwise distinguish the occupants of positions of domination and their interest groups from those of positions of subjection? It appears useful to discuss this problem with reference to the theories of three sociologists whose work is here representative and has heretofore in this discussion deliberately been mentioned only occasionally. I mean Pareto (25), Mosca (24), and Aron (34), whose conceptions resemble ours in several points. Of the three, Mosca takes the most explicit stand on the problem at hand, and his conception will therefore require particular attention.

The chief element of the model of class formation consists in the explanation of conflicts of interest groups in terms of quasi-groups determined by the distribution of authority in imperatively coordinated associations. We share this emphasis on authority structures with all three authors mentioned, whose work might therefore be described as the proximate origin of a theory of conflict of the type here proposed.[26] Since they argue in terms of authority, Pareto, Mosca, and Aron also operate with a two-class model. It is characteristic of all of them, however, that they concentrate their attention —unlike Marx, Weber, and many others—on the group possessing authority, the members of which occupy, in other words, positions of domination. We shall presently consider some of the implications of this emphasis on dominating groups for the analysis of subjected groups and of group conflict in general. In describing dominating conflict groups the authors in question use primarily two concepts. Mosca refers almost exclusively to the "political class" which, in the German and English translations of his *Elementi di Scienza Politica*, has become a "ruling class." Pareto introduces for this group the much-disputed category of "elite"; however, he distinguishes "governing" and "nongoverning" elites (25, p. 222) and devotes as much attention to the latter as to the former. Aron has narrowed down the notion of "elite" to the "minority" that "exercises power" (34, p. 567); elsewhere, he speaks of "ruling classes." Without entering into terminological disputes, I propose to examine the general characteristics ascribed by these three authors to dominating groups and the validity of their analyses.

In their way of posing the problem, the approaches of Pareto, Mosca, and Aron entail at many points indications of the sociological theory of group conflict as we understand it. All three authors deal with the problem of inertia, i.e., the tendency of dominating groups to maintain and defend their domination. They also deal with the role of legitimacy in the maintenance or change of authority structures. Mosca and Pareto, in particular, emphasize the problem of social mobility to which we shall have to return. As to the psychology of conflict groups, their works contain many a useful suggestion. They discuss in some detail the formation and disintegration of "aristocracies" as well as other types of social change, basing their analyses on thorough historical documentation. If for the discussion

---

[26] To this list other names would obviously have to be added, among them, above all, Max Weber. However, Weber has failed to connect his theory of power and authority with the analysis of conflict. Contrary to Aron's, Pareto's, and Mosca's, his work is suggestive rather than directly indicative of the approach of the present study.

of this section I select only five aspects of the theories of Pareto, Mosca, and Aron, it is because this selection is guided by the intention to combine a critical examination of these theories with some discussion of the general characteristics of dominating conflict groups.

(1) Even in his definition of dominating groups, Aron refers to these as "minorities." Mosca does not hesitate to elaborate this into the general thesis that the ruling class is "always the less numerous" group. The notion of an elite appears to evoke almost automatically the idea of the "chosen few," of a small ruling stratum. Thus, even Marx describes the action of the proletariat as the "independent movement of the overwhelming majority in the interest of the overwhelming majority" (14, pp. 20 f.), and almost as a matter of course Geiger, in his graphical schema of class structure (46, p. 43), represents the ruling class by a segment of the whole (circle) much smaller than the subjected class. That dominating groups are by comparison with their subjected counterpart often insignificantly small groupings is an assumption which to my knowledge has never been contested in the literature. Not all authors state as clearly as Machiavelli how small, exactly, these groups are: "In any city, however it may be organized politically, no more than 40 or 50 men attain real power" (see 24, p. 271). Mosca, in particular, supplements his political class by "another, much more numerous stratum including all those who are suited for leading positions" (p. 329); but by this extension he merely obliterates his analysis without abandoning the minority character of elites. In fact, the assumption that in any association the number of those subjected to authority is larger than the number of those in possession of authority does seem capable of generalization. It seems hard to imagine an association in which the "rulers" outweigh the "ruled" in number. In every state, the number of cabinet ministers is smaller than the number of citizens; in every enterprise there are fewer executives than employees. However, this seemingly general statement requires qualification for industrial societies at an advanced stage of development. Today, one is hardly surprised to find that in many modern industrial enterprises almost one-third of all employees exercise superordinate functions. Delegation of authority in industry, in the state, and in other associations makes possible in industrial societies dominating groups which are no longer small minorities but which in size hardly fall short of subjected groups. We have earlier examined some of the problems of delegated authority and we shall return to this point. By way of generalization, these phenomena justify at least the negative statement that it seems

to be one of the characteristics of industrial societies that those who are plainly subjected to authority in imperatively coordinated associations of many types not only do not any longer amount to the "overwhelming majority" but actually decrease steadily. Pareto's, Mosca's, and Aron's thesis of a small ruling minority requires correction. Legitimate power may be distributed, if with considerable gradations of spheres of authority, over a large number of positions.

(2) Pareto and Mosca characterize dominating groups by a number of peculiar properties which are alleged to be necessary for a group to attain and successfully defend its position of power. Pareto emphasizes "energy" and "superiority" (25, p. 230), an "instinct of combination," concentration on the proximate, and similar "properties" (e.g., pp. 242 f.). Mosca goes even further; for him "the ruling minorities usually consist of individuals who are superior to the mass of the ruled in material, intellectual, and even moral respects, or they are at least the descendants of individuals who had such virtues. To put it differently, the members of the ruling minority generally have real or apparent properties which are highly esteemed and convey great influence in their societies" (24, p. 55). This kind of thesis illustrates that pre-sociological character of Mosca's analyses, i.e., the speculative recourse from social structures and roles to individuals and their "properties," which hardly helps our insight into social relations. Without the full consistency of the Aristotelian argument, Mosca approximates the notion that certain people are "by nature" rulers or ruled, freemen or slaves. This notion, however, in whatever variant it may appear, has to be banned radically and finally from the sociological theory of group conflict.

Whether dominating conflict groups are characterized by attributes and patterns of behavior other than common manifest interests is a question that can be answered only by empirical observation and in relation to specific social conditions. This is in fact the question with which we have dealt above in terms of "class culture." It is certainly possible that there are societies in which dominating groups are also distinguished by patterns of behavior crystallized hypothetically in "properties"; but it is at least equally possible that the coherence of such groups is confined to the defense of common interests within well-defined units of social organization without significantly affecting other spheres of the behavior of the members of ruling groups. From the point of view of the theory of group conflict, the "properties" of individual group members are in principle indeterminate and variable.

(3) Mosca consistently derives from two untenable postulates—the minority character of ruling groups and the existence of a common culture among them—the conclusion that dominating conflict groups are always better organized than subjected groups. "The minority is organized simply because it is the minority" (p. 55). Like its premises, this conclusion can by no means be assumed; it is, rather, an empirical generalization, and one demonstrably false. Within the association of industry, for example, it would appear that there are greater obstacles to the formation of an interest group on behalf of the incumbents of positions of domination (because of the far-going internal differentiation of this quasi-group?) than is the case for the subjected workers. At the very least, we can say that we know of no point of view that would permit the postulate that a transition from quasi-groups to interest groups is easier for dominating than for subjected groups.[27]

(4) Mosca, and to some extent Pareto, means by the name "ruling class" only the incumbents of positions of domination in the political society. Pareto recognizes elites in all spheres and associations of society, but "governing elites" are for him politically governing elites. Mosca limits the field of his analyses by the very concept of "political class." It is only Aron who intimates an extension of this approach by emphasizing "the distinction between the political power of classes, founded on the position occupied in the state by their representatives, and their economic power, determined by their place in the process of production" (34, p. 572). Yet Aron also presupposes the unity of a class ruling in all spheres in which authority is exercised. In so far as this presupposition implies a restriction of conflict analysis to the association of the political state, it is unnecessary and, indeed, disadvantageous; in so far as it implies the assertion that the "political class" is *eo ipso* the ruling group in all other spheres of society, it is once again an untenable empirical generalization. One of the shortcomings of the theories of Mosca, of Pareto, and, to some extent, of Aron is that although these authors derive conflict groups from relations of authority, they fail to relate these to the crucial category of imperatively coordinated associations.

Ruling groups are, in the first place, no more than ruling groups

[27] To clarify this problem fully one would have to consider all the conditions of organization. Thus it might be feasible to make an empirical generalization to the effect that in pre-industrial societies ruling groups were (above all because of easier communication) provided with better conditions than subjected groups. In industrial societies, however, this clearly does not hold.

within defined associations. In theory, there can be as many competing, conflicting, or coexisting dominating conflict groups in a society as there are associations. Whether and in what way certain associations—such as industry and society—are connected in given societies is a subject for empirical analysis. Without doubt, such analysis is of considerable significance for a theory of conflict. Nevertheless, it is analytically necessary and empirically fruitful to retain the possibility of a competition or even conflict between the ruling groups of different associations. In this sense, the expression "ruling class" is, in the singular, quite misleading.

(5) Of the three authors under discussion, Mosca in particular has fallen victim to a Marxian overestimation of class analysis. If Pareto claims that history is "a cemetery of aristocracies" (25, p. 229), he leaves it open whether group conflicts or other forces caused the death of ruling elites. But Mosca is quite explicit: "One could explain the whole history of civilized mankind in terms of the conflict between the attempt of the rulers to monopolize and bequeath political power and the attempt of new forces to change the relations of power" (24, pp. 64 f.). This is hardly more than a reformulation of the Marxian thesis "the history of all hitherto society is the history of class struggles" (14, p. 6). Mosca's statement is therefore subject to the same objections. Ruling groups in the sense of the theory here advanced do by no means determine the entire "level of culture of a people" (Mosca, 24, p. 54). As coercion theory emphasizes but one aspect of social structure, thus the distinction between ruling and subjected groups is but one element of society. It would be false to identify the upper stratum of a society unequivocally with its ruling conflict group. There is no need for these two to be identical with respect to their personnel, nor do these categories, even if the personnel of upper stratum and ruling conflict group are the same, describe the same aspect of social behavior. In any case, ruling classes or conflict groups decide not so much the "level of civilization" of a society as the dynamics of the associations in which they originated.

"MASSES" AND "SUPPRESSED CLASSES"

It is a significant if confusing trait of the theories of Pareto and Mosca that both of them are concerned less with the explanation of social change than with that of stability or, as Pareto explicitly says at many points, of "equilibrium." By concentrating their attention primarily on the "elite" or "ruling class," they tend to reduce all changes to changes in the composition of the ruling class, i.e., to one type of social mobility.[28] Pareto's "circulation of elites" and Mosca's emphasis on the "ability" of a people "to produce in its womb new forces suited for leadership" (24, p. 227) aim at the same phenomenon, i.e., the regeneration of a leading stratum which is assumed to be universally procured by individual mobility. By virtue of this emphasis the theories of Pareto and Mosca take a strange turn of which their authors are probably not aware. Although both of them originally refer to two classes (Pareto, p. 226; Mosca, p. 52), their approach gradually and barely noticeably reduces itself to a "one-class model," in which only the ruling group functions as a class proper. Pareto characteristically speaks, by way of introducing the notion of "circulation of elites," of "two groups, the elite and the *rest of the population*" (p. 226), and Mosca similarly distinguishes at one point "the subjected *masses*" and "the political class" (p. 53).[29] Both notions, however—that of a "rest of the population" and that of "masses"—are basically residual categories defined by privation and not considered as independently operative forces. It need hardly be mentioned that this procedure robs any theory of conflict of its substance. At this point we see the crucial difference between elite theories and conflict theories in the sense of the present study.

The almost unnoticed transition from conflict theory to elite theory in the works of Pareto and Mosca has one aspect of some significance for our context. This becomes apparent if we contrast this modification with Marx's approach (which at times almost appears to commit the opposite mistake and to recognize only the proletariat as a class). The thesis might be advanced that in post-classical history of Europe the industrial workers of the nineteenth century constituted, indeed, the first subjected group that managed to establish itself as such, i.e., that left the stage of quasi-group and organized itself as an interest group. Thus, earlier "suppressed classes" could quite properly be described as "masses" or "rest of the population," that is, as quasi-groups such as the French peasants of Marx's "18th Brumaire," who provided—as Mosca (p. 104) argues along lines similar to Marx's in his study of Louis Bonaparte—merely a basis of legiti-

[28] Quite consistently, then, revolutions are, for Pareto and Mosca, abnormal events which betray the weakness of an elite, namely its inability to rejuvenate by absorbing new members.

[29] Italics in both quotations mine.

macy and "support" of competing "groups within the political class."
We need not settle this question here. But the fact that it can be
raised provides a further reason why I have chosen to limit this study
—contrary to Pareto and Mosca as well as Marx—to industrial societies. Perhaps it is feasible to make the general assertion that, in
principle, ruling and suppressed classes have, in industrial societies,
equal chances of organization, because in these societies one obstacle
to the organization of subjected groups characteristic for most earlier
societies is removed: the impossibility of communication. Although
I suspect that the theory formulated in this study might be extended
in such a way as to apply to pre-industrial societies also, I shall confine
myself to applying it to societies in which manifest conflicts of organized interest groups are empirically possible.

Subjected conflict groups must therefore not be visualized as essentially unorganized masses without effective force. In analogy to
the characteristics of ruling groups we can state (*a*) that they do not
necessarily comprise the majority of the members of an association,
(*b*) that their members are not necessarily connected by "properties"
or a "culture" beyond the interests that bind them into groups, and
(*c*) that their existence is always related to particular associations, so
that one society may display several subjected conflict groups. Beyond
these, one distinguishing feature of subjected groups must be emphasized. The Marxian expression "suppressed classes" might appear
to mean that any such group is characterized by the attributes which
Marx ascribed to, or found present in, the proletariat of his time.
However, this implication is by no means intended here. "Pauper-
ism," "slavery," absolute exclusion from the wealth and liberty of
society is a possible but unnecessary attribute of the incumbents of
roles of subjection. Here, again, the connection is indeterminate, i.e.,
variable, and its particular pattern can be established only by empirical
observation and for particular associations. It is not only conceivable
that members of the subjected group of one association belong to the
dominating group of another association, it is above all possible that
"suppressed classes" enjoy, despite their exclusion from legitimate
power, an (absolutely) high measure of social rewards without this
fact impeding their organization as interest groups or their participation in group conflicts. Even a "bourgeoisified proletariat" can
function as a subjected conflict group, for conflict groups and group
conflicts are solely based on the one criterion of participation in or
exclusion from the exercise of authority in imperatively coordinated
associations. Difficult as it may be for minds schooled in Marx to

separate the category of "suppressed class" from the ideas of poverty and exploitation, a well-formulated theory of group conflict requires the radical separation of these spheres.

CLASSES OR CONFLICT GROUPS?

Up to this point I have postponed and at times avoided the question whether the concept of class is a useful concept to employ and, if so, what its precise meaning is in the context of the theory of conflict group formation. The reader will not have failed to notice that I have in fact strenuously avoided the word "class" in the present chapter wherever possible. Before turning now to an attempt to settle this rather disturbing question, I want to emphasize one point. In my opinion, the problem of the applicability of the concept of class is a purely terminological problem. In positive terms, this means that it is in part a matter of arbitrary decision, and in part a matter of convenience. Logically, there is no reason why we should not call quasi-groups and interest groups classes or anything else. Pragmatically, of course, the usage and history of words has to be considered; it is unwise to provoke misunderstandings by choosing words which carry associations that are not intended. In negative terms, the terminological nature of this problem means that I see no meaning in the statement that class is a "historical concept" in the sense of being inseparably tied to a definite historical entity such as the industrial proletariat of the nineteenth century. "Historical concepts" of this kind are fictions of Hegelianism or, more generally, conceptual realism. If I shall therefore try to bring together, in the following pages, the arguments that can be advanced for and against using the concept of class for conflict groups other than those described by Marx, the ensuing discussion is concerned exclusively with problems of pragmatic convenience, and the conclusion it reaches remains reversible.

So far in our considerations there have emerged four main reasons why the concept of class should not be applied to the analysis of conflicts in post-capitalist societies. The first of these is of a historical nature. We have seen that the changes which have occurred since Marx's time have in several ways affected the classes with which he was concerned. Bourgeoisie and proletariat are no longer uniform blocs of identically situated and oriented people if, indeed, they can be said to exist at all in post-capitalist society. The progressive institutionalization of the values of achievement and equality has removed many barriers which for Marx were associated with the concept of class. Without anticipating the results of empirical analysis we can already conclude that conflict groups in modern society are likely to be rather loose aggregations combined for special purposes and within particular associations. In view of factual developments of this kind, it seems certainly questionable whether it is useful to employ for the conflict groups of advanced industrial society the concept used for the Marxian classes of the nineteenth century.

This doubt is strengthened by a second argument accruing from our theoretical considerations in the present chapter. We have deliberately restricted our model of group formation to elementary and highly formal features of the phenomenon. Most of the empirical characteristics of conflict groups are subject to a wide range of variability the limits of which may be fixed in terms of a constructed model but the substance of which needs to be determined by observation and experience. Conflict groups may, but need not be, immobile entities; they may, but need not be, characterized by a "class culture"; they may, but need not, engage in violent conflicts. Moreover, we have endeavored to detach the category of conflict groups and the whole notion of social conflicts from economic determinants both in the Marxian sense of relations of production and ownership and in the Weberian sense of socioeconomic class situations. Conceptually, the similarity between Marx's and even Weber's concepts of class and our concept of conflict group is but slight. There is reasonable doubt as to whether there is a chance for the concept of class not to be misunderstood if it is applied to conflict groups in the sense of this study.

Thirdly, in addition to these general conceptual difficulties, the question must be raised: what precisely do we mean by class even if we decide to apply this term to conflict groups? Are we to follow Ginsberg and conceive of classes as quasi-groups, i.e., unorganized aggregates of the occupants of positions endowed with role interests? Or are we to follow Marx in calling classes only such groups as have attained political organization and coherence, and which are interest groups? Distinctions such as those between "collectivity" and "class," or "class" and "party," or "class in itself" and "class for itself" are necessary, but they do not exactly help to render the concept of class unambiguous.

Finally, the history of the concept in sociological literature has to be considered. One may deplore the fact that the terms "class" and "stratum" have tended to become interchangeable categories in sociological studies, but it remains a fact. While the existence of a difference between the study of social conflict and the study of social stratification is probably plausible to anybody, the concepts of "class" and "stratum," as they are often used today, fail to express this difference. Under these conditions, it may not be wise to try to restore to the concept of class a meaning which for many it lost long ago.

There are, on the other hand, three arguments that might be held against these doubts about the applicability of the concept of class to conflict groups in the sense of our model. First, the alternative category of conflict group is so general as to be almost embarrassing. We have explicitly distinguished from other conflicts those conflicts arising out of the distribution of authority in associations. Yet there is no conceivable reason, other than an inconveniently narrow definition, why the contestants in conflicts between Protestants and Catholics, Negroes and whites, town and country should not be called conflict groups. Short of using a more specific, but extremely clumsy, expression (such as "conflict groups arising from authority structures in associations"), the concept of class seems to provide a convenient tool for emphasizing the limitations of scope of the theory advanced in this study.

This is, secondly, all the more plausible, since the heuristic purpose originally associated with the concept of class is also the heuristic purpose of this study. When Marx adapted the word "class" to the requirements of his theories, he used this word as a term for structurally generated groups that engage in conflicts over existing arrangements of social structure. It is true that before Marx the term "class" was used by a number of authors in a rather less specific sense; but it is probably fair to say that it was Marx's category which became germinal for later students in the field and which therefore represents its original version. The essential importance of this heuristic purpose has been emphasized at many points in our considerations. Since there is no other concept that expresses this purpose with equal clarity, one might consider it reasonable to retain the concept of class despite all qualifications necessitated by the arguments against it.

One of these arguments has referred to the history of the concept in sociological literature. Thirdly, however, there is one not entirely insignificant branch of sociological thinking which has consistently used (and uses) the term "class" in the form, if not the substance, assigned to it by Marx. This is true not only for many Marxist scholars whose work is, as we have seen, often pitifully barren and fruitless, but also for eminent non-Marxist (although possibly Marxian) sociologists such as Renner and Geiger, Aron and Gurvitch, Pareto and Mosca, Marshall and Ginsberg, Lipset and Bendix, and many others. We might go even further and assert that the trend of conceptual development in the work of these scholars anticipates in many ways the theses advanced in the present study. Many of them have tried to refine the concept of class by maintaining its heuristic purpose while altering its substance; quite often, this altering of substance meant a shift from property to power as a determinant, or other attempts at generalization. In using the concept of class for Marx's bourgeoisie and proletariat as well as for modern and utterly different conflict groups, one could refer not only to the origin of this concept with Marx, but also to a great and unbroken tradition in sociological analysis.

It is hard to weigh the "pros and cons" of the preceding argument entirely rationally; an element of personal preference will probably enter into any decision. Without trying to argue for this decision at any length, I will therefore state immediately that in my opinion the case in favor of retaining the concept of class is still sufficiently strong to warrant its application to even the most advanced industrial societies. This decision does involve, of course, a polemical stand against all those who "falsify" the term "class" by applying it to what should properly be called social strata. It also involves considerable extensions of the concept as it was used by Marx as well as by all Marxists and Marxians. But it emphasizes that in class analysis we are concerned (*a*) with systematic social conflicts and their structural origin, and (*b*) with but one specific type of such conflicts.

In terms of our model, the term "class" signifies conflict groups that are generated by the differential distribution of authority in imperatively coordinated associations. This definition implies no assumption as to the looseness or rigidity of their coherence, the presence or absence of a common culture or ideology (beyond specific interests) among their members, and the intensity or lack of intensity of their engagement in social conflicts.

It will be noted that this definition is inconclusive with respect to the differentiation of quasi-groups and interest groups. I would suggest that it is useful to leave it so. The category of class is a general term for groupings of the kind described more specifically in our model of conflict group formation. For all particular purposes of analysis, it is necessary to abandon this general category in favor of the more specific concepts of quasi-group and interest group. The attempt to confine the concept of class to either of these is bound, indeed, to provoke misunderstandings. Classes, like conflict groups, indicate an area and type of sociological analysis rather than its substance. Both terms are more useful in compounds such as "class analysis," "class structure," or "class conflict" than on their own. This is but one further illustration of the essential insignificance of a terminological dispute about these matters. For purposes of the present study, and without any dogmatic insistence on terms, I propose to dissolve the alternative "classes or conflict groups" into the definition "classes as conflict groups."

VI

Conflict Groups, Group Conflicts, and
Social Change

THE "FUNCTIONS" OF SOCIAL CONFLICT

Classes, understood as conflict groups arising out of the authority structure of imperatively coordinated associations, are in conflict. What are—so we must ask if we want to understand the lawfulness of this phenomenon—the social consequences, intended or unintended, of such conflicts? The discussion of this question involves, almost inevitably, certain value judgments. I think that R. Dubin is right in summarizing at least one prominent attitude toward the functions of social conflict as follows: "From the standpoint of the social order, conflict is viewed from two positions: (*a*) it may be destructive of social stability and therefore 'bad' because stability is good; (*b*) it may be evidence of the breakdown of social control and therefore symptomatic of an underlying instability in the social order. Both positions express a value preference for social stability" (77, p. 183). I would also agree with Dubin's own position: "Conflict may be labeled dysfunctional or symptomatic of an improperly integrated society. The empirical existence of conflict, however, is not challenged by the stability argument. . . . The fact of the matter is that group conflict cannot be wished out of existence. It is a reality with which social theorists must deal in constructing their general models of social behaviour" (p. 184). But I think that in two respects Dubin might have been rather less cautious. First, I should not hesitate, on the level of value judgments, to express a strong preference for the concept of societies that recognizes conflict as an essential feature of their structure and process. Secondly, and quite apart from value judgments, a strong case can be made for group conflict having consequences which, if not "functional," are utterly necessary for the social process. This case rests on the distinction between the two faces of society—a distinction which underlies our discussions throughout this study. It is perhaps the ultimate proof of the necessity of distinguishing these two faces that conflict itself, the crucial category in terms of the coercion model, has two faces, i.e., that of contributing to the integration of social "systems" and that of making for change.

Both these consequences have been admirably expressed by L. Coser. (Although, to my mind, Coser is rather too preoccupied with what he himself tends to call the "positive" or "integrative functions" of conflict.) On the one hand, Coser states in the unmistakable terminology of the integration theory of society (for which see my italics): "Conflict may serve to remove dissociating elements in a relationship and to *re-establish* unity. Insofar as conflict is the resolution of tension between antagonists it has *stabilizing functions* and becomes an *integrating component* of the relationship. However, not all conflicts are *positively functional* for the relationship. . . . Loosely structured groups, and open societies, by allowing conflicts, institute safeguards against the type of conflict which would *endanger basic consensus* and thereby *minimize the danger of divergences* touching core values. The interdependence of antagonistic groups and the crisscrossing within such societies of conflicts, which *serve to 'sew the social system together'* by cancelling each other out, thus *prevent disintegration* along one primary line of cleavage" (81, p. 80). On the other hand, Coser follows Sorel in postulating "the idea that conflict . . . prevents the ossification of the social system by exerting pressure for innovation and creativity" and states: "This conception seems to be more generally applicable than to class struggle alone. Conflict within and between groups in a society can prevent accommodations and habitual relations from progressively impoverishing creativity. The clash of values and interests, the tension between what is and what some groups feel ought to be, the conflict between vested interests and new strata and groups demanding their share of power, wealth and status, have been productive of vitality" (80, pp. 197 f.).

Conflict may, indeed, from a Utopian point of view, be conceived as one of the patterns contributing to the maintenance of the *status quo*. To be sure, this holds only for regulated conflicts, some of the conditions of which we shall try to explore presently. Coser's analysis of Simmel (81) has convincingly demonstrated that there is no need to abandon the integration theory of society simply because the phenomenon of conflict "cannot be wished away" but is a fact of observation. In this sense, conflict joins role allocation, socialization, and mobility as one of the "tolerable" processes which foster rather than endanger the stability of social systems. There seems little doubt, however, that from this point of view we can barely begin to understand the phenomenon of group conflicts. Were it only for its "positive functions," for which Coser found so many telling synonyms, class conflict would continue to be rather a nuisance which the sociologist would prefer to dispense with since it may, after all, "endanger basic consensus." So far as the present study is concerned, "continuing group conflict" will be regarded as "an important way of giving direction to social change" (Dubin, 77, p. 194). Societies are essentially historical creatures, and, because they are, they require the motive force of conflict—or, conversely, because there is conflict, there is historical change and development. The dialectics of conflict and history provide the ultimate reason of our interest in this phenomenon and at the same time signify the consequences of social conflict with which we are concerned.

Dubin's observation that conflict is a stubborn fact of social life is undoubtedly justified. Earlier, we have made the assertion explicit that social conflict is ubiquitous; in fact, this is one of the premises of our analysis. Possibly, this premise permits even further generalization. There has been in recent years some amount of interdisciplinary research on problems of conflict. In specific features the results of these interdisciplinary efforts remain as yet tentative; but one conclusion has been brought out by them with impressive clarity: it appears that not only in social life, but wherever there is life, there is conflict.[1] May we perhaps go so far as to say that conflict is a condition necessary for life to be possible at all? I would suggest, in any case, that all that is creativity, innovation, and development in the life of the individual, his group, and his society is due, to no small extent, to the operation of conflicts between group and group, individual and individual, emotion and emotion within one individual. This fundamental fact alone seems to me to justify the value judgment that conflict is essentially "good" and "desirable."

If I here assume social conflict, and the particular type of group conflict with which we are concerned in the present study, to be ubiq-

[1] This and numerous other statements in the present chapter are based on discussions with and publications of psychologists, anthropologists, lawyers, and social psychologists at the Center for Advanced Study in the Behavioral Sciences, Stanford, California. John Bowlby, M.D., and Professor Frank Newman, LL.D., have been particularly helpful in making suggestions. In support of the statement in the text I might also refer, however, to the symposium published in *Conflict Resolution* (77), which includes contributions by economists, sociologists, social psychologists, anthropologists, and psychologists, and strongly supports my point.

uitous, I want this statement to be understood more rigidly than is usual. At an earlier point I have intimated what I mean by rigidity in this sense. One or two remarks in addition to these earlier hints seem in order. In summarizing earlier research, Mack and Snyder state with some justice that by most authors "competition is not regarded as conflict or a form of conflict" (77, p. 217). The alleged difference between the two is identified differently by different authors. T. H. Marshall emphasizes common interests, rather than divergent interests, as characteristic of states of competition or conflict (59, p. 99). For Mack and Snyder, "competition involves striving for scarce objects . . . according to established rules which strictly limit what the competitors can do to each other in the course of striving; the chief objective is the scarce object, not the injury or destruction of an opponent per se" (77, p. 217). It seems to me, however, that it is not accidental if Mack and Snyder state a little later that "conflict arises from 'position scarcity' and 'resource scarcity,' " and that therefore "conflict relations always involve attempts to gain control of scarce resources and positions" (pp. 218 f.). Despite terminological traditions, I can see no reason why a conceptual distinction between competition and conflict should be necessary or, indeed, desirable.[2] Like competition, conflict involves a striving for scarce resources. From the point of view of linguistic usage, it is perfectly proper to say that conflicting interest groups compete for power. As far as the "established rules" of competition are concerned, they emphasize but one type of conflict, namely, regulated conflict. In the present study, the notion of conflict is intended to include relations such as have been described by many other authors as competitive.

Another distinction almost general in the literature is that between changes "within" and changes "of" or conflicts "within" and conflicts "about" the system. Many authors have been at pains to define these differences. Coser, e.g., proposes "to talk of a change *of* system when all major structural relations, its basic institutions and its prevailing value system have been drastically altered," but admits that "in concrete historical reality, no clear-cut distinctions exist" (80, p. 202). Marshall distinguishes more specifically "conflict that arises out of

---

[2] At least, no such reason has been put forward. It might be argued, of course, that the concept of competition employed in economic theory is rather different from that defined by Marshall or Mack and Snyder, and does not carry any conflict connotation. I am not entirely sure that this argument is justified, but for purposes of the present analysis competition in a technical economic sense will be excluded.

the division of labor, conflict, that is to say, over the terms on which cooperation is to take place, as illustrated by a wage dispute between employer and employed," from "conflict over the system itself upon which the allocation of functions and the distribution of benefits are based" (59, p. 99). Thinking in terms of inclusive epochs like "feudalism" and "capitalism" as well as in terms of the existence of political parties that propose to change "the whole system" can probably explain the widespread feeling that a distinction between "changes within" and "changes of" is necessary. But apart from these, it is surely no coincidence that it was Parsons who emphasized that "it is necessary to distinguish clearly between the processes *within* the system and processes of change *of* the system." This very distinction betrays traces of the integration approach to social analysis. If conflict and change are assumed to be ubiquitous, there is no relevant difference between "changes within" and "changes of," because the "system" is no longer the frame of reference. It may be useful to distinguish more or less intense or violent conflicts and major and minor changes, but these are gradations to be accounted for in terms of intervening variables of an empirical nature. In the present study, no assumption is implied as to the type of change or conflict effected by the antagonism of conflict groups. Wage disputes as well as political conflicts "over the system itself" will be regarded as manifestations of class conflict, i.e., of clashes of interest arising out of and concerned with the distribution of authority in associations.

As with the theory of class formation, the real problems of the theory of class conflict consist in the identification of the empirical variables delimiting the range of variability of forms and types. Change and conflict are equally universal in society. But in historical reality we always encounter particular changes and specific conflicts, and these, even in the more limited sphere of class conflict, present a varied picture of manifold types and forms. Assuming the ubiquity of conflict and change, we have to try to discover some of the factors that influence its concrete shapes.

INTENSITY AND VIOLENCE: THE VARIABILITY OF CLASS CONFLICT

The substance of the theory of class action, or class conflict, can be summarized in one statement: conflict groups in the sense of this study, once they have organized themselves, engage in conflicts that effect structure changes. The theory of class action presupposes the complete formation of conflict groups and specifies their interrelations.

However, this tautological statement is evidently not all that can be said about group conflicts, nor is it all that one would expect a theory of group conflict to provide. Beyond a basic assumption of this kind, a theory of class conflict has to identify and systematically interrelate those variables that can be shown to influence patterns of intergroup conflict. In the present chapter several such variables will be discussed in some detail, their selection being guided by the significance they suggest for the course and outcome of class conflict. Before we embark upon this discussion, however, there is one preliminary question that has to be settled. The statement that class conflicts are empirically variable is sufficiently vague to be almost meaningless. What is it— we must ask—about class conflicts that is variable and therefore subject to the influence of factors to be identified? In this question, the categories of intensity and violence are essential. In some connection or other, the terms "intensity" and "violence" can be found present in any discussion of conflict. Here is one example. Mack and Snyder, in their summary of earlier research, on the one hand derive the proposition "a high degree of intimacy between the parties, as contrasted with a high degree of functional interdependence, will *intensify* conflict" (77, p. 225), while, on the other hand, they suggest "the more integrated into the society are the parties to conflict, the less likely will conflict be *violent*" (p. 227). The distinction between the two concepts is not perhaps entirely clear from these statements, and, indeed, many authors use them almost synonymously. Yet there is an important difference between them, as Simmel knew when he said: "It is almost inevitable that an element of commonness injects itself into . . . enmity once the stage of open *violence* yields to another relationship, even though this new relation may contain a completely undiminished sum of *animosity* between the two parties" (see 81, p. 121). That conflict is variable means that its intensity and violence are variable; but the two may vary independently and are, therefore, distinct aspects of any conflict situation.[3]

The category of intensity refers to the energy expenditure and degree of involvement of conflicting parties. A particular conflict may be said to be of high intensity if the cost of victory or defeat is high for the parties concerned. The more importance the individual participants of a conflict attach to its issues and substance, the more intense is this conflict. For class conflict a continuum might be constructed ranging, e.g., from a conflict within a chess club which involves but

---

[3] All italics in the quotations of this paragraph are mine.

a small segment of the individual personalities concerned to the overriding class conflict, in Marx's analyses, in which individuals are engaged with almost their entire personalities. In operational terms, the cost aspect is here crucial. Members of a group that strives to upset the authority structure of a chess club stand to lose less in case of defeat than members of a trade union who endeavor to change the authority structure of the enterprise (or their own social conditions by way of this authority structure).[4] The cost of defeat, and with it the intensity of conflict, differs in these cases.

By contrast to its intensity, the violence of conflict relates rather to its manifestations than to its causes; it is a matter of the weapons that are chosen by conflict groups to express their hostilities. Again, a continuum can be constructed ranging from peaceful discussions to militant struggles such as strikes and civil wars. Whether or not class conflict expresses itself in militant clashes of interest is in principle independent of the intensity of involvement of the parties. The scale of degree of violence, including discussion and debate, contest and competition, struggle and war, displays its own patterns and regularities.[5] Violent class struggles, or class wars, are but one point on this scale.

While violence and intensity of conflict vary independently, several of the factors shortly to be discussed affect both. This fact can be illustrated with reference to one factor which has been mentioned already and which need not therefore be discussed again at any length. I have mentioned in the preceding chapter that the conditions of organization of interest groups continue to affect group conflict even after the complete formation of conflict groups. They are, in this sense, a factor which, among others, accounts for variations of intensity and violence. With respect to the intensity of class conflict, the political conditions of organization appear especially relevant. It may be suggested that, for the individuals concerned, involvement in con-

---

[4] I have as yet not given a systematic exposition of the patterns of change effected by class conflict; the formulation in the text may therefore give rise to misunderstandings. These will, I hope, be cleared up in the section on "class conflict and structure change" later in this chapter.

[5] In terms of the distinction thus introduced, we are now able to reformulate the contrast between the conception of conflict here assumed and that of several other authors. The latter tend to confine the term "conflict" to one point on the scale of degree of violence, namely, highly violent clashes. In the present study, however, conflict is conceived as including the whole scale, i.e., any clash of interest independent of the violence of its expressions.

flicts decreases as the legitimacy of conflicts and, by implication, their issues become recognized. However, in the ensemble of factors affecting intensity of conflict, the specific weight of the conditions of organization is probably not very great. By contrast, it is considerable among the variables involved in determining the violence of conflict manifestations. As soon as conflict groups have been permitted and been able to organize themselves, the most uncontrollably violent form of conflict, that of guerrilla warfare, is excluded. Moreover, the very fact of organization presupposes some degree of recognition which in turn makes the most violent forms of conflict unnecessary and, therefore, unlikely. This is not to say, of course, that conflicts between organized groups cannot be highly intense and violent. The conditions of organization are but one, and not the most important, factor among many. Of these I have selected four which seem to me of particular importance and which will be dealt with separately in the following sections of this chapter.

PLURALISM VERSUS SUPERIMPOSITION: CONTEXTS AND TYPES OF CONFLICT

One of the crucial elements of the theory of group conflict consists in the strict relation of conflicts to particular associations. Any given conflict can be explained only in terms of the association in which it arose and, conversely, any given association can be analyzed in terms of the conflicts to which it gives rise. In theory, this approach would suggest that inclusive societies present the picture of a multitude of competing conflicts and conflict groups. The two-class model applies not to total societies but only to specific associations within societies (including, of course, the inclusive association of the state, i.e., the whole society in its political aspect). If, in a given society, there are fifty associations, we should expect to find a hundred classes, or conflict groups in the sense of the present study. Apart from these, there may be an undetermined number of conflict groups and conflicts arising from antagonisms other than those based on the authority structure of associations. In fact, of course, this extreme scattering of conflicts and conflict groups is rarely the case. Empirical evidence shows that different conflicts may be, and often are, superimposed in given historical societies, so that the multitude of possible conflict fronts is reduced to a few dominant conflicts. I suggest that this phenomenon has considerable bearing on the degree of intensity and violence of empirical conflicts.

The pluralism-superimposition scale which might thus be constructed has two distinct dimensions. One of these relates to the separation or combination of conflicts of the class type in different associations. Let us restrict ourselves, for purposes of illustration, to the three associations of the state, industry, and the church in countries in which one church dominates the sphere of religious institutions. It is conceivable that the ruling and the subjected groups of each of these associations are largely separate aggregations. The dignitaries of the church may be mere citizens of the state and may have no industrial property or authority. Similarly, the citizens of the state may be church dignitaries or industrial managers. This is the kind of situation here described as pluralistic. Within each of the three associations there are (class) conflicts, but, as between these, there is dissociation rather than congruence. Evidently, complete dissociation and pluralism are, in the case mentioned, empirically rather unlikely. It is more probable that the workers of industry are at the same time mere members of the church and mere citizens of the state. One might expect that the dignitaries of the church are in some ways connected with the rulers of the state and possibly even with the owners or managers of industry. If this is the case, (class) conflicts of different associations appear superimposed; i.e., the opponents of one association meet again—with different titles, perhaps, but in identical relations—in another association. In this case, the personnel of the conflict groups of different associations is the same.

Such congruence may also occur with conflict groups of different types. Again, a realistic example may serve to illustrate the point. We might suppose that in a given country there are three dominant types of social conflict: conflict of the class type, conflict between town and country, and conflict between Protestants and Catholics. It is of course conceivable that these lines of conflict cut across each other in a random fashion, so that, e.g., there are as many Protestants among the ruling groups of the state as there are Catholics and as many townspeople in either denomination as there are countrypeople. However, here, too, we might suspect that dissociation and pluralism are empirically rather unlikely to occur. One would not be surprised to find that most Protestants live in towns and most Catholics in the country, or that only one of the denominations commands the instruments of political control. If this is so, we are again faced with a phenomenon of superimposition in the sense of the same people meeting in different contexts but in identical relations of conflict.

With respect to the violence of manifestations of conflict, the pluralism-superimposition scale is not likely to be a factor of great significance. While there is a possible (negative) correlation between the degree of pluralism and the violence of conflicts in a given society, there is little reason to believe that dissociation of types and contexts of conflict makes industrial strikes, for example, impossible. Only in the inclusive association of the state would there seem to be a probability of pluralism reducing and superimposition increasing the violence of interest clashes.

At the same time, this scale is of the utmost importance for variations in the intensity of class conflict. The proposition seems plausible that there is a close positive correlation between the degree of superimposition of conflicts and their intensity. When conflict groups encounter each other in several associations and in several clashes, the energies expended in all of them will be combined and one overriding conflict of interests will emerge. The situation with which Marx dealt is a case in point. If incumbents of subjected positions in industry are also subjected in all other associations; if they are, moreover, identical with conflict groups other than those determined by authority relations, a "division of society into two large hostile classes" may indeed result—a situation, that is, in which one inclusive conflict dominates the picture of the total society. If, on the other hand, the inevitable pluralism of associations is accompanied by a pluralism of fronts of conflict, none of these is likely to develop the intensity of class conflicts of the Marxian type. There is in this case, for every member of the subjected class of one association, the promise of gratification in another association. Every particular conflict remains confined to the individual in one of his many roles and absorbs only that part of the individual's personality that went into this role.[6] The empirical analysis of pluralism and superimposition of contexts and types of conflict is one of the important problems suggested by the theory of social classes and class conflicts.

PLURALISM VERSUS SUPERIMPOSITION: AUTHORITY AND THE DISTRIBUTION OF REWARDS AND FACILITIES

In connection with the concept of class situation, we have briefly (and, for the most part, critically) considered the relation between class structure and social stratification at several points in the pre-

---

[6] This type of analysis seems to me to provide one of the answers to the question why there is no socialism in the United States. Throughout her history, the pluralism of associations and conflicts has made inclusive conflict groups held together by quasi-religious ideologies unnecessary. There has been no single group that enjoyed universal privilege or suffered universal alienation.

ceding chapters. It is not my intention to repeat here what has been said before. Rather, I propose to summarize and extend these earlier discussions with particular emphasis on the problems of intensity and violence of class conflicts. It is evident that in the context of a theory of group conflict of the type under discussion, "class situation" is an unnecessary concept. It means no more than what we have described as the authority position of aggregates in associations. The condition of a quasi-group in terms of the distribution of authority signifies the "situation" that underlies class conflict. However, the traditional concept of class situation includes a number of elements which, while irrelevant for the formation of social classes, affect their patterns of conflict in ways to be defined. Property, economic status, and social status are no determinants of class, but they do belong to the factors influencing the empirical course of clashes of interest between conflict groups.

As with contexts and types of conflict, the problem of rewards and facilities can be seen in terms of a contrast between divergence and parallelism, or pluralism and superimposition. Thus, property can, but need not, be associated with the exercise of authority. It is conceivable that those who occupy positions of domination in industry do not own industrial property—and, indeed, that those in positions of subjection do own such property. The separation of ownership and control, and certain systems of the distribution of shares to industrial workers, are cases in point. While neither of these structural arrangements eliminates the causes of (industrial) conflict, they have an impact on its intensity and violence. Once again, a certain parallelism between authority and property ownership may seem more probable, but it is not necessary.

The same holds for the economic status of persons in different authority positions. By economic status I shall here understand status in terms of strictly occupational rewards such as income, job security, and general social security as it accrues from occupational position. It is both possible and reasonably probable that those in positions of domination enjoy a somewhat higher economic status, and that these two attributes of social position are in this sense superimposed. But numerous illustrations could also be given for divergences between the two. In the early labor unions, and for many shop stewards and local union secretaries today, authority involves a comparative loss of income and security. In the Roman Catholic church, authority is supposed, in theory if not in practice, to be accompanied by low economic status. In totalitarian countries, political authority usually conveys high incomes but also a high degree of insecurity which lowers the economic status of dominant groups. Such divergences of authority position and economic status make for a plurality of noncongruent scales of position in a society, which constitutes one of the critical facts of class analysis.

Divergences of position are even more evident if we contrast authority positions with people's social status in the sense of the prestige attached to their position by themselves and by others in relevant universes of ranking. The prestige of power is a highly precarious quantity in all societies. Unless all existing studies are wrong in their findings, there would in fact seem to be, for persons in the upper ranges of the status scale, an inverse relation between the authority and the prestige. The judge (United States), the doctor (Britain), and the university professor (Germany) enjoy a markedly higher prestige than the cabinet minister or the large-scale entrepreneur.[7] Probably, the theory of class conflict with its assumption of opposing role interests would account for this phenomenon. On the other hand, there are and have been associations in which the division of authority and the scale of prestige followed identical lines. In the industrial enterprise, this would still seem to be the case in most countries (and with the possible exception of scientifically trained staff members). Thus, we also find here an empirically variable relation that is likely to affect the course of class conflict.

All examples chosen in the preceding paragraphs serve to illustrate the phenomenon of relative deprivation, i.e., the situation in which those subjected to authority are at the same time relatively worse placed in terms of socioeconomic status. However, in nineteenth-century Europe, and in some countries even today, we encounter what by contrast may be called an absolute deprivation of groups of people in socioeconomic terms. If the social condition of industrial workers, who are as such excluded from authority, falls below a physiological subsistence minimum or "poverty line," the effects of such deprivation are likely to be different in kind from those of relative deprivation. I would suggest that in this case, and in this case only, the superimposition of scales of status and the distribution of authority is likely to increase the violence of class conflict. This is a subtle and complex relation. So far as we know, oppression and deprivation may reach a point at which militant conflict motivation gives way to apathy and lethargy. Short of this point, however, there

[7] For relevant data, cf. the studies by the National Opinion Research Center (120), Glass (107), and Bolte (103).

is reason to believe that absolute deprivation coupled with exclusion from authority makes for greater violence in conflict relations.

Relative deprivation, on the other hand, tends to affect the intensity of conflict rather than its violence. If incumbents of positions of subjection enjoy the countervailing gratification of a relatively high socioeconomic status, they are unlikely to invest as much energy in class conflicts arising out of the authority structure of associations as they would if they were deprived of both authority and socioeconomic status. Dominant groups are correspondingly not so likely to be as involved in the defense of their authority unless their high socioeconomic status is simultaneously involved. In terms of the intensity of conflict, pluralism would again seem to make for a decrease, and superimposition or congruence for an increase:[8] the lower the correlation is between authority position and other aspects of socioeconomic status, the less intense are class conflicts likely to be, and vice versa.

MOBILITY VERSUS IMMOBILITY:
THE "CLASSLESS" SOCIETY

Since Marx, the idea of a "classless society" has remained an often-used category in sociological literature. By "Marxist" scholars it is applied to a number of existing societies as an allegedly valid category of description. But among "non-Marxist" social scientists, too, the concept of classless society is occasionally used for describing empirical states of society. Thus S. Landshut (53) has tried to demonstrate the classlessness of present-day Western industrial societies. In a rather more definite sense, a number of sociologists have employed the concept of a classless society to describe more limited phenomena, such as the agricultural cooperatives of Israel. J. Ben-David, for example, speaks on this basis of a "collectivist," "classless" stage of the social development of Israel (125). We have now assembled the materials for examining the sense and nonsense of the sociological category of a classless society. This examination will reveal an additional factor affecting the intensity and violence of class conflict.

On the basis of the assumptions and models introduced in this

---

[8] This proposition must be opposed to the assumption of integration theorists that the congruence of different scales of social position is a requisite of stable, integrated societies (cf. Parsons, in 35). The exact opposite seems true, even from the point of view of integration theory. I cannot help feeling that this is one of the points at which integration theorists display—unwillingly, to be sure—almost totalitarian convictions.

study, the concept of classless society can mean either of two things. First, it may be intended to describe societies in which there are no structures of authority that give rise to the formation of conflict groups and group conflicts. A society is classless if it is "powerless," i.e., if there is no authority exercised in it at all, or if such authority is distributed equally among all citizens. But in this sense the category of classless society is sociologically meaningless. It may be possible to conceive of a society in which all differences of *income* and *prestige* are leveled and which is therefore "stratumless," but it is hardly possible to imagine a society in which there is no differentiation of roles in terms of legitimate *power*. Permanent anarchism is socially Utopian. Any society, and, indeed, any social organization, requires some differentiation into positions of domination and positions of subjection. No matter what the formal nature of the authority mechanism, it is a functional imperative of social organizations. Since classes *can* be explained in terms of the differential distribution of authority, there is no sociological substance in the assumption of a classless society devoid of differentiated authority structures.

However, the idea of a classless society may be understood in a second sense. It is possible to conceive of a society whose structure contains positions equipped with different authority rights but which does not enable any group of persons to occupy these positions regularly and exclusively. The same might hold in imperatively coordinated associations other than the state, e.g., in industry. Associations may be governed by the principle of an alternating chairmanship, according to which the incumbency of positions of domination may or may not be patterned. The collective settlements (*kibbutzim*) of Israel seem to provide a case in point. At least originally it was stipulated that every member in turn was to occupy the positions of leadership for relatively short periods of time.[9] In view of examples of this kind, it seems plausible to argue that where there is no group which is capable of monopolizing the positions of authority, it is virtually impossible for coherent conflict groups to emerge, and the society or association in question is therefore classless. To be sure, this is a kind of classlessness rather different from that of the Utopian anarchy; still, it cannot be denied that it makes sense to speak of class-

---

[9] The same principle (of "annuity") may also be found in other organizations, such as in German universities where the administrative and scholastic head (*Rektor*) changes every year, and every full professor must (or may) expect to be elected in his time.

lessness in this case also. We might say that societies and associations governed by a permanently "alternating chairmanship" are classless so far as social mobility is concerned, for it is not the structure of positions but the fluctuation of personnel that in this case prevents the formation of classes and conflict between them. The example of classlessness by fluctuation provides a welcome opportunity to try to settle the intricate problem of the relationship of social mobility to class conflict.

Here, as elsewhere, the concept of social mobility is too general to be useful. Different types of mobility have to be distinguished, and their relation to class conflict examined separately. For purposes of this analysis, it seems sufficient to distinguish between intergeneration mobility—i.e., fluctuations that from the individual's point of view occur at the beginning of his occupational (or even educational) career—and intrageneration mobility, i.e., fluctuations during the occupational life of the individual. Either of these, if present to any considerable extent, of course characterizes societies in which class membership is not an inescapable and inherited fate. We shall presently have to return to this other extreme of the mobility scale which, according to our theory, suggests a very high intensity of class conflict.

Intergeneration mobility seems fully compatible with class formation and class conflict. If a man's position in the authority structure of an association remains the same throughout his membership in this association, it appears likely that he belongs to a quasi-group as well as to an interest group growing out of this, even if his son or his father belongs to a different class. Schumpeter's comparison of classes with "a hotel or an autobus" which "are always occupied, but always by different people," is here pertinent (27, p. 171). Where the personnel of classes changes between generations only, there is a sufficient degree of stability to permit the formation of conflicting interest groups. Janowitz's finding that intergeneration mobility has no detrimental consequences for the coherence of secondary groupings may be regarded as an empirical confirmation of this thesis.

The case of societies in which there is a high degree of intrageneration mobility is rather more difficult. To begin with, further distinctions are here required. Not all types of intrageneration mobility affect class formation and class conflict. At least potentially, classes are large groupings which may display, from the point of view of social stratification, considerable differentiation within themselves. Mobility within classes, however, is entirely irrelevant for our context. Thus, upward and downward movements between skilled, semiskilled, and unskilled industrial occupations do not affect the stability of the conflict group of industrial workers. Moreover, single upward or downward moves by individuals, even if they involve a change of class allegiance, do not appear destructive of classes. It is only the institutionalized principle of an alternating chairmanship that may give rise to a state of quasi-classlessness. If the individual can change his class belongingness at will, or is even forced to do so regularly; if, e.g., the worker can become an entrepreneur merely if he wants to; or if every member of the community has to be mayor at least once— then we encounter a type and a degree of intrageneration mobility that makes class formation and class conflict impossible. In this case, class belongingness becomes an accidental or merely temporary occurrence. Although there still is a quasi-group structure of authority roles, the continuous exchange of their incumbents makes impossible the organization of interest groups defending or attacking the legitimacy of authority structures: there is no class conflict, and there are no classes in the strict sense.

As a mobile society (of the intrageneration variety), the classless society is thus a sociological category of realistic significance. However, one qualification to this conclusion is necessary. There is something to be said for an empirical generalization which Mosca calls the "law of inertia": "All political forces have the property which in physics is called inertia, i.e., a tendency to stay in a given state" (24, p. 61). Ben-David has specified this "law" with respect to Israel. For him, classlessness in the indicated sense characterizes "revolutionary periods" of social development rather than lasting types of social order (125, p. 303). Usually, these periods last but a few years. Then, that "articulation of the power structure" and "functional differentiation" sets in which Ben-David demonstrates for the social structure of the professions in Israel (p. 309). Although the rulers of totalitarian states like to operate with an "ideology of perpetual national emergency," as demonstrated impressively by Bendix (138, p. 443), for which the well-known theory of the "permanent revolution" is an example, it is plausible that the indicated state of quasi-classlessness is never more than a combination of transitory processes of radical change (which soon gives way to a minimum of stability) and of monopolization of power that makes possible the formation of classes and conflict between them. Classlessness by (intrageneration) mobility is, in sociological analysis, a limiting case that always tends toward its own abolition and that may therefore be ignored. There is no reason to assume that a stable society can operate on the principle of the continuous patterned exchange of the personnel of authority positions.[10]

While social mobility, apart from its limiting case of permanent exchange between the classes within generations, cannot thus be said to present an obstacle to the formation of classes and the existence of class conflict, there can be little doubt that it affects the intensity of class conflict. From the point of view of mobility two distinct types of classes may be distinguished. With respect to dominant conflict groups, Mosca calls one of these the "aristocratic class" bent on the "maintenance of authority for the descendants of those who possess it at a given point of time," and distinguishes it from the "democratic class" characterized by the "tendency to rejuvenate the ruling class by upward mobility of persons from the ruled class" (24, p. 322). G. D. H. Cole confines the term "class" to the first of these types and refers to the second as "elite" (39). In analogy to those terms of Max Weber's frequently used in connection with social mobility I would recommend speaking here of "closed" and "open" classes. Where allocation to authority positions is based on ascriptive criteria, we find closed classes. By contrast, open classes are recruited anew in every generation. These types are nevertheless but two points on a scale of numerous gradations. From caste-like rigidity to quasi-classlessness there is a continuum of types of social classes determined by degrees of inter- and intrageneration social mobility. It seems plausible that this continuum also defines a scale of conflict intensity. There is an inverse relation between the degree of openness of classes and the intensity of class conflict. The more upward and downward mobility there is in a society, the less comprehensive and fundamental are class conflicts likely to be.[11] As mobility increases, group solidarity is increasingly replaced by competition between individuals, and the energies invested by individuals in class conflict decrease.

It is easy to see that the correlations between conflict intensity and empirical variables suggested in the preceding sections of this chapter

[10] There is possibly some connection between the size of associations and the feasibility of the principle of alternating chairmanship: the larger the association, the smaller the probability that complete openness of the authority positions will be maintained for longer periods of time. It may be noted, here, that even in the Soviet Union purges have become more difficult technically today than they were in 1935.

[11] From this point of view, the limiting case of quasi-classlessness becomes part of the intensity scale; it is distinguished in this sense not by the absence of classes, but by an intensity of conflict amounting to zero. In view of our assumption that class conflicts are universal, this seems the most plausible formulation of the case.

all involve a psychological factor as well. The intensity of conflicts is a function of the involvement of individuals. Earlier I have suggested that this involvement is likely to be greater if the individual participates in specific conflicts with several of his roles than if he participates only with one. With respect to mobility, our proposition might be reformulated in psychological terms also. If the individual sees for his son, or even for himself, the chance of rising into the dominant or falling into the subjected class, he is not as likely to engage his whole personality in class conflicts as he is when class position is of a more permanent nature. While in general these psychological assumptions are probably safe to make, it has to be recognized that from the individual's point of view nonstructural factors may also influence his involvement in group conflict. Without doubt there are psychological constellations that make one individual more "quarrelsome" than another. I would suggest that individual variations of this kind are of but minor significance for the over-all intensity of class conflict; at the same time, their presence must not be overlooked in a comprehensive analysis.

THE REGULATION OF CLASS CONFLICT

All the factors discussed so far have been related primarily to variations in the intensity of class conflict. Their effect on the violence of conflict manifestations seems but slight. The reverse is true with respect to the final, and in many ways most crucial, factor affecting the empirical patterns of class conflict: conflict regulation. Probably, effective conflict regulation is also of some consequence for the intensity of group conflict; but this important process is above all concerned with expressions or manifestations of conflict, and it therefore determines degrees of violence rather than intensity. In discussing the regulation of social conflict I shall start with a number of seemingly terminological problems. As the patient reader will soon realize, however, every one of these is tied to substantial problems of patterns of conflict, so that the distinction between terminological and substantial discussions becomes largely spurious.

There are a number of competing concepts for what we shall call conflict regulation, some of which have connotations not intended here. This is especially true with respect to the concept of conflict *resolution*. The idea that conflicts may be resolved could mean, and often is thought to imply, that it is possible to eliminate given conflicts altogether. As used by some, the notion of conflict resolution addresses itself to the causes rather than the expressions of social conflict. This notion is at the very least misleading, and I propose to reject it on theoretical grounds. There is one, and only one, sense in which one might say that a conflict has been resolved: the specific issues of a specific conflict, e.g., the claim of a union for a certain wage increase on a certain date, may be settled in such a way as not to reappear again. But it should by now be abundantly evident that from the point of view here suggested such specific settlements do not in the least affect the causes and determinants of even the specific conflict of the example; if, with changing issues, this conflict persists it has not therefore been resolved. The concept of conflict resolution will be rejected as reflecting a sociologically mistaken ideology according to which complete elimination of conflict is possible and desirable.[12]

A second notion that has to be rejected as sociologically meaningless is that of the *suppression* of social conflict. It is perhaps evident without discussion that suppression cannot be thought of as an effective (or indeed desirable) means of regulating social conflicts. However, I would go one step further and assert that effective suppression of conflict is in the long run impossible. This assertion contains the invariably awkward expression "in the long run." Even in our own century, history has shown that for totalitarian regimes it is possible to suppress opposition both in industry and in the state for what are, for the people concerned, very considerable periods of time. By using the phrase "in the long run," I do not want to be misunderstood as taking a cynical view of facts of this kind. It seems to me, however, that the very history of contemporary totalitarian states has demonstrated that the "long run" in this case extends to no more than a decade at the most. To the superficial observer this may seem a surprising statement; unfortunately, I can here substantiate it only by one or two rather gross assertions. Where an attempt is made to suppress conflict altogether, either of two consequences is likely to occur within at most a decade. Either suppression amounts to complete nonrecognition and exclusion of opposition, in which case revolutionary changes of the Hungarian type are virtually bound to occur; or suppression of opposition is coupled with a careful and continuous scrutiny of the embryonic manifest interests of the potential opposition, and changes are introduced from time to time which incorpo-

---

[12] I recognize of course that the term "conflict resolution" might be defined differently. Thus, I have no doubt that the editors of the journal *Conflict Resolution* are really concerned with conflict regulation. However, it seems to me necessary to emphasize in the strongest possible terms the assumption of the universality of conflict—regulated or not.

rate some of these interests.[13] In the latter case, suppression is not complete, and violent conflicts may simmer under the surface for a long time before they erupt; the ineffectiveness of the former type of suppression needs no comment.

We are here concerned not with resolution and suppression but with the *regulation* of social conflict. By this we mean such forms of conflict control as address themselves to the expressions of conflicts rather than their causes, and as imply the continued existence of antagonisms of interest and interest groups. Effective conflict regulation in this sense presupposes the presence of at least three factors, each of which in itself influences the violence of conflict manifestations.

First, for effective conflict regulation to be possible, both parties to a conflict have to recognize the necessity and reality of the conflict situation and, in this sense, the fundamental justice of the cause of the opponent. In a way, this is a value premise. Recognizing the justice of one's opponent's cause does not mean of course that the substance of the opponent's interests has to be recognized as justified at the outset. Rather, recognition means, here, that both parties accept their conflict for what it is, namely, an inevitable outgrowth of the authority structure of associations. Wherever the attempt is made to dispute the case of the opponent by calling it "unrealistic," or denying the opponent the right to make a case at all, effective regulation is not possible. This is also true, however, where conflicts are not recognized for what they are, and where too great an emphasis is put on what are often misleadingly called "common interests." It seems to me that the London *Economist* was well-advised when it "reproached British unions for their 'moderation' which it declared in part responsible for the stagnation and low productivity of British capitalism; it compared their policies unfavourably with the more aggressive policies of American unions whose constant pressure for higher wages has kept the American economy dynamic" (see 80, p. 198). Without doubt, there are "common interests" in any conflict situation; without community, no conflict, and vice versa. However, the crucial factor for effectively regulating conflicts is recognition, and even emphasis, of systematic divergence and opposition. The attempt to obliterate lines of conflict by ready ideologies of harmony

[13] This "subtle totalitarianism," as one might call it, can be amply illustrated by the history of the Soviet Union. The most striking example is perhaps provided by the history of land collectivization (under Stalin), where the peasants' interests were increasingly recognized by the government.

and unity in effect serves to increase rather than decrease the violence of conflict manifestations.[14]

A second prerequisite of effective conflict regulation is the organization of interest groups. So long as conflicting forces are diffuse, incoherent aggregates, regulation is virtually impossible. Here, Coser's (or Simmel's) point is quite pertinent, namely, that despite the paradox of the situation, conflict groups are often actually intent on fostering each other's unity and organization. "A unified party prefers a unified opponent" (81, 132). Guerrilla warfare is not susceptible of effective regulation.[15] Dubin believes that it is feasible to make a general proposition to the effect that "conflict between groups becomes institutionalized" (77, p. 287). Once again, however, the problem of the time span (covered by Dubin's "becomes") arises. Possibly, the inertia principle applies to this aspect of group conflicts also, so that "in due course" most conflict groups come to be organized. We have seen, however, that this organization depends above all on certain structural conditions which are not universally present. From the point of view of effective conflict regulation, these conditions of organization may be said to be one of its prerequisites, since the organization of conflict groups itself is one of its prerequisites.

Thirdly, in order for effective regulation to be possible, the opposing parties in social conflicts have to agree on certain formal rules of the game that provide the framework of their relations. Again, Dubin seems to think that such agreement invariably comes about: "Continuous conflict between groups leads to standardized modes of conflict. . . . Continuous conflict between groups leads to routinized interactions" (77, p. 190). Here, too, however, Dubin's propositions seem overly optimistic. By rules of the game we shall understand such procedural norms as are binding for the contestants without prejudicing the outcome of the contest. Normally, they would include stipulations as to where and how to meet, how to proceed, how to reach decisions, what sanctions to apply in case of noncompliance, and when and how to change the rules themselves. Kerr has pointed out that such rules are generally advantageous for conflict regulation as well as for the interest groups involved: "These rules normally protect the survival of both parties, reduce the potential injury to each, intro-

---

[14] One illustration of such ill-conceived attitudes and their consequences will be given in the discussion of the German codetermination experiment in Chapter VII.

[15] I am sure that this point will be confirmed emphatically by all Colonial Secretaries of mid-twentieth century governments. Very often, it is the absence of an organized opponent that makes the regulation of colonial disputes in the contemporary world so difficult.

duce some predictability into their actions, and protect third parties from undue harm" (84, p. 235). Examples for the establishment of such rules are numerous in industrial and political as well as international conflict. It is important to note, however, that rules of the game can serve their function only if and as long as they put both parties on an equal footing and do not imply any substantive stipulations disabling one or the other conflict group.[16]

Once these prerequisites of conflict regulation are present, varying forms of regulation itself can come into operation. While a comprehensive survey of such forms is neither possible nor necessary here, it seems useful to examine some of the more frequent types of conflict regulation in terms of their effect on the violence of class conflict. In this field, generalization is of course as difficult as it is unsatisfactory. The conditions of different associations differ greatly, and analogies between types of conflict regulation in, say, industry and the state, are bound to do injustice to the specific requirements of either of these associations. Moreover, there are significant differences even between societies of similar forms of government; no generalization is feasible, e.g., about the place of the legal institutions of the United States, France, and Germany, in the regulation of political and industrial conflicts. For these and similar reasons, I shall confine myself in the following discussion of forms of conflict regulation to a few highly abstract remarks which require both extension and modification with respect to specific associations and societies.[17]

[16] The rules of the game are, from this point of view, always precarious. What is a formal agreement at one point may turn out to prejudice the case of one of the opponents at a later point. For this reason, rules for changing the rules are perhaps the most important element of rules of the game (such as, e.g., constitutions).

[17] To facilitate the following discussion, it may be useful to present a schematic picture of forms of conflict regulation. The following—highly tentative—schema represents an extension of a table given by Moore (157, p. 446) and includes a list of terms suggested by Kerr (84, p. 236). It is evidently derived from conditions of conflict regulation in industry, and its adaptation to other associations presents certain difficulties. The schema is based on the role of third parties in conflict regulation. For further discussion of the type of regulation see the text.

ROLE OF THIRD PARTY IN THE REGULATION OF SOCIAL CONFLICT

Type	Invitation of 3rd Party Advice	Acceptance of 3rd Party Advice	Kerr's Terms
A	none	none	conciliation
B	voluntary	voluntary	mediation
C	voluntary	compulsory	} arbitration
D	compulsory	voluntary	(suppression)
E	compulsory	compulsory	

The first and foremost form of conflict regulation appears to consist in the operation of certain institutions which provide the framework for discussions of and decisions about conflicting issues. In general these institutions may be described as parliamentary or quasi-parliamentary bodies in which conflicting interest groups or their representatives meet in order to carry on their conflict in a relatively peaceful and patterned manner. For such institutions to be effective, they have to comply with at least four standards: they must be autonomous bodies invested with the right to reach decisions without having recourse to outside agencies of any kind; their place in a given association has to be monopolistic in the sense that they are the only institution of its kind; their role must be obligatory both in that conflicting interest groups have to refer to these institutions in case of acute conflicts, and in that decisions reached in them are binding for both interest groups and their members; and they have to be democratic, i.e., both parties have to be heard and be given a chance to state their claims before decisions are reached. Further procedural arrangements as to the modes of discussion and decision are part of the rules of the game.

It seems evident that the very creation of parliamentary or quasi-parliamentary bodies of this kind involves a considerable reduction in the violence of group conflicts. Those who have agreed to carry on their disagreements by means of discussion do not usually engage in physical violence. Moreover, the violence of conflicts would seem to decrease as the effectiveness of parliamentary institutions increases. At the same time, the presence of such institutions does not generally guarantee that violent conflicts will be avoided altogether.[18] In many cases, in order for the violence of group conflict to be effectively reduced, autonomous conciliation has to be supplemented by other forms of conflict regulation. These other forms differ from conciliation in that all of them involve the intervention of "third parties," i.e., outside agencies.

The mildest form of outside interference with group conflicts would seem to consist in what in industry is usually called mediation. Here, both parties agree to consult an outsider who is asked to give

---

[18] The feasibility of majority decisions and, underlying this, the relative permanence of authority structures are relevant here. In the association of the state where periodical elections are part of the rules of the game, majority decisions are an acceptable norm, although they may put one of the parties at a permanent disadvantage during one election period. In industry, majority decisions are not feasible, because the authority structure of the enterprise is not subject to changes by elections. The likelihood of breakdowns of autonomous conciliation is therefore considerably greater.

advice but whose advice will have no binding force for the parties. At first sight, this type of regulation may seem to promise little effect; yet experience in many spheres of social life has shown that mediation in fact often is the most successful type of conflict regulation.[19] Kerr's excellent analysis of mediation suggests that this kind of third party interference generally has at least five favorable consequences for conflict regulation: reduction of irrationality, removal of nonrationality, exploration of solutions, assistance in graceful retreat, and raising the cost of conflict (see 84, pp. 236-39). Examples of this form of conflict regulation are frequent in industrial and international conflicts, but rather rare in political conflict, although in some cases either certain legal institutions or the incumbents of highly representative positions (king, president) may serve as mediators between political parties.

The place of legal institutions in conflict regulation is more accurately described, however, by what in industry is usually called arbitration. There are two types of arbitration, differing in the kind of commitment to an arbitrator to which conflicting parties have agreed. The rules of the game may stipulate either that conflicting parties are obliged to call in an arbitrator in case of breakdown of conciliation and mediation but are free to accept or reject the arbitrator's decision, or that they are free to call in an arbitrator but must accept his decision once they have done so. In either case, arbitration is likely to be an effective means of reducing the violence of class conflict, although arbitration in general can, as Lockwood has pointed out (86), become a problematical form of conflict regulation. There is, according to Lockwood, a "political" and a "judicial" conception of arbitration. The first suggests that it is the task of arbitration to find a workable compromise between conflicting issues accepted as such; in terms of conflict theory, this approach promises success. The second conception, however, views conflicts from a legalistic point of view, i.e., ascribes to the arbitrator the task of judging the merits of conflicting issues in terms of fixed standards of "right" and "wrong." Where this is the case, the rules of the game are likely to prejudice the case of one or the other party, for if one side or claim is declared right in an ultimate legal and moral sense, conflict itself is not recognized and the other party is likely to feel so frustrated as to resort to violence. From in-

---

[19] Incidentally, this holds not only in social life, but also in psychological matters. Many psychoanalysts interpret their role as that of a mediator of conflicting emotions within their patients.

dustry, this dichotomy may be transposed to the political and legal systems. Thus, a comparative analysis of the legal systems of Anglo-Saxon and Continental European countries would probably show that whereas in the former a political conception of legal arbitration prevails, the latter display the judicial conception to an extent which is dangerous from the point of view of effective conflict regulation.[20]

The three forms of conflict regulation thus indicated, i.e., conciliation, mediation, and arbitration, may operate as successive stages of conflict regulation or be applied individually in given situations. If they are understood as a succession of stages, their logical conclusion would appear to be that type of arbitration in which both the invitation of an arbitrator and the acceptance of his decision are compulsory for the parties involved. However, compulsory settlement of disputes is not, in the sense of conflict theory, an effective mode of conflict regulation. Even if agreed upon by conflicting parties as a rule of interaction, it seriously restricts their chances of defending their respective cases. There is, in compulsory settlement, at least a danger of one or the other party being dominated by an outside agency, e.g., government. In other words, compulsory settlement may lead to the suppression of conflict, with all the consequences indicated earlier.[21]

There is an immense variety of empirical modes of conflict regulation; but I suggest that most of these concrete forms represent some modification or combination of the general types outlined in this section. Conciliation, mediation, and arbitration, and their normative and structural prerequisites, are the outstanding mechanisms for reducing the violence of class conflict. Where these routines of relationship are established, group conflict loses its sting and becomes an institutionalized pattern of social life. For revolutionary upheavals to be transformed into evolutionary changes, there is, contrary to Marx's belief, no need for a classless society (that is, for a Utopian fiction); by effective regulation, class conflict may become the element of regularity in a continuously changing world. Even if the intensity of conflict remains undiminished its manifestations may be channeled in such a way as to protect the individual from the physical threat of a *bellum omnium contra omnes*. In this sense, conflict regulation seems a more

[20] Short of a comprehensive study, this point could be brought out, I think, by a detailed analysis of the position of defense counsels in Anglo-Saxon and Continental European courts of law.

[21] This conclusion is borne out by two prominent experiences in the compulsory settlement of industrial disputes: that of Germany in the 1920's and that of contemporary Communist states.

satisfactory solution, both theoretical and political, of the "Hobbesian problem of order" than the solution offered by Talcott Parsons.[22]

GROUP CONFLICT AND STRUCTURE CHANGE

Throughout the abstract considerations of the preceding chapters, we have assumed that group conflicts of the class type result in structure changes. We have moreover rejected attempts to distinguish between allegedly different kinds of change such as "changes within" and "changes of" the structure of associations. Having now assembled the elements of a theory of class conflict, it is our task, in conclusion, to specify how structure changes are brought about by class conflict and under which specific conditions particular modes of structure change must be expected. Again, this involves supplementation of a model by terminological distinctions and empirical generalizations.

Like the stability of social structure, changes in class structure must be investigated on the two levels of analysis which we have called the normative, or ideological, and the factual, or institutional, levels. Interests may become values, but, also, realities. If, for example, one of the manifest interests of a conflict group consists in equality in the sense of Marshall's citizenship rights, there are two levels on which this interest may become realized. First, it may become a more or less general value orientation of the citizens of a society; Tocqueville's "manly and lawful passion for equality" may spread so "that [it] incites men to wish all to be powerful and honored" (232, p. 56). Secondly, equality may be incorporated in institutional arrangements, as by the socialization of medicine, the abolition of school and university fees, etc. Both processes are processes of change, and it would be a uselessly speculative undertaking to try and establish a primacy of either the normative or the institutional level. While, therefore, neither of these levels must be neglected in any analysis of structure change, it nevertheless seems necessary to use an operational approach that specifies modes of structure change in terms of but one of these levels. In the present context, all structure changes will be understood as changes involving the personnel of positions of domination in imperatively coordinated associations.

[22] The problem of conflict regulation constitutes the most important consequence of conflict theory in terms of social policy. I have only intimated this aspect of the problem in the preceding discussion, and its conclusions should not be regarded as automatically applicable to the political problem of conflict regulation. Thus, violent conflict may at times actually be desirable in some associations. Generally speaking, however, it would seem to be the task of social policy to try to regulate the inevitable conflicts of social life by means other than resolution or suppression.

The immediate effect of class conflicts is brought to bear on the incumbents of positions of domination, and changes are introduced by way of these positions.

This operational specification seems tenable in view of the role and definition of authority in the theory here proposed. Insofar as the distribution of authority in associations can be described as the formal object of class conflict, changes resulting from class conflict are in their formal aspect always changes in these authority structures or in their personnel. Moreover, authority is, from the point of view of sociological analysis,[23] an instrumental value. In class theory, the possession of authority does not figure as a value sought for its own sake but as an opportunity to realize specific interests. This conception of authority is in keeping with our distinction of power and authority by the central category of legitimacy. It follows from it that, e.g., an exchange of the personnel of positions of domination has to be viewed not only as a process of rejuvenation of a basically constant "ruling class" or "elite," but above all as the instrumental aspect of a process which substantively represents structure change. In this sense, exchanges of personnel are not in themselves structure changes, but merely a condition for (from the point of view of the *status quo*) "new" interests becoming values or realities. Problems of changing patterns of recruitment to an upper stratum are meaningful only in the context of integration theory. For coercion theory, changes of the personnel of authority roles are merely the formal or instrumental aspect of changes of social structure on both the normative and the institutional levels.

The operational approach suggested permits the distinction of at least three modes of structure change, each of which requires some comment. A first mode of change, in this sense, consists in the total (or near-total) exchange of the personnel of positions of domination in an association. This is clearly the most sudden type of structure change. For purposes of illustration we might use the association of the state, and assume a specific state to be divided in such a way that there are three political parties, two of which are in opposition and one in power. A total exchange of the personnel of positions of domination would involve, then, the replacement of all cabinet ministers, higher civil servants, and other incumbents of political office by members of

---

[23] As against, e.g., psychological analysis, where "lust for power" and the possession of power are of considerable interest, also, as immediately gratifying values.

the opposition parties. In modern states, such sudden changes are a comparatively rare occurrence; the last outstanding example was probably provided by the Bolshevik revolution in Russia. Generally speaking, total exchange of ruling personnel might also be described as revolutionary change. It is at this point that the sociology of revolution ties in with the theory of group conflict.

Far more frequently we encounter in history, and especially in modern history, a second mode of structure change, namely, the partial exchange of the personnel of positions of domination. Such partial exchange signifies evolutionary rather than revolutionary change. In terms of our illustration, it would be present if the majority party chose to form a coalition with, say, the smaller one of the two opposition parties. In this case, some representatives of the hitherto subjected class penetrate the ruling class and influence the policies adopted and decisions made. Coalitions are of course not the only example of partial exchange; if elections in democratic countries reverse the majority relations, they usually result in but partial exchanges of government personnel, so that, e.g., cabinet ministers are exchanged, but some of the judges, diplomats, and higher civil servants of the previous majority party remain in office.[24]

But probably more important than either of these is a third mode of structure change by class conflict which does not involve any exchange of personnel. It is possible for structure changes in directions intended by subjected groups to be inaugurated without any members of these subjected groups penetrating into dominant positions. This seemingly accidental consequence of the process of social conflict occurs in democratic and totalitarian countries alike. In terms of our example, it would mean that majority and opposition remain stable and distinct over long periods of time, but the majority party incorporates proposals and interests of the opposition in its legislation and policies. Strange as it may initially appear that structure change should ever occur without an exchange of ruling personnel, there are nevertheless numerous illustrations in the history of states, enterprises, churches, and other associations. To be sure, this third mode of structure change marks the slowest type of evolution and requires particular skill on

[24] There are considerable differences between different countries in this respect, ranging from the German case where judges and civil servants cannot be fired, to the American case where replacement of leading personnel tends to include even not-so-senior civil servants.

the part of the rulers to avoid such suppression of opposing interests as thereby to provoke revolts[25]; it can nevertheless enable a dominant class to maintain the legitimacy of its authority over long periods of time.

Possibly, these three modes of structure change indicate the end points and center of a scale that measures the suddenness of change. Partial exchange of personnel is evidently a broad category that covers the whole field between total exchange and complete stability. However, while it may be said that structure change is more sudden in the extent to which more personnel is exchanged, this does not necessarily mean that it is also more radical. Suddenness and radicalness of structure change are two dimensions of this phenomenon which can vary independently, much as the intensity and violence of class conflicts can vary independently. There are examples of relatively sudden changes that are accompanied by but slight modifications of values and institutions, and there are examples of extremely radical, although comparatively slow, evolutions.[26] Majority shifts in democratic states illustrate the former case, while the latter is illustrated by such deep changes in class structure as we have analyzed earlier in this study.

The relation between the radicalness-suddenness dimension of structure change and the intensity-violence dimension of class conflict is more than merely logical. It may be argued that the suddenness of change varies directly with the violence of conflict. The more violent class conflicts are, the more sudden are the changes wrought by it likely to be. In this sense, effective conflict regulation serves to reduce the suddenness of change. Well-regulated conflict is likely to lead to very gradual change, often near the third mode distinguished above. Conflict regulation may, in fact, constitute a machinery for forcing on dominant groups recognition of the interests of subjected groups, which interests are then incorporated in policy. The example of a wage claim settled by conciliation is a case in point. Uncontrolled conflict, on the other hand, always threatens the incumbents of posi-

---

[25] The history of the Catholic church provides examples of both: the skillful handling of slow changes of policy without exchange of personnel, and the degeneration of this pattern into suppression and consequent revolt.

[26] In fact, the two concepts of revolution so often interchanged in the literature may be differentiated in terms of the distinction between suddenness and radicalness. The Industrial Revolution was probably more radical than the French Revolution, yet it was not nearly as sudden. The term "revolution" is often used indiscriminately for both particularly radical and particularly sudden changes. I should prefer to use it in the latter sense only.

tions of domination in their very possession of authority; it aims at a total exchange of leading personnel, and, in this sense, at sudden change.

At least in theory, there is also a scale of the radicalness of structure change. However, an operational formulation of such a scale offers particular difficulties. In general, the radicalness of structure changes is evidently a function of what in particular historical situations represents the *status quo*. In eighteenth-century Europe, the peaceful utilization of nuclear energy would certainly have made for extremely radical changes, both technical and social. In twentieth-century Europe, the same process, although still involving some change, has no really radical consequences but simply ties in with continuing trends of rationalization, automation, etc. Similarly—and more immediately to the point here—changes resulting from conflicts within the association of the Catholic church are, in most countries of today, far less radical than they were at earlier times. Thus, the radicalness of structure change is not merely a consequence of the intensity of class conflict. Within certain limits, however, this relation does obtain. The more strongly people are involved in given conflicts, the more far-reaching are their demands likely to be, and the more radical will be the changes resulting from this conflict, irrespective of the suddenness of such changes. Radicalness and suddenness of change, like intensity and violence of conflict, may coincide, but more often they diverge; and in any case their divergence presents more interesting problems of social analysis than their coincidence.

Apart from historical conditions, the co-variance of the intensity of conflict and radicalness of change as well as of the violence of conflict and suddenness of change is further restricted by the structural requisites of associations. This will become immediately apparent if we contrast industrial and political conflict. In political associations, exchange of leading personnel is a realistic possibility, so that the whole scale of suddenness of change can be applied here. In industrial associations, exchange of leading personnel is, except within certain very narrow limits, not possible.[27] There are no elections (and there cannot be) as a result of which the members of management become

---

[27] These limits will be further explored in Chapter VII, below. In a formula: individual members of the subjected class can be taken into management, and the personnel of management can be totally replaced by revolutionary action. However, both these phenomena indicate structure changes of a special type, namely, changes that do not satisfy the interests of a subjected group.

workers, and representatives of labor become managers. Structure changes in industry will therefore almost invariably take the form of changes of policy unaccompanied by exchanges of personnel. To some extent, similar conditions obtain in most church organizations. Before investigating processes of structure change by class conflict in specific associations, we must therefore ascertain the range of possible modes of change in these associations.[28]

In general, however, and without losing sight of additional intervening variables, we can propose that different modes of structure change co-vary with different modes of class conflict. The more intense class conflict is, the more radical are the changes likely to be which it brings about; the more violent class conflict is, the more sudden are structure changes resulting from it likely to be. Structure change is the final element of the theory of group conflict under discussion. Like all other elements of this theory, it represents but a segment of more inclusive phenomena of conflict and change. Possibly, the typology of change introduced in the preceding pages is applicable also to the consequences of kinds of conflict other than that between classes. As everywhere in this study, however, I have confined myself here to exploring the causes, forms, and consequences of conflicts generated by the authority structures of imperatively coordinated associations.

THE THEORY OF SOCIAL CLASSES AND CLASS CONFLICT

It may appear premature, if not overambitious, to have used the word "theory" in connection with the approach outlined in the last two chapters. I have suggested a number of premises, concepts, models, and empirical generalizations which appear to have a bearing on problems of social conflict and social change, but these suggestions do not display a degree of formalization and rigidity that would warrant calling them a theory. I may say that this shortcoming was partly deliberate, partly unavoidable. It was deliberate in that attempts at formalization in sociology have, in my opinion, remained to the present day more pretentious than useful, and that I understandably wanted to avoid seeing the approach suggested in this study exposed to the same criticism. At the same time, I would admit that formalization in so-

---

[28] The specific conditions of industrial associations are clearly related to the fact that whereas it is possible to conceive of modes of regulation which exclude civil war forever, strikes cannot be completely avoided. There is, so to speak, no outlet for intense conflicts within the social structure of industry, so that intensity is sometimes transformed into violence.

ciology is desirable. From this point of view, I regret not to have been able to give a more rigid formulation to the approach discussed in the last two chapters. If in conclusion of this abstract analysis I shall try now to summarize the main points of my approach to group conflict, the seemingly systematic character of this summary should not be mistaken as a statement that complies with the methodological standards of scientific theories. Rather, I hope that this summary may enable other students in the field to advance beyond the limits of my own capabilities of formalization.

1. The approach of this study has to be understood in terms of two premises—one formal, one substantive—which, although they are of a meta-theoretical or methodological nature, provide the necessary frame of reference of its elements.

1.1. The heuristic purpose of the approach proposed in the present study is the explanation of structure changes in terms of group conflict. This purpose is therefore neither purely descriptive nor related to problems of integration and coherence in or of society.

1.2. In order to do justice to this heuristic purpose it is necessary to visualize society in terms of the coercion theory of social structure, i.e., change and conflict have to be assumed as ubiquitous, all elements of social structure have to be related to instability and change, and unity and coherence have to be understood as resulting from coercion and constraint.

2. Within this frame of reference, the theory of social classes and class conflict involves a number of concepts to be defined.

2.1. "*Authority* is the probability that a command with a given specific content will be obeyed by a given group of persons" (M. Weber, 33*a*, p. 152).

2.1.1. By *domination* shall be understood the possession of authority, i.e., the right to issue authoritative commands.

2.1.2. By *subjection* shall be understood the exclusion from authority, i.e., the duty to obey authoritative commands.

2.2. "An association shall be called *imperatively coordinated association* insofar as its members are, by virtue of a prevailing order, subject to authority relations" (M. Weber, 33*a*, p. 153).

2.3. Orientations of behavior which are inherent in social positions without necessarily being conscious to their incumbents (role expectations), and which oppose two aggregates of positions in any imperatively coordinated association, shall be called *latent interests*.

2.4. *Quasi-group* shall mean any collectivity of individuals sharing positions with identical latent interests without having organized themselves as such.

2.5. *Manifest interests* shall mean orientations of behavior which are articulate and conscious to individuals, and which oppose collectivities of individuals in any imperatively coordinated association.

2.6. *Interest group* shall mean any organized collectivity of individuals sharing manifest interests.

2.7. By *social class* shall be understood such organized or unorganized collectivities of individuals as share manifest or latent interests arising from and related to the authority structure of imperatively coordinated associations. It follows from the definitions of latent and manifest interests that social classes are always conflict groups.

2.8. Any antagonistic relationship between organized collectivities of individuals that can be explained in terms of patterns of social structure (and is not, therefore, sociologically random) shall be called *group conflict*.

2.9. *Class conflict* shall mean any group conflict that arises from and is related to the authority structure of imperatively coordinated associations.

2.10. Any deviation of the values (normative structure) or institutions (factual structure) of a unit of social analysis at a given point of time $(T + n)$ from those of a preceding point of time (T) shall be called *structure change*, insofar as it involves the incumbents of positions of domination.

2.10.1. By *radicalness of structure change* shall be understood the significance of consequences and ramifications of structure change.

2.10.2. By *suddenness of structure change* shall be understood the extent to which incumbents of positions of domination are replaced.

3. The formation of conflict groups of the class type follows a pattern that can be described in terms of a model involving the following partly analytical, partly hypothetical steps:

3.1. In any imperatively coordinated association, two, and only two, aggregates of positions may be distinguished, i.e., positions of domination and positions of subjection.

3.2. Each of these aggregates is characterized by common latent interests; the collectivities of individuals corresponding to them constitute quasi-groups.

3.3. Latent interests are articulated into manifest interests; and the quasi-groups become the recruiting fields of organized interest groups of the class type.

3.3.1. Articulation of manifest interests and organization of interest groups can be prevented by the intervention of empirically variable conditions of organization.

3.3.2. Among the conditions of organization, technical conditions (personnel, charter), political conditions (freedom of coalition), and social conditions (communication, patterned recruitment) can be distinguished. To these, certain nonstructural psychological conditions (internalization of role interests) may be added.

4. The course of group conflict of the class type also follows a pattern that can be described in terms of a model involving both analytical and hypothetical elements.

4.1. Once the formation of conflict groups of the class type is complete, they stand, within given associations, in a relation of group conflict (class conflict).

4.1.1. The intensity of class conflict varies on a scale (from 0 to 1) according to the operation of certain factors.

4.1.1.1. The intensity of class conflict decreases to the extent that the conditions of class organization are present.

4.1.1.2. The intensity of class conflict decreases to the extent that class conflicts in different associations are dissociated (and not superimposed).

4.1.1.3. The intensity of class conflict decreases to the extent that different group conflicts in the same society are dissociated (and not superimposed).

4.1.1.4. The intensity of class conflict decreases to the extent that the distribution of authority and the distribution of rewards and facilities in an association are dissociated (and not superimposed).

4.1.1.5. The intensity of class conflict decreases to the extent that classes are open (and not closed).

4.1.2. The violence of class conflict varies on a scale (from 0 to 1) according to the operation of certain factors.

4.1.2.1. The violence of class conflict decreases to the extent that the conditions of class organization are present.

4.1.2.2. The violence of class conflict decreases if absolute deprivation of rewards and facilities on the part of a subjected class gives way to relative deprivation.

4.1.2.3. The violence of class conflict decreases to the extent that class conflict is effectively regulated.

4.2. Group conflict of the class type effects structure changes in the associations in which it occurs.

4.2.1. The radicalness of structure change co-varies with the intensity of class conflict.

4.2.2. The suddenness of structure change co-varies with the violence of class conflict.

I must leave it to the reader to judge whether the preceding list of abstract statements provides a satisfactory summary of the approach suggested in the last two chapters of this study. Obviously, both the summary and its more elaborate basis are, as they stand, tentative and in need of many a refinement. I would nevertheless claim that even in this preliminary and tentative form the approach to group conflict proposed here provides a useful tool of analysis. It directs our attention to a specific set of problems and furnishes these with a coherent explanation. It is, in this sense, a searchlight that illuminates one sector of reality. In the following chapters I shall try to substantiate this claim by applying the theory of social class and class conflict to some of the significant problems of post-capitalist society.

VII

Classes in Post-Capitalist Society
I: Industrial Conflict

CAPITALIST SOCIETY IN THE LIGHT OF THE THEORY
OF GROUP CONFLICT

Formulation and application of a theory are two different matters, each of which obeys its own laws and patterns. While the theory itself can be set out in a highly schematic and "logical" fashion, the analysis of facts would lose much of its color and interest if forced into the strait jacket of theoretical exposition. Although I shall indicate when the following analysis of conflict in advanced industrial society is guided by the theory of social class and class conflict, I shall not attempt to rearrange facts so as to fit the order of postulates, models, and hypotheses resulting from the considerations of the last two chapters. The order of reality rather than of theory will guide our analysis in the final chapters of this study, except in this section of this chapter, which serves a special purpose in the context of the following analysis.

It is proper to demand that if we dismiss an old theory—as we did Marx's—and replace it with a new one, the new theory should be capable of explaining both the facts accounted for and the facts left unexplained by the old theory. Thus, one of the tests of the usefulness of our theory of group conflict lies in its applicability to the conditions with which Marx dealt. There is, of course, no intrinsic reason why it should be possible to deal more schematically with this historical material than with post-capitalist society. However, in the present context I propose to simplify the task of reconsidering class conflict under capitalism. I shall refrain from questioning the facts described by Marx, and, instead, concentrate on how these facts appear in the light of the theory of group conflict. This would appear to be a doubtful procedure. All too often the societies that appear in the work of sociologists are merely historical constructions borrowed from earlier works or even invented in order to provide an impressive contrast for contemporary data. Were it not for the thorough documentation of Marx's work, and for the deliberate sketchiness of this initial section, I should do everything to avoid the suspicion of having an uncritical attitude toward history. As it is, I must ask the reader's indulgence if the next few pages leave much to be desired in terms of historical accuracy and detail.

The starting point of Marx's analyses consists in what he himself variously calls the "sphere of production," the "relations of production," or "property relations." Clearly, all these expressions refer to the industrial enterprise and the social relations obtaining within it. For Marx, the enterprise is the nucleus of class war. In terms of our approach, the relevant feature here is that the industrial enterprise is an imperatively coordinated association. Marx, of course, emphasized the property aspect. This seems reasonable, in retrospect, since at his time it was legal possession of the means of production that provided both the foundation of capitalist power and the main issue of industrial conflict; but this is nevertheless too specific an approach to the problem. Industrial enterprise, being an imperatively coordinated association, has in it two quasi-groups which we may designate, following Marx, as those of capital or the capitalists and of wage labor or the wage laborers. Both capital and labor were united by certain latent interests which, being contradictory, placed them on the opposite sides of a conflict relation. While the most formal objective of the opposing interests was, in capitalist society, either the maintenance or the change of the *status quo* of authority, the precise substance of the conflict might, in relation to the specific conditions of this period, be described as a clash between capital's profit orientation and labor's orientation toward an improvement of their material status.

The intensity of conflict in capitalist society was increased by the superimposition of authority and other factors of social status, especially income. Domination meant, for the capitalists, a high income, while subjection involved for labor extreme material hardship. There was a clear correlation between the distribution of authority and social stratification.

Despite this initial position, large obstacles were in the way of organization for both quasi-groups in the early stages of industrialization. We find here that constellation of factors described above (p. 188) which makes the organization of interest groups virtually impossible. Lack of leaders and ideologies (technical conditions), heterogeneous modes of recruitment to authority positions (social conditions), and, in the case of labor, the absence of freedom of coalition (political conditions)—all these hold industrial conflict for some considerable time in a stage of latency, in which there are only occasional attempts at organization. As industrial associations stabilize, the conditions of organization gradually emerge, and both capital and labor form organizations (employers' associations, trade unions) in defense of what are now articulate manifest interests. Industrial class conflict enters a manifest phase of which strikes and lockouts are the most telling symptoms.

The situation described so far is that of the sphere of industry. It is characteristic of conflict in capitalist societies, however, that not only authority and social status, but also industrial and political conflict are superimposed one on the other.[1] The dominating groups of industry were at the same time the dominating groups of the state, either in person, through members of their families, or by other agents. Conversely, the subjected groups of industry were as such excluded from political authority. Industry is the dominating order of society; its structures of authority and patterns of conflict therefore extend to the whole society. Consequently, the quasi-groups of industry also extend to the political sphere. The industrial quasi-group of capital becomes, as bourgeoisie (to use the Marxian terms once again), the dominant group of the state, whereas wage labor is, as proletariat, subjected in the political sphere as well. Since, under the particular conditions of capitalist society, conflict fronts that characterized industry and society were identical, the conflict was intensified to an extraordinary degree.

In the political field, too, organization of conflict groups proved difficult in the beginning. Insofar as industrial and political quasi-groups were identical, the same factors were at work in the state that tended to prevent industrial organization. Moreover, political restrictions, such as electoral systems, made it difficult for the proletariat to form effective interest groups. Thus, class conflict was smoldering below the surface of society for some time, until all restrictions fell and the two classes met openly in the political arena.

By virtue of the superimposition of various lines of differentiation this conflict was, as we have seen, extremely intense. Its intensity was further increased by the fact that both classes were relatively closed units. Mobility within and between generations remained an excep-

---

[1] This is one of the points where detailed historical analysis would probably come to correct the factual statements of Marx. While in English society in the nineteenth century industrial power may, indeed, almost automatically have conveyed political power, this is not true, e.g., for Germany, where, on the contrary, entrepreneurs were restricted in their exercise of industrial power by the impact of older political elites.

tion.[2] Bourgeoisie and proletariat were strictly separate and largely self-recruiting groups. But in this period it was not merely the intensity of the conflict but the violence as well that was extraordinarily great. In industry and the state, there were virtually no accepted modes of conflict regulation. In the absence of a democratic process that put both parties to a conflict on an equal footing, the subjected class increasingly became a suppressed class which faced as a solid but powerless bloc the absolute rule of the incumbents of roles of domination. Because of this hardening of the class fronts, there were widespread demands for a complete and revolutionary change of existing structures. For structure changes could not slowly grow out of class conflict in this stage. Immobility and lack of regulation made the penetration of the ruling class by members of the subjected class impossible. At the same time, there were neither institutional channels nor ideological provisions for the ruling class to accept and realize any of the interests of the proletariat. Thus, it seemed justified to predict that class conflict in capitalist society tended toward both sudden and radical changes, i.e., a revolution promoted by the proletariat which replaces in one stroke the dominant groups of industry and society.

Marx carried his analysis of capitalist society approximately to this point. Although he went considerably further in detail, his whole work converges on the prediction of the proletarian revolution. We have seen earlier how at this point Marx became a prisoner of preconceived philosophical and, perhaps, political convictions. Thus he did not, or would not, notice that factual developments followed the course of his predictions only up to a point. The ossification of conflict fronts and the intensification of conflict began to be checked both by the very fact of organization of interest groups on the part of the proletariat and by the structure changes to which this organization led. Within industry in particular, signs of the development of modes of regulation became apparent; trade unions managed to make some of their claims effectively heard and accepted. Marx showed himself a consistent philosopher but a poor sociologist when he tried to ridicule such "partial results" and the operation of trade unions (i.e., industrial conflict, as distinct from political class conflict) in general. His

---

[2] Here, again, the correctness of Marx's factual assertions is doubtful. It is hard to see how a new ruling class—capital—can be recruited without mobility, including mobility between the classes. It is obvious here that, even in the sense of our theory, Marx has geared his facts in such a way as to make plausible the extreme civil-war type of conflict which he anticipated.

attempt to advocate, despite such tendencies, an intensification of the class war, and his insistence on the revolutionary goal of the proletariat, document his prophetic and political rather than his scientific self. At this point, we have to reject not only the substance, but the very intention of his work.

Before we try to follow the indicated lines of class conflict somewhat beyond the point of Marx's analysis, one clarifying remark seems in place. It should now be abundantly clear that the traditional, Marxian concept of class is but a special case of the concept advanced in the present study. For Marx, classes are conflict groups under conditions of (*a*) absence of mobility, (*b*) superimposition of authority, property, and general social status, (*c*) superimposition of industrial and political conflict, and (*d*) absence of effective conflict regulation. Thus, classes are conflict groups involved in extremely intense and violent conflicts directed toward equally extremely sudden and radical changes. This is the "traditional" or "historical" concept of class. As against this concept, we have removed all four conditions mentioned from its definition and included them as empirically variable factors in a theory of social class and class conflict. In this way, the concept itself becomes a highly formal and—in this sense—"unhistorical" category; but the theory gains in fruitfulness, range, and applicability.

Thus, what has happened since Marx are in fact changes in the factors that contributed to the intensity and violence of the conflicts of his time. Patterns of conflict regulation emerged in both industry and the state. More and more, the democratic process of decision-making gave both parties a chance to realize their goals. The violence of class conflict was thereby effectively reduced. The institutionalization of social mobility made for a certain degree of openness in both classes. Absolute deprivation on the scales of social stratification gave way, for the proletariat, to relative deprivation, and later, for some, to comparative gratification. Finally, the associations of industry and the state were dissociated to some extent. All these changes served to reduce both the intensity and the violence of class conflict in post-capitalist society, and to make sudden and radical structure changes increasingly improbable. New patterns of class conflict emerge, to which we shall turn presently.

It must, of course, be emphasized that, whatever concept or theory one employs, history cannot be explained solely in terms of class. The changes that separate capitalist and post-capitalist society are not wholly due to the effects of class conflict, nor have they merely been changes in the patterns of conflict. Thus, the subdivision of authority positions stimulated by an ideology of rationalization in both the enterprise and the state is an autonomous process. The decomposition of capital and labor by the separation of ownership and control, and by the emergence of new differentiations of skill, has consequences for class conflict but is due to other factors. As a comprehensive process, the development from capitalist to post-capitalist society remains outside the scope of the present analysis. But it should be clear from the preceding sketch that in principle our theory of group conflict is applicable, also, to the facts with which Marx dealt—and I hope it will be clear from the following rather more elaborate analysis in what sense it lends itself, by generalizing earlier approaches, to a coherent account of industrial and political conflict in the contemporary world.

DO WE STILL HAVE A CLASS SOCIETY?

In a sense, Schelsky is undoubtedly right in calling the "often heard question . . .: Have we still got a class society today?" a "naïve" question (72, p. 62). However, this question is naïve not so much because it is too general to be answered with a plain "yes" or "no," but because it can be answered without thereby stating anything significant or exciting about post-capitalist society. Are there still classes? Or, as we can ask more precisely now: Are there still interest groups and quasi-groups in the sense of class theory? That there are interest groups in contemporary society can be affirmed immediately. There are, for example, trade unions and employers' associations, progressive and conservative political parties. It is not difficult to show that all these organizations are interest groups in the sense of our definition. Quasi-groups, on the other hand, may be assumed to exist wherever there are authority relations and imperatively coordinated associations. Is it necessary to prove that there are such associations and relations in contemporary society? The state, the industrial enterprise, the churches—to mention only a few—are imperatively coordinated associations which exist in all modern societies and which, if our theory is right, justify the assumption that there are quasi-groups with conflicting latent interests within them. And if post-capitalist society has quasi-groups and interest groups, it has classes also. Like its precursor, advanced industrial society is a class society. Concept and theory of class are still applicable.

By taking this position we differ from a number of sociologists whose work has been discussed above. But is this difference, as described so far, more than a difference of terminology? Cannot the charge be leveled against us that we presuppose the existence of classes by definition instead of demonstrating it empirically? Can we really answer the question of whether we still have a class society as easily as we did?

The assertion that there still are classes because there are quasi-groups and interest groups is indeed less than a definition. It is, on the basis of class theory, a mere tautology. On the other hand, the assertion that there are still classes because there are imperatively coordinated associations is more than a definition. Although it presupposes the theoretical—and perhaps definitional—connection between classes and authority relations, it asserts the empirical presence of relations of authority. Social classes and class conflict are present wherever authority is distributed unequally over social positions. It may seem trivial to state that such unequal distribution exists in associations of post-capitalist society, but this assertion nevertheless establishes both the applicability of class theory and the radical difference from all attempts to describe contemporary society as classless.

Nevertheless, to conclude merely that we are still living in a class society is as insufficient as it is unsatisfactory. It marks the beginning, not the end, of an analysis of advanced industrial society. For many people, the notion of a class society immediately evokes such definite associations that to apply it to a particular society might appear to involve a substantial statement of fact. I should like to emphasize therefore that I do not regard it as such. I am concerned, here, not with asserting the applicability of class theory, but with applying it. If imperatively coordinated associations can be shown to be a functional requisite of social structures, then the universal existence of classes is postulated by the same token. By way of empirical generalization we can maintain at the very least that in many societies there are associations and classes, and in all known societies social conflicts. Societies do not differ by the fact that in some there are classes and in others not. Just as in the sociology of the family we are concerned not with the existence but with the patterns and functions of the family, so here we are dealing not with the presence of classes but with their nature and effect. By confronting capitalist with post-capitalist society we want to discover the changed patterns and conditions of class formation and class conflict. Historically, the problem of an analysis of post-capitalist society in terms of class may be formulated as one of the destiny of the "old" conflict between capital and labor, bourgeoisie and proletariat. If we project the historical problem into the present it becomes transformed into the task to apply the tool of class theory to some critical features of post-capitalist society and to try to contribute in this way to the understanding of the society in which we live.

The "society in which we live" covers a multitude of generalities. It is as awkward as it can be fruitful to lump together, in sociological analysis, a number of societies under a general term, such as "advanced industrial" or "post-capitalist society." Most of the data presented so far in this study relate to contemporary British, American, and German society. It is an open question whether these data, or the conclusions derived from them, apply to French, Italian, Japanese, or Russian society as well—and indeed, whether there are not significant differences between Germany, Britain, and the United States which would have to be taken into account. I am well aware of this problem, and of the criticism to which I lay myself open in not discussing it more elaborately. It is nevertheless my intention to try to consider some of the features of the industrial and political life of "post-capitalist society" without referring to specific countries or periods in more definite terms than by stating my belief that the conclusions of our analysis apply at least to those democratic countries of the West that underwent industrialization in the nineteenth century, and at most to all societies at an advanced stage of industrial development. In this analysis, I shall avoid generalities by specifying subject rather than time and place. By concentrating on a few salient points, I hope to pave the way for more detailed investigations. This essay—for such it is—does not pretend to answer all problems of conflict in post-capitalist society.

THE AUTHORITY STRUCTURE OF THE INDUSTRIAL ENTERPRISE

One social institution to which Marx devoted a great deal of attention has survived capitalist society: the industrial enterprise. Trivial as this statement may sound, there is no reason to avoid it. There can be no doubt that many changes have occurred in the century between 1850 and 1950 both outside and inside the industrial enterprise. It may appear meaningless to identify the small factory of a capitalist entrepreneur in 1850 with the large corporation of 1950 in terms of productive capacity and number of employees, technical perfection and spatial extension, complexity of organization and conditions of work. However, although these changes are by no means irrelevant for conflict analysis, we have to start with a more fundamental relation which remains, or has remained so far, unchanged. In capitalist as in post-capitalist society, in the Soviet Union as in the United States, the industrial enterprise is an imperatively coordinated association.[3] Everywhere it displays those conditions of social structure which give rise to social conflict in terms of class theory. Wherever there are industrial enterprises, there are authority relations, latent interests, quasi-groups, and (industrial) classes.

In dealing with the formal organization of the enterprise a distinction is usually made between the "functional" aspect of the division of labor and the "scalar" aspect of super- and subordination. Both are functionally necessary; they are complementary aspects of industrial organization. One of the secrets of the increase of productivity by mechanized factory production lies in the subdivision of the total process of production into cooperative detail processes. Every one of these is equally indispensable for the accomplishment of the total process. From a strict functional point of view, the unskilled laborer, the foreman, and the executive stand on one level; the enterprise cannot function if one of these positions remains vacant. However, for purposes of the organization, coordination, and leadership of such subdivided detail processes a principle other than the division of labor is needed. A system of super-and subordination guarantees the frictionless operation of the total process of production—a system, in other words, which establishes authority relations between the various positions. The incumbents of certain positions are endowed with the right to make decisions as to who does what, when, and how; the incumbents of other positions have to submit to these decisions. Nor are the commands given and obeyed in the industrial enterprise confined to technical work tasks: hiring and firing, the fixing of wage rates and piecework systems, introduction and control of disciplinary regulations, and other modes of behavior are part of the role expectations of the incumbents of authority positions in the enterprise and give rise, therefore, to its scalar or authority structure. For the industrial worker, the labor contract implies acceptance of a role which is, *inter alia,* defined by the obligation to comply with the commands of given persons. Industrial authority does not, of course, involve the subordination of total persons under other persons; it is restricted to persons

[3] I deliberately neglect in the following analysis the often overstressed tendencies of automation and their social implications. It is of course conceivable that automation will change not only the conditions of work, but also the authority structure of the enterprise, but this is today without doubt a distant dream which need not and must not be taken into account, unless we want sociological analysis to evaporate into the skies of fantasy or science fiction.

as incumbents of given, limited roles; but it is therefore no less authority, i.e., a "probability that a command with a given specific content will be obeyed by a given group of persons." Although, in other words, the foreman cannot legitimately command his workers to collect stamps in their leisure time, there exist in the industrial enterprise, within a definable range, authority relations in the strict sense of class theory.

Some industrial sociologists have denied the applicability of the category of authority to industrial enterprises either in general or in specific instances. Thus, Neuloh confronts "unilateral industrial organization" characterized by authority relations with the (sociologically contradictory) notion of "bilateral organization," where "superordinates and subordinates or their representatives participate with equal rights in the process of decision-making" (160, p. 54), so that the "subordinates" become "superordinates" and there are no real "subordinates" at all. Mueller goes even further if he states categorically that "relations of subordination in the enterprise" are essentially "not authority relations" (158, p. 171). "The thesis . . . that the enterprise is a 'sphere of authority' must . . . be rejected," Mueller asserts (p. 172), although a little later he remarks that "super- and subordination in industrial organization is essential to the enterprise" (p. 173). This latter remark shows quite clearly that Mueller is concerned not with the fact but with the concept of authority. The same holds for Neuloh, who states with excessive caution at the end of his work: "It would seem to be a general conviction that total coordination [i.e., total lack of subordination—R.D.] is impossible in any kind of enterprise, particularly in the industrial enterprise," since this would "involve the abolition of hierarchies in the enterprise, i.e., of any discipline and authority" (160, p. 249). This is, indeed, not merely general conviction, but an indispensable condition of the structure of the enterprise. By contrast, it is "general conviction" that Mueller's "super- and subordination" and Neuloh's "discipline and authority" describe authority relations in the strict sense of the term, and that there is no reason not to call them by this name. Schelsky rightly emphasizes the "particular authority foundation" of the industrial enterprise as distinct from such structures as are founded on technical requirements (164, p. 87). "Wherever enterprises are set up, a few command and many obey," Bendix states as a matter of course in the second sentence of his work on industrial authority (138, p. 1). Later he repeats more specifically: "All economic enterprises have in common a basic social relation between the employers who exercise authority and the workers who obey" (p. 13). However one may resent the word authority, substantively there can be no doubt that industrial enterprises are at all times and in all places imperatively coordinated associations. In this sense Mueller is involuntarily right when he refers to Marx and remarks: "Even Karl Marx had to admit: 'All immediate social or communal labor on a larger scale requires more or less leadership. . . . An individual violinist conducts himself, but an orchestra requires a conductor' " (158, p. 170).

Since the industrial enterprise has an authority structure and is therefore an imperatively coordinated association, we are entitled to assume that the incumbents of positions of domination and subjection within it are united in two conflicting quasi-groups with certain latent interests. This inference follows from the model of class formation. If the theory of group conflict proves useful, its validity is as universal as the imperative character of the enterprise itself. Wherever there are industrial enterprises, there is a quasi-group of the incumbents of roles of domination, the latent interests of which are in conflict with those of a corresponding quasi-group of incumbents of roles of subjection. If W. E. Moore states that "the interests of management and labor may be 'basically the same,' and yet the relations between the two groups be anything but harmonious" (157, p. 400) and adds that "in a complete absence of like interests, there can be no conflict: there is nothing to fight about" (p. 399), he merely expresses the fact of the two faces of society with specific reference to the enterprise. Like all other units of social structure, industrial enterprises may be described in terms of integration theory. Their stability presents itself, then, as based on a "common value system" or "common interests." But for certain purposes of analysis this approach is insufficient; we need the parallel approach of coercion theory. From the point of view of coercion theory, however, the interests of the incumbents of different authority positions appear as conflicting. Thus, Taylor's "firm conviction that the true interests of the two [management and labor] are one and the same" (167, p. 10), that employers and workers are not opponents but partners, does not constitute an objection to class analysis. As opposed to Taylor, we do not postulate any "true interests." We merely assert that Taylor's exclusive emphasis on the community of interests among all participants of the enterprise is plainly insufficient for the explanation of certain phenomena, such as strikes, and that it is therefore necessary to assume a conflict of latent interests in the enterprise emerging from the differential distribution of authority.

Speaking of "common interests," Taylor and others usually specify the substance of these interests: "In the ordinary course of affairs it is mutually advantageous to management and labor for an industrial establishment to continue in operation" (Moore, 157, p. 400). Analogously, the question of the substance of conflicting latent interests in industry must be raised. This question may appear unnecessarily abstract at a time at which everybody knows that the conflict of interests between employers and workers manifests itself in the form of disputes over wages and conditions of work. Yet it is questionable whether the substantive interest in higher wages or higher profits defines the substance of the latent interests of industrial classes sufficiently clearly. In an acute argument Drucker has tried to reduce wage disputes to their "real basis": "The wage rate is the traditional symbol for the real conflict rather than the issue itself. The basic problem is a conflict between the enterprise's view of wage as cost, and the employee's view of wage as income. The real issue is not, properly speaking, an economic one, but one over the nature and function of wage: shall the need of the enterprise or the need of the employee be the basis for determining the function of wage?" (144, p. 58). Drucker comes close to our problem, but not quite close enough. In reducing known manifest interests to latent interests at their basis we must abstract even further from substantive contents connected with specific social conditions. "It is clear that a conflict is always concerned with a distribution of power. An exertion of power is necessary in order to retain a share in the determination of future relations, as well as for the acquisition or retention of other benefits which may be the immediate 'reasons' for the conflict. This is to say that the immediate and necessary goal of any conflict is complete or partial victory" (Moore, 157, p. 400). If we formulate, as we must, the latent interests of industrial quasi-groups on an equally formal and general level as the "common interest" in the continued operation of the enterprise, their substance can be described as the maintenance or change of the *status quo* by conservation or modification of existing relations of authority.

In disputes between trade unions and employers, an argument is often put forward by the employers which has found its way into sociological literature also. Employers like to assert that they represent the interests of the total enterprise whereas the unions merely stand for partial interests. It might appear that there is no convincing refutation of this argument.[4] However, in the light of the theory of group conflict it becomes apparent what the basis of this argument is and why it is ideological, i.e., demonstrably false—a fact which is of considerable significance for class analysis. We have seen earlier that the interests of a ruling group assume, as ruling interests, the character of accepted values in a unit of social structure. They are a reflection of the real structure, the existing conditions, although these are upheld and guaranteed by the rule of but one class. They might therefore appear as binding for all elements of a unit of social structure. Yet the theory of class exposes the fact that the existing conditions are themselves in a sense merely "partial," that they exist by virtue of the authority of one part, or class. As the prime minister is both representative of the whole nation and exponent of the majority party, the entrepreneur is both "the enterprise" and one partial interest in the conflicts generated by its structure—depending on the image of society underlying our analysis. In this sense, "conservation" and "modification" of a *status quo* are, from the coercion point of view, strictly equivalent "partial" interests the conflict of which can be conceived as one of the determinants of the dynamics of social structure.

Two objections are frequently raised these days against the universal reality of conflicting latent interests in industry. They are easily disposed of, yet it may further clarify the issue to discuss them briefly. The first of these objections is based on the thesis that what is often called the "bourgeoisification of the proletariat," i.e., the improvement of the economic situation of industrial workers, makes the assumption of continuing conflict unreasonable and, indeed, nonsensical. If, it is argued, the workers are no longer proletarians, if they do not live in poverty and suppression, they no longer have reason to revolt against their employers. The public of post-capitalist societies realizes, with baffled surprise, the continued reality of strikes and yet insists, at the same time, on the theory that industrial conflict has lost its causes and issues where the standard of living is high. This paradox testifies to a remarkable consistency of conviction, if not to insight. The theory of group conflict does not postulate any connection between class conflict and economic conditions. For the emergence of social conflicts the standard of living of their participants is in principle irrelevant, for conflicts are ultimately generated by relations of authority, i.e., by the

---

[4] At any rate, many trade union leaders have found it difficult to argue against this point, except by dogmatic insistence on their power. Cf. 42.

differentiation of dominating and subjected groups. Even if every worker owns a car, a house, and whatever other comforts of civilization there are, the root of industrial class conflict is not only not eliminated, but hardly touched. The fact that economic demands may provide the substance (a substance situationally specific and in that sense incidental) of manifest interests must not give rise to the erroneous notion that satisfaction of these demands eliminates the causes of conflict. Social conflict is as universal as the relations of authority and imperatively coordinated associations, for it is the distribution of authority that provides the basis and cause of its occurrence.

A second objection against the assumption of the persistence of a latent conflict of interest consists in the thesis that the replacement of capitalists by managers has removed the basis of industrial class conflict. Upon closer inspection, this thesis, too, proves untenable. As we have seen, latent interests can be conceived of as quasi-objective role expectations. They are held not by persons, but by positions, or by persons only insofar as they occupy certain positions. If a person occupies a position of domination in an enterprise, it is irrelevant in principle[5] whether his authority is based on property, election by a board of directors, or appointment by a government agency. For the latent interests of the incumbents of positions of authority, their incumbency of these positions is the sole significant factor. Although, therefore, their modes of recruitment and bases of legitimacy make for significant differences between capitalist and manager in other contexts, their authority positions in the enterprise are alike, and their places in conflicts of interest identical. For the explanation of group conflict, the factual relations of authority are the crucial factor. To this extent I agree with Burnham's thesis and with Marx's and Renner's analysis of joint-stock companies; the replacement of functioning owners or capitalists by propertyless functionaries or managers does not abolish class conflict, but merely changes its empirical patterns. Independent of the particular personnel of positions of authority, industrial enterprises remain imperatively coordinated associations the structures of which generate quasi-groups and conflicting latent interests.

Apart from such inconsequential objections, there is one rather difficult problem, which becomes apparent if we try to define the bor-

---

[5] If I refer here and elsewhere to the "irrelevance" of certain social changes, I always mean irrelevance in terms of the theoretical model of class analysis. This is of course not to say that the changes in question may not be relevant as intervening variables affecting the intensity or violence of conflicts.

derline between the quasi-groups of industrial associations. Bendix remarks that in every enterprise there are "a few" who command and "many" who obey. Presumably, he has the capitalist enterprise in mind when he says so. But the same criticism applies to his statement as was raised against Pareto's and Mosca's thesis of a ruling "minority." In the enterprises of post-capitalist society, authority is typically no longer exercised by one individual, or even by a few. A complex system of delegation of responsibility obliterates virtually to invisibility the dividing line between positions of domination and subjection. Even if we ignore for the moment the place of labor representatives in the formal organization of the enterprise, there are two groups that stubbornly resist allocation to one or the other quasi-group. One of these consists of the so-called "staff" of the enterprise, the engineers, chemists, physicists, lawyers, psychologists, and other specialists whose services have become an indispensable part of production in modern firms. Occasionally, these specialists have a defined place in the scalar structure of authority in the enterprise, usually by the inclusion of specialist qualifications in the definition of the expectations associated with managerial roles.[6] More frequently, however, the staff is linked with the line of authority by an intricate system of cross-relations without its members having immediate authority except over their secretaries and assistants ("line-staff system"). In this case the class situation of specialists in the enterprise remains as uncertain as the class situation of intellectuals in society. They are neither superordinates nor subordinates; their positions seem to stand beyond the authority structure. Only insofar as they can be identified as (often indirect) helpers of management, can they be called a marginal part of the ruling class of the enterprise.

The number of staff positions in industrial enterprises is usually fairly limited. But there is another troublesome group of positions in the modern enterprise which is far more numerous, namely that of all salaried employees, of department heads and typists, accountants, and foremen, etc. Few of these positions can be described as positions of subjection in the sense in which those of workers are. But are they positions of domination? Do salaried employees participate in the exercise of authority? Do they belong to the ruling class of the industrial enterprise? In the first place, the distinction introduced earlier between bureaucrats and white-collar workers is here of im-

[6] Not infrequently, it is expected of the technical manager today that he be a trained engineer, of the business manager that he be a trained economist, of the general manager that he be a lawyer, etc.

portance. The latter clearly belong to the quasi-group of the subjected and do not therefore present a special problem. But what about the bureaucrats? In the following chapter we shall have to investigate the place of bureaucrats in social conflict rather more extensively. Anticipating the result of this investigation, however, I think that with certain qualifications the conclusion is indicated and, indeed, forced upon us that the positions of bureaucrats in the enterprise have to be counted among the positions of domination. The theory advanced by Renner and others since the turn of the century, and called "theory of delegation" by Croner, provides the only consistent explanation of the authority position (although not of the social status or economic situation!) of bureaucratic roles. Bureaucratic roles in the enterprise must be described as differentiated management roles. The total process of the exercise of authority appears, in the modern enterprise, subdivided into a multitude of positions coordinated by a peculiar type of organization. In the analysis of bureaucratic roles below we shall see that this subdivision and coordination bears striking similarities to the division of labor in technical production. In both cases, differentiation has the effect of splitting up a totality into a multitude of elements to the extent of almost entirely alienating each of the elements from the totality of which it is a part. Here, appearances are deceptive, for the fact remains that industrial bureaucracy or, as Renner calls this group, the "service class," stands as a whole on this side of the borderline which separates the possessors of authority in the enterprise from the subjected workers, both manual and white-collar. By virtue of their positions, bureaucrats are members of the ruling class of industry and share its latent interests.[7]

It may appear superfluous to devote so extensive a discussion to the structural origins of industrial conflict in view of the fact that the organized interest groups of trade unions and employers' associations belong to the accepted institutions of post-capitalist society. Yet this appearance is deceptive. Only if we manage to identify the structural origins of industrial conflict unambiguously can we hope to be able to assess the place of organized interest groups in post-capitalist society with sufficient accuracy. The authority structure of the industrial enterprise generates, in every social order and at all times, independent of the socio-economic status of labor and the modes of recruitment of

[7] Clearly, there are nevertheless significant differences, even from the point of view of social conflict, between managers and bureaucrats. How these affect analysis in terms of conflict theory will be shown in the discussion of bureaucratic roles in Chapter VIII.

management, latent interests and quasi-groups in the sense of class theory. Their conflict may be described as the ultimate source of class antagonisms in industry. At the same time, this statement leaves out of consideration whether industrial conflict becomes acute or remains latent, whether it assumes regulated patterns or is of the civil-war type, whether it is confined to industry or molds the whole of society. Empirically, these are the crucial questions, and the answers to them cannot be derived from the authority structure of the enterprise. For them to be satisfactorily answered, we now have to look at the empirical conditions of industrial conflict in post-capitalist society.

INDUSTRIAL DEMOCRACY

In connection with the brief re-analysis of Marx's data above, I have indicated that there is a tendency toward decreasing intensity and violence in industrial conflict by virtue of the "institutionalization of class conflict" and the development of "industrial democracy." This assertion must now be made specific and documented. Without entering into a detailed historical account of the development of conflict patterns in various countries, I shall try in this section to trace some of the typical (and universal) elements of conflict regulation in industry as they affect the violence of manifestations of conflict. My thesis is that in post-capitalist society industrial conflict has become less violent because its existence has been accepted and its manifestations have been socially regulated. Today, industrial conflict is recognized as a necessary feature of industrial life. This recognition, as well as the establishment of regulatory institutions, constitutes in itself a structure change which is due to no small extent to the effects of industrial conflict.

The establishment of "industrial democracy" consists of a number of structural arrangements, each of which warrants brief inspection. In the following pages, I propose to analyze five elements of industrial democracy in advanced countries which seem to me of particular importance: (1) the organization of conflicting interest groups itself; (2) the establishment of "parliamentary" negotiating bodies in which these groups meet; (3) the institutions of mediation and arbitration; (4) formal representations of labor within the individual enterprise; and (5) tendencies towards an institutionalization of workers' participation in industrial management. The purpose of the following analysis, as of the whole chapter, is to stimulate thought and research rather than to present conclusive solutions; thus, we shall concentrate on significant facts rather than present all relevant data.

(1) In the sphere of industry we encounter the conflicting classes in full formation. In a way, the conditions of industry in post-capitalist society might be described as an empirical analogue of the model of class theory, an ideal type come true. The authority structure of the enterprise generates the two quasi-groups of management and labor, along with their latent interests; from these are recruited the interest groups of employers' associations and trade unions, with their specific manifest interests. For many decades, now, the disputes between trade unions and employers' associations have presented the well-known picture of industrial conflict.

There are a number of problems in connection with the formation of industrial classes which, although well worth investigating, we can only touch upon here. (*a*) It would be interesting to investigate why trade unions typically attempt to recruit all members of the quasi-group of labor into their organization ("closed shop") and to actualize their interests permanently, whereas employers' associations are much looser organizations composed of a few representatives of their underlying quasi-group. One would have to inquire whether this pattern indicates a general regularity of manifest conflict, or whether it might not be conceivable that a subjected class is also represented by a small interest group of delegates.[8] (*b*) Complex problems are raised by the relation between employers' associations and industrial bureaucrats, particularly their union-type organizations, if we introduce the premise that the service class is part of the ruling class. (*c*) In many countries, the relation between different (often conflicting) interest groups based on the same quasi-group, such as Christian and Socialist trade unions, presents important problems. (*d*) Finally, we cannot here discuss the extremely significant consequences of the fact that organized trade unions are themselves imperatively coordinated associations which potentially generate within themselves the same conflicts between dominant and subjected groups ("bosses" and members) as other associations.

Other problems might be added to these. However, we are here concerned merely with a more limited question: in what sense does even the organization of conflict groups itself contribute to a decrease in the intensity and violence of class conflicts? It is worth pursuing the

---

[8] There is some indication today that trade unions develop from membership organizations to offices staffed with a few functionaries who professionally represent the interests of labor. It is just possible that the trade union of the future will look more like American than like European political parties, i.e., that it will be a "latent" organization actuated only for special purposes.

subject that every act of organization is as such a process of institutionalization. The organization of an interest group creates an entity in time, endowed with a "charter," certain norms, a material instrumentarium, and a personnel that constitute—if we accept Malinowski's definition—an institution. This fact has certain prerequisites; and certain consequences flow from it. Thus, the organization of trade unions presupposes, apart from the presence of a quasi-group of latent interests, those technical, political, and social conditions which we have described as conditions of organization and the presence of which signifies in itself a minimum of recognition of the legitimacy of conflict and its issues. The organization of trade unions is in this sense the first structure change of industrial society caused by class conflict; by its completion class conflict loses some of its intensity and violence.

This conclusion is supported by the consequences of the organization of interest groups. Organized groups stand in open, and therefore in controllable, conflict. As long as the organizations of subjected groups are not dissolved, their political prerequisites not abolished, absolute suppression of this class is no longer possible. Organized interest groups of subjected classes have means to enforce recognition of their interests at their disposal; moreover, they are in principle accessible for negotiations, i.e., regulated disputes. One cannot negotiate with unorganized, loosely connected "rebels"; for conciliation comprehensive organization growing out of a quasi-group is indispensable. Thus, the conclusion is suggested that the "democratization" of industrial conflict begins with the organization of industrial classes.

(2) In fact the formation of industrial interest groups has soon been followed, in all industrial countries, by the emergence of negotiating bodies in which the representatives of both parties convene for settling their disputes by discussion. In some countries these negotiating bodies, originally formed *ad hoc* whenever necessary, have stabilized into persistent institutions; there is a machinery for collective bargaining and joint negotiation. "The term 'collective bargaining' is applied to those arrangements under which the wages and conditions of employment are settled by a bargain, in the form of an agreement made between employers or associations of employers and workpeople's organizations" (156, p. 15). The structure of these negotiating bodies differs in different countries. "The area regulated by collective contract is, for example, much wider in America than in Germany. In the latter country many of the relations between employer and employee are regulated on the basis of mutual under-

standing without this anywhere being put down in writing; many other conditions are fixed preferably by law and less by collective contracts" (McPherson, 155, p. 69). Apart from this latter qualification, the significance of collective bargaining for industrial conflict can be asserted in general for all post-capitalist societies.

Occasional or statutory negotiating bodies of employers' associations and trade unions serve a quasi-parliamentary function in industrial class conflict. In them the representatives of both parties meet in order to articulate their disputes on the basis of certain rules of the game (such as an order of procedure, but also according to other norms and forms of behavior)[9] and, if possible, to arrive at a common decision. T. H. Marshall has demonstrated convincingly how radically this structural principle differs from a private-law conception of the labor contract (cf. 57). For us, the essential fact is that by collective bargaining the frozen fronts of industrial conflict are thawed. If the representatives of management and labor meet regularly for negotiations, gradual changes of social structure replace the tendency toward revolutionary explosions and civil war.

(3) However, this possibility is by no means entirely removed where collective bargaining bodies exist. The rules of the game of political democracy can only partly be applied to the industrial conflict of interests. "The whole of this collective system rests upon the principle of mutual consent, and the value of the agreements and the machinery for settling disputes has depended upon the loyal acceptance by the constituent members on both sides of the decisions reached" (156, p. 16). Not only the acceptance of agreements once reached, but even more the difficulty of reaching agreement endangers the effectiveness of conciliation. Majority decisions are structurally impossible in the negotiating bodies of employers' associations and unions; decisions are reached unanimously or not at all. To the extent to which agreement between conflict groups cannot be attained by negotiation, industrial conflict threatens the democratic process itself. Violent conflict—strike and lockout—remains its background and, often, its result.

In order to remove the possibility of outbreak of violent conflict even further, most advanced industrial societies have developed a

---

[9] These are nicely brought out when a bitter wage dispute which has no result ends in an exchange such as that found in the minutes of an English negotiation which I have analyzed elsewhere (42), where the union representative (a man known for his radical views) says, "I presume we say Good morning then!" and the employers' representative replies, "I am sorry, Mr. T."

second line of institutional safeguards, a system of mediation and arbitration. It is the declared aim of arbitration to make a last non-violent attempt at regulating conflicts in case of breakdown of conciliation. In connection with the general discussion of conflict regulation I have presented a schema of types of third-party interference in conflict, ranging from (voluntary) mediation through (partly compulsory) arbitration to compulsory arbitration. Apart from the last type, such interference may operate as an effective means of reducing the violence of industrial conflict. There are many empirical illustrations of this fact. However, for arbitration to be effective, it is necessary that it be based on the acceptance of the conflict itself, i.e., that it follow a political rather than a legal conception of its task, to use Lockwood's distinction (cf. 86). If, and only if, mediation and arbitration are conceived of as mechanisms for facilitating legitimate decision-making on the part of both parties to a conflict, do they contribute to industrial democracy.

(4) The three factors mentioned so far form a coherent pattern. Its *rationale* lies in the autonomous, in that sense democratic, regulation of conflict. This pattern can be found in most post-capitalist societies, but particularly in Britain and the United States. The two remaining factors, representation within the enterprise and co-determination, also form a coherent pattern. Again, traces of the pattern are present in most industrial countries, but it is particularly prominent in Germany. Its most general principle can be described as the attempt to institutionalize industrial conflict by modifying the authority structure of the enterprise itself. So far as we can see today, the range of variability of possible modifications of the authority structure of the industrial enterprise is relatively limited.[10] Yet there is the possibility of supplementing the authority structure by what Schelsky called an "institutionalized side-hierarchy of employees' representatives" (165, p. 187), such as shop stewards, *comités d'entreprise*, *Betriebsräte*, or, in Communist countries, party cells in the enterprise. Schelsky states on the basis of this important structure change of modern industry that "a dualistic authority structure belongs to the hierarchical constitution of the modern enterprise" (165, p. 185). It is worth following up some of the consequences of this development for violence and intensity of industrial conflict.

In Germany, labor representation within the enterprise found its

[10] This conclusion is brought out with great clarity by Bendix in his study of industrial authority (138).

way into legislation as early as 1920. Special legislation defines the task of shop councils[11] by two main expectations. Shop councils are established "in order to defend the common economic interests of employees . . . vis-à-vis the employer, and in order to support the employer in realizing the functions of the enterprise." The striking ambiguity of the position of shop councils—and, to a lesser extent, of British and American shop stewards—becomes apparent in this formulation. The first part of the legal definition, ascribing to shop councils the task of defending the interests of labor, seems to bear out Schelsky's and Drucker's comparison of this institution with a parliamentary opposition. From this point of view, the institution of shop councils neither modifies nor supplements the authority structure of the enterprise; leaders of opposition have no legitimate power within the state. There is, however, a second aspect of the position of shop councils. Apart from defending the interests of labor, shop councilors have also to give certain commands to the workers; they have to "support the employer in realizing the functions of the enterprise." More apparently than with the shop stewards of English and American industry, German shop councils occupy a curiously ambiguous place in the enterprise. They are both opposition and side-government, representatives of the interests of labor and agents of management. For this reason, much the same problems are associated with their roles as Roethlisberger and others found characteristic for the foreman. At least in Germany, the shop councilors are, even more than the foreman, "men in the middle," "masters and victims of double talk."[12]

In so far as the representation of labor within the enterprise follows the double definition of German shop councils, its effect on the intensity and violence of industrial conflict is as ambivalent as its position in the authority structure of the enterprise. On the one hand, class theory would lead one to assume that the establishment of institutions designed to "defend the common economic interests of employees" serves to reduce the violence of conflict by providing peaceful channels of expression for antagonistic interests. On the other hand, the

---

[11] The German term *Betriebsrat* will in the following analysis be translated by "shop council," so as to avoid confusion with the shop steward system, which is different in several respects. The following quotation stems from the *Betriebsrätegesetz* of 1920, section 1 of which defines the functions of shop councils.

[12] This situation is most pronounced in German industry. However, the comparative analyses by McPherson (155) and A. Philip (161, Chapter II) show that shop stewards and *comités d'entreprise* also serve certain managerial functions, so that the present analysis applies to other countries as well.

very design of shop councils tends to alienate this institution from those whose interests it is supposed to serve. By necessity, the representatives of labor get entangled with the tasks, decisions, and—at least indirectly—interests of management. What appears to be an interest group of the subjected turns out to be an agent of the dominating group as well. It seems probable that this kind of perverted conflict regulation will increase rather than diminish both the violence and the intensity of conflict by simultaneously opening and blocking one of its channels of expression.

This latter point is most clearly illustrated by the relationship of labor representatives within the individual enterprise to the larger organizations of labor, i.e., the trade unions. In England and the United States "shop stewards are appointed by and subject to the control of their unions" (156, p. 66). They are in this sense delegates of the comprehensive interest group of labor within the enterprise. As such, they are symptom and tool of the institutionalization of class conflict and serve to decrease its violence. Although in actual fact there are in Germany, also, many enterprises where the trade unions have at least informal control over selection, election, and work of the shop councils, these are in principle independent of the unions. There are therefore at least two distinct interest groups of labor,[18] the relations between which may be friendly, competitive, or conflicting. The theory of group conflict would suggest that the closer the connection between labor representatives in the enterprise and comprehensive interest groups, the better do these interest groups serve their purpose of regulating industrial conflict and thereby reducing its violence. The shop councilor, as an incumbent of roles of domination, becomes part of the ruling class of industry, deprives labor of one of its channels of expression, and provides the cause for new conflicts of the class type within the enterprise and industry as a whole.

(5) This conclusion holds *a fortiori* for a final element of industrial democracy which we have to discuss and which, once again, is most prominent in West German industry: workers' participation in management. Apart from strictly syndicalist tendencies in a number of

---

[18] Strictly speaking, the shop council cannot be called an interest group but is merely the head of an otherwise nonexistent group. What happens is that the comprehensive quasi-group of labor functions as such with respect to trade unions, and is at the same time split up into innumerable smaller units and recruiting fields within the walls of individual enterprises. Thus, every worker functions as industrial worker and as worker of factory X, or as (potential) trade union member and as (potential) shop councilor.

historical and contemporary societies, the coal, iron, and steel industry of post-war Germany provides the first large-scale example of an attempt to furnish labor with a share in the management of industrial enterprises. There have been numerous studies, sociological and otherwise, of the German co-determination experiment in recent years, and I do not intend to review here these investigations or the problems they have raised. There is, however, one element of co-determination which is of immediate relevance for our problem and requires some consideration. One of the crucial stipulations of the "Law Concerning Co-Determination of Employees in the Boards of Directors and of Executives in the Enterprises of Coal Mining and the Iron and Steel Industry of May 21st, 1951" relates to the inclusion of a labor representative in the executive board. Section 13 of the third part of the law, dealing with executive boards, says: "1. A labor manager (*Arbeitsdirektor*) is appointed with rights equal to those of the other members of the legally representative executive board. The labor manager cannot be appointed against the votes of those members of the board of directors elected in accordance with section 6 [i.e., the representatives of labor in the board of directors —R.D.]. . . . 2. The labor manager, like the other members of the legally representative executive board, has to fulfill his tasks in close cooperation with the total board." What are the structural consequences for industrial conflict of this stipulation, and the real conditions created on its basis?

Two conclusions can immediately be derived from the wording of the law. First, this law stipulates the creation of a new position. It does not define in any detail the role, the behavior expectations attached to this position. However, its designation "labor manager" implies an indication that the legislators had in mind an executive who is primarily concerned with personnel matters in the widest sense.[14] The law states quite explicitly, however, that the role of the labor manager is a role of domination, a leadership or management role equipped "with equal rights." The position of labor manager is clearly defined as belonging to the ensemble of positions endowed with the right to issue authoritative decisions and commands. Secondly, the wording of the law stipulates a mode of recruitment of persons to this position. Here, again, the text remains purely formal. It is not suggested, e.g., that the labor manager has to be a (former)

---

[14] To the present day, the German trade unions eagerly disclaim this implication, which, in their opinion, puts the labor manager at a disadvantage with his colleagues. Despite this fact, I should maintain my interpretation.

worker or trade union member, although this idea may have played a part. It is merely said that he must have the confidence of the labor representatives on the board of directors, that he cannot be appointed against their votes. What, then, is the class position of the labor manager in terms of conflict theory?

With respect to his position and role, and quite apart from its specific incumbent, the answer to this question is evident. As a position of domination it belongs to the plus-side of the zero-sum distribution of authority positions in the enterprise; the position of labor manager is, to all intents and purposes, a managerial or entrepreneurial position. "Like the other members of the legally representative executive board," the labor manager belongs, by virtue of his position, to the ruling quasi-group of those whose objective role interests aim at the maintenance of existing conditions. In this sense, the institution of labor manager is, as Pirker justly observes, "nothing but the continuation of the process of rationalization of large-scale enterprises and of the specialization and centralization of management connected with it" (162, p. 417). Like his older, but similarly defined, colleague in English and American industry, the personnel manager, the labor manager is an entrepreneur.

These facts, which are so obvious that it is truly surprising how rarely they are recognized, are complicated by that further stipulation of the law which prescribes a mode of recruitment. In order to articulate the consequences of this prescription, let us assume hypothetically the extreme case of a worker—say, a fitter—who is also an active unionist, being appointed labor manager of a steelworks by its board of directors. From the point of view of class theory, this means, in the first place, that a man who belongs to the quasi-group of the subjected becomes mobile, rises socially, and assumes a position that automatically puts him into the quasi-group of the rulers. His latent interests change from one extreme to the other. This seemingly nonsensical statement becomes reasonable if we realize that latent interests are associated with positions, not persons, and that they are therefore in principle exchangeable with positions. The individual can abandon his class position, as he can his occupational position. Our fitter has become, by the decision of a board of directors, an entrepreneur. His interests are no longer represented by a trade union but by an employers' association. Once again we must agree with Pirker, who says: "Enforcing loyalty with the union would be incompatible with the functions [better: the role—R.D.] of the labor manager which are, and must be, directed towards the optimal social constitution of the enterprise within the existing economic and social order" (162, p. 420).

In one respect our analysis might be charged with a certain lack of realism. One might ask how the fitter of our example will react to his new role. Will he be able or willing to forget, once he is labor manager, that he was a fitter before? This is a psychological question. However, it appears to me that we may formulate a number of alternatives of behavior that are open to the newly made labor manager of our hypothetical example. (*a*) He may try to continue acting as if he were a member of the subjected class from which he came. This would mean that he does not adapt himself to his new role and does not fulfill its tasks as he should, so that he may be a good unionist but will certainly be a bad labor manager. (*b*) On the other hand, he may try to adapt himself to his new role very rapidly (and succeed in doing so). By forgetting his origin he may indeed become an extreme example of an industrial ruler and soon display all the status symbols of a manager. (*c*) Finally—and this may be the most probable case—our fitter may gradually adapt himself to his new role as labor manager, live through what may easily be a painful conflict between the old and the new role, and try to solve this conflict by increased efforts on behalf of his former colleagues (thereby doing what is his task, as a labor manager, in any case). He becomes an entrepreneur, a member of the ruling class of industry, but he remains an employer concerned about the welfare of labor.

I have deliberately tried to assess the significance of co-determination in the light of class theory without reference to the unending discussion of the virtue or vice of this structure change. This, it seems to me, is the only way of gaining an impression unbiased by wishes or aversions. Thus, the much-discussed problem of the "conflict of loyalties" (union vs. enterprise) is reduced to the psychological conflict of a man—who in reality is a rare exception[15]—who turns over-

---

[15] No exact figures are available about the origin of the (roughly 100) labor managers in West Germany. There are, however, some figures about the occupations of labor representatives on the boards of directors (170, p. 1). According to these, of the representatives in all co-determination enterprises in 1955, 22 per cent were trade union employees, 24.8 per cent higher salaried employees, managers, civil servants, cabinet ministers, members of parliament etc. (persons, in other words, who were in leading positions before), 7.1 per cent experts (professors, lawyers, etc.), 14 per cent bureaucrats, 31.5 per cent skilled workers and foremen, and 0.6 per cent semiskilled workers. Here, our hypothetical case would not be typical, but neither would it be exceptional. However, it is more than likely that the proportion of former workers is much smaller among the labor managers.

night from worker to entrepreneur. Neuloh's "totally bilateral process of decision-making" (160, p. 58) is revealed as an extremely inaccurate description of the actual conditions. But it becomes evident, also, that the large number of workers who (according to a survey of the Frankfurt Institute of Social Research) expect from co-determination "equal participation in decision-making" or even "rights of control and veto on the part of labor" (149, p. 212), are voicing Utopian wishes rather than structurally justified expectations.

In many ways, co-determination in the basic industries of West Germany is the most insignificant of the factors of industrial democracy discussed in this section. This conclusion certainly holds for the creation of the position of labor manager. The strengthening of shop councils effected by a supplementary law of 1952 as well as the participation of labor representatives in the boards of directors stipulated by the co-determination law may be regarded as contributions to the effective regulation of industrial conflict. Here, negotiating bodies are erected or invigorated which serve to remove conflict from the streets to conference rooms. But the very significance of institutions of this latter type supports our general view that any attempt to eliminate conflict altogether is bound to fail as such and, in fact, intensifies existing cleavages. Regulation requires acceptance of conflict; but co-determination is based on a conviction that conflict is bad and must be abolished. From the point of view of effective conflict regulation, it is an ill-conceived pattern that contradicts rather than supports a general trend toward the reduction of violence and intensity of industrial conflict.

THE INSTITUTIONAL ISOLATION OF INDUSTRY AND INDUSTRIAL CONFLICT

"I believe," says Parsons in one place, "that class conflict is endemic in our modern industrial type of society" (67, p. 333). With respect to industry, our analysis suggests that this belief is indeed well-founded. But while the existence of class conflict is indubitable, its manifestations have changed. The analysis of industrial democracy reveals some such changes, namely, those in the violence of interest clashes. At several points we have suggested that with decreasing violence the intensity of industrial conflict was also reduced. However, the latter tendency is rather less apparent than the former. It is necessary, here, to define its extent and limits as precisely as possible. In this problem, the relationship between industry and society is crucial.

We have seen that one of the reasons why industrial conflict was exceptionally intense in capitalist society rested with the fact that the lines of industrial and political conflict were superimposed. The opponents of industry—capital and labor—met again, as bourgeoisie and proletariat, in the political arena. Clearly, the relations between industry and society are close in all modern societies; in this sense, the term "industrial society" is fitting. At the same time, industry and society are, at least for purposes of analysis, discrete associations, the interrelations between which are not a priori definable. It is one of the central theses of the present analysis that in post-capitalist society industry and society have, by contrast to capitalist society, been dissociated. Increasingly, the social relations of industry, including industrial conflict, do not dominate the whole of society but remain confined in their patterns and problems to the sphere of industry. Industry and industrial conflict are, in post-capitalist society, institutionally isolated, i.e., confined within the borders of their proper realm and robbed of their influence on other spheres of society. In post-capitalist society, the industrial enterprise is no longer the model after which all other relations are fashioned. From this thesis (which, for this reason, one might call a "theory" by contrast to the "propositions" or "hypotheses" derived from it) a number of significant consequences follow for class analysis. Before we consider these in some detail, however, the theory itself requires some elucidation.

At an earlier point in this study we have described three sets of facts which would seem to suggest that Marx and Burnham are right in believing industry and society to be virtually identical in the modern world. The first of these was the purely physical extent of industry and industrial enterprises as well as the manifest significance of industrial production for life in contemporary society. Whatever changes may have occurred with respect to the relation of industry and society, they have evidently supported rather than contradicted this tendency. In ever larger enterprises an ever growing number of workers produces ever more numerous goods. Yet this fact does not contradict the theory of institutional isolation of industry, as will become apparent if we look at the other two factors mentioned in our earlier analysis. We have stated there that the occupational role dominates the social position of people in industrial society, and in particular that of workers. Here, a counter-trend cannot be ignored. The time spent by the average worker on his job has decreased and will probably continue to decrease. Although his work plays a prominent part in the daily life of the worker, there are indications that other roles besides his occupation gain in importance. In a sense, his occupation has been confined to a set place in the life of the worker, just as industry has been confined to a set place in the structure of society. We shall return to this problem presently. With respect to the sanctions available to employers to enforce conformity with the values of the ruling class of industry, we can note an analogous development. The quasi-governmental police supervision of early capitalists has been restricted considerably in post-capitalist society. The ruling class of industry rules over a rather more limited part of the lives of its workers; its sanctions are confined to properly industrial penalties and are, even here, subject to legal regulations. Employers shooting their workers with their own police force are as hard to imagine today as corporal punishment, arrest, or even dismissal without reason and reduction of wages.[16] The loss on the part of management of quasi-governmental rights of control which penetrate deeply into the life of the individual also marks a reduction of the formerly all-embracing significance of industry. Here, too, confinement to a specific, limited sphere can be demonstrated.

That industry and industrial conflict have been institutionally isolated means that they have settled down in society, have found a stable and definite place within it. Parallels to other institutional spheres suggest themselves. One might argue, for example, that in the secularized societies of today the church has been displaced from the all-embracing part it played at earlier times and confined to a proper, defined sphere in society; the church, too, has been institutionally isolated. In all countries directly or indirectly affected by the French Revolution, the relation of church and state is one of delimitation of competence between two separate institutional orders and imperatively coordinated associations. According to the thesis here advanced, we are witnessing, in post-capitalist society, a similar development with respect to industry and the enterprises of industrial production. Here, too, a process of confinement—that is, of delimitation of basically separate competences—takes place. With a somewhat daring but illustrative comparison from modern medicine, one might say that, like a stomach the ulcers of which are deprived of their influence on the total organism by the severance of vagus and sympathicus and which is left to regulate itself, industry in post-capi-

---

[16] This—it has to be emphasized—holds for post-capitalist societies. It emphatically does not hold for industrializing countries, Communist or otherwise, where all the worst symptoms of European capitalism reappear.

of an undiminished, even intensified, presence of the class conflict between employers (as managers) and workers, Schelsky believes that the question of the significance of the "old" classes for the present has to be answered "unequivocally in the negative." These incompatible conclusions cannot be argued away by ridiculing one or the other student of the matter. Rather, the incompatibility of these theories challenges the sociologist to develop a new and better theory. This is precisely what the theory of the institutional isolation of industrial conflict affords. It supports, so to speak, Burnham with respect to the sphere of industry where the old conflict persists (although not, as we have seen, in an intensified form), and it confirms, at the same time, Schelsky's notion by disputing the binding force of industrial conflict for the inclusive society. In this way, the claim for general validity implicit in both theories is rejected. The "old" conflict persists; but its effects are limited to the institutional sphere of industry. Outside industry, in the political society, the prolongation of "capital" and "wage labor" into "bourgeoisie" and "proletariat" in the Marxian sense no longer describes the dominant patterns of social conflict.

EMPIRICAL CONSEQUENCES OF THE THEORY OF INSTITUTIONAL ISOLATION OF INDUSTRIAL CONFLICT

As formulated so far, the theory of institutional isolation of industrial conflict is a general orientation, a point of view rather than a scientific theory. Above all, it is not, as such, susceptible of refutation by empirical test. One may argue for or against it—but such arguments can finally neither confirm nor reject its validity. The theory proves testable only if we succeed in deriving certain testable propositions from it, and in confronting them with known or accessible facts. Some of the assumptions which may thus be derived from the theory of institutional isolation of industrial conflict, and which promise to further the process of our analysis, will now be formulated and, insofar as possible, at least illustrated by empirical data.

(1) If it is correct that with industry itself industrial conflict has been institutionally isolated in post-capitalist societies, it follows that his occupational role has lost its comprehensive molding force for the social personality of the industrial worker, and that it determines only a limited sector of his social behavior. Even today, occupation is generally assumed to be the decisive social role of at least the man in industrial society. "A man's job—occupying nearly one-third of his daily life—is more than just a means of livelihood or an outlet

for his creative energy; it is a vital influence on his existence even beyond working hours. His social position, his economic welfare, and even his daily habits are all determined by the kind of job he holds" (120, p. 411). While there can be no doubt that income and prestige are in all industrial societies to a definable extent functions of occupation, and that many daily habits, such as the time of rising and going to bed, are determined by the requirements of the job, the thesis is advanced here that in the special case of industrial workers[17] that sector of social behavior which is not immediately determined by occupation is extending steadily. In post-capitalist society, the worker, when he passes the factory gate, increasingly leaves his occupational role behind him with the machines and his work clothes; outside, he plays new roles defined by factors other than his occupation. The occupation and the expectations connected with it dominate less and less the life of the industrial worker, and other expectations mold his social personality. The job has become exactly what it is denied in the above quotation: a means for the end of life which as such assumes a fixed and limited place in the workers' behavior.

Here, the "convergence of social science in highly industrialized countries" emphasized by Schelsky has its place; it aims at "putting the structures of consumption and leisure-time behavior into the center of the interpretation of contemporary society" (72, p. 65). One may (and must) doubt whether consumption roles are becoming— as Schelsky thinks (72, pp. 65 ff.)—"the central determinant of all patterns of behavior instead of class status." I should think that the undoubted trend toward increasing the importance of his consumer's position in the life of the worker in post-capitalist society develops at the expense of occupational position and testifies to the isolation of occupationally determined patterns of behavior, i.e., their restraint to a specific context confined in time and space. If it is possible to show, by empirical investigation, that consumption status does indeed assume a more prominent place in the consciousness and factual behavior of the worker than his occupational status, the proposition formulated here may be regarded as confirmed.

(2) A special case of the matter formulated in this proposition and a further consequence of the theory of the institutional isolation of industrial conflict can be found in the hypothesis that the participants of industry, upon leaving the factory gate, leave behind them

---

[17] Probably this thesis is also valid for other occupational groups; however, in the present context I want to restrict it to industrial workers.

with their occupational role their industrial class interests also. The manifest contents of industrial class interests are no longer identical with those of political class interests. At a time when the one and only manifest interest of those subjected to industrial authority was an economic subsistence minimum, defined either physiologically or socially, this interest accompanied the workers to all spheres of their social behavior. But the significance for class conflict of the tendency toward equality, toward leveling the differences between strata, lies in the fact that the increasing equalization of living conditions and the institutionalization of the right to a minimum wage have provided a basis for separating the manifest interests of industrial and political conflict. Two aspects of this tendency are clearly visible today. First, the issues of industrial conflict in post-capitalist society are typically no longer of the kind that would divide the whole society into "two large hostile camps." They divide only the participants of industry into two hostile camps; they are confined to goals in which only these are "interested" by virtue of their occupational and, more specifically, authority roles. This is true not only of wage claims based on higher productivity, but also for demands to prolong paid vacations, shorten working hours, establish participation in management—to say nothing of the more technical issues of conflict (job evaluation, problems of time and motion study, of wage system, etc.) which, outside industry, are hardly understood as conflict issues. In terms of its issues, industrial conflict increasingly becomes *industrial* conflict without reference to general social and political problems. Secondly, this narrowing down of the issues of industrial conflict means that the individual worker is concerned with them only in his role as worker. In other roles he is moved by other things; as consumer or citizen, he is no longer worker. If, for the sake of clarity, an overstatement is permitted, one might say: as the bowling fan may get heated over certain problems in his bowling club which leave his behavior outside the bowling club totally unaffected, so the issues of industrial conflict become increasingly irrelevant outside the sphere of industry.[18]

(3) One of the consequences of this fact and of the theory of institutional isolation is that industrial strikes no longer affect the so-called public of post-capitalist societies immediately; indeed, that strikes in one branch of industry leave workers in another branch rela-

[18] Tendential assumptions always require qualification; this one is no exception. Obviously, matters of wage disputes affect the economic position of people; this in turn affects consumption chances and thereby the total social life. In historical perspective, a separation of spheres seems apparent, however, even here.

tively unaffected. If industry and society are two discrete social contexts, conflicts in one do not lead to conflicts in the other, i.e., the public does not identify itself with the striking parties on the basis of the respective class situation, but for completely different motives (e.g., harm to the economy, to one's own position, temporary discomforts, etc.). Geiger's "new line" of a conflict between those who participate immediately in production and the "mere consumers" plays a part here: events within the institutionally isolated sphere of industry may be regarded as threatening by the unconcerned public precisely because of this isolation; they are not identified with political conflicts. It is a telling fact that in a German opinion survey in 1954 almost one-half of those interviewed took a stand against strikes and expressed their belief that "the workers get, by strikes, advantages only for themselves and never even consider the interests of the general public" (see 229, p. 235).[19]

(4) Within the sphere of political organization it follows from the theory of the institutional isolation of industrial conflict that trade unions and progressive (socialist, labor) parties are no longer identical; that, indeed, the notion of a workers' party has lost its political meaning. If it is true that industrial conflict is, in post-capitalist society, confined to its own specific sphere, if, therefore, the role distribution and the issues of industrial conflict have lost their embracing social significance, then the interest groups of industry and society are also discrete organizations. They may still be connected by the bond of tradition, but they are no longer united by a common cause and field of recruitment. The validity of this thesis is most evident in the United States and least evident in Britain. In all post-capitalist societies, however, there is the double tendency to establish the political independence of trade unions as interest groups in industrial conflict and to extend socialist or progressive parties as interest groups in political conflict beyond the boundaries of an industrial class to "people's parties" or "mass parties." Many people are still surprised to find active unionists among the voters, or even functionaries, of conservative parties; but this is merely a consequence of the trend of development which we have tried to describe as one of institutional isolation.

(5) If this theory proves a useful explanatory tool, it follows— to formulate a last derivation—that in post-capitalist society the ruling

[19] It has to be noted, however, that this latter attitude is probably more characteristic for Germany (where conflict is notoriously regarded as "bad" and undesirable) than for Britain and the United States.

and the subjected classes of industry and of the political society are no longer identical; that there are, in other words, in principle two independent conflict fronts. Outside the enterprise, the manager may be a mere citizen, the worker a member of parliament; their industrial class position no longer determines their authority position in the political society. According to this assumption it is by no means true that "the relation to the instruments of production . . . decides the issue of class dominance, of power and privilege, in society" (Burnham, 140, p. 97); political authority is, rather, allocated independent of a man's industrial authority position. Moreover, this holds increasingly as within industry the separation of ownership and control increases and as the more universal capitalists are replaced by managers.

It was the intention of this analysis to push the theory of institutional isolation of industrial conflict to the point at which testable hypotheses can be formulated. Since no quantity of empirical data, however large, is capable of verifying these hypotheses, it seems sensible to present them for criticism and, perhaps, refutation by empirical research. As long as they are not refuted, we may maintain that in post-capitalist society the associations of industry and society have to be understood as discrete universes of class conflict. "Wage labor" and "capital," the industrial classes of capitalist society, determine the social conflicts of industry even today as labor and management, or trade unions and employers' associations, although the forms of these conflicts have been subject to many a change in the last hundred years. The fronts of social conflict, however, can no longer be extrapolated by merely extending the lines of industrial conflict beyond the boundaries of industry. Neither is "capital" extended into the "bourgeoisie," the ruling class, nor "wage labor" extended into the "proletariat," the subjected class, of post-capitalist society in its political aspect. Rather, this is a problem for separate investigation.

INDUSTRIAL CONFLICT: TRENDS AND COUNTERTRENDS

The history of industrial conflict provides illustrations and examples for most of the patterns and types suggested by the theory of group conflict in imperatively coordinated associations. These illustrations and examples are all the more interesting, since the protagonists of industrial conflict have in many ways remained the same throughout industrial development. We have seen that both capital and labor underwent a process of decomposition in the course of the last hundred years. The unified capitalist class of the time of Marx dissolved into various elements, such as the managers, the mere owners, the finance capitalists; the homogeneous working class of a hundred years ago evolved within itself new lines of differentiation according to skill, income, prestige; both classes were extended and complicated by the emergence of a "new middle stratum" of bureaucrats and white-collar workers. However, all these developments have modified the authority structure of the industrial enterprise but slightly. There still are employers and employees, entrepreneurs and workers; and management and labor are even today the quasi-groups underlying the organizations that carry on the dynamics of the social development of industry.

But the modes of their interrelations have changed in many ways since the time the Luddites in England fought their alienation by trying to break machines in isolated factories, or even since the time when a hired police force of management tried to disperse workers on strike by force. For one thing, the violence of industrial conflict has diminished considerably. This is due, in the first place, to the very fact of organization of the conflicting parties. Secondly, trade unions and employers' associations have established an often intricate system of routines of conflict regulation. Before they have recourse to violent manifestations of conflict, they meet to discuss their claims, they call in a mediator and, perhaps, an arbitrator; in short, they try to settle their disagreements by talking rather than fighting. This reduction of violence has been greatly helped by improvements in the standard of living of the workers. In most of the countries that might today be described as post-capitalist societies, absolute deprivation on the part of industrial labor gave way, early in this century, to relative deprivation, so that the "cost" of victory or defeat in conflict decreased. There is a peculiar dialectics in the fact that this reduction of violence is both cause and effect of the institutionalization of industrial conflict: by forming organizations and defending their claims, management and labor have been able to introduce changes which in turn helped their chances of peacefully settling disputes.

With the violence, although for different reasons, the intensity of industrial conflict has decreased also. Here, the dissociation of patterns that were superimposed in capitalist society is crucial. Above all, in contemporary societies industrial conflict and political conflict are no longer identical. The protagonists, issues, and patterns of industrial conflict make for a discrete set of social relations. Industrial conflict has been severed from the antagonisms that divide political society; it is carried on in relative isolation. In many (though not all) countries, this dissociation of formerly superimposed patterns has also occurred with respect to the relations between class conflict and other types of conflict,[20] and with respect to the relations between authority position and social status. Characteristically, the social status of a skilled man devoid of authority is higher than that of a low-level bureaucrat who participates, if in a distant way, in the exercise of managerial authority. We have not here analyzed the incidence of social mobility between the classes in industry. However, what little data we have[21] suggest strongly that there is a great deal of exchange between the classes in industry, between, as well as within, generations. Industry is, of course, by no means "classless," but there is enough mobility to suggest that from this point of view, too, the intensity of conflict has diminished rather than increased. The conclusion that the energies invested in industrial conflict by management and labor in post-capitalist society are rather smaller than a hundred years ago is confirmed, moreover, by numerous surveys showing a steadily decreasing interest and participation in union affairs on the part of labor.

Diminishing intensity and violence of conflict have their effect on the modes of structure change in industry. They would suggest that sudden as well as radical changes are largely absent on the contemporary scene. Changes of conditions and structures occur gradually and remain piecemeal. In part, they take the form of penetration of the ruling groups by members of the subjected groups, but more often what happens in industry is that interests of labor are (if grudgingly) accepted by management and made part of the existing structure.

In the foregoing analysis, I have confined myself to indicating such developments as point in the direction of decreasing intensity and violence. As always in social affairs, however, development is by no means unilinear. There are undoubtedly countertrends, also, and our analysis is not intended to suggest that all trouble in industry is past. For one thing, it is never possible simply to extrapolate social developments. The fact that industrial conflict has become less vio-

[20] This is still not entirely true in Britain with respect to the position of the Irish in industry, and above all in the United States with respect to both colored workers and immigrant workers. In these cases the management-labor conflict is even today often intensified by other lines of division.

[21] Cf., above all, the data presented by G. Thomas for Britain (123, p. 30), according to which only 5 per cent of the "managerial" category in his representative national sample have been managers all their lives, whereas no less than two-thirds of all managers have been in manual laboring occupations at some time.

lent and intense in the last century does not justify the inference that it will continue to do so. On the contrary, experience shows that in the history of specific conflicts more and less violent, more and less intense periods follow each other in unpredictable rhythms. It is certainly conceivable that the future has more intense and violent conflicts in store.

To some extent there are already indications of such a development. I have tried to show that not all changes introduced in order to regulate industrial conflict have been well-conceived. The German shop council and co-determination systems block rather than open channels of expression of conflicting interests. It would not be surprising if these ineffective modes of regulation should lead to new and at first uncontrolled outbreaks of violence; indeed, it would, from the point of view of conflict theory, be surprising if this did not happen. Moreover, the institutionalization of trade unions brings with it that phenomenon which Michels (see 200) so aptly described as the "iron law of oligarchy," i.e., the stabilization of an unequal authority distribution within the unions. This, again, promotes a new type of conflict, intra-union conflict, and one for which wildcat strikes already provide some evidence. It is hard to see how trade unions propose to check this development. Finally, there is always, of course, the possibility that totalitarian forms of government will interfere with the industrial order and change its patterns of conflict. It will be evident to the reader that most of the analysis of the present chapter presupposes a democratic political system. Once this system is abolished, a new situation arises inside as well as outside industry—a system (as I shall try to show in the following chapter) that promotes extremely intense and violent conflicts. Whatever trends toward reduction of violence and intensity of conflict there may be in the industry of post-capitalist society, there are countertrends also, and it is hard, if not impossible, to derive predictions in that sphere from the analysis of this chapter.

VIII

Classes in Post-Capitalist Society
II: Political Conflict

HOW PEOPLE SEE SOCIETY

Few people, sociologists or otherwise, deny that there still are conflicts in industry. Wage claims, demands for a share in management, strikes, and lockouts are too clearly in evidence to be argued away. But there are many people who claim that so far as political life in post-capitalist society is concerned, issues and lines of division other than class have become far more important for an understanding of society. Where this is argued, half-truths are usually intermingled with untruths. It is said that the problems of industry no longer concern every citizen; this is true, but it does not mean that there are no longer issues that divide the political community. It is said that political parties have become more and more similar in their programs; this is true, but it does not mean that they have become interchangeable either from the point of view of the voter or from that of policy. It is said that people no longer respond to ideologies; this is true, but it does not mean that they have no divergent convictions. At the bottom of such arguments there is often a vague assertion to the effect that by comparison with their attitude during the golden or gruesome age of capitalism, the people have changed their attitudes, views, and outlook on society. It is said that people no longer look at society in terms of divisions and antagonisms but now judge everybody on his merits from the point of view of a happy cooperative whole; and that sociologists who insist on cleavages and conflict merely again stir up troubles that have just been overcome. This assertion, to be sure, is not a half-truth but an untruth. Since it refers to people's feelings, however, rather than to sociological interpretations of reality, it is both necessary and appropriate that we begin our analysis of political conflict in contemporary societies with a look at some studies that are explicitly concerned with ascertaining how people see society. Discussion of these studies will link the sociological aspects of our problem with its psychological dimension and at the same time add some color and verisimilitude to statements which as assertions, assumptions, and hypotheses remain by necessity vague, abstract, and, perhaps, unconvincing.

I have indicated earlier at which points the sociological analysis of conflict may be fruitfully and legitimately supplemented by (social) psychological data. I have then emphasized what I again affirm here, that psychological evidence does not and cannot provide a conclusive test for our theory. Primarily, our theory refers not to what people think but to what they do; and while it may often be difficult to separate the two, the validity of our theory is in no way dependent on whether a representative sample thinks it is valid. The data to be discussed in this section illustrate some points of our theory, they are suggestive of further problems, they help to round off the picture of conflict in post-capitalist society presented here, but they must not be understood as either confirming or refuting the theory of conflict or any of its derivations. Between the scientific explanation and the popular view of a phenomenon there remains a gap which is hard to bridge.

With respect to the question of how people see society, we are today in the fortunate position of having at our disposal a number of competent studies which provide suggestive and comparable data for various countries. Of these, I have singled out four that seem to me of particular import: those of Centers in the United States (38), Popitz and associates in Germany (69), Willener in French Switzerland (76), and Hoggart in Britain (52). Although these studies have been conducted almost entirely independently of each other,[1] their authors formulate the object of their research in surprisingly similar terms. Above all, there are two notions that come up in most of them, namely, those of "class" and of "images of society" (*images de la société, Gesellschaftsbilder*). These studies are, in other words, directly to the point of our own investigation. Although similar in subject, these four studies differ in their techniques of investigation and methods of interpretation. Centers presents and briefly interprets[2] the quantified findings of a (multiple-choice) questionnaire survey.

[1] Willener explicitly refers to Centers but not to Popitz and Hoggart. All others are apparently (and, considering the dates of publication, understandably) ignorant of one another. The studies appeared in the following sequence: Centers (1949), Hoggart, Willener, Popitz (all 1957). The co-authors of Popitz's study were H. P. Bahrdt, E. A. Jüres, and H. Kesting; but since the parts in question here have been written by Popitz alone, it seems justified to refer to the study by his name.

[2] I am neglecting, here, the sketchy and rather out-of-place theoretical introduction and conclusion of Centers' work. Contrary to the author's belief, these have, in my opinion, virtually no relation to his data.

Willener used a questionnaire also, but an open-ended one; his more varied findings are quantified and interpreted. The study of Popitz and his team is based on depth interviews following a general schema; in his interpretation, Popitz largely avoids quantitative conclusions and instead presents a brilliant discussion. Hoggart's study, finally, is of a different kind altogether. It is an outstanding "impressionistic" account of what the author himself calls "aspects of working-class life," based on intimate personal knowledge but evidently entirely qualitative. In all cases, we shall confine ourselves in the following discussion to presenting in a summary fashion a small selection of the findings and conclusions—those that are relevant for the progress of our own investigation.

One of the first conclusions reached by these studies is that, by and large, people do have an image of society. In a sense, this is perhaps not very surprising. The need to assess one's place in the world is presumably an existential need; it includes the necessity to place oneself in the social universe of reference. At the same time, though in general there exists an image of society, this does not come about merely as a matter of course, nor is it easily or precisely defined for the individual. However vague or stereotyped this image may be, it requires some considerable effort of reflection and of dissociation from one's most personal sphere. Let us look at how a man who lacks such reflection views the world. Popitz reports the case of a roll-caster in a steelworks who, in his opinion, has no image of society: "(What do you think of technical progress?) I do not think that far. I always say, after us the deluge. (How does technical progress come about?) The foremen do that, and the engineers and employers. . . . (What does co-determination mean to you?) Co-determination? Has that been carried out? I have very little interest in that . . ." (69, p. 227). This is certainly a pathetic statement; but should we not expect to find it often? It would seem that in fact it is anything but commonplace to find that people have by and large a fairly articulate view of the society in which they live.

A second uniform finding of the four studies in question is that people's images of society differ, and that such differences as there are are not random. Popitz and Willener each distinguish six types of approach. Those of Willener are directly related to problems of social stratification and class structure. According to him, people see society in terms of: (*a*) socioeconomic categories, (*b*) socio-occupational categories, (*c*) a dichotomy of dependence, (*d*) class struggle, (*e*) social prestige, or (*f*) political categories (see 76, p. 153). Popitz's classification of types is more general. According to the dominant idea in different images of society he distinguishes: (*a*) static order, (*b*) progressive order, (*c*) dichotomy as collective fate, (*d*) dichotomy as individual conflict, (*e*) reform of the social order, (*f*) class struggle (see 69, p. 233). In both studies, the (Marxist) notion of society torn by class strife was found to be of but minor importance: 10 per cent of those interviewed by Willener and 1 per cent (!) of those interviewed by Popitz still adhered to this idea.[3] The data presented by Centers and Hoggart do not allow a comparison here.

Willener and Popitz agree, however, that their six types may be further reduced to two basic images of society which underlie the empirical variety found. Here, Centers' work may be adduced also. As we have done in this study, Centers distinguishes strictly between social strata and social classes, between a "static" and a "dynamic" view of society (38, pp. 26 ff.). For Centers, as for us, this is a theoretical decision. However, the studies of Popitz and Willener show that this decision is reproduced in the views different people have of society. "Strata (or levels)," states Willener, "imply the image of a *continuity* . . . whereas classes indicate *antagonistic* groups" (76, p. 206), and he adds that, on the basis of his findings relating to this distinction, "there can be no doubt that there are fundamental differences between the image of individuals situated at the top of the social scale and those situated at the bottom" (p. 208). More precisely: "The 'inferior' categories of respondents predominantly respond in terms of social classes rather than strata; conversely, the respondents of 'superior' categories have a tendency of referring more frequently to strata than to classes" (p. 206). This conclusion bears a striking similarity to that of Popitz when he expresses the notions of "class" and "stratum" by the terms "dichotomy" and "hierarchy": "All workers with whom we have spoken and who develop an image of society in the sense of our definition at all see society as a *dichotomy*, incontrovertible or subject to change, unbridgeable or susceptible of mediation by 'partnership.' . . . By contrast, the white-collar man knows a 'top' that is above him, and a 'bottom' that is below him. He places himself in the middle, and develops a remarkably acute sense

---

[3] The reason for this otherwise surprising difference between Switzerland and Germany is that whereas Popitz characterizes by the "class struggle" image only those who profess strictly Marxist views, Willener also includes those who vaguely refer to "capital," "exploitation," etc.

of distinction and of social gradations. One may assume, therefore, that he sees society not as a dichotomy like the industrial worker, but as a *hierarchy*" (69, pp. 237, 242).

In these views, our two models of society reappear. The continuity of a hierarchical system of stratification represents order and integration. There may be problems and strains, but there are no deep cleavages in society thus conceived. By contrast, the antagonisms of a dichotomous structure of class evoke the ideas of conflict, dissensus, and coercion. But, in the empirical findings of Popitz and Willener, these views are not complementary approaches to the same object. To be sure, even here they are not contradictory. But they are held by different people. Those "above" visualize society as a comparatively ordered continuous hierarchy of positions; those "below" are, above all, struck by the gap between them and "the others." Several interpretations of this strange and important fact are possible. In terms of our theory of conflict, however, it would seem that the dominant groups of society express their comparative gratification with existing conditions *inter alia* by visualizing and describing these conditions as ordered and reasonable; subjected groups, on the other hand, tend to emphasize the cleavages that in their opinion account for the deprivations they feel. At least potentially, there is an ideological element in the models of society distinguished by us and, apparently, by people generally. The integration model, the hierarchical image, lends itself as an ideology of satisfaction and conservation; the coercion model, the dichotomous image, provides an expression for dissatisfaction and the wish to change the *status quo*. Even at a time at which revolutionary ideologies of the Marxist type have lost their grip on workers everywhere, there remains an image of society which, in its political consequences, is incompatible with the more harmonious image of those "above," whether they be called "capitalists," "ruling class," or even "middle class."

Little need be added about the hierarchical image of society as expressed predominantly by middle-class people. It is, clearly, derived from the notion of a bureaucratic hierarchy in which everybody has his defined place both above and below others. The whole is an ordered, well-organized system in which one can rise but not fall, and which has an accepted, institutionalized scale of symbols, titles, statuses. Such conflicts as are recognized are individual, highly personal conflicts; and all other cleavages are banned from consciousness as unpleasant also-realities.

As against this, even the more stereotyped versions of the dichotomous image of society are rather more colorful. From the studies under discussion it would seem that there are, in many languages, simple but descriptive terms by which to characterize the two sides of the dichotomy: *them* and *us* in Britain, *ceux qui sont en haut* and *en bas* in Switzerland (and, probably, in France), *die da oben* and *wir hier unten* in Germany—these are expressions that belong to the stock-in-trade of working-class language. This is, for example, what some of the workers interviewed by Popitz had to say about co-determination: " 'One can always corrupt the workers' representatives. Where there is money, there is power. And if the workers' representatives have really pushed through a decision, one can twist its execution in such a way that nothing comes of it. . . . They don't want others to look at their cards. . . . If they ever go in for co-determination, then to their own advantage: for the worker as much co-responsibility and as little co-determination as possible.' . . . 'We have nothing to co-determine. That is determined by management. What they say, will be done—and that is that.' . . . 'All that is just talk. We have nothing to co-determine. It's been managed by the unions, and if anybody co-determines, it is at best the union secretaries and bosses. . . . They up there don't care anyway' " (69, pp. 202 f.). Hoggart summarized the attitude apparent from these statements in a splendid selection of stereotypes: " 'They' are 'the people at the top,' 'the higher-ups,' the people who give you your dole, call you up, tell you to go to war, fine you, made you split the family in the 'thirties to avoid a reduction in the Means Test allowance, 'get yer in the end,' 'aren't really to be trusted,' 'talk posh,' 'are all twisters really,' 'never tell yer owt' (e.g., about a relative in hospital), 'clap yer in clink,' 'will do y' down if they can,' 'summons yer,' 'are all in a click [clique] together,' 'treat y' like muck' " (52, p. 62).

The criteria of distinction between the two groups that make up the dichotomy of society are varied. Hoggart's list of idioms carries a strong connotation of resentment of authority, so that differences of power might indeed appear to mark the dividing line between "them" and "us": " 'Them' is the world of the bosses, whether those bosses are private individuals or, as is increasingly the case today, public officials" (52, p. 62). Willener emphasizes the criterion of power also, but he adds others: "Certain interviewees conceive essentially two classes: the salaried and the nonsalaried, in other words those who are dependent and those who are independent. To this may be added the formula 'those who work and those who do not work' which is given more rarely with the same meaning" (76, p. 155).

Popitz again stresses the importance of the "stereotype alternative of power and impotency" (69, p. 244), but regards another criterion as equally significant: the dichotomy between manual and nonmanual labor. This dichotomy is, for Popitz, closely related to the "formula" Willener encountered among his respondents: "Even very intelligent workers who make a point of judging white-collar people justly and who concede that there have to be such people, too, remain mistrustful in one respect: it seems extremely questionable to them whether white-collar people really work" (69, p. 238; cf. 68). White-collar work lacks "publicity," it is not susceptible of the same kind of control as manual work, it is not as visibly *work*; and a line is drawn between those who do "visible" and those who do "invisible" work. In this question of criteria for social dichotomies the study of Centers is also relevant, for, although he did not intend to do so, Centers also found, in effect, that for most people (American) society consists of but two classes: the middle class and the working class. Ninety-four per cent of his original interview population assigned themselves to these two classes.[4] Among the criteria of distinction between these classes, Centers found "beliefs and attitudes," "family," and "money" most prominent. But, like Willener, Centers emphasizes: "To the members of the working class the most important criterion of middle class membership after money or income is the ownership of a small business, profession or trade; in sum, being an independent operator or proprietor of some kind" (38, p. 99). By contrast, "it cannot help but strike one as highly significant that the most distinctive criterion given for membership in [the working] class is 'working for a living' " (38, p. 100).[5] Not surprisingly, Centers, much like Popitz and Willener, concludes that "the effect is to make the white-collar work vs. manual work and salaried work vs. wage work dichotomies both important bases for class distinction in virtue of their importance as criteria for working class affiliation, and the psychological effect is to push white-collar workers toward identification with the middle class" (38, p. 102).

---

[4] In a later study Centers reports only 88 per cent did so, while there was a slightly larger proportion of interviewees that "didn't know" or ranked themselves as "upper" or "lower class," the four alternatives presented to them being "upper," "middle," "working," and "lower class" (see 38, p. 77).

[5] Even more striking, perhaps, is the comparative evidence which seems to agree even in the details of everyday language: "working for a living and not working for a living" (Centers, U.S.A.), "ceux qui travaillent et ceux qui ne travaillent pas" (Willener, Switzerland), "wirklich arbeiten und nicht wirklich arbeiten" (Popitz, Germany).

However, all four authors stress the fact that these criteria of distinction do not permit of an entirely unequivocal identification of all persons and occupations as "middle class" or "working class," "above" or "below." The studies seem to agree that the dividing line between "them" and "us" runs somewhere through the group of salaried employees. "The class position of office workers seems also[6] to be an equivocal one, for they are claimed almost as often by working class people as they are by the middle class. The difficulty of assigning them to class membership appears thus no less a one with the members of actual classes than it has been to social scientists" (38, pp. 81 f.). Willener thinks that by the "below" most people mean wage-earning as well as salaried employees (see 76, p. 163), but I think more probable Popitz's and Hoggart's suggestion that in people's minds the phenomenon of social distance is crucial for distinguishing between "them" and "us." According to Popitz, the foremen and immediate supervisors of industry, whose work is visible to most workers, are usually counted among the working class, and "above" begins with the shop supervisors and the shop councilors and union secretaries, for these no longer "belong" (see 69, pp. 243 f.). According to Hoggart, for the worker the world of "them" begins even earlier: "So, when working-class people are asked to become foremen or N.C.O.'s they often hesitate. Whatever their motives, they will be regarded now as on the side of 'them' " (52, p. 64). It will be well to remember, in the following analysis, that for those who visualize society as dichotomous, the upper part of the dichotomy begins not far from the bottom layer of social stratification and includes all those who have even a minimal share in the exercise of authority.

Whatever changes may have occurred in the last hundred years, the idea that there is a fundamental division of society into "haves" and "have-nots," "above" and "below," "them" and "us" is still a force in the minds of many people. One might be tempted to think that the dichotomous image of society is a relic of Marxism or, more generally, of the conditions of early capitalism and their interpretation. However, Ossowski has shown that "the dichotomous view of social stratification"—as an essay of his is entitled (96)—is both older and more general than capitalism. "The spatial metaphor which represents society as an aggregate of men of which some are above and others below belongs to those images which do not lose their

---

[6] Centers had just discussed the position of farmers.

pertinence in the course of the centuries and which, as the history of cultures seems to prove, impose themselves to the imagination" (96, p. 16). Ossowski follows this image through the myths and religions of mankind, through literature and philosophy. Three aspects of the social dichotomy run like a thread through its many manifestations: the divisions into rulers and ruled; rich and poor; those for whom one works, and those who work (96, p. 19). We might feel inclined to replace, in the medieval English quatrain, the word "God" by "society" and thereby take the worst sting out of the dichotomy, but its substance remains essentially true even today:

> The rich man in his castle,
> The poor man at his gate,
> God made them high or lowly,
> And ordered their estate.

The assertion that a dichotomous image of society is an archetype of human understanding cannot, of course, be supported by the evidence presented in this section. Rather, there would seem cause for qualifying the conclusions already drawn. We have seen earlier that not everybody has an image of society at all; there are people who get along with a minimum of reflection on matters beyond the immediate horizon.[7] Of those who have an image of society, only a few visualize society as a dichotomous entity. If one breaks down people's views by their own occupational or class position, there are indications of "deviance" from the point of view of class theory: workers rank themselves as "middle class," white-collar people profess a dichotomous image of society. There are problematic groups, groups that are not easily placed in terms of the dichotomy, such as salaried employees and farmers. Finally, the consequences people draw from their images of society differ greatly. Centers believes that "the top occupational strata are marked by their adherence to the *status quo* in the order of politico-economic relations. In contrast, the lowest occupational groups are distinguished by their lack of support of the *status quo* and by their endorsement of views clearly radical in character" (38, p. 208). Plausible as this sounds, it is as much a direct derivation from Centers' theory as it is a summary of evidence. Very likely,

---

[7] Popitz found that about 20 per cent of those interviewed by him have no real image of society (69, p. 233); 24 per cent of those interviewed by Willener responded negatively, without clear idea, or not at all (76, p. 161); by comparison, the 2 per cent who "didn't know" or "didn't believe in classes" in Centers' study are surprisingly few (38, p. 77).

Popitz is closer to the truth in concluding that the "consciousness" of workers "may still admit to itself and to others that industrial workers have their own interests which are in conflict with those of others" (69, pp. 247 f.), but that there are also many phenomena, both social and personal, that make workers hesitant to draw pronouncedly radical political conclusions from their dichotomous image of society. This is confirmed by Glantz, who found in an independent empirical study in the United States that "a latent tendency towards radicalism undoubtedly exists among some workers, but there is little or no historical evidence to indicate that it has recently been developing into a conscious ideology" (195, p. 378).[8] Ossowski has shown that the dichotomous image of society may be activated into an ideology of political conflict, but it is as such no more than an interpretation of the social world.

As a way of seeing society, however, the dichotomous view is a solid and, probably, powerful social fact. It may lend itself toward giving additional force to the considerations offered in this study. In a way, it provides a second foothold for our analysis of post-capitalist society: on the one hand, there are the suggestions and assumptions derived from the theory of conflict; on the other hand, there are indications and problems furnished by the findings of systematic empirical observation. In any case, these findings dispose of the half-truths and untruths mentioned at the outset of this section. That from one point of view society presents a dichotomous image, an image of conflict and dissensus, is by no means an invention of sociologists imposed on a basically harmonious and cooperative social reality. The dichotomies of post-capitalist society may have little to do with those asserted by Marx: there is no disagreement here between sociological and public opinion. But there still are dichotomies, and they are very real to those who experience society in terms of them. Here, as elsewhere, sociological analysis is more than a disengaged and noncommittal exercise of the mind: it is an attempt to explain rationally and systematically those facts which to men in society are real stumbling blocks on their path.

THE AUTHORITY STRUCTURE OF THE POLITICAL STATE

"An imperatively coordinated association will be called political association if and so far as the enforcement of its order is carried out

---

[8] Glantz is explicitly—and rightly—critical of Centers' conservatism-radicalism scale and characterizes most of the conclusions based on this scale as "methodologically derived fiction" (195, p. 378 n.).

nected with the authority structure of the state, we have to be able to identify this structure as one of super- and subordination of persons in their capacity as incumbents of social positions.

This approach seems realistic in a second sense, too. The statement that the force of the law has replaced the authority of persons provokes the question: Why was there this difference in other societies? The notions of "anonymous" ruling forces or of a society that runs itself seem to document no more than that it is difficult, or that Schelsky and Riesman find it difficult, to identify the seat of political authority in post-capitalist societies. But does this mean that there is no authority? Does it mean that there are no persons who, by virtue of their positions, are entitled and expected to make authoritative decisions? It seems to me that a Hegelian reification of the state as liberty incarnate is required in order to answer these questions in the affirmative. Can there be any doubt that there still are governments, parliaments, and courts of law in the contemporary world? And— since this is obviously an entirely rhetorical question—can there be any doubt that cabinet ministers, members of parliament, and judges lend their authority to decisions that affect the lives of those subjected to them? If there is any truth in attempts to dispute the continued presence of political authority in the contemporary world, it is in the empirical generalization that many people find it hard to name and, perhaps, identify those "above." But surely it is not the task of the sociologist to hypostasize the confusions of public opinion into ambiguities of social structure itself.

However we may eventually describe and delimit the ruling class of the polity of post-capitalist society, we maintain that the presence of an unequal distribution of political authority over persons as incumbents of positions is both a useful assumption and a descriptive fact. Furthermore, most of the elements of the authority structure of the polity are easily identified and clearly visible to anybody. There is, in the first place, the large quasi-group of those who have no share in the exercise of political authority. They may be described as the "mere" citizens, i.e., those who occupy no political position other than that common to all members of the polity.[9] It is a characteristic fea-

---

[9] Strictly speaking, citizenship is of course dependent on more conditions than mere residence in a given territory. Children, lunatics, criminals, in some countries women, new immigrants, and certain other groups do not enjoy citizenship rights. In modern democratic societies we can neglect these groups in an analysis of political conflict; in some earlier societies, however, such as classical Athens, the very possession of citizenship rights involved political authority, and the dividing line between dominance and subjection could be defined by possession or nonpossession of citizenship rights.

ture of political conflict in post-capitalist society that even the "bottom" of its authority structure is not entirely deprived of rights. A citizen is not only eligible for political office, he has, above all, the right to vote; and the act of voting may be described as an exercise of control over others. Legitimacy was, in all societies, a necessary requisite of the exercise of authority. In modern democracies the presumption of legitimacy has been converted into a continuous process of legitimation through regular elections and, in some cases, plebiscites. It may therefore be argued that no citizen of a democratic state is entirely powerless with respect to its political affairs. However, despite this basic power common to all, a clear line can be drawn between those who enjoy nothing but this minimum and those who are in the position to exercise regularly control over the life chances of others by issuing authoritative decisions. The citizens of a democratic state are not a suppressed class, but they are a subjected class, or quasi-group, and as such they constitute the dynamic element in political conflict.[10]

By contrast to "mere" citizens, members of the three classical branches of government have authority and, therefore, constitute the quasi-group of those in domination.[11] There is, first, the legislative branch. *De jure*—if not *de facto*—it is, in most present-day advanced societies, embodied in parliaments, chambers of deputies, houses of representatives, and the like. Deputies, representatives, members of parliament belong, by virtue of their position, to the ruling quasi-group of the polity. Strictly speaking, however, this does not hold for all members of parliament in a given situation: only those members represent a more or less permanent part of the authority structure of the state who belong either to the majority party or to those parties which make up a governing coalition. Opposition members also have some degree of authority by virtue of their parliamentary position; they may sanction decisions of the government in power, assent to, or even inaugurate legislation and thereby exercise authoritative control; but theirs is an authority that might legitimately be

[10] Laski, in his definition of the state quoted above, emphasizes that those who execute orders are themselves affected by them. This important clause indicates a peculiarity of the constitutional (as against the absolute) state: in it, even the incumbents of positions of domination are at the same time citizens. They have authority only in one of their (political) roles; by this duplicity of roles they control themselves, so to speak.

[11] This statement will presently be qualified in two respects: first, by the assessment of the class position of political bureaucracies, and, second, by the discussion of the phenomenon of representation, or the relation between power and interests in the modern state.

described as "situational." Members of the parliamentary opposition exercise authority only if and when they are in agreement with the majority or convince the majority to agree with them. Otherwise, they represent the interests of those excluded from domination. By contrast to members of the parliamentary majority, they do not, by virtue of their positions, permanently belong to the ruling quasi-group of the polity. Obviously, this subtle distinction is blurred in reality by relations of personal influence, complications of specific situations,[12] and, above all, by the implications of a representative system in which group interests are regularly, and sometimes institutionally, represented by nonparliamentary organizations. We shall turn to these and other complications presently.

As far as the judiciary branch of government is concerned, delimitation of "mere" citizens and carriers of authority presents least difficulty, although here, too, a "situational" element of the exercise of authority is not absent. In the first place, the judiciary consists of all positions and persons who are permanently in the service of the state in order to enforce, and sometimes modify, the law: legal advisers, judges on all levels, public prosecutors. To these are added the two groups—solicitors and juries—whose authority is confined to specific situations and who cannot therefore as such be included in the ruling quasi-group of the polity. To refer to the judiciary as part of the ruling class is of course a somewhat doubtful way to express this idea. I do not mean to imply a Marxian view of the legal system as an incarnation of the ideology of the ruling class. Rather, the position of the judiciary would seem to be somewhat similar to that of the bureaucracy in that both are branches of government without being the seat of particular interests except for a vague general orientation to uphold the *status quo*. In other words, the judiciary need not be conceived of as a militant part of the dominant conflict group of the polity, but its members are in the position to exercise control over others. They are therefore placed on the plus-side of the zero-sum distribution of authority in the state.

Finally, the executive branch represents an integral part of the dominant positions in the political state. Executive positions are, above all, government positions. Cabinet ministers and secretaries of state constitute the visible expression of the chief executive, and by

---

[12] Such as, e.g., very small majorities dependent on the attendance of members, or the independence of legislative and executive in the American sense which makes a contradictory balance of power in the two branches possible.

virtue of this fact they are rightly considered the real exponents of political authority. But the executive complex of the modern state extends beyond the members of a cabinet. It includes a large number of positions which might be described as those of white-collar employees. And it is these positions that require our special attention in an analysis of political conflict in post-capitalist society.

BUREAUCRATIC ROLES AND POLITICAL AUTHORITY

Even in his definition of the political association, Max Weber referred to the "administrative staff" as executor and instrument of authority. An administrative staff can today be found in all three branches of government. There are bureaucrats associated with the legislative, with the judiciary, and with the executive, although their number is probably greatest in the various branches of the executive. Bureaucracies are moreover characteristic not only of the political system but also of all other institutional orders and associations of post-capitalist society. We have already seen that the rapid growth of an industrial bureaucracy introduced new elements into the patterns of conflict in industry. The analysis of the class position of bureaucracies presented in this section applies, therefore, to the administrative staff of all associations; its immediate reference, however, is to the authority structure of the political state.

It is perhaps appropriate to recall at this point that in our survey of historical developments in the last hundred years we have divided the large group usually referred to as "white collar" or "new middle class" into two distinct parts. One of these, that of white-collar workers, clearly belongs to the subjected quasi-groups of imperatively coordinated associations. There are of course white-collar workers in the service of the state also. In many countries, railway and post-office employees, workers in public enterprises and municipal utilities, etc., have salaried or even civil service status. The following discussion, however, is concerned not with these occupations and persons whose class position is unambiguous, but with bureaucrats of all levels, i.e., with those salaried white-collar employees whose position places them on a step of the ladder of administrative jobs. What is their position in political conflict? Are they, as administrators of the means of industrial authority, a part or even the whole of the ruling class? Or are they, as dependent, often subordinate salaried employees, an element of the subjected class? There are few subjects which have been dealt with as thoroughly and extensively by sociologists as that of bureaucracy. True, most investigations are not explicitly related to the problem of class, but they are no less useful in our context for this restriction. More than elsewhere in this study we can fall back, here, on studies by other authors and claim empirical verisimilitude for our conclusions.[18]

Bureaucratic organizations differ from industrial organizations in one important point. Whereas the authority structure of industrial organizations *ipso facto* defines the borderline that divides the two aggregates of those in positions of dominance and those in positions of subjection, and whereas industrial organizations are in this sense dichotomous, bureaucratic organizations typically display continuous gradations of competence and authority and are hierarchical. Within dichotomous organizations class conflict is possible; within hierarchical organizations it is not. This difference has an important consequence for the definition of bureaucratic roles. Insofar as bureaucratic roles are defined in the context of a career hierarchy, they do not generate a (class) conflict of interests with other bureaucratic roles. Tensions within bureaucratic role structures arise characteristically from frustrations of expected opportunities, from "blocked or 'once-for-all' mobility" (Tropp, 132, p. 322). If, for example, there are in a bureaucratic hierarchy several points of entry which divide the total career into subsections separated by insurmountable barriers, these tensions may of course lead to social conflicts also, i.e., to conflicts between groups. However, one of the distinctive features of bureaucratic role structures is the principle of competition between individuals, and the psychological strains and tensions resulting from it (cf. Merton, 136). Structural conflicts based on latent antagonisms of interest in the sense of class theory are absent from bureaucratic organizations by virtue of their hierarchical character. This means that all incumbents of bureaucratic roles in the association of political society belong on the same side of the fence that divides the positions of dominance from those of subjection. Since a break such as generates class conflict cannot be demonstrated within bureaucratic structures, it follows that bureaucracies stand in their entirety either on the side of dominance or on that of subjection—no matter how differentiated bureaucratic roles may be according to qualification, status, and sphere of authority.

---

[18] The following discussion has been inspired largely by the works of Weber (33), Bendix (126 and 138), Merton (136), Lockwood (135), Gouldner (131), and Croner (129), as well as by a number of further essays brought together in the reader edited by Merton and others (136).

It is hardly necessary to emphasize that it would be nonsensical to describe the roles of political bureaucracy in their entirety as roles of subjection. At least the highest civil servants are unequivocally bearers of political authority; and what is true for the highest civil servants is also true—in accordance with the premise just introduced —for all other employees of political administration. Bureaucratic roles are roles of political dominance. Their definition includes certain latent interests which aim at the maintenance of existing institutions and valid values. The incumbents of bureaucratic roles are members of one and the same ruling quasi-group. At this point the analytical value of a rigidly formulated "theory of delegation" becomes apparent: the development which Weber described as one of " 'socialization' of authority relations" (33*b*, p. 669) has made for a "division of labor" of the total process of the exercise of authority. Like the division of labor in industrial production, this has led to the creation of numerous specialist positions, every one of which bears but slight traces of the process of which it is a part. Who produces the car in an automobile factory? The director? The fitter? The foreman? The typist? Every one of these questions has to be answered in the negative, and one might therefore be tempted to conclude that nobody produces the car at all. Yet the car is being produced, and we can certainly identify people who do not participate in its production. In relation to authority, both industrial and political, we encounter a strictly analogous situation. Nobody in particular seems to exercise "the authority," and yet authority is exercised, and we can identify people who do not participate in its exercise. Thus the superficial impression of subordination in many minor bureaucratic roles must not deceive us. All bureaucratic roles are defined with reference to the total process of the exercise of authority to which they contribute to whatever small extent. Differentiation of spheres of authority (i.e., of how many people are controlled to what extent) permits of manifold gradations; but the possession of authority itself does not. The strange structural state emerging for these reasons in post-capitalist society has been described by Weber as a "leveling of the ruled vis-à-vis the ruling, bureaucratically differentiated group" (33*b*, p. 667). While the "mere" citizens, those excluded from political authority, are in this respect a uniform (quasi-) group, the ruling class presents an image of far-reaching hierarchical differentiation.

It is clear that this type of analysis of the class position of clerks and bureaucrats confirms the subjective experience of people described earlier in this chapter, where we have seen that for many "ordinary" citizens and workers the world of "above" or "them" begins with the white-collar employee. " 'Being dressed up to go to work,' 'sitting down to work,' 'having it cushy,' 'pushing pens,' 'being bosses' men,' 'being one of *them* up *there*,' from whom orders come and authority emanates, are terms which working men frequently use of office workers, irrespective of their actual positions in the office hierarchy" (Lockwood, 135, p. 131). The fact that white-collar people do not usually regard themselves as being "on top" or "upper class," far from contradicting the attitude of those "below," adds a further element which we have here discussed: the very nature of bureaucratic organization makes everybody feel that although some are "below" him, there are also others "above," so that he is "in the middle." Whatever the ruling class of post-capitalist society may be, it seems probable that it will tend to deny its own rule on account of its internal differentiation, which places every one of its members between two others. However, while this internal differentiation of the ruling class complicates the situation, sociological analysis and people's "class consciousness" converge in the conclusion that "the clerk is the man on the other side of the desk who is somehow associated with authority" (Lockwood, 135, p. 132).

According to Weber's conception—which, more recently, has been adopted and further elaborated by Bendix—bureaucracy has not only a share but a monopoly of political authority. In support of this thesis, both sociologists refer, above all, to the monopoly of specialized expert knowledge on the part of bureaucracies which makes their replacement (say, in a revolution) as impossible as their effective control by others who invariably find themselves, "in face of the schooled civil servant who stands in the process of administration, in the position of the 'dilettante' vis-à-vis the 'expert' " (Weber, 33*b*, p. 671). This monopoly position is further strengthened by the attributes characteristic of bureaucratic status, and by tenure, pension rights, and similar privileges. It would be misleading to think of bureaucracies as a ruling caste because of their monopoly of authority; a class becomes a caste only if entry to it remains, for many generations, an exclusive privilege of the children of its members. This is decidedly not the case in highly mobile advanced industrial societies. Nevertheless, the monopoly of authority founded in expert knowledge provides the incumbents of bureaucratic roles at any given time with a degree of exclusiveness which underlines their unity as members of the same quasi-group and may be conceived of as a condition of conscious solidarity.

Does all this mean that the incumbents of bureaucratic roles in public administration are the ruling class of post-capitalist society? The attempt to answer this question reveals in the class position of bureaucracy a strange paradox which explains many otherwise incomprehensible modes of behavior of the clerk, the administrator, and the civil servant. "The fact that bureaucratic organization is technically the most advanced instrument of power in the hands of those who control it does not as yet say anything about how forcefully the bureaucracy as such is capable of pushing through its conceptions within the social organization in question" (Weber, 33*b*, p. 671). Bendix states even more incisively: "The bureaucracy is all-powerful and at the same time unable to determine how its power should be used" (126, p. 129). In other words, the bureaucratic monopoly of authority is a mere potential, mere possibility of authority without a structurally defined goal.

Weber and Bendix have tried to explain this fact. Both of them argue that the indispensability of bureaucracies for the administration of the modern state (i.e., the very basis of their authority) has led to the development of a professional ethos, the dominant values of which are duty, service, and loyalty—in other words, values of subordination, not of autonomous domination. Bendix emphasizes, moreover, the significance of formal efficiency of administration for the definition of bureaucratic roles. Bureaucracies are oriented toward the smooth functioning of the machinery of administration irrespective of which interests are administrated according to which substantive principles. For bureaucracies, what exists is what exists at any given time; as an interchangeable constant it enters into the definition of bureaucratic roles. The so-called "nonpolitical civil service" is an expression of this attitude. Its consequences, however, are manifold and highly significant for conflict analysis. First, by its monopoly of authority unaccompanied by independent substantive interests, the bureaucracy of the state is, so to say, the law of inertia of social development become real. Bureaucracies persist as a constant force in all changes of the personnel of leading political positions. Following Weber, Bendix has emphasized the impossibility, which has its cause here, of revolutions in bureaucratically governed states. Secondly, the trend toward "purposive rationality" and "managerialism" which is so characteristic for the ruling values in wide areas of post-capitalist society is embodied in bureaucracies and their formalism of orientation toward the "how," not the "what," of authority. Thirdly, the state administered by a bureaucracy functions almost without restriction even if political governments change rapidly, for the indispensability of bureaucracies makes these into ever ready and ever available regents or temporary plenipotentiaries of authority.[14]

Thus, a peculiar position must be assigned to bureaucracies in the light of the theory of conflict. Although they always *belong* to the ruling class, because bureaucratic roles are roles of dominance, bureaucracies as such never *are* the ruling class. Their latent interests aim at the maintenance of what exists; but what it is that exists is not decided by bureaucracies, but given to them. In two respects—and it will prove useful to separate these two aspects—the incumbents of bureaucratic roles are dependent on forces beyond them. First, their authority is borrowed or delegated authority which ultimately refers back to certain roles, endowed with most general authority, outside the orbit of bureaucracy. Although all commands are channeled, specified, perhaps adapted and even modified by bureaucracies, these commands originate outside their hierarchy. Second, the interests which define the substance of their authority are also given to bureaucracies. These merely administer, by virtue of their delegated authority, general orientations which are conceived and formulated elsewhere and by others. Because of this double dependence, bureaucracy represents what might be called a political reserve army, a reserve army of authority. Domination without a bureaucracy is no longer possible, but domination merely by a bureaucracy is impossible, too. As a medium and instrument of domination, bureaucracy stands at the disposal of anybody who is called upon to control it. As a constant in political conflict it accompanies and supports whatever group is in power by administering its interests and directives dutifully and loyally. It is, as Renner rightly says, a "service class," defined by its service relation to authority.

In the preceding remarks I have deliberately overstated my case a little. In actual fact, bureaucracies are by no means as powerless as our analysis might suggest. In a different context, it would be worth exploring the conditions of refusal of service by bureaucracies as well

---

[14] This is what Riesman might have meant by his remark about the state that runs itself (although he does not say so). Even so, a note of caution is in order. For some time, a state may be effectively ruled by a bureaucracy without a head; but soon the impossibility of innovation will make for intense and violent conflict. This problem will be taken up again below.

as the structural consequences of the immanent conservatism of incumbents of bureaucratic roles. With respect to both these questions,
Bendix has provided an approach in terms of the conditions and limits
of bureaucratic autonomy (cf. 126, pp. 131 ff.). Many an insight
into the regularities of social change in modern societies might be
gained by further investigating these problems.

Here, however, one final aspect of bureaucratic roles seems more
important. Being incumbents of roles of dominance, the civil servants of public administration always belong to the ruling political
quasi-group. However, being a reserve army of authority, the bureaucratic members of this quasi-group are not potential members of
an interest group of those in power. For structural reasons, the process
of class formation is always abortive in the case of bureaucracies.
Their members are, by virtue of their positions, united by certain
(formal) latent interests. Their (substantive) manifest interests,
however, are, again by virtue of their position, always derived from
those of the group that represents the existing state of affairs and that
controls bureaucracy. In principle, these manifest interests are therefore interchangeable; they change with changing ruling groups. In
this sense, too, bureaucracies are merely a potential; they are, in a
paradox, a class which can never be a class, a quasi-group whose path
to organization is blocked by the social definition of the roles of its
members. This does not mean, of course, that civil servants cannot
have political convictions and become members of political parties.
But it does mean that, as civil servants—as incumbents of roles of
dominance, that is—they cannot consistently profess a definite set of
manifest interests. The bureaucratic reserve army of authority is a
mercenary army of class conflict; it is always in battle, but it is forced
to place its strength in the service of changing masters and goals.

THE RULING CLASS

Who, then, constitutes the ruling class of post-capitalist society?
The attentive reader will have noticed that we have given at least
part of the answer already—although this simple-sounding answer
may not meet with his approval. Obviously, we have to look for the
ruling class in those positions that constitute the head of bureaucratic
hierarchies, among those persons who are authorized to give directives
to the administrative staff. This head of the hierarchy, however, is
clearly defined: it consists of precisely those positions in the three
branches of government which we have described above as the top
of the pyramid of authority in the polity. The clerk in a court of law,

the parliamentary private secretary, and the office director in a ministry have delegated authority; they are bureaucrats. But the Speaker of Parliament, the Prime Minister, and the Supreme Court Judge have immediate authority; their decisions provide legitimation and substance to the work of the administrative staff. It is true that, in the constitutional state, judge, minister, and member of parliament are each responsible to somebody, too. Each is, in Laski's words, "subject to the scrutiny of their fellow-citizens," either through representatives or directly through public opinion. But within the formal hierarchies of political authority they are the ones to whose roles attaches the expectation of authority, who make decisions binding upon all. In this sense, the leading positions of executive, legislative, and judiciary are the obvious places in which to look for the core of the ruling quasi-groups of the polity.

I have said that this is obvious, and I should like to emphasize this point. It seems to me that one of the main shortcomings of analyses such as those by Burnham and Mills (and of Marx, for that matter, although there the mistake was less consequential) is that they do not pay enough attention to the evident seat of authority in the political state, and to its occupants. Managerial or capitalist elites may be extremely powerful groups in society, they may even exert partial control over governments and parliaments, but these very facts underline the significance of governmental elites: whatever decisions are made are made either by or through them; whatever changes are introduced or prevented, governmental elites are their immediate object or agent; whatever conflicts occur in the political arena, the heads of the three branches of government are the exponents of the *status quo*. It is admittedly not sufficient to identify a ruling class solely in terms of a governmental elite, but it is necessary to think of this elite in the first place, and never to lose sight of its paramount position in the authority structure of the state. In this sense, I should agree with Riesman's point about the analysis of ruling classes in post-capitalist society: "We cannot be satisfied with the answers given by Marx, Mosca, Michels, Pareto, Weber, Veblen, or Burnham, though we can learn from all of them" (230, p. 252).

Of course, this insistence on governmental elites as the core of the ruling class must be truly shocking to anybody thinking in Marxian terms, or, more generally, in terms of the traditional concept of class. To some extent, the apparent incompatibility of the traditional and of our notion of class will be bridged presently. Basically, however, it is important to recall at this point that the present study is concerned not with the concept of class and its current applicability, but with the problem of conflict in industrial society. I believe that the traditional concept of class may be incorporated as a special case into the analysis suggested here; but the concept as such is irrelevant to our discussion. If it sounds strange that cabinet ministers, judges, and members of parliament should be the exponents of a ruling class, this strangeness is, in my opinion, due to the strangeness of reality, and not to the faultiness of the approach proposed in this study. Ruling classes, in many countries today, no longer behave as their predecessors did in capitalist society; they are, for this reason, no less ruling classes or, if one prefers these terms, dominant groups in political conflicts.

It is true, of course, that, much like bureaucracies, governmental elites provide but an incomplete description of any ruling class or dominant conflict group. Bureaucracies are heteronomous; they are therefore a reserve army of authority. Governments represent people and interests; they are therefore the exponents and not the whole of the ruling class. The phenomenon of representation, which complicates so many problems of political analysis in contemporary society, has two complementary aspects. First, governmental elites are the exponents of certain persons, the visible head of a body of men who through government have a share in authority. Cabinet members, judges, and members of parliament do not make up an autonomous group that exists by itself; they rule on behalf of somebody. Second, the substance of government policy incorporates interests which originate outside the rather limited circle of governmental elites. The exercise of authority always involves both the chance to issue authoritative commands and certain interests which constitute the substance of these commands. In order to identify those who are represented by governmental elites, we have to find the sources of their substantive policies as well as the group or groups behind them. In abstract, therefore, the ruling political class of post-capitalist society consists of the administrative staff of the state, the governmental elites at its head, and those interested parties which are represented by the governmental elite.

This conclusion is obviously so abstract and formal as to be utterly useless for our understanding of the societies in which we live; and I do not propose to leave it at that. However, this abstract conclusion marks the limit beyond which a general analysis of post-capitalist society cannot go. All modern societies have bureaucracies and governments; in this respect, our conclusion holds for the United States as for the Soviet Union, for West Germany as for East Germany. But the "interested parties" behind the governments of these countries differ greatly. Rather than describe their composition in general, we must here try to determine the range of variability of possible structures. "Post-capitalist society" in the singular dissolves here into a variety of political systems. One of the most important of those criteria which define the range of variability of political conflict seems to me the homogeneity of the groups represented by governments. In terms of their homogeneity, we can construct a scale of types of ruling classes which seems to cover the empirical patterns found in the modern world.

At one extreme of this scale we find the situation envisaged by Marx, Burnham, and others. Here, the governmental elite is part and parcel of a homogeneous and organized larger entity. Cabinet ministers, judges, and members of parliament—if such exist—are chosen from among this larger group, and the substance of their decisions is defined by the interests held by the larger group. Although not part of the formal hierarchy of political administration, the members of this group are incumbents of positions of political domination on account of their continuous, if indirect, participation in the business of government. This is roughly the situation described by Djilas as characteristic of modern totalitarian states.[15] A state party controls the instruments and positions of government (including, in this case, the administrative staff). In terms of personnel and interests, the members of this party constitute the recruiting field of government. They are the quasi-group which attempts to maintain the *status quo* of authority relations, and their exponents at the top of the administrative hierarchies are interchangeable representatives of identical interests.

At the other extreme of the scale that defines possible types of ruling classes we encounter the condition so aptly described by Riesman. Here, the governmental elite does not represent a stable, organized quasi-group. There are, to be sure, political parties, but these are themselves heterogeneous to the extent of losing their identity. Instead, society is split up into a large number of organizations, "veto

---

[15] It has to be realized, of course, that the extremes of the scale described here are ideal types which we are unlikely to find in reality. If we identify, therefore, the two extremes with the analyses presented by Djilas (here) and Riesman (below), this implies a critical appraisal: both Djilas and Riesman have—perhaps deliberately, and in that sense justifiably—overstated their cases by claiming reality for ideal-typical models.

groups," which "by their very nature . . . exist as defense groups, not as leadership groups" (230, p. 245), but which have situational authority. Any one act of government reveals an "issue" which has been advocated by somebody; veto groups enter the structure of authority when and as long as an interest or person of their choosing is adopted by government. This is a peculiar state of affairs, in which it is indeed virtually impossible to locate the ruling class. Government itself is here bureaucratized; its heads merely provide channels of expression for varying aggregations of interests. The governing elites represent nobody in particular, or everybody, except in specific situations and decisions in which they associate with specific veto groups. Rather than an exponent, they are but a switchboard of political authority. Thus the ruling class consists of two constants, bureaucracy and government, and one variable, the veto group whose claims are, in particular situations, incorporated in government policy. Conversely, the subjected class consists of all those who in a given situation do not associate with government, but again it is a situational class, every element of which has its chance to exercise authority.[16]

However, these extremes of the scale, and particularly the latter, are ideal types, and emphatically do not describe the conditions of any existing society. Within totalitarian state parties, there are invariably competing subgroups representing sectional interests with varying degrees of success. The "new class," far from being an entirely homogeneous entity, is a highly explosive unit in which local and central, industrial and agricultural, dogmatic and adaptive, bureaucratic and entrepreneurial "pressure groups" struggle for domination. If the ruling class of present-day totalitarian societies nevertheless comes close to the first extreme of our scale, this is largely because experience shows that when the existing order itself is threatened, most of its subgroups abandon their differences in favor of the common goal to uphold the *status quo*.

With respect to Western societies, on the other hand, Riesman overstated his case in several respects. For one thing, political conflict in post-capitalist society has grown out of the fierce ideological battles of the capitalist period, and it is at the very least unlikely that these have entirely ceased to play a part. For another thing, there

[16] Riesman's exposition of this situation in the chapter on "Who Has the Power?" (230, pp. 242–55) is really excellent, and little need be added to it, except for two things: first, Riesman underemphasizes the place and importance of governmental elites as switchboards of power; second, he describes an ideal type and not an actual situation.

still are political parties. While it is certainly true that these are less and less inspired by all-embracing ideologies, there still are differences between them. Perhaps political parties, too, tend to become switchboards rather than holders of authority, but they are switchboards with a bias. Riesman believes that "unlike a party that may be defeated at the polls, or a class that may be replaced by another class, the veto groups are always 'in'" (230, p. 254). Undoubtedly, lobbyists of every description try to keep up good relations with all political parties. But for the parties, there still are hierarchies of interest, there is a rank order of veto groups. With respect to specific issues, a party cannot simultaneously satisfy trade unions and employers' associations, veterans' organizations and pacifist groups, Protestant and Catholic churches, competing minorities, etc. Even if the manifest interests of political parties are reduced to an order of precedence for lobbyists, these still provide a general direction of policy in matters both of personnel placement and of the substance of political decisions.

Thus, if the ruling class of post-capitalist countries in the West is "situational," this is not because it consists of ever changing veto groups, but because political parties "may be defeated at the polls." It has but one stable element, the bureaucracy of the state. While the bureaucracy is an impotent participant of political conflict in the ordinary course of affairs, its conservative effect on all modern societies, and especially on those whose governments change rapidly, must not be overlooked.[17] The governments of Western societies are often mere switchboards of authority; decisions are made not by them but through them. In this respect, the political parties from which the personnel of governmental elites is recruited do not differ very greatly from these elites. But there is, associated with every party, a number of veto groups that enjoy the particular favor of this party. If this party is in power, then the ruling class of the society in question consists of the four elements: bureaucracy, governmental elite, majority party, and its favored veto groups. If it is not in power, then its favored veto groups are, like its members, defense groups that represent the interests of the subjected class.

[17] This effect was particularly evident, of course, in France before de Gaulle assumed power—and its consequences for political conflict are still in evidence. Generally speaking, however, bureaucracies may promote stability, but stability and stagnation are never very far apart; and where social development is arrested, political conflict is likely to increase rapidly in both intensity and violence.

It might appear as if we were trying to avoid the question of who is the ruling class in post-capitalist society. Having first reduced its composition to some constant and some empirically variable elements, we have now described these elements in a manner exactly as formal as before. However, even on the reduced level of the generality of the last part of our analysis, we can go no further. The ruling quasi-groups of post-capitalist societies differ from country to country, and from election to election, depending on the party (and veto groups) in power. Otherwise put, political conflict is always situational conflict between those who at a given point of time are excluded from authority and those who are "in." It is a characteristic feature of most Western societies that the "ins" and the "outs" change places, or *can* at least change places. If they do not do so for prolonged periods of time, if, in other words, one party stays in power for several election periods, it is likely that both the intensity and the violence of political conflict will grow, because certain interests (and veto groups) are continuously and systematically neglected. If there is a regular exchange of personnel and policy, conflict will remain situational and mild, because all interests (and veto groups) are recognized. In any case, the stable elements of the ruling class of contemporary Western societies are politically impotent, and the dynamic elements are empirically variable.

POLITICAL DEMOCRACY

Many of the features characteristic of the political class structure of Western societies are both a consequence and an index of a process which, without undue extension of the term, might be described as political democracy. More generally, our analysis of ruling classes in post-capitalist societies reveals by implication different modes of institutionalizing political conflict; and it is to these that I propose to turn in the concluding sections of this study. We have seen that, empirically, conflict has two major aspects, those of violence and of intensity. These in turn determine the ways in which group conflict leads to structure change. How do the factors influencing violence and intensity of political conflict, and suddenness and radicalness of structure change, present themselves in post-capitalist society? Which future trends seem indicated in the patterns of conflict and change of present-day industrial countries?

Once again—to start, in this section, with the violence aspect of conflict—it will help our analysis if we begin by constructing ideal types in order then to confront real societies with them. There is, to begin with, the democratic type of society. In it the conditions of organization are present for most subjected groups. There is freedom of coalition and free communication, and for most political groups leaders and ideologies are readily available. In fact, there are organizations—political parties—representing the interests of the opposing quasi-groups (with the qualifications introduced above). Moreover, absolute deprivation of any group of the population in terms of socio-economic status has become rare, if not impossible. Finally, there is an elaborate system of conflict regulation in the political sphere. In fact, the institutions of the democratic state reflect very nearly the model of effective conflict regulation: conflicting parties and interests are institutionally recognized; parliamentary bodies furnish the setting of regular conciliation between the parties; the rules of the game, including a constitution as well as statutory procedural arrangements, enable decisions to be made; certain personages, often the head of state, may act as mediators if autonomous conciliation breaks down; finally, there is the legal system to arbitrate unsolved disputes which threaten to break down the machinery of parliamentary negotiation.

Under these conditions, we should expect political conflict to be entirely nonviolent, and structure change to be entirely gradual. There is always a chance for the subjected class, or its parliamentary representatives, to take over government, or to penetrate into the governing elites, or to make its claims heard and accepted without any change in the government personnel. The effect of political democracy can be convincingly illustrated by one of its crucial, and paradoxical, rules of the game. If, as the result of an election, the governing elite is replaced in its entirety and forced into the opposition, structure change would (according to our criteria) appear to be extremely sudden, indeed. On a single day the personnel of all but the bureaucratic positions of dominance is exchanged. Why does this revolution fail to have the effect of a revolutionary change? A complete change of government in a democratic country is, to be sure, invariably an event of great consequence. But it is mitigated by a number of factors. First, there is the fact that whatever changes may occur, they do not affect the rules of the game agreed upon by both parties. Secondly, these rules of the game include for all parties the legitimate expectation of attaining power in the future. Finally, the larger part or the whole of the administrative staff provides, in all democratic states of the post-capitalist period, an element of stability that survives every change. Thus, social structure and the political rules of the game combine to mitigate and smooth out the comparative suddenness of changes resulting from elections and help to preserve the gradual nature of social development arising from institutionalized conflict.

This is the ideal pattern of democracy; in practice, of course, there are strains and distortions in it, and it would be well, here, to point out the various deviations from the democratic pattern—departures that are found in the actual political structure of all or some Western countries. These deviations are all the more serious since they arise directly from the structure of democratic institutions or from the rules of the game of the democratic process themselves. One example of such deviations has already been mentioned and discussed briefly: in its most limiting aspect, the process of political democracy allows for a rapid succession of governments which can prevent any one ruling group from remaining in power long enough to make its influence felt. For all practical purposes, the top of the political hierarchy of authority is unoccupied. In this case, the bureaucracy of the state becomes its own master. Since it is unable to inaugurate anything new, it goes on administering the commands it was given by the last more permanent government. The *status quo* is frozen, and all parties and veto groups are unable to realize their interests. This is the kind of development which may lead an ever-growing subjected class to consider the abolition of "the system itself," i.e., the rules of the game that are (rightly, to some extent) blamed for the existing conditions.[18]

Secondly, there are no provisions in the democratic rules of the game to prevent a party that is supported by, say, 30 per cent or even 45 per cent of the electorate from staying out of office indefinitely. As A. Downs has shown (193), this would not happen in a perfectly "rational" world of certainty. But in the real world there have been and are political parties which regularly gather a substantial and often stable share of the popular vote without ever becoming quite strong enough to form a government. This was (and still is, here and there) notoriously the case with Socialist parties in European countries. Unless such permanent minorities have alternative channels of ex-

[18] There are certain constitutional remedies, certain rules of the game, designed to cope with this situation; again, France (but also the German Federal Republic) might be cited as an example. These rules usually take the form of restrictions imposed on parliament with respect to voting governments out of office.

pression,[19] they will be increasingly alienated from "the system" that prevents them from getting "in" and increasingly irritated by the rules of the game according to which they have no right to demand a share in the exercise of authority. Such permanently excluded subjected groups are very likely to become more and more radicalized, to introduce an element of violence into political conflict, and to aim at a sudden replacement of all incumbents of positions of dominance—if not of the whole framework of political conflict that they blame for their ill fortunes.[20]

Finally, the system of representation in modern democratic states may lead to a situation in which all political conflict either is, or is believed to be, reduced to a struggle between competing governmental elites. The functionaries of political parties are so alienated from their members that these lose all confidence in their representatives. There is already, in many Western countries, a widespread feeling that "it does not matter for whom one casts one's vote," because "whatever one votes, the same people will always rule." This state of affairs corresponds suspiciously closely to the dichotomous image of society according to which it makes no difference whether "they" call themselves representatives of the workers or of the employers. It also corresponds to the actual collusion which is so general a feature among the representatives of political parties. What happens, here, is that the ruling class becomes a small elite of functionaries of nominally different or even conflicting organizations, while the overwhelming majority of the people form a subjected class whose every access to authority is blocked. The blocking is done by their so-called representatives who, when the position of the "insiders" is threatened with dislodgment, jealously guard the "inside" position not only of themselves but even of their competitors. Under these conditions, the subjected class has no channel of organization but one: the one described by Marx in his "18th Brumaire of Louis Bonaparte." There may come to the fore one man, or a small group of men, who succeeds in convincing the many that they are the "real" representatives of their

---

[19] Such as a federal political structure which enables them to control at least state governments. This possibility serves as a compensating force, e.g., in West Germany and in Canada (cf. Lipset, 199).

[20] There are no formal rules of the game to provide for this eventuality; but there is the possibility of the (presumably equally permanent) government incorporating demands of the permanent opposition to its policies so as to thaw the fronts of conflict somewhat. In any case, a permanent minority—Socialist, Communist, or otherwise— remains a disturbing element of political democracy.

interests, and who promises to do away with the whole "system" of parties, parliaments, and democratic governments. Whatever the substantive outcome of such a process, it is certain that it will lead to increasingly violent conflicts.[21]

It would seem that all the inherent dangers of political democracy point to an alternative of conflict regulation which may be described as an ideal type opposite to democracy. In the terms of classical political thought this other extreme of the scale is oligarchy, or tyranny. In a modern state organized along oligarchic and authoritarian lines, the conditions of organization for opposing groups are absent. There is but one "official" organization, if any, and outside this organization freedom of coalition is drastically curtailed. Above all, however, such states have no accepted routines of conflict regulation, because their governments do not recognize the legitimacy of political conflict itself. Wherever there are signs of "rebellion" these are forcefully suppressed. The rule of the few is upheld at all costs.

Conflict theory would suggest that this kind of political organization would make for extremely violent political conflicts as well as sudden structure changes. However, this is clearly a self-contradicting conclusion. There cannot be violent conflict and effective suppression at the same time. Either one or the other, the principles of either conflict theory or of the ideal type of tyranny, must be wrong if their results contradict each other. I suggest that what is wrong here is the picture of the ideal type: there is, in reality, no country in which all conflict is effectively suppressed by force, and in which the arbitrary rule of a small group is upheld by sheer brutality. In fact, I should claim that one of the important consequences of the approach to conflict analysis proposed in this study is that it exposes as mistaken the view that there are political systems based on force

---

[21] Considering Michels' "iron law of oligarchy," the latter perspective would seem to be not only a very real, but almost an inevitable, result of representative democracy. "If we accept Michels' formulation of the problem, we are faced with the fact that modern democracies do not constitute a government by the people. Instead, this form of government consists of conflicts of power among oligarchic organizations, with the result that the average citizen exercises his rights of citizenship only in the sense that he chooses among alternatives presented to him by these competing oligarchies" (Bendix and Lipset, 191, p. 95). This would, however, be an overdrawn conclusion. Depending on the rules of the game in force, some countries are in fact more affected than others by the tendency toward collusion among the representatives: those with proportional representation more than those with a relative majority system of election; those with a multiparty system more than those with a two-party system. Once again, however, there is no absolute safeguard.

alone. Instead, conflict theory directs our attention to those phenomena in existing nondemocratic countries which can only be understood as attempts to regulate political conflict. More than in the case of democratic countries, such approximations to the ideal type of tyranny as there are deviate from its patterns.

It is obvious that in those countries (post-capitalist or otherwise) which are under Communist rule, the conditions of organization are lacking, there is to some extent absolute deprivation, and political conflict is not officially recognized as a social force. It is therefore also true that a tendency toward violent conflict and sudden change accompanies these totalitarian countries in every phase of their development. After the events of the last decade, there is no need to elaborate on these facts—which, by implication, testify to the ultimate ineffectiveness of brutal suppression. However, the modern tyranny called totalitarianism is not as simple as we have made it here. Suppression and nonrecognition of conflict are merely the visible facets of a far more complex reality.

In our attempt to identify the dominant groups of contemporary societies, we have described the ruling class of totalitarian countries as particularly homogeneous and organized. By virtue of this fact there is, in totalitarian countries, a clear line of demarcation between the rulers and the ruled. Where the party ends, the subjected class begins. And the subjected class constitutes a large quasi-group whose many partially divergent interests are combined into one demand—a change in the *status quo* of authority. But this group is unable to organize itself; there is no freedom of coalition. Whatever conflicts exist are therefore forced to remain latent or under cover. Yet even the "official" structure of political authority provides this subjected quasi-group with channels of expression. In order to recognize these, we must remember that "discussion" is one of the crucial features of totalitarian government. Nowhere is there as much "discussion" as in the one-party countries of the modern world: meetings in one's factory or office, street or house, trade union, cooperative society, choir or football club, school, etc., serve the one purpose of "discussing" things. These "discussions" are not, to be sure, opportunities for a free exchange of ideas. They are above all attempts at indoctrination and at soliciting that brand of "voluntary cooperation" so peculiar to modern totalitarian states. But *inter alia* and in a minor way the meetings and "discussions" which loom so large in the life of every subject of totalitarian government provide a chance to voice, cautiously and in the accepted language, criticisms of individuals and policies, suggestions, and demands. From the point of view of the ruling class, this fact is both "functional" and "dysfunctional." On the one hand, the party organization and its varied affiliations serve as a gigantic institute of opinion research which, through meetings and "discussions," tries to explore the "wishes and feelings of the people." On the other hand, the same meetings and "discussions" that are necessary for this as well as for many another purpose bring into contact the otherwise scattered members of the subjected quasi-group and form the nuclei of actual and future conflicts. It is no accident that the revolts in Communist countries originated among those who meet most often in large numbers: building workers, steel workers, students.[22]

Undoubtedly, meetings and "discussions" as channels of conflict are, from the point of view of the ruling class, largely a pretext. It may well be that state parties explore their subjects' wishes and feelings not in order to incorporate these in their policies, but in order to see how much further they can push their own plans. However, here again the ruthlessness of oligarchic rulers must not be exaggerated. The skillfully ruled totalitarian countries[23] are by no means stagnant. Change and development play almost as great a part in them as they do in democratic societies. Here, the institution of "purges" is crucial. Some naïve observers believe that purges within the new class of totalitarian countries are merely an expression of personal or group rivalries. These may in fact provide the motivation of those who are either actively or passively engaged in them, but purges serve another purpose as well. Like elections in democratic states they involve a partial replacement of the governing elite, and this replacement means in fact, or appears to mean to the subjected class, a change of policy which incorporates interests hitherto unacknowledged. We have defined structure change operationally in terms of changes affecting the personnel of leading authority positions. I would insist on this definition, and I suggest at the same time that an investigation of frequencies and rates of change in democratic and totalitarian countries would reveal very little difference between the two.

All this is emphatically not to say that totalitarian political systems are not as bad as they are made out to be in the West. It *is* to say,

---

[22] Apart from using this mechanism of channeling social conflict, totalitarian rulers are of course experts in redirecting conflict energies and providing safety-valve institutions. Coser's study of conflict (81) supplies many examples of such patterns.

[23] Nazi Germany was not, in this sense, "skillfully ruled"; but most Communist countries of eastern Europe are.

however, that we must appraise their political structure realistically, and that the sociological theory of conflict can help us do so. While there is an undercurrent of potentially violent conflict aiming at sudden change in all totalitarian countries, it does not follow that this latent antagonism will break out into the open. The reason for this is not, as so many believe, the effectiveness of suppression in totalitarian states, but the existence of a hidden system of conflict regulation in which meetings and "discussions" as well as purges play an important part. Horrible as this idea may be, it is possible to establish a totalitarian rule in which the violence of political conflict is reduced almost as effectively as by the democratic process of conflict regulation.[24] Suppression of conflict, however, far from helping to control political conflict, defeats its own ends: totalitarian governments are in "danger" of being violently overthrown to the extent to which they resort to suppression as a means of dealing with conflict.

TOTALITARIAN SOCIETIES VS. FREE SOCIETIES

Their modes of conflict regulation constitute one of the most important distinguishing features of democratic and totalitarian political systems. By looking at these in terms of the institutional arrangements set up in order to control political conflict, we are able to relate different forms of government to different patterns of social structure. This is *a fortiori* the case with respect to the factors that influence the intensity of political conflict. The antithesis of pluralism vs. monism with respect to associations, scales of differentiation, and patterns of conflict seems especially suited to describe the social bases of political freedom. A free society encourages diversity in its institutions and groupings to the extent of actually promoting divergence; conflict is the life breath of freedom. A totalitarian society insists on unity to the extent of uniformity; conflict is a threat to its coherence and survival.

First, the intensity of political conflict depends on the presence of the conditions of organization. We have already seen that while in free societies subjected quasi-groups are free to organize themselves

---

[24] The "almost" in this statement is of course deliberate. Clearly, the danger of systematically ignoring certain interests and groups is much greater for even the cleverest totalitarian government than it is for the government of a country in which everybody is free to voice his discontent. Here, as elsewhere, it is safer to trust the spontaneity of individuals and groups than to trust a "plan." In any case, Communist countries have not succeeded in setting up an effective hidden machinery of conflict regulation.

in defense of their interests, their counterparts in totalitarian societies have to search out devious channels to make possible even a minimum of expression of their interests. Due to the lack of the conditions of organization, there is a permanent, and often growing, quantity of unreleased pressure in totalitarian states which imbues their latent political conflicts with an intensity unknown in free societies, where pressure is released almost as soon as it is created. There can be little doubt that repression of conflict by force raises the cost of victory or defeat.

A second determinant of the intensity of conflict is the amount of mobility found in a given society. Without once again entering into a detailed discussion of available evidence, we can maintain that, in the post-capitalist societies of the West, rates of social mobility are fairly high. There are still, to be sure, barriers in the system of social stratification which are hard for the individual to overcome; but the educational institutions operate as agents of role allocation, and such biases as there are in the educational system are increasingly being removed. Mobility through education includes mobility between the classes: from manual to clerical and professional occupations, and vice versa. Insofar as intergeneration mobility constitutes the predominant type of fluctuation, class position may still be a largely inescapable reality for the individual; but it is no longer a collective fate. The hope that one's son might rise to the position one has oneself failed to attain is one of the most widespread feelings of people in post-capitalist society. Insofar as mobility affects it, the intensity of political conflict has diminished considerably in the last decades.

The extent of social mobility in totalitarian societies is not altogether easy to assess. For all we know, there is a high amount of movement up and down the status scale in existing totalitarian countries; in the East, as in the West, the educational system plays an important part. Some observers of Soviet society have claimed that in Russia social mobility is indeed so widespread as to make for the type of "classlessness" described above as the society made classless by mobility. This, however, is open to doubt. T. Bottomore, who reports a statement to this effect, holds two convincing objections against it. First, "the high level of mobility may . . . be regarded as a phenomenon resulting from the needs of industrial development and not any conscious attempt to promote it" (37, p. 42). Thus, many of the present-day totalitarian countries are in fact not post-capitalist societies but societies at an early stage of industrialization, and they therefore display the symptoms characteristic of the industrial revolution.

Secondly, "there is in fact some evidence that social mobility is now being restricted" (37, p. 42). In any case, "there is no evidence that social mobility is, at the present time, any greater than in the Western democracies, and much evidence that it is being deliberately reduced" (p. 43). If we can believe Djilas, this reduction of mobility would seem, moreover, to involve, above all, the "new class" in totalitarian countries which increasingly closes itself to any influx from other strata, especially from the subjected class. We can assume that to the extent that this trend of closure continues, political conflict in totalitarian countries is becoming more intense.

Of all factors influencing the intensity of political conflict, those of the pluralism-superimposition scale are by far the most effective. In order to assess their consequences, I shall resort, for a last time, to constructing contrasting ideal types. At one extreme of the scale thus emerging, we should find a society in which all patterns, issues, and contexts of political conflict are superimposed and combined into two large hostile camps. There is superimposition with respect to the structure of authority and to the scales of rewards that make up social stratification. Whoever occupies a position of authority has wealth, prestige, and other emoluments of social status at his disposal, too; whoever is excluded from political authority has no hope of climbing very far on the scale of social status. Furthermore, the conflicts arising from different associations are superimposed. Power is generalized in the sense that a homogeneous and interchangeable elite governs an identical subjected class in the state, in industry, in the army, and in all other associations. Finally, such nonclass conflicts as exist in society are congruent with the conflicts arising out of the unequal distribution of authority. Political class conflict, industrial class conflict, regional conflicts, conflicts between town and country, possibly racial and religious conflicts—all are superimposed so as to form a single and all-embracing antagonism. Under these conditions, the intensity of political conflict reaches its maximum.

As with our earlier ideal types, there is no actual society in which this is fully realized. There are, however, many indications that superimposition of patterns, and the monism of social structure resulting from it, are a characteristic feature of modern totalitarian states. The ruling and the subjected groups of industry and the state are identical; the party exercises its power in both associations. With respect to the military, the same condition is aimed at, although—as the Russian example shows—it is not attained without a struggle. In any case, generalized authority is the constant goal of the state party.

This generalized authority includes the attempt to monopolize every scale of socioeconomic status for the "new class." Its members enjoy, apart from, or perhaps by virtue of, their authority, high incomes and considerable prestige—although the latter is less subject to manipulation than the former.[25] With respect to the superimposition of class and other conflicts, no unequivocal pattern seems discernible in totalitarian countries, although a tendency to alienate minorities as well as subjected groups in terms of authority is not uncommon under oligarchic rule. *Divide et impera* is an old and supposedly useful imperative of despotism; but with respect to the social structure of their countries, present-day totalitarian rulers have not followed its prescription. They have, instead, aimed at a uniform and monistic organization of society. Moreover, in the Communist countries of the East they have adopted an ideology of intense conflict. The two go together well: on account of the monistic structure of conflict (and many other) relations in totalitarian countries, these relations have gained, and continue to gain, in intensity. Whatever conflicts do occur involve both rulers and ruled with their whole personalities; and if these conflicts become open and violent, the cost of defeat is too high for both parties to allow graceful retreat. "Totality" distinguishes the totalitarian state in more than one respect, including the extent of the changes desired by those who, for the time being, are its powerless subjects.

The ideal type opposite to that of totalitarianism is that of a free society. Here, the intensity of political conflict is reduced to a minimum. The scales of social stratification are largely separate; possession of authority does not necessarily imply wealth, prestige, security. There are competing elites at the top of the various scales. Conflicts in different associations are dissociated. Leadership in the state does not imply leadership in industry, in the army, or in other associations, nor does exclusion from authority in one context imply exclusion in all others. Class conflict and other clashes between groups are dissociated, too; being a member of a particular minority, race, or church does not automatically convey certain privileges or disabilities with respect to the distribution of political authority. Pluralism of institutions, conflict patterns, groupings, and interests makes for a lively, colorful, and creative scene of political conflict which provides an opportunity for success for every interest that is voiced.

[25] They do not enjoy high "job security" nor will they be able to achieve this under totalitarian conditions. In view of possible revolts and the role of the ruling class in them, this fact must not be underestimated.

Needless to say, there is no society which corresponds in all respects with this ideal-typical picture. With respect to minorities, in particular, there still is a great deal of superimposition of conflict fronts in all Western countries. Being a member of this or that church, race, or ethnic group puts many people at a disadvantage in the struggle for political authority. Regarding the other two factors, however, we have seen that a pluralist structure of society is in fact progressing in the post-capitalist world. One of its symptoms consists in the institutional isolation of industry; this in turn involves some dissociation of the scales of wealth and authority. By these and similar factors, the involvement of people in political conflict decreases; individuals, veto groups, and political parties can, so to speak, afford to lose; and if they win, the changes they introduce are piecemeal rather than radical. History is a permanent guest in a free society, not an unwanted intruder whose presence signals revolutionary upheavals.

I concur with the common belief that the struggle between free societies and totalitarian societies is the dominant issue of political conflict in our time. Contrary to many, however, I do not believe that this struggle is confined to international relations. The struggle between freedom and totalitarianism occurs within societies as well as between them. No real society can be found at one or the other extreme of our ideal types. There are very nearly free and very nearly totalitarian countries, but more often we find intermediate forms. In the modern world, there are such paradoxical states as democracy without liberty and liberty without democracy. Everywhere, however, the struggle between freedom and totalitarianism may be regarded as one between different attitudes toward social conflict. Totalitarian monism is founded on the idea that conflict can and should be eliminated, that a homogeneous and uniform social and political order is the desirable state of affairs. This idea is no less dangerous for the fact that it is mistaken in its sociological premises. The pluralism of free societies, on the other hand, is based on recognition and acceptance of social conflict. In a free society, conflict may have lost much of its intensity and violence, but it is still there, and it is there to stay. For freedom in society means, above all, that we recognize the justice and the creativity of diversity, difference, and conflict.

Bibliography

CONCEPT AND THEORY OF SOCIAL CLASSES

EARLY WORKS (BEFORE 1900)

1. Friedrich Engels, *Die Lage der arbeitenden Klassen in England*. New ed. Berlin, 1952.
2. Adam Ferguson, *Essay on the History of Civil Society*. London, 1767.
3. Karl Marx, *Nationalökonomie und Philosophie*. Ed. by E. Thier. Cologne and Berlin, 1950.
4. ——— *Die heilige Familie, oder Kritik der kritischen Kritik*. In *Marx-Engels Gesamtausgabe*, Section I, Vol. III. Berlin, 1932.
5. ——— "Die moralisierende Kritik und die kritische Moral," in Franz Mehring, ed., *Aus dem literarischen Nachlass von Karl Marx und Friedrich Engels*. 3d ed. Stuttgart, 1920.
6. ——— *Das Elend der Philosophie*. New ed. Berlin, 1947.
7. ——— *Zur Kritik der politischen Ökonomie*. New ed. Berlin, 1947.
8. ——— *Der 18. Brumaire des Louis Bonaparte*. New ed. Berlin, 1946.
9. ——— *Die Klassenkämpfe in Frankreich*. New ed. Berlin, 1951.
10. ——— Letter to Bolte (November 1871), in *Zur Kritik des Gothaer Programms*. New ed. Berlin, 1946.
11. ——— "Zirkularbrief" to Bebel and others (September 1879), in *Zur Kritik des Gothaer Programms*. New ed. Berlin, 1946.
12. ——— *Das Kapital*. New ed. Berlin, 1953.
13. Karl Marx and Friedrich Engels, "Die deutsche Ideologie," in Siegfried Landshut, ed., *Der historische Materialismus*. Stuttgart, 1953.
14. ——— *Manifest der kommunistischen Partei*. New ed. Berlin, 1953.
15. John Millar, *An Historical View of the English Government*. London, 1787.
16. Thorstein Veblen, *The Theory of the Leisure Class*. New York, 1899.

RECENT WORKS (BEFORE 1930)

17. Gerhard Albrecht, *Die sozialen Klassen*. Leipzig, 1926.
18. Käthe Bauer-Mendelberg, "Stand und Klasse," *Koelner Vierteljahreshefte für Soziologie*, Vol. III, No. 4 (1924).
19. Pontus Fahlbeck, *Die Klassen und die Gesellschaft*. Jena, 1922.
20. Theodor Geiger, "Zur Theorie des Klassenbegriffs und der proletarischen Klasse," in *Schmollers Jahrbuch*, Vol. LIV (1930).
21. Georg Lukacs, *Geschichte und Klassenbewusstsein*. Berlin, 1923.
22. Robert Michels, "Beitrag zur Lehre von der Klassenbildung," *Archiv für Sozialwissenschaft*, Vol. XLIX (1920).

23. Paul Mombert, "Zum Wesen der sozialen Klasse," in *Hauptprobleme der Soziologie: Erinnerungsgabe für Max Weber.* Munich, 1923.

24. Gaetano Mosca, *Die herrschende Klasse.* Bern, 1950.

25. Vilfredo Pareto, *Allgemeine Soziologie.* Transl. and ed. by C. Brinkmann. Tübingen, 1955.

26. Karl Renner, *Die Wirtschaft als Gesamtprozess und die Sozialisierung.* Berlin, 1924.

27. J. A. Schumpeter, "Die sozialen Klassen im ethnisch homogenen Milieu" (1927), in *Aufsätze zur Soziologie.* Tübingen, 1953.

28. Werner Sombart, *Der moderne Kapitalismus.* 4th ed. Munich and Leipzig, 1921.

29. ———— "Die Idee des Klassenkampfes," *Schriften des Vereins für Sozialpolitik*, Vol. CLXX (1925).

30. Pitirim Sorokin, *Contemporary Sociological Theories.* New York, 1928.

31. Othmar Spann, "Klasse und Stand," in *Handwörterbuch der Staatswissenschaften*, Vol. V. 4th ed. 1923.

32. Max Weber, "Der Sozialismus," in *Gesammelte Aufsätze zur Soziologie und Sozialpolitik.* Tübingen, 1924.

33a. ———— *The Theory of Social and Economic Organization.* Transl. by A. M. Henderson and Talcott Parsons. New York, 1950.

33b. ———— *Wirtschaft und Gesellschaft* (Grundriss der Sozialökonomik, section III). 4th ed. Tübingen, 1947.

RECENT WORKS (SINCE 1930)

34. Raymond Aron, "Social Structure and the Ruling Class," in 35 below.

35. Reinhard Bendix and S. M. Lipset, eds., *Class, Status and Power: A Reader in Social Stratification.* Glencoe, 1953.

36. Reinhard Bendix and S. M. Lipset, "Karl Marx's Theory of Social Classes," in 35 above.

37. T. B. Bottomore, *Classes in Modern Society.* London, 1955.

38. Richard Centers, *The Psychology of Social Classes.* Princeton, 1949.

39. G. D. H. Cole, *Studies in Class Structure.* London, 1955.

40. O. C. Cox, "Estates, Social Classes and Political Classes," *American Sociological Review*, Vol. X (1945).

41. Ralf Dahrendorf, "Gibt es noch Klassen? Die Begriffe der 'sozialen Schicht' und 'sozialen Klasse' in der Sozialanalyse der Gegenwart," *Annales Universitatis Saraviensis*, section Philosophie, Vol. II, No. 4 (1954).

42. ———— "Klassenstruktur und Klassenkonflikt in der entwickelten Industriegesellschaft," *Die neue Gesellschaft*, Vol. II, No. 4 (1955).

43. ———— "Social Structure, Class Interests and Social Conflict," in *Transactions of the Third World Congress of Sociology*, Vol. III. London, 1956.

44. Milovan Djilas, *The New Class: An Analysis of the Communist System.* New York, 1957.

45. P. N. Fedoseyev, "Laws of Social Changes in the Twentieth Century," in *Transactions of the Third World Congress of Sociology*, Vol. VIII. London, 1957.

46. Theodor Geiger, *Die Klassengesellschaft im Schmelztiegel.* Cologne and Hagen, 1949.

47. Morris Ginsberg, *Sociology*. London, 1953.

48. M. M. Gordon, "Social Class in American Society," *American Journal of Sociology*, Vol. LV (1950).

49. Llewellyn Gross, "The Use of Class Concepts in Sociological Research," *American Journal of Sociology*, Vol. LIV (1949).

50. Georges Gurvitch, "Le Dynamisme des classes sociales," in *Transactions of the Third World Congress of Sociology*, Vol. III. London, 1956.

51. Maurice Halbwachs, *Les Classes sociales*. Paris, 1937.

52. Richard Hoggart, *The Uses of Literacy*. London, 1957.

53. Siegfried Landshut, "Die Gegenwart im Lichte der Marxschen Lehre," in H.-D. Ortlieb, ed., *Hamburger Jahrbuch für Wirtschafts- und Gesellschaftspolitik*, Vol. I . Tübingen, 1956.

54. G. E. Lenski, "American Social Classes—Statistical Strata or Social Groups?" *American Journal of Sociology*, Vol. LVIII (1952).

55. S. M. Lipset and Reinhard Bendix, "Social Status and Social Structure," *British Journal of Sociology*, Vol. II (1951).

56. T. H. Marshall, ed., *Class Conflict and Social Stratification*. London, 1938.

57. ———— *Citizenship and Social Class*. Cambridge, 1950.

58. ———— "Social Class: A Preliminary Analysis," in 57 above.

59. ———— "The Nature of Class Conflict," in 56 above. (See also 35 and 57.)

60. K. B. Mayer, "The Theory of Social Classes," in *Transactions of the Second World Congress of Sociology*, Vol. II. London, 1954.

61. ———— *Class and Society*. New York, 1955.

62. C. W. Mills, *The New Men of Power*. New York, 1954.

63. ———— *The Power Elite*. New York, 1956.

64. V. S. Nemchinov, *Changes in the Class Structure of the Population of the Soviet Union*. Mimeographed for the Third World Congress of Sociology (1956).

65. ———— "Changes in the Class Structure of the Population of the Soviet Union" (abridged version), in *Transactions of the Third World Congress of Sociology*, Vol. VIII. London, 1957.

66. Stanislaw Ossowski, "Old Notions and New Problems: Interpretations of Social Structure in Modern Society," in *Transactions of the Third World Congress of Sociology*, Vol. III. London, 1956.

67. Talcott Parsons, "Social Classes and Class Conflict in the Light of Recent Sociological Theory," in *Essays in Sociological Theory*. Rev. ed. Glencoe, 1954.

68. Heinrich Popitz, "Zum Begriff der Klassengesellschaft," in H.-D. Ortlieb, ed., *Hamburger Jahrbuch für Wirtschafts- und Gesellschaftspolitik*, Vol. III. Tübingen, 1958.

69. Heinrich Popitz, H. P. Bahrdt, E. A. Jueres, and H. Kesting, *Das Gesellschaftsbild des Arbeiters*. Tübingen, 1957.

70. Karl Renner, *Mensch und Gesellschaft: Grundriss einer Soziologie*. Vienna, 1952.

71. ———— *Wandlungen der modernen Gesellschaft: zwei Abhandlungen über die Probleme der Nachkriegszeit*. Vienna, 1953.

72. Helmut Schelsky, "Gesellschaftlicher Wandel," *Offene Welt*, No. 41 (1956).

73. J. A. Schumpeter, *Capitalism, Socialism and Democracy*. London, 1943.

74. Paul Sering, *Jenseits des Kapitalismus*. Nürnberg, 1947.
75. W. L. Warner, *Social Class in America*. Chicago, 1949.
76. Alfred Willener, *Images de la société et classes sociales*. Bern, 1957.

ON SOCIAL CONFLICT

77. "Approaches to the Study of Social Conflict: A Colloquium," *Conflict Resolution*, Vol. I, No. 2 (June 1957).
78. John Bowlby, "A Psychoanalytic View of Conflict and Its Regulation" (mimeo.), *Center for Advanced Study*, 1958.
79. J. S. Coleman, *Community Conflict*. Glencoe, 1957.
80. L. A. Coser, "Social Conflict and Social Change," *British Journal of Sociology*, Vol. VII, No. 3 (September 1957).
81. ———— *The Functions of Social Conflict*. London, 1956.
82. Ralf Dahrendorf, "Toward a Theory of Social Conflict," *Conflict Resolution*, Vol. II, No. 2 (June 1958).
83. International Sociological Association, *The Nature of Conflict*. With contributions by J. Bernard, T. H. Pear, R. Aron, and R. C. Angell. Paris, UNESCO, 1957.
84. Clark Kerr, "Industrial Conflict and Its Mediation," *American Journal of Sociology*, Vol. LX, No. 3 (November 1954).
85. A. W. Kornhauser and others, eds., *Industrial Conflict*. New York, 1954.
86. David Lockwood, "Arbitration and Industrial Conflict," *British Journal of Sociology*, Vol. VI, No. 4 (1955).
87. H. L. Sheppard, "Approaches to Conflict in American Industrial Sociology," *British Journal of Sociology*, Vol. V, No. 4 (1954).

ON PROBLEMS OF CLASS STRUCTURE

SOCIAL STRATIFICATION

88. C. J. Barnard, "The Functions and Pathology of Status Systems in Formal Organizations," in W. F. Whyte, ed., *Industry and Society*. New York and London, 1946.
89. A. M. Carr-Saunders and D. C. Jones, *A Survey of the Social Structure of England and Wales*. 2d ed. Oxford, 1937.
90. Kingsley Davis and W. E. Moore, "Some Principles of Stratification," in Logan Wilson and W. L. Kolb, *Sociological Analysis*. New York, 1949.
91. Theodor Geiger, *Die soziale Schichtung des deutschen Volkes*. Stuttgart, 1932.
92. D. G. MacRae, "Social Stratification (Bibliography)," *Current Sociology*, Vol. II (1953/54).
93. Heinz Markmann, "Sozialstruktur im Allgemeinen," in Alfred Weber, ed., *Einführung in die Soziologie*. Munich, 1955.
94. T. H. Marshall, "A Note on 'Status,'" in K. M. Kapadia, ed., *Professor Ghurye Felicitation Volume*. Bombay, 1954.
95. ———— "General Survey of Changes in Social Stratification in the Twentieth Century," in *Transactions of the Third World Congress of Sociology*, Vol. III. London, 1956.
96. Stanislaw Ossowski, "La Vision dichotomique de la stratification sociale," *Cahiers Internationaux de sociologie*, Vol. XX (1956).

97. H. W. Pfautz, "The Current Literature on Social Stratification: Critique and Bibliography," *American Journal of Sociology*, Vol. LVIII (1952).

98. Helmut Schelsky, "Die Bedeutung des Schichtungsbegriffes für die Analyse der gegenwärtigen deutschen Gesellschaft," in *Transactions of the Second World Congress of Sociology*, Vol. I. London, 1954.

99. J. A. Schumpeter, "Das soziale Antlitz des Deutschen Reiches" (1929), in *Aufsätze zur Soziologie*. Tübingen, 1953.

100. W. L. Warner and P. S. Lunt, *The Social Life in a Modern Community*. New Haven, 1941.

SOCIAL MOBILITY

101. Reinhard Bendix and S. M. Lipset, *Social Mobility in Industrial Society*. Berkeley and London, 1958.

102. K. M. Bolte, "Ein Beitrag zur Problematik der sozialen Mobilität," *Kölner Zeitschrift für Soziologie und Sozialpsychologie*, Vol. VIII, No. 1 (1956).

103. ———— *Sozialer Aufstieg und Abstieg. Eine Untersuchung über Berufsprestige und Berufsmobilität*. Stuttgart, 1959.

104. ———— "Some Aspects of Social Mobility in Western Germany," in *Transactions of the Third World Congress of Sociology*, Vol. III. London, 1956.

105. Ralf Dahrendorf, "Die soziale Funktion der Erziehung in der industriellen Gesellschaft," *Speculum: Saarländische Studentenzeitschrift*, Vol. I, No. 7 (1956).

106. Jean E. Floud, "The Educational Experience of the Adult Population of England and Wales as at July 1949," in 107 below.

107. D. V. Glass, ed., *Social Mobility in Britain*. London, 1954.

108. D. V. Glass and J. R. Hall, "Social Mobility in Britain: A Study of Inter-Generation Changes in Status," in 107 above.

109. J. R. Hall and D. C. Jones, "The Social Grading of Occupations," *British Journal of Sociology*, Vol. I (1950).

110. J. R. Hall and D. V. Glass, "Education and Social Mobility," in 107 above.

111. J. R. Hall and W. Ziegel, "A Comparison of Social Mobility Data for England and Wales, Italy, France, and the U.S.A.," in 107 above.

112. Hilde T. Himmelweit, "Social Status and Secondary Education since the 1944 Act: Some Data for London," in 107 above.

113. Alex Inkeles and P. H. Rossi, "National Comparisons of Occupational Prestige," *American Journal of Sociology*, Vol. LXII, No. 4 (1956).

114. Morris Janowitz, "Some Consequences of Social Mobility in the United States," *Transactions of the Third World Congress of Sociology*, Vol. III. London, 1956.

115. Japan Sociological Society, *Social Mobility in Japan*. Mimeographed for the Third World Congress of Sociology (1956).

116. S. M. Lipset and H. L. Zetterberg, "A Theory of Social Mobility," in *Transactions of the Third World Congress of Sociology*, Vol. III. London, 1956.

117. Gerhard Mackenroth and K. M. Bolte, "Bericht über das Forschungsvorhaben 'Wandlungen der deutschen Sozialstruktur (am Beispiel Schleswig-Holstein),'" in *Transactions of the Second World Congress of Sociology*, Vol. II. London, 1954.

118. C. A. Moser and J. R. Hall, "The Social Grading of Occupations," in 107 above.

119. Ramakrishna Mukherjee, "A Study of Social Mobility between Three Genera tions," in 107 above.

120. National Opinion Research Center, "Jobs and Occupations: A Popular Evaluation," in 35 above.

121. Natalie Rogoff, *Recent Trends in Occupational Mobility*. Glencoe, 1953.

122. Helmut Schelsky, *Soziologische Bemerkungen zur Rolle der Schule in unserer Gesellschaftsverfassung*. Unpublished, mimeographed (1956).

123. G. Thomas, "Labour Mobility in Great Britain 1945–49" (An Inquiry carried out for the Ministry of Labour and National Service), *Report No. 134 of The Social Survey*. London, n.d.

MIDDLE STRATA

124. H. P. Bahrdt, *Industriebürokratie: Versuch einer Soziologie des industrialisierten Bürobetriebes und seiner Angestellten*. Stuttgart, 1958.

125. Joseph Ben-David, "The Rise of a Salaried Professional Class in Israel," in *Transactions of the Third World Congress of Sociology*, Vol. III. London, 1956.

126. Reinhard Bendix, "Bureaucracy and the Problem of Power," in 136 below.

127. John Bonham, *The Middle Class Vote*. London, 1954.

128. Lewis Corey, *The Crisis of the Middle Class*. New York, 1935.

129. Fritz Croner, *Die Angestellten in der modernen Gesellschaft*. Frankfurt a.M. and Vienna, 1954.

130. Michel Crozier, "Le Rôle des employés et des petits fonctionnaires dans la structure sociale française contemporaine," in *Transactions of the Third World Congress of Sociology*, Vol. III. London, 1956.

131. Alvin Gouldner, "Eine Untersuchung über administrative Rollen," in *Kölner Zeitschrift für Soziologie und Sozialpsychologie*, Vol. VIII, No. 1 (1956).

132. R. K. Kelsall, D. Lockwood, and A. Tropp, "The New Middle Class in the Power Structure of Great Britain," in *Transactions of the Third World Congress of Sociology*, Vol. III. London, 1956.

133. Emil Lederer and Jakob Marschak, "Der neue Mittelstand," in *Grundriss der Sozialökonomik*, Section IX, Part I. Tübingen, 1926.

134. Roy Lewis and Angus Maude, *The English Middle Classes*. London, 1949.

135. David Lockwood, *The Blackcoated Worker*. London, 1958.

136. R. K. Merton, A. P. Gray, B. Hockey, and H. C. Selvin, eds., *Reader in Bureaucracy*. Glencoe, 1952.

137. C. W. Mills, *White Collar: The American Middle Classes*. New York, 1951.

LABOR, MANAGEMENT, INDUSTRY, AND SOCIETY

138. Reinhard Bendix, *Work and Authority in Industry: Ideologies of Management in the Course of Industrialization*. New York and London, 1956.

139. Goetz Briefs, *The Proletariat*. New York, 1938.

140. James Burnham, *The Managerial Revolution*. New York, 1941.

141. Theodore Caplow, *The Sociology of Work*. Minneapolis, 1954.

142. Ralf Dahrendorf, "Industrielle Fertigkeiten und soziale Schichtung," *Kölner Zeitschrift für Soziologie und Sozialpsychologie*, Vol. VIII, No. 4 (1956).

143. Ralf Dahrendorf, *Unskilled Labour in British Industry*. Ph.D. Thesis. London, 1956.

144. P. F. Drucker. *The New Society: The Anatomy of the Industrial Order*. New York, 1950.

145. Henri Fayol, *Administration industrielle et générale*. Paris, 1916.

146. Georges Friedmann, *Zukunft der Arbeit*. Cologne, 1953.

147. Peter Gay, *Das Dilemma des demokratischen Sozialismus*. Nürnberg, 1954. (Translated from *The Dilemma of Democratic Socialism*. New York, 1952.)

148. H. H. Gerth and C. W. Mills, "A Marx for the Managers," in 136 above.

149. Institut für Sozialforschung, Frankfurt a.M., *Betriebsklima*. Frankfurt a.M., 1954. Mimeographed. (Abridged version: Frankfurt a.M. 1956.)

150. Heinz B. Kluth, "Arbeiterjugend—Begriff und Wirklichkeit," in Helmut Schelsky, ed., *Arbeiterjugend—gestern und heute*. Heidelberg, 1955.

151. ——— "Empirische Studien im Industriebetrieb," in H.-D. Ortlieb, ed., *Hamburger Jahrbuch für Wirtschafts- und Gesellschaftspolitik*, Vol. I. Tübingen, 1956.

152. Jürgen Kuczynski, *Die Geschichte der Arbeiter in Deutschland von 1789 bis in die Gegenwart*. Sixth ed. Berlin, 1954.

153. Emil Lederer and Jakob Marschak, "Die Klassen auf dem Arbeitsmarkt und ihre Organisationen," in *Grundriss der Sozialökonomik*, Section IX, Part II. Tübingen, 1926.

154. Elton Mayo, *The Social Problems of an Industrial Civilization*. London, 1949.

155. W. H. McPherson, "Betrachtungen zur deutschen Arbeitsverfassung," in H.-D. Ortlieb and Helmut Schelsky, eds., *Wege zum sozialen Frieden*. Stuttgart and Düsseldorf, 1954.

156. Ministry of Labour and National Service, *Industrial Relations Handbook*. London, 1953.

157. W. E. Moore, *Industrial Relations and the Social Order*. New York, 1947.

158. F. H. Mueller, *Soziale Theorie des Betriebes*. Berlin, 1952.

159. National Resources Committee, "The Structure of Controls," in 35 above.

160. Otto Neuloh, *Die deutsche Betriebsverfassung und ihre Sozialformen bis zur Mitbestimmung*. Tübingen, 1956.

161. André Philip, *La démocratie industrielle*. Paris, 1955.

162. Theo Pirker, Siegfried Braun, and others, *Arbeiter, Management, Mitbestimmung*. Stuttgart and Düsseldorf, 1955.

163. Helmut Schelsky, "Die Jugend der industriellen Gesellschaft und die Arbeitslosigkeit," in *Arbeitslosigkeit und Berufsnot der Jugend*, Vol. II. Cologne, 1952.

164. ——— "Berechtigung und Anmassung in der Managerherrschaft," in H.-D. Ortlieb, ed., *Wirtschaftsordnung und Wirtschaftspolitik ohne Dogma*. Hamburg, 1954.

165. ——— "Industrie- und Betriebssoziologie," in Arnold Gehlen and Helmut Schelsky, eds., *Soziologie*. Düsseldorf and Cologne, 1955.

166. W. H. Scott, *Industrial Democracy: A Revaluation*. Liverpool, 1955.

167. F. W. Taylor, "The Principles of Scientific Management," in *Scientific Management*. New York and London, 1947.

168. Beatrice and Sidney Webb, *Industrial Democracy*. London, 1913.

169. W. H. Whyte, *The Organization Man.* New York, 1957.
170. "Zahlen zur Mitbestimmung," *Das Mitbestimmungsgespräch*, Vol. II, No. 11 (1956)
171. "Die Möglichkeiten der betrieblichen Mitbestimmung nach dem Mitbestimmungs- und Betriebsverfassungsgesetz," *Das Mitbestimmungsgespräch*, Vol. II, No. 11 (1956).

ON CAPITALISM AND INDUSTRIAL SOCIETY

172. Charles Babbage, *On the Economy of Machinery and Manufactures.* London, 1832.
173. A. A. Berle and G. C. Means, *The Modern Corporation and Private Property.* New York, 1932.
174. Colin Clark, *The Conditions of Economic Progress.* London, 1951.
175. Barbara and J. L. Hammond, *The Bleak Age.* London, 1946.
176. Eduard Heimann, *Wirtschaftssysteme und Gesellschaftssysteme.* Tübingen, 1954.
177. —— "Kapitalismus," in *Handwörterbuch der Sozialwissenschaften*, Vol. I. Stuttgart, Tübingen, and Göttingen, 1956.
178. Carl Jantke, "Vorindustrielle Gesellschaft und Staat," in Arnold Gehlen and Helmut Schelsky, eds., *Soziologie.* Düsseldorf and Cologne, 1955.
179. —— "Industriegesellschaft und Tradition," in *Verhandlungen des 13. deutschen Soziologentages.* Cologne, 1957.
180. Hargreaves Parkinson, *Ownership of Industry.* London, 1951.
181. P. J. Proudhon, *Système des contradictions économiques, ou Philosopie de la misère.* 3d ed. Paris, 1867.
182. Lionel Robbins, "The Economic Basis of Class Conflict," in 56 above.
183. F. Rosenstiel, "Der amerikanische 'Volkskapitalismus,'" *Frankfurter Allgemeine Zeitung*, November 11, 1956.
184. Karl Schwantag "Aktiengesellschaft: (II) AG in wirtschaftlicher Hinsicht," in *Handwörterbuch der Sozialwissenschaften*, Vol. I. Stuttgart, Tübingen, and Göttingen, 1956.
185. Adam Smith, *An Inquiry into the Nature and Causes of the Wealth of Nations.* New ed. New York, 1937.
186. Fritz Sternberg, *Kapitalismus und Sozialismus vor dem Weltgericht.* Hamburg, 1951.
187. R. H. Tawney, *Religion and the Rise of Capitalism.* London, 1926.
188. Andrew Ure, *The Philosophy of Manufacturers.* London, 1835.
189. Max Weber, *The Protestant Ethic and the Spirit of Capitalism.* London, 1930.

ON POLITICAL SOCIOLOGY

190. Hannah Arendt, *The Origins of Totalitarianism.* New York, 1951.
191. Reinhard Bendix and S. M. Lipset, "Political Sociology," *Current Sociology*, Vol. VI, No. 2 (1957).
192. Carl Brinkmann, "Revolution," in *Handwörterbuch der Sozialwissenschaften*, Vol. IX. Stuttgart, Tübingen, and Göttingen, 1957.
193. Anthony Downs, *An Economic Theory of Democracy.* New York, 1957.
194. Theodor Eschenburg, *Herrschaft der Verbände?* Stuttgart, 1955.

195. Oscar Glantz, "Class Consciousness and Political Solidarity," in *American Sociological Review*, Vol. XXIII, No. 4 (1958).

196. F. A. von der Heydte and Karl Sacherl, *Soziologie der deutschen Parteien*. Munich, 1955.

197. Harold Laski, *A Grammar of Politics*. 6th impr. London and New Haven, 1934.

198. Harold Lasswell, *Politics—Who Gets What, When, and How?* New York, 1936.

199. S. M. Lipset, *Agrarian Socialism*. New York, 1950.

200. Robert Michels, *Zur Soziologie des Parteiwesens in der modernen Demokratie*. 2d ed. Stuttgart, 1925.

201. Talcott Parsons, "The Distribution of Power in American Society," *World Politics*, Vol. X, No. 1 (October 1957).

202. André Philip, *Le Socialisme trahi*. Paris, 1957.

203. Bertrand Russell, *Power: A New Social Analysis*. London, 1938.

204. Werner Sombart, *Warum gibt es in den Vereinigten Staaten keinen Sozialismus?* Tübingen, 1906.

205. J. L. Talmon, *The Origins of Totalitarian Democracy*. London, 1952.

ON THEORY AND METHOD OF SOCIOLOGY

206. Ralf Dahrendorf, "Struktur und Funktion: Talcott Parsons und die Entwicklung der soziologischen Theorie," *Kölner Zeitschrift für Soziologie und Sozialpsychologie*, Vol. XII, No. 4 (1955).

207. ———— "Out of Utopia: Towards a Re-Orientation of Sociological Analysis," *American Journal of Sociology*, Vol. LXIV, No. 2 (September 1958).

208. Kingsley Davis, *Human Society*. New York, 1949.

209. M. J. Levy, "Some Sources of the Vulnerability of the Structures of Relatively Non-Industrialized Societies to Those of Highly Industrialized Societies," in B. F. Hostelitz, ed., *The Progress of Underdeveloped Areas*. Chicago, 1952.

210. David Lockwood, "Some Remarks on 'The Social System,'" *British Journal of Sociology*, Vol. VII, No. 2 (1956).

211. R. M. MacIver, *Society*. New York, 1937.

212. Bronislaw Malinowski, *A Scientific Theory of Culture and Other Essays*. Chapel Hill, 1944.

213. ———— *The Dynamics of Culture Change: An Inquiry into Race Relations in Africa*. Ed. by P. M. Kaberry. New Haven, 1945.

214. R. K. Merton, *Social Theory and Social Structure*. 2d ed. Glencoe, 1957.

215. R. K. Merton and P. F. Lazarsfeld, *Continuities in Social Research*. Glencoe, 1950.

216. Talcott Parsons, *The Structure of Social Action*. 2d ed. Glencoe, 1949.

217. ———— "The Present Position and Prospects of Systematic Theory in Sociology," in *Essays in Sociological Theory*. Rev. ed. Glencoe, 1954.

218. K. R. Popper, *Logik der Forschung*. Vienna, 1935.

219. ———— *The Open Society and its Enemies*. 2d ed. (rev.). London, 1952.

220. A. R. Radcliffe-Brown, "On the Concept of Function in Social Science," in *Structure and Function in Primitive Society*. London, 1952.

221. A. R. Radcliffe-Brown, "On Social Structure," in *Structure and Function in Primitive Society*. London, 1952.
222. Bertrand Russell, "Structure," in *Human Knowledge, Its Scope and Limits*. London, 1948.

OTHER LITERATURE

223. Henri Bergson, "Die Wahrnehmung der Veränderung," in *Denken und schöpferisches Werden*. Meisenheim, 1948.
224. Ralf Dahrendorf, *Marx in Perspektive: Die Idee des Gerechten im Denken von Karl Marx*. Hannover, 1953.
225. ———— "Philosophie und Soziologie bei Karl Marx: Marx-Kritik und ihre Bedeutung," *Geist und Tat*, Vol. X, No. 3 (1955).
226. G. W. F. Hegel, *Phänomenologie des Geistes*. 5th ed. Leipzig, 1949.
227. Max Horkheimer and T. W. Adorno, *Dialektik der Aufklärung*. Amsterdam, 1947.
228. Karl Mannheim, *Ideology and Utopia*. London, 1946.
229. Elisabeth Noelle and E. P. Neumann, *Jahrbuch der öffentlichen Meinung, 1947 bis 1955*. Allensbach, 1956.
230. David Riesman, *The Lonely Crowd*. New Haven, 1950.
231. Helmut Schelsky, *Wandlungen der deutschen Familie in der Gegenwart*. 3d ed. Stuttgart, 1955.
232. Alexis de Tocqueville, *Democracy in America*. Ed by P. Bradley. New York, 1945.

Subject Index

Author Index